LITERARY LIFE IN TŌKYŌ
1885-1915

A Stringful of Writers. (See p. 239)
From the left: Hasegawa Tenkei, Tayama Katai, Kunikida Doppo, Kawakami Bizan, Oguri Fūyō, Kanbara Ariake (February 1903).

LITERARY LIFE IN TŌKYŌ 1885-1915

TAYAMA KATAI'S MEMOIRS ('THIRTY YEARS IN TŌKYŌ')

TRANSLATED WITH FULL ANNOTATIONS
AND AN INTRODUCTION BY

KENNETH G. HENSHALL

E.J. BRILL
LEIDEN • NEW YORK • KØBENHAVN • KÖLN
1987

Library of Congress Catologing-in-Publication Data

Tayama, Katai, 1871-1930.
Literary life in Tōkyō, 1885-1915.

Translation of: Tōkyō no sanjūnen.
Bibliography: p.
Includes index.
1. Tayama, Katai, 1871-1930—Biography.
2. Authors, Japanese—20th century—Biography.
I. Henshall, Kenneth G. II. Title. III. Title: Thirty years in Tōkyō.
Pl817.A8Z46813 1987 895.6'34 [B] 87-703
ISBN 90-04-08119-4

ISBN 90 04 08119 4

PRINTED IN THE NETHERLANDS BY E. J. BRILL

CONTENTS

ACKNOWLEDGEMENTS

I am extremely grateful to the Suntory Foundation for a generous donation to assist with the publication of this book. I am also grateful to the Japan Foundation for its financial support, and for the Fellowship which enabled me to complete the research and translation of Katai's memoirs at Kōbe University. I am indebted to Kōbe University for extending its facilities to me, and in particular I am indebted to Professor Nishigaki Tsutomu, Professor of Modern Japanese Literature, for his enthusiastic and painstaking assistance on a whole range of obscure topics. My thanks are also due to Mr Okamoto Yoshio, a private scholar based in Kōbe, to Mr Suzuki Michio, of the Chiyoda-ku Library, Tōkyō, and to the numerous specialists who have helped with various points of detail.

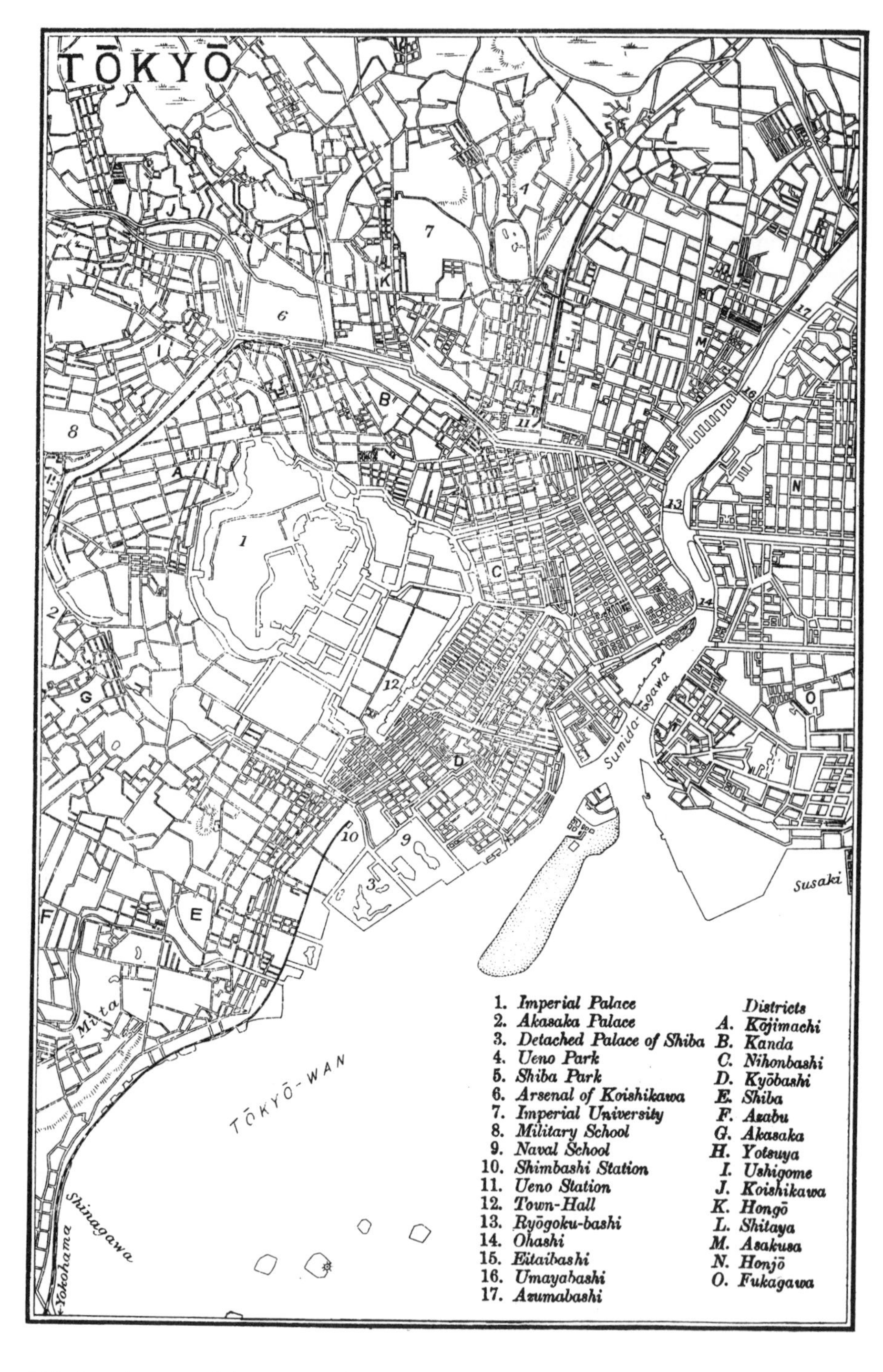

Tōkyō at the turn of the century. From Papinot's *Historical and Geographical Dictionary of Japan*, 1910. (*Courtesy of Charles E. Tuttle Co. Inc.*)

INTRODUCTION

1. General introduction

a) *The significance of 'Thirty Years in Tōkyō'*

'Thirty Years in Tōkyō' was published on June 15th 1917 by Hakubunkan, the publishing company for which Katai worked between September 1899 and December 1912. Inspired in part by Alphonse Daudet's 'Thirty Years in Paris' (Trente Ans de Paris, 1888), it is a personal account of the changes Katai had seen in Tōkyō over the thirty or so years since his arrival there in 1881 as an errand-boy for a bookstore, and naturally the emphasis is placed on the literary scene. Many of the chapters are modified versions of reminiscences and critical articles which Katai had published over the previous few years in various Hakubunkan magazines, particularly 'Bunshō Sekai' (World of Writing, March 1906-December 1920, of which Katai was chief editor from its inception till his retirement in 1912). Some later editions of the work omit the lengthy chapter 'K and T', which first appeared in 'Bunshō Sekai' on January 1st 1917 and is rather different in content from the other chapters (being set in Nikkō, for example), but since it was included in the original edition and is anyway of considerable interest I have included it in this translation.

The work is of interest and value to various types of reader at various levels. Obviously, for those with a special interest in Katai it is essential reading, especially in view of the fact that the vast majority of his writings were so closely linked to actual events in his life. As just a few examples from among many, the chapter 'My Own Anna Mahr' gives valuable background information on his best-known work 'The Quilt' (Futon, 1907), 'When I wrote 'Life'' gives similar information on his well-known autobiographical novel 'Life' (Sei, 1908), and in a more general sense, the account of his struggle to escape from relative poverty and establish himself as a writer by making use of the patonage system (see 'Visiting Kōyō Sanjin' in particular) illustrates clearly Katai's practical approach to literature, as well as shedding light on the patronage system in general. To assist such readers to place the work in context relative to Katai's career, I have given later in this introduction a brief account of his life, works, and personality. Readers are also referred to the introduction to my translation of his ''Quilt' and Other Stories' (1981, Tokyo U.P.), where I have discussed Katai's life and works and gone into considerable detail regarding the literary movement with which he was most associated, naturalism.

The next group of readers to whom 'Thirty Years in Tōkyō' will be of value are those who are not necessarily interested in Katai himself but rather in the literature of Meiji Japan (1868-1912) in general, especially those already familiar to some extent with that field. For amongst other things the work is a rare *first-hand* account of the world of Meiji literature, providing interesting comments, personal judgements, and snippets of information about contemporary writers and their works. In this respect it has a dimension not found in standard reference works. For example, we are told that the powerful critic Saitō Ryokū was generally "thought of as a nuisance and a crank" and that "some writers even loathed him like some nasty little insect" ('The Author of 'Hide and Seek''), while we are also told that, in the opinion of the then aspiring poet-novelist Kunikida Doppo, the renowned senior novelist Hirotsu Ryūrō wrote "cow's drivel" ('K and T'). At the same time we are told how Ryūrō went about his writing — mostly, it would seem, churning out vast amounts late at night in a Yoshiwara brothel — and how much he received for his manuscripts. Similar interesting comments are made about scores of writers and publishers, and offer a fascinating insight into relatively hard-to-gauge aspects of the literary world of the day such as the personal relationships between writers of various factions, the effect of a specific work or event on a writer's reputation or attitude, the power of the publishing houses, the problems of copyright, the role of the illustrators, the pressures and rewards of writing for a living, and so on and so on.

While on the subject of the Meiji literary world in general, a point which should not be overlooked by the reader is the vast number of writers whom Katai mentions. He refers to literally hundreds, many of whom have now become largely forgotten and certainly neglected, even by Japanese researchers. This neglect may perhaps prove to be justified in some cases, at least from the point of view of significance to literary history, but nevertheless it would be nice to see research done on such intriguing if unimportant figures as the engineer-writer Nakazawa Rinsen or the 'Russian student type' Takase Bun'en. And even if one does confine one's thinking to those who apparently did figure prominently in Meiji literary history, 'Thirty Years in Tōkyō' draws attention to at least a dozen such figures, with Ozaki Kōyō, Kawakami Bizan, Oguri Fūyō, and Ueda Bin being particularly prominent amongst those currently neglected. It is one of my hopes that 'Thirty Years in Tōkyō' will help to broaden the approach of those undertaking research into Meiji literature, sufficiently at least for them to realise that there is more to life than Sōseki.

The reader who is *not* familiar with Meji literature to any great extent will still, I believe, find the work of interest. Partly with such readers in mind I have given extensive annotations and, later in this introduction, a brief account of the main developments in the Meiji literary world, while the work itself can also be read from a wide, socio-historical angle rather than a relatively narrow literary one. It offers, in this respect, valuable insights into the society of the day, not just in terms of well-documented matters such as public attitudes on occasions like the wars with China (1894-5) and Russia (1904-5) or the death of Emperor Meiji (1912), but in rather more 'day to day' terms. For example, those who think that 'dance fever' was a phenomenon first brought about by John Travolta and Olivia Newton-John (or was it the Bee Gees?) might be surprised to learn about Inoue Kaoru ('Return to Tōkyō' and notes), while those who think that scruffy students first appeared in the beatnik era in the West might be surprised to read about student life in Tōkyō in the 1880's. Similarly, information such as the need to queue at public toilets is not normally the sort of thing found in the average history book.

Nor would such information be found in a standard history of Tōkyō, which is another valuable secondary role of the work. While it is primarily a history of Katai and his relationship with the literary world, which happened to be based in Tōkyō, rather than a history of Tōkyō itself (as the title might suggest), 'Thirty Years in Tōkyō' nevertheless offers from time to time fascinating illustrations of the Tōkyō of old. 'Out in the Western Suburbs' is particularly informative in this regard, and such accounts as that of the early 'campus' of Waseda University make one aware of just how green and undeveloped much of Tōkyō was in those days. The metamorphosis of the city is a recurrent theme in the work.

In short, 'Thirty Years in Tōkyō' is by no means a dull, dry history of Meiji literature and/or Meiji society and/or Meiji Tōkyō, but a living record of one individual's course through those fascinating, frenetic worlds, and an album of people and events encountered along the way.

b) *Regarding the translation and annotations*

In writing the notes I have tried to explain obscurities while avoiding judgements or evaluations, as the inclusion of these would erode the first-hand character of the text and its own judgements and evaluations. That is, when for example annotating a reference to a writer I have simply, in the vast majority of cases, given such factual data as dates and pseudonyms and such basic information as whether they were chiefly poets, playwrights, novelists or critics. Other literary characteristics I have tried to let emerge naturally from the text.

As part of the same attempt to keep the original flavour of the text I have not altered anything which Katai wrote, even if it is obviously in error, but have indicated anything erroneous, unusual or irregular in the notes. Katai's cavalier attitude towards details such as dates was, while often infuriating to the researcher, an important reflection of his impressionistic approach, and it is similarly important for the reader to appreciate the degree of clinical inaccuracy which this entailed.

An equally infuriating — though less misleading — aspect of Katai's impressionistic approach is his occasional tendency to use bland and vague terminology that leaves the reader wishing for more specific detail. Where possible I have tried to give extra detail in the notes, but unfortunately the missing detail is sometimes of a type that simply cannot be given by anyone other than the original writer. For example, he often talks loosely of 'new trends', and one is in some cases unsure as to what exactly he is intending. Similarly, he often refers to discussions with people like Tōson and Doppo over vague issues like 'love', 'life', and 'faith'. Sometimes, as in parts of 'K and T', he does give more specific detail, and records such points as specific differences in attitudes to women, but the reader will, I am afraid, have to be prepared to encounter a number of frustrating imprecisions. For better or for worse, that is the way Katai wrote, and it is not the translator's part to interfere.

To avoid interrupting the text unnecessarily I have put notes at the end of sentences or occasionally paragraphs rather than against each item, with the result that some notes cover several different items. (Originally I had over two thousand annotations.) Items are explained in detail in the first note only; in other cases it will be necessary for the reader to consult an appendix or index. In most cases I have not given notes for place-names that can be found in present-day maps of Tōkyō, but nonetheless, since Tōkyō has seen perhaps more changes over the last hundred years than any other major city in the world and since many of the names Katai mentions no longer exist, the number of 'geographical' notes is far from inconsiderable. In a further attempt to reduce the number of notes, I have on occasion resorted to square brackets, especially for 'sic' when irregularities are blatant.

I have retained Katai's usage of initials, with explanatory notes where necessary (his 'O', for example, can refer to any one of at least five different people). I have also retained his nomenclature, and used surnames where he has and pseudonyms where he has. I have not, however, retained suffixes such as '-san' and '-kun' unless these indicate a special relationship (as with '-sensei'). I have also kept all foreign language terms used by Katai, such as 'Sturm und Drang' (usually with accompanying note). Where Katai has given the title of a non-Japanese work in a language other than Japanese I have retained the language he himself used (ie. French or German), while all titles he gives in Japanese I have put into English, including Japanese works. I have not, however, translated magazine titles (except where useful in notes) owing to the confusing similarity of many of these titles when put into English. There are, for example, at least three magazines which can be translated as 'World of Literature', so it is a dangerous policy to use anything other than the original Japanese titles. An index of these magazines has been attached for convenience.

It has been impossible to achieve objective consistency over such items as '-gawa' for 'river', '-ji' for 'temple', and '-hashi/-bashi' for 'bridge'. Purist theory maintains that tautology should be avoided and that one should, for example, write 'Kyō Bridge' for 'Kyōbashi'. This is, however, difficult if not impossible in practice as it is necessary to appreciate that 'Kyōbashi' can also refer to an area as well as a specific bridge and that the Japanese do not always differentiate between the two. When one further considers that there are other bridges within the Kyōbashi district, and such vague terms as 'Kyōbashi no hashi', the difficulties become even more apparent. Even when clarity is not a problem, euphony often is. While one can normally replace '-gawa' by 'River', as in 'Sumida River' for 'Sumidagawa', it simply does not sound right to say 'No River' instead of 'Nogawa'. I have therefore taken the easy way out and written the form that at the time seemed most appropriate, indicating tautology by square brackets. It has similarly been difficult to achieve consistency over word division, even with regard to the same term in different contexts. For example, the word 'shū' (meaning 'collection') sometimes seems more appropriate joined to the preceding word, sometimes not, depending on the degree of usage of that preceding word as an independent unit.

I have retained Katai's usage of proper nouns even though these may at times be considered unusual. Thus I have used the term 'Genyūsha' instead of the more common 'Kenyūsha', since Katai clearly intended this pronunciation by his use of the abbreviated 'G-sha'. (It may always be possible that Katai's is in fact the more accurate pronunciation, though I have found only one reference book listing a reading 'Gen' for the first character of the term.)

Throughout the translation I have taken the liberty of avoiding slavishly literal rendition of common terms that might be considered figurative. For example, where I refer to a writer sitting pensively with 'pen in hand' it should be appreciated that the original text gives 'brush in hand'. I have also avoided awkwardnesses in English arising from attempts to translate what is in effect untranslatable, notably certain items of clothing and foodstuffs. I have appended a glossary of such terms, excluding those listed in English dictionaries (eg. 'geisha').

To write the notes for 'Thirty Years in Tōkyō' I consulted over five hundred books, and conferred with numerous specialists. Nevertheless, some half-dozen items remain obscure (apart from 'dates unclear'), including the mysterious 'Kerē Shōkai' business on the very first page. Should any reader be able to cast any light on these obscure matters, I would be grateful for the illumination, as indeed would the specialists concerned.

Among the books consulted, those I found most useful were 'Tayama Katai Kenkyū' (A Study of Tayama Katai, ten volumes, 1976-84, Ōfūsha), by Kobayashi Ichirō, 'Nihon Kindai Bungaku Daijiten' (Dictionary of Modern Japanese Literature, six volumes, 1978, Kōdansha), and the Tōkyō volume of 'Nihon Chimei Daijiten' (Dictionary of Japanese Place-names, Vol. 13, 1978, Kadokawa).

2. The Meiji Literary World and 'Thirty Years in Tōkyō'

a) *General developments in the history of Meiji literature*

Though the 1890's saw the dramatic rise of writers to youth idol status, in the mid-1880's, when Katai's thoughts first turned towards the prospect of a literary career, literature per se was probably not the sort of career that most ambitious young men would have chosen. Writers generally did not enjoy a high social standing or high financial rewards, and they had inherited from the Tokuwaga period (1602-1868) a literature that was not inspiring. Though some Tokugawa writers, such as Saikaku and Chikamatsu, were soon to enjoy a more favourable reassessment, at the time in question Tokuwaga literature was often felt to be either a frivolous mode of trite entertainment or a distorted means of sermonising and moralising, and either way certainly not an art form (with the exception of some forms of poetry). In fact, this view of literature continued to be held by some well into the later part of the Meiji period, and in 'Geographical Editing' we find that as late as 1903 no less a 'literary figure' than the owner of Hakubunkan, Ōhashi Shintarō, tells Katai that it is a waste of time his (Katai's) being a novelist, and that he should choose instead an academic career. "Academics were greatly esteemed," writes Katai, "whereas people like me, who chose to follow the path of literature, were looked down upon."

The same trivial type of writing did indeed continue into the early Meiji period with 'gesaku', which were largely forgettable satires of the changes being wrought in society as a result of the Westernisation process. In 'The Author of 'Hide and Seek'' Katai tells us that, among other reasons for his being disliked, Saitō Ryokū "was despised as a gesaku writer."

It was that same Westernisation process, however, that eventually contributed to an amelioration of literary standards. At first, Western literature was translated primarily for its functional value, with Samuel Smiles' guide to becoming a good gentleman, 'Self Help' (1859, translated 1871), standing as a good example of the utilitarian selection (see Note 245). But then, as interest — or perhaps one should say rather 'curiosity' — in Westerners grew, so too did interest in their literature and the characters depicted therein. Before too long translations of a wider range of works appeared, albeit fanciful interpretations, and novels by writers like Scott and Bulwer-Lytton became quite popular.

In those early days, when Japan was struggling to reorientate and reshape itself in a Western-dominated world, strong leadership was naturally an essential requirement. Accordingly politics was seen as THE career to follow, and novels with a political flavour were particularly popular. 'Return to Tōkyō' touches on this, referring to the popularity of such 'political novels' as Tōkai Sanshi's 'Strange Encounters with Beautiful Women' (started 1885) and Suehiro Tetchō's 'Plum Blossoms in the Snow' (1886). The same chapter also makes clear, along with 'The Champions of a New Type of Literature', the popularity of novels actually written by politicians themselves, with British writer-politicians such as Disraeli and Macaulay being seen as particularly good models for a young man to follow. If there *were* any wish amongst significant numbers of young men to follow the path of literature in the 1880's, then it was certainly a path that ran in conjunction with that of politics. Katai, we are told, was no exception.

England seems to have been the favoured country initially, and it was a knowledge of English literature that lay behind the would-be reformist Tsubouchi Shōyō's attempt, from about 1885 on, to advocate a serious and realistic approach to literature and to elevate it to a serious art form. The best known work to present these views was his 'Essence of the Novel' in 1885, and it is interesting that Katai makes no reference to it. Shōyō seems to have largely failed in his attempted reform, however, especially since he was unable to escape from a 'gesaku' type flavour in his own creative writing. It is clear from Katai's remarks throughout the first half of 'Thirty Years in Tōkyō' that while Tsubouchi was respected as an academic — a point which certainly did no harm to the cause of literature — he was felt to be too old-fashioned in his literature to be truly representative of a modern age. In particular, he was felt to be too bound up with pedantic aspects of style and with English classics, whereas such stylistic considerations were soon to give way to those of content and informality of expression, and England was even sooner to lose ground in the popularity stakes (especially in literature) to Russian, French, German, and even Japanese models. Thus, while Tsubouchi's call for a more serious approach to literature was no doubt a significant development, at least in a theoretical sense, it seems from Katai's writings that the actual reform in literature was carried out without Tsubouchi, or even *despite* Tsubouchi and his limitations. It also serves to show just how quickly trends changed at the time, with English literature being abandoned before it had really had a chance to be properly absorbed, and a would-be reformist being considered old-fashioned almost before he had completed the very draft of his reform.

Ironically, one of the main reasons for the failure of the budding Tsubouchi to actually blossom was a man who was, despite enormous differences in attitudes, an admirer of his, Futabatei Shimei (Hasegawa Tatsunosuke). As Katai makes clear in 'Futabatei's Death', it was this man who was responsible for the first proper introduction of foreign literature to Japan, through some superb translations of epoch-making accuracy, backed up with remarkably detailed knowledge of the literature he was translating. The translations ('Rendezvous' and 'Chance Encounter') were of Turgenev, and appeared in 1888/9. In addition to these translations Futabatei wrote his own novel, 'The Drifting Cloud', between 1886-1889. It has often been called Japan's first modern novel, since it revealed a depth of psychological awareness, developed a concept of individuality, had an anti-hero as its protagonist (under the influence of Turgenev's 'superfluous man'), and pioneered a new informal style known as 'genbun'itchi' ('combination of written and spoken word'). Katai observes that just about every writer over the next few decades was influenced to a greater or lesser degree by these early works of Futabatei's, and that it was felt to be a matter of great regret that, as a result of a personal conviction of inadequacy concerning both himself and the value of literature, Futabatei should withdraw from the literary scene for the next fifteen years, reemerging only a few years before his death in 1909.

It is from this point of the late 1880's on that Japanese literature became characterised by overt factionalism, with the 1890's being particularly extreme in this regard. As Katai discusses in chapters such as 'The Literary World in those Days', there were at least six distinct groups in this period, created partly by fundamental differences in literary attitudes per se, which in turn in some cases were reflections of differing literary stances at various new universities and colleges, and partly by the personal experiences and convictions of various literary figures, including their reaction to foreign ideology. In fact, it could be said that the factionalism resulted in large part specifically from differences in reactions to foreign literature and ideology. It was during this period that a particularly vast and varied range of Western literature and ideology entered Japan, and it was also at this time that Christianity, which had of course been introduced much earlier, enjoyed a resurgence in popularity. Christianity had especially strong links with the romantic Jogaku Zasshi and Bungakukai groups and with the politically aware Kokumin Bungaku group (being seen as an ideological basis for early moves towards people's rights and free expression, etc). Perhaps the main group, however, was the Genyūsha. Its leader was Ozaki Kōyō (also known as Kōyō Sanjin and by his real name of Ozaki Tokutarō), who was one of the most dominant figures of his time. The group itself was in many respects a compromise between old and new, Japanese and Western, and combined the literary flavour of a reappraised Saikaku (especially his metaphoric language and 'down-to-earth' content) with a Western-influenced realism and specifically a Zola-influenced respect for minutely detailed depiction. The chapter 'Visiting Kōyō Sanjin' gives a good illustration of Kōyō's personality and his attitude to Zola.

Kōda Rohan was another major figure, being associated with the decidedly old-fashioned, pro-Japanese Negishi group, while Tsubouchi Shōyō continued, despite limitations on his popularity, to enjoy prominence through his association with the pro-English and *relatively* old-fashioned Waseda (University) group. But perhaps the greatest figure of all — a rare man who had actually spent some time in Europe — was Mori Ōgai. This extraordinary man — accomplished linguist, translator (from German), writer, critic, and later Surgeon General — had a profound influence on literary developments from the time of his return in 1888 from four years' medical study in Germany, not only through his prodigious criticisms, translations, and original writings, but through his personality. Even though Katai was invariably on the receiving end of Ōgai's cutting criticisms, at frequent points throughout 'Thirty Years in Tōkyō' he makes it abundantly clear that he respected Ōgai more than any other literary figure, admiring the range of his knowledge and the sharpness of his mind but in particular the strength of personality that allowed him to stand unflinchingly by his beliefs and principles, with no need for the customary group support from sundry acolytes. In fact, Katai treats Ōgai as to all intents and purposes comprising a faction — the Sendagi faction — all by himself.

Many of these factions had their own publishing outlets, the côterie magazines, although circumstances often led to members of a particular faction publishing in a magazine associated with another faction. (On at least two occasions in 'Thirty Years in Tōkyō' Katai refers to members of the Bungakukai group publishing in other magazines simply for the fees.) In any event, the relative abundance of these magazines was one reason for the emergence of the short story as a major genre in Meiji literature. Other publishing outlets were newspapers such as the Yomiuri, which were often characterised by a particular literary flavour, and which helped to develop the genre of the serialised novel. There were also a limited number of publishing houses, such as Kinkōdō, Shunyōdō, and Hakubunkan, which published their own magazines as well as 'tankōbon' (novels in book form). 'Thirty Years in Tōkyō' contains numerous references to the role of these various publishing outlets.

Around the middle of the 1890's the romantic movement, centering by this stage on the Bungakukai magazine, grew particularly strong. Katai discusses his first contact with members of this faction — including the famed Shimazaki Tōson — in the chapter 'Our Group'. The romanticism fostered through the magazine was largely of a lyrical, emotional nature, but there was also present an increasing awareness of the concept of the individual and the self. This self-awareness, combined with the development of individualism as an ideological phenomenon, gained strength throughout the 1890's in direct proportion to the introduction of appropriate foreign literature, such as Rousseau's 'Confessions' (read by Tōson in 1894), and became especially strong around the turn of the century with the introduction of Nietzsche by the critics Hasegawa Tenkei and Takayama Chogyū. Together with the death of Kōyō in 1903 this new trend to all intents and purposes brought to an end the 'old-fashioned' movements — at least those whose old-fashionedness was attributed to an excessive adherence to Japanese traditions (such as the Genyūsha's attention to ornateness of style rather than the development of ideological depth with a serious bearing on the individual and real life). The three successive chapters 'Buds of a New Ideology', 'Kōyō's Death', and 'The Second Floor of Maruzen' are particularly informative with regard to this development of individualism and self-awareness, and Katai's thoughts at Kōyō's graveside ('Kōyō's Death') are often quoted as an illustration of individualism 'squaring up' against socio-moral norms of Confucianist tradition that tended to efface the self:

> At the time, deep with me, individualism was awakening. Through the medium of foreign literature I had been profoundly influenced by the belief that we are lone individuals in the universe and that communal living is a compromise, and by naturalistic ideology, new ideology that tried to suppress standardised grief. As I stood in attendance at Kōyō's funeral I thought to myself: 'This splendid ceremony, this public sympathy, this grief based on a sense of duty and humanity, this sorrow shown by friends and colleagues and pupils alike — I wonder how it would all look in the light of new ideology? Isn't the ceremony simply a display of old morality?

> ... In a world where new ideology reigned there would be none of this strength of formalism and obligation. ... We have been too bound up with standardised morality. From now on we must live our own lives as our own individual selves.'

Similarly, in 'The Second Floor of Maruzen' he tells us how "Nietzsche's fire, and Ibsen's defiance, and Tolstoi's 'self'" were amongst "the surging currents of thought of nineteenth century Europe that broke relentlessly through onto the shores of this remote Far Eastern island," currents of thought that had come "full of energy and might" into "a calm little world of chivalry and Confucianism, Buddhism and superstition, duty and humanity, humiliating self-sacrifice and forbearance, compromise and social etiquette." In 'Brief Comments on Certain Writers' he tells us that those writers who were not able to cope with self-awareness and self-understanding "were all swept away — big figures, little figures, and whole groups of figures alike."

Katai's concern for the individual, and especially for the self as a symbol of the individual, is a key factor in the character of Japanese naturalism, which became established with his 'Quilt' of 1907. As mentioned earlier, I have dealt with this question at some length in the introduction to my translation 'The Quilt and Other Stories by Tayama Katai', as well as in various specialist articles, so I will refrain here from going into detail and quoting extensively from material other than 'Thirty Years in Tōkyō' (in which Katai does not make a special point of discussing naturalism per se). It is, however, quite clear from a study of Katai's critical writings that his concept of Japanese naturalism was not, as is commonly and erroneously believed, merely an attempted Japanese version of Zola's pseudo-scientific analytical determinism, but one that was influenced by writers (admittedly sometimes including Zola in *this* regard) who wrote with directness, bluntness, and simplicity — as opposed to artificially elaborate and ornate texts full of fanciful fiction and lacking a valid link with fact and reality — and especially by writers who wrote in such vein of the basic INDIVIDUAL. For, during his naturalist period at least, Katai felt that man the free individual was closer to nature than man the social unit, and that society and its rules — ie. morality, tradition, etc. — were artificial. His ideal naturalist was a writer who could depict the natural individual bluntly and truthfully, regardless of the fact that the work might be considered 'anti-social' and might materially harm the writer's career, and he had great admiration for any writer who showed courage in this regard. (It is for this reason that he often refers to Ibsen as a naturalist, feeling that the basic truths defiantly exposed in his work outweighed the melodramatic contrivances used as tools in the process.)

Katai was especially influenced by the 'pro-individual, anti-societal' form of German naturalism represented by Hauptmann and Sudermann (a form little studied and little known even in the West), and 'Thirty Years in Tōkyō' contains frequent references to these two writers. 'The Little House in the Suburbs', for example, reveals his enthusiasm for Sudermann's 'Cat's Bridge' and Hauptmann's 'Sunken Bell', while 'The Old Castle Ruins of Komoro' contains the revealing statement that he and Tōson — considered the other major representative of the naturalist movement — found Hauptmann's 'Lonely People' to be "a particularly interesting source of discussion, as we were concerned about the problem of 'family'." Hauptmann's 'Lonely People' — the story of Johannes Vockerat, who, misunderstood by his old-fashioned wife and parents, kills himself when various moral restraints prevent him from pursuing a relationship with a modern-minded girl student (Anna Mahr) who comes to stay in his house — was in fact probably the single most influential foreign work in the formation of Japanese naturalism, and its relationship to Katai's 'Quilt' is discussed to some extent in 'My Own Anna Mahr'.

When read in the light of the above comments regarding the character of the naturalism which Katai tried to establish, the remarks which Katai makes at various points in 'Thirty Years in Tōkyō' about writers depicting life bluntly (such as Maupassant, in 'The Second Floor of Maruzen') take on an extra significance. It is also significant that Katai makes nothing of the works of Kosugi Tengai, whose works between 1900 and 1902 have been called 'naturalist' by some literary historians. In fact, they merely amounted to a superficial Zola-inspired realism, and Katai merely makes a brief passing condemnation of Tengai as such in 'The Old Castle Ruins of Komoro'.

As described in 'My Own Anna Mahr', Katai decided to write 'The Quilt' as a desperate make-or-break work, after years of failure to achieve any real fame as a writer. It recounts with remarkable veracity the stay in Tōkyō of a girl pupil of his, Okada Michiyo, and his feelings of desire towards her — feelings that were immoral by the standards of the day. It was primarily a cathartic work rather than a reasoned embodiment of his views on the individual, and its popularity no doubt owed more — at least initially — to mere morbid curiosity on the part of the average reader than to any bona-fide appreciation of the ideological issues raised, but nevertheless the work did succeed in portraying the frustration of the natural desires of an individual by the moral restraints imposed by a convention-bound society. It also established the new genre of the 'I' novel. Autobiography in itself was far from new in Japanese literature, but what WAS new about 'The Quilt' was the exhaustive extent of the self-exposure, with the writer portraying himself (and later his family and friends), vices and all, as a real living individual who could symbolise the clash between the would-be free individual and the social roles he was forced to enact. Following the establishing of this trend Katai and Tōson — who had, in his 'Broken Commandment' of 1906, similarly attacked the repression of the individual by social convention, but had focussed on a third party instead (specifically an 'eta', fated to be treated by society as a non-person) — went on to write a number of works dealing exhaustively and ruthlessly with members of their family and circle of friends. In 'When I Wrote 'Life'' 'Katai tells us in some detail about his labours in writing one such work, 'Life', which immediately followed 'The Quilt'.

The naturalist movement petered out around 1910-11, to be replaced by the aesthetic/decadent trend led by Nagai Kafū and Tanizaki Junichirō and the Shirakaba humanitarian movement under Mushanokōji Saneatsu. It is interesting that Katai makes no reference to either of these movements or to any of the three above-mentioned writers (except for an unconnected passing reference to one of Kafū's works). This may be taken as a lingering reluctance on his part to acknowledge that naturalism had in fact had its day, for he himself went on, under the influence of writers such as Huysmans (referred to somewhat cryptically in the later chapters of the work), to produce a "spiritual naturalism" that sought by religious meditation to define man's natural quintessence and his role in the natural order of the universe — in other words, a different type of literature, but still a naturalism of sorts. It is also interesting that he makes no comment on Natsume Sōseki, felt by many present-day critics to have been the leading figure of the literary world from 1905 to 1915, and moreover a writer who dealt with the theme of the individual. Katai never liked Sōseki either as a writer or a man, and while his failure to mention Sōseki in 'Thirty Years in Tōkyō' (except in an unconnected context) may well be seen as a reflection of that dislike, it may also indicate that, while Sōseki was undoubtedly popular amongst the reading public, he was not perhaps as influential amongst his fellow writers as is commonly believed (a point made by Katai himself in another of his critical writings, 'Modern Novels' [Kindai no Shōsetsu] of 1923). Katai does, however, refer to young writers such as Masamune Hakuchō and Tokuda (Chikamatsu) Shūkō, who were associated with a nihilist type off-shoot of naturalism, and, interestingly, he remarks that they represent the first generation of writers TRULY free from the encumbrances of the old approach to literature, with its concern for ostentatious character-usage and the like. It should be noted that he considers that even he himself suffers to some extent from being old-fashioned in this latter regard.

Some of the reasons for the demise of naturalism proper can be found, then, in Katai's personal change of attitude towards life, not just literature. Some of his attitudinal problems — though not his more profound concerns with individualism — are described in 'The Crisis at Forty' which also makes some interesting points about naturalism and attitudes to Western literature. For example, he writes that "There had been cries for naturalism, but had there actually been a form of art produced that would change everything?" thereby indicating his awareness that his earlier type of naturalism contained an element of anti-conventional defiance — "cheap confessions and petty defiance" are the obviously self-denigratory words that he himself uses. On two occasions he also openly admits to the attempt to imitate Western literature, though, as discussed earlier, this should not be taken as denying the indigenous characteristics of Japanese naturalism and should also be appreciated in the context of Katai's tendency to exaggerate when being critical of himself.

'A Certain Grave' touches, with extraordinary crypticism, upon another possible factor in the demise of naturalism, namely the Treason Incident of 1911, in which a number of young persons suspected of harbouring anti-State thoughts were executed without proper trial. Some commentators see this as having in practice 'called the bluff' of naturalist writers who were developing an anti-social attitude, and Katai's extreme vagueness in this chapter (together with a number of self-exculpatory works of his not mentioned in 'Thirty Years in Tōkyō') tends to suggest that there may indeed be some truth in such a view. Sadly, he himself may have lacked the courage he so admired in Western writers.

Such, then, are the main literary developments in the period covered by 'Thirty Years in Tōkyō'. As well as providing an at times illuminating commentary on these developments in the Meiji world of letters, 'Thirty Years in Tōkyō' contains interesting 'pen-pictures' of some of the protagonists, including chapters (or substantial passages) devoted to figures such as Kōyō, Rohan, Takase Bun'en, Ueda Bin, Kunikida Doppo, Kawakami Bizan, Futabatei Shimei, Masamune Hakuchō, and Tokuda Shūkō. These passages may be read as virtually independent texts if necessary, though they are obviously best appreciated in context. Indeed, I have not been able to discuss in these brief introductory pages more than a handful of the writers involved, for it has been my job merely to outline the plot, and Katai's job to tell the story and develop the characters.

b) *Other background characteristics of the Meiji literary scene*

'Thirty Years in Tōkyō' is, perhaps by virtue of its personalised approach, very revealing of the *actual* character of the world of Meiji letters. Some aspects of that character, such as factionalism and the rapid turnover of trends, have emerged through the discussion of general developments, and it has already been stated that 'Thirty Years in Tōkyō' provides valuable background information in these regards, such as the personal relationships between members of the various factions. There are also, of course, characteristics which are not quite so apparent from a discussion confined to chief developments, but which are nevertheless significant to a proper understanding of Meiji literature, and which feature prominently in 'Thirty Years in Tōkyō'. One such characteristic — not unconnected with factionalism — is the patronage system, whereby aspiring writers attached themselves to an established senior writer (or group of writers) and received from them practical help and advice, especially the benefits of the senior writers' contacts in the publishing world. In return for this help their duty was, not unlike that of apprentices in other walks of life, often of a domestic rather than professional nature, such as performing household tasks and running errands. Obviously they also had the duty of flattering their masters, singing their praises and defending their causes. The humiliation involved in this process of securing a patron is well illustrated in the chapter 'Visiting Kōyō Sanjin', and one can well imagine the life-style of the various acolytes consigned to the tiny room next to Kōyō's front door. 'My First Translation' illustrates how these mentors could use their publishing contacts to get the work of young aspirants into print — in this particular case Kōyō's friend and colleague Emi Suiin getting Ōhashi Otowa of Hakubunkan to publish a translation by the then unknown Katai. 'My First Manuscript Fee' provides a similar illustration, with Emi Suiin getting Fujimoto Tōin, editor of the magazine 'Miyako no Hana', to publish the unknown Katai's first-ever professional story:

> Through Emi Suiin's introduction I once sent him (Fujimoto Tōin) a rather poor short story. It left much to be desired, but Suiin was a good friend of his and so, after I'd been asked to amend various parts of the manuscript, it scraped through and was published in the November issue of the magazine.

In the same chapter we also find reference to Higuchi Ichiyō's first major work carrying an introduction by her particular mentor, Miyake Kaho. Such introductions were a typical practice, and are of course not unknown today.

Although patronage was by no means unheard of in Europe, as evidenced for example by Zola's Médan group (who, it should be noted, later 'disowned' him), in terms of degree it can be considered a distinguishing characteristic of the Japanese literary world. Few authors appear to have established themselves in Meiji Japan without first attaching themselves to some higher authority (or at least rapidly gathering group support around themselves), and for that reason the achievement of those few who did manage it alone, such as Mori Ōgai, is all the more remarkable.

One of the effects of this patronage system was, of course, that an acolyte had to do his master's bidding, which must necessarily have imposed restrictions on the aspirant's literary freedom and creativity and, ironically in some cases, career. In 'The Literary World in Those Days', for example, we learn of Kōyō using his German-speaking pupil Sazanami Sanjin to attack — remarkably unsuccessfully — his rival Mori Ōgai in the arena of German literature, and one can only wonder to what extent the unfortunate Sazanami himself was a willing participant in those self-destructive exercises in which he was "invariably torn to shreds."

Of course, it was not mentors and patrons alone who could direct the literary inclinations of the young aspirants. The editors and publishers too wielded great power, and this is another feature of the literary world amply illustrated by 'Thirty Years in Tōkyō'. Naturally, publishers anywhere in the world have considerable influence in the final version of what they publish, but in the case of Meiji Japan it seems once again that in terms of degree their power becomes a distinguishing characteristic. There were the editors of the côterie magazines, which were associated with some faction or other and whose editors therefore often had strong and predetermined views; there were the editors of newspapers like the Yomiuri, which were again often associated with particular elements of the literary scene and whose editors could similarly be prone to being swayed by criteria other than pure literary merit; and there were the superlatively powerful 'bosses' of the big publishing houses, notably such concerns as Shunyōdō, Kinkōdō (early on), Hakubunkan, Shinseisha, and (from 1904) Shinchōsha, who could virtually dictate terms (and everything else for that matter) to the writers. The pressure which these figures could put on writers seems, however, to have had particular effect with regard to length of manuscript and — more importantly — time taken to write same, with an appropriate effect on the quality. At various points in 'Thirty Years in Tōkyō', such as in the discussion of Doppo's first work in 'K and T', we are told of editors taking or requesting a work of a certain length, while the pressure to meet deadlines is well illustrated by chapters such as 'Doppo's Death' or 'Desk'. 'Desk' also reveals how pressure to meet a deadline at all costs can indeed cost the quality of the work, with a writer producing something trivial at the eleventh hour which the publisher nevertheless accepts and publishes. One is left with the unfortunate feeling that the Meiji literary world might have done better to pay more attention to quality and less to quantity and mechanical completion of contract, as if literary art could be produced like goods in a factory. In 'Desk' and elsewhere Katai touches on this problem, but never seems to have taken positive measures to give priority to artistic quality. 'The Reception-Room of the H Publishing Company' gives a good account of the humiliating serf-lord relationship between the less established (or less favoured) writers and the figures of power and authority in the publishing world, while 'The Room Upstairs' describes the system whereby publishing houses physically detained writers in order to ensure completion of production targets/contracted work (a system still in existence nowadays, and now known as 'canning' — 'kanzume').

The critics too — often but not always one and the same as the established writers who patronised the young aspirants — could naturally influence careers and trends. Obviously this could apply to any literary or art scene in any country, but yet again it seems that in the matter of degree it is a prominent feature of the world of Meiji literature. 'The Big Names at the Time' is a good illustration of the power wielded by the critics, in this case particularly those writing in Ōgai's 'Mesamashigusa' (notably Ōgai himself, Kōda Rohan, and Saitō Ryokū). Katai writes how he was invariably vilified by them and always felt insulted and angry, but how he nevertheless respected the perceptiveness shown in their criticisms and benefited from some of the more constructive remarks. Were such influence always constructive it might be a matter for admiration rather than regret, but there is ample evidence given in 'Thirty Years in Tōkyō' that the approach of the critic often degenerated to the personal, negative, often destructive style of some present-day Hollywood gossip columnists. 'Social Intercourse amongst Writers' mentions the destructive effect gossippy type criticism — as popular then as now, it would seem — could have on a career, while in 'K and T' Doppo is shown expressing his far from benign view of certain critics.

Some of the senior figures in the world of Meiji literature feature in yet another characteristic of that world touched upon in 'Thirty Years in Tōkyō', a characteristic which may be considered perhaps as an unfortunate extension of the role of the mentor/patron. Namely, major writers would on occasion lend — or, a cynic might observe, 'sell' — their name to aspiring writers in order to facilitate publication of that aspirant's manuscript. In 'The Author of 'Hide and Seek'' Katai quite openly describes Saitō Ryokū's approaching him with a view to lending his name to a work in the writing of which Ryokū himself had no part. There is mention of the fact that Ryokū then passed the publisher's money to Katai, and although it does not state what percentage of it he passed on one would have to be somewhat naive to assume that he passed on ALL of it in a spirit of utter altruism (especially in view of the fact that the money was sent to him rather than Katai). In Note 468 I touch upon a further intriguing example, which saw a 'joint' work produced by Katai and Kōyō despite the open antipathy between them at that stage, and one can only speculate as to what exactly went on behind the scenes in such a case (there is rarely much documentation for the researcher to work off). To Western readers such a practice is at best artistically undesirable and misleading, rather like an extreme form of 'ghost writing', and at worst downright fraudulent, but the fact that Katai writes about it openly indicates that it was, presumably, known and tolerated by the reading public. (As further examples, from beyond 'Thirty Years in Tōkyō', one might raise the matter of transfer of ownership of a manuscript in Sōseki's 'Autumn Wind', or the peculiar 'fusing of identity' between Futabatei Shimei and his mentor Tsubouchi Shōyō with regard to the authorship of early versions of Futabatei's (Shōyō's?) 'Drifting Cloud'.) It does not seem to have been the case that the reading public were simply interested in the work and not the writer, for chapters such as 'Kōyō and Rohan' make it clear that writers had their own fan clubs and were the subject of much interest as to their personal as well as professional lives. Perhaps one can only conclude that the public accepted such things as necessary extensions of the mentor-novice relationship, and were prepared to turn a blind eye to the occasional incongruity.

'Thirty Years in Tōkyō' touches upon another feature of the world of letters which can distract the reader from the material actually written by the writer, and that is the matter of the illustrating. This is an aspect of literature which often seems overlooked, but 'Thirty Years in Tōkyō' makes it clear that illustrators played a fairly significant role in the Meiji literary world, both in terms of their social involvement with the writers (eg. Kosugi Misei, who features in 'Doppo's Death' and elsewhere) and in terms of their influence on readers' interpretation of the written word. In 'When I Wrote 'Life'' Katai gives a good illustration of this influence and the problems it can create, while in Note 550 accompanying that chapter I also discuss the disastrous role of the illustrator of Katai's 'Quilt'.

There are a number of other features of the Meiji literary world which become clear through the pages of 'Thirty Years in Tōkyō', such as the intense competitiveness, the enormous role played by newly adopted

Western literature and ideology, the psychological problems raised by the latter, and so on and so on. To some extent these have been touched upon already and, rather than discuss them in specific detail in this section, I think they will be more meaningfully treated by showing the part they played in the career of Katai himself, in the following sections.

3. Tayama Katai and 'Thirty Years in Tōkyō'

a) *The main developments in Katai's career*

Katai was born Tayama Rokuya on January 22nd 1872 (texts that give December 13th 1871 have overlooked the calendrical change in 1872), in Tatebayashi, present-day Gunma Prefecture. His family, both on his father's and mother's sides, had traditionally been samurai retainers to the Akimoto clan, then lords of the fief. As retainers they had belonged to a class known as 'shizoku', and had enjoyed warrior-noble privileges not dissimilar to those of medieval European knights. However, shortly before Katai's birth the feudal structure of society had been drastically changed as part of the Restoration process from 1868 on, and the rank of 'shizoku' was abolished along with the fiefs themselves. Many former 'shizoku' were plunged into desperate straits as a result, since in most cases they had little aptitude for any other profession. Katai's father Shōjūrō was no exception, and after a brief and unsuccesful attempt to farm he left for Tōkyō, used family connections to become a policeman, and presently enlisted for service in the Seinan Civil War of 1876-7. He was killed in action in April 1877, plunging the already improverished Tayama family into severe financial distress. Relying on just a war-widow's pension and occasional income from weaving brought in by Katai's paternal grandfather Hoyata, Katai's mother Tetsu strove to support a family comprising herself, Katai/Rokuya, his elder brother Miyato and infant brother Tomiya, his elder sister sister Katsuyo, and Hoyata and his wife. (A further sister Itsu had in 1876 married a police colleague of Shōjūrō's, Ishii Osamu, and had moved to Tōkyō.)

Life was obviously not easy for the Tayamas, and, as soon as they were old enough, the scholastically inclined Miyato was sent to Tōkyō in order to complete his studies and obtain clerical work with the minimum delay, Katai was sent to Tōkyō as a bookstore apprentice, and his sister Katsuyo was sent to Tōkyō as a serving-maid. Miyato's studies were supported by Itsu's husband Ishii Osamu, and his life at this stage is touched upon in 'The Sound of Voices Reading'. Katai's life as a nine-year old errand-boy — a position secured again by family connections, namely the owner of the bookstore's being a friend of the employer of an uncle of Katai's — is described in particular detail in the first chapter, 'In Those Days'.

Katai did not like the work, preferring to become a scholar, and appears to have deliberately got himself dismissed for persistent stealing. His sister Katsuyo had also proved unsatisfactory as a serving-maid, and the two returned together in disgrace to Tatebayashi early in 1882. Two years later, aged fifteen, Katsuyo was to marry a local weaver and eventually bear him nine children, while Katai was to continue his schooling.

He proved to be a good scholar with a bent for language and literature, and soon started writing poetry, inspired by the famed natural beauty of the Tatebayashi area. Most of his poems were published in the amateur magazine 'Eisaishinshi', as described in the early part of the chapter 'Return to Tōkyō'.

The same chapter mainly deals with the Tayama family's return to Tōkyō in 1886 (they had briefly spent some time there while Shōjūrō was alive) following Miyato's securing of a clerical position in the Department of Historical Documents. This position too had been found through family connections (in fact the same connections as in the case of Katai's apprenticeship), namely through the historian Okanoya Shigezane, who was formerly the Tōkyō-based vassal of Lord Akimoto and was the employer of Katai's uncle Yokota Ryōta.

While being supported in Tōkyō by his brother Miyato Katai attended various English schools, with the intention of becoming a lawyer, politician, or military officer, and continued to write poetry. His life at the time is described in such chapters as 'Return to Tōkyō' and 'The Late 1880's'. Again through family connections — specifically the historian Ishii Kakyū, the father of his brother-in-law Osamu — he was able to join the poetry classes of Matsuura Tatsuo, described in 'The Sunflower Hedge'. Not only was Matsuura himself an influence on Katai, emphasising such points as respect for nature and avoidance of elaborateness in depiction, but attendance at his classes also gave Katai the opportunity to make the aquaintance of fellow pupils such as the literary figures Miyazaki Koshoshi and Yanagita Kunio. Yanagita, who was then regarded as a child genius, was to become a particularly good and lifelong friend.

As a result of his poor eyesight Katai failed to embark upon a military career, and late in 1890 enrolled in a law school with a view to pursuing his alternative plan of becoming a politician and/or lawyer, only to find himself forced to withdraw soon afterwards as a result of lack of funds. Late 1890 and early 1891 was indeed a gloomy period for him, for to add to his troubles both he and his younger brother Tomiya contracted typhoid and were invalided for several months, and his mother was becoming increasingly cantankerous because of the pressures upon her, criticising Katai in particular for not getting a job and bringing home a proper income. The chapter 'Kōyō and Rohan' contains ample illustration of the difficulties he and the rest of the family were experiencing at the time:

> Even living in a place like that [a little house with overhanging eaves and dark rooms] it was difficult to make ends meet on my brother's salary, and we were in fairly desperate straits. ... I was always envious of others. ... To cap it all my younger brother and I caught typhoid. ... Lack of funds led to my withdrawal from the Japan Law School, which I'd just started going to... . In addition to that things were not going at all smoothly between my mother and elder brother and his wife, which upset me greatly. ... And I was forever hearing my mother complaining: "How long's he going to keep on playing around, our Roku?! It'd be nice if he went out somewhere and brought back a few yen!"

On May 14th that year (1891) Miyato's wife Tomi, of whom Katai was very fond, died in childbirth, and this seems to have been the final spur to action for Katai. He decided to put into effect an idea he had been entertaining of late, namely to endeavour to establish himself in a literary career by requesting help from Ozaki Kōyō, a leading literary figure of the day who happened to live nearby. Around May 20th Katai wrote him a letter requesting patronage, and, as described in 'Visiting Kōyō Sanjin', was fortunate in that his timing coincided with Kōyō's plan to form a new group of protégés, the Seishunsha, and to launch a new magazine, 'Senshibankō', as a publishing vehicle for it. Katai was accordingly accepted, and put in touch with Kōyō's 'right-hand man', the writer Emi Suiin, who was to be editor of the magazine. Suiin seems from the outset to have felt a strong sympathy for Katai, hailing himself from a former 'shizoku' family, having also lost his father when young, and having also spent some considerable time in the Tatebayashi region, and he was to prove of great help to him. It was just as well for Katai that Suiin was so benignly disposed, for Kōyō soon took a dislike to Katai's presumptuousness, ceased to consider him a protégé, and on at least one occasion actually prevented the publication of his works. In fact, a rift soon developed between Kōyō and Suiin himself, apparently over Kōyō's treatment of Katai, and Suiin ended up publishing his own magazine 'Kozakuraodoshi', specifically to help launch the much abused Katai. In addition, he was to use his contacts in the publishing world at large to help Katai become established as a professional writer (both 'Senshibankō' and 'Kozakuraodoshi' being amateur magazines). Though 'Thirty Years in Tōkyō' does not discuss such matters as the founding of 'Kozakuraodoshi' or Suiin's wise and timely assistance when Katai tried to publish an early work that was clearly a plagiarism of Saikaku, it nevertheless refers to Kōyō's shunning Katai in favour of other protégés such as Izumi Kyōka and Oguri Fūyō (see the final section of

'Visiting Kōyō Sanjin'), and to the fact that it was Suiin's introductions that led to Katai's first professional work, late in 1892 ('My First Manuscript-Fee'), and first professional translation, that of an English version of Tolstoi's 'Cossacks' in 1893 ('My First Translation').

One of Suiin's contacts was Ōhashi Otowa (Ōhashi Watanabe), a former Genyūsha writer who was to marry into the Hakubunkan publishing concern and consequently acquire enormous power and influence, and in fact become arguably the single most important figure in the publishing world in those days. Fortunately for Katai Ōhashi too proved to be reasonably well disposed towards him, as is made clear by such chapters as 'The Road Along the River' and 'The Reception-Room of the H Publishing Company', and subsequently bought many of his manuscripts despite their questionable artistic level.

As a result of these contacts and acts of assistance, and a certain identifiable if limited literary skill, by the mid 1890's Katai was able to consider himself a professional writer, especially of travelogues. Together with occasional translation-fees and income earned from transcribing documents for the earlier-mentioned historian Okanoya Shigezane (see 'The Road Along the River'), he was able to earn enough to take himself off on various enjoyable and educative trips (described in such chapters as 'Myself and Travel') even though he and his family were still relatively poor.

Katai's fictional works in the 1890's were either thinly disguised adaptations of other writers' works, or works of a highly emotional, lyrical vein, usually depicting a love affair doomed to remain unrequited through the cruel hand of fate (separation by death, duty, irreconcilable differences in social standing, etc.) and leaving the unhappy protagonist to seek consolation in the bosom of beautiful nature. They were hardly inspiring creations, and in 'The Reception-Room of the H Publishing Company' Katai tells us that Ōhashi considered them "wishy-washy and naive."

Nevertheless, that sort of work did have an appeal to the youth of the day, and it was a type frequently found in the pages of such magazines as 'Bungakukai', one of the major vehicles of the romantic movement that dominated the latter half of the 1890's. As Katai was no longer a member of the Genyūsha group and as it was difficult, even with contacts, to survive in the literary world of Meiji as a free-wheeling novice writer, it was not unnatural that he should gravitate towards the Bungakukai group, finally joining it early in 1896. His early contact with the group, which led among other things to his meeting the writer Shimazaki Tōson, is described in 'Our Group'.

The following year, through the mutual friendship of his old poetry classmate Miyazaki Koshoshi, Katai got to know one of his greatest friends-to-be, the writer Kunikida Doppo. It was shortly after Doppo's notorious and disastrous affair with Sasaki Nobuko, his wife for a few months only, and Doppo was badly in need of friendship. Though they shared a love of poetry, travel, and certain foreign works, Katai and Doppo were very different in terms of character and experiences, with Doppo being very worldly-wise (especially with regard to women), sharp, and decisive, as opposed to Katai's tendency to dream naively rather than act. However, these very differences seem to have bonded the friendship together, with the two friends acting as foils for each other. 'The House on the Hill' and the long chapter 'K [Kunikida] and T [Tayama]' reveal both the differences in their characters and the strength of their friendship.

Partly through his friendship with Doppo, partly through his increased exposure to foreign literature and ideology (especially individualism), and partly through his acquiring greater responsibilities in life associated with growing older, Katai's idealistic, fanciful, romantic outlook on life began to change to a more realistic one during his late twenties. In February 1899 he married Risako, the sister of one of his old poetry classmates Ōta Gyokumei, and underwent what appears to have been his first physical experience of women. In August that year his mother died, severing a link with the past and in a sense enforcing independence upon him. The following month, through contacts, he joined Hakubunkan's editorial staff for his first and only proper salaried employment (discounting a few months he had spent several years earlier on the staff of a newspaper). In February 1901 his first child was born (a daughter Reiko), adding parental responsibility to his new sense of reality.

It was just at this time that he was profoundly influenced by Maupassant's complete works, as described in 'The Second Floor of Maruzen', and, influenced in particular by Maupassant's cynical 'man of the world' attitude, decided to adopt a more mature and realistic approach both in his personal life and in his writing:

> My amazement over these stories brooked no comparison. I felt as though I had been struck over the head with a club. My way of thinking was turned topsy-turvy. ... Up till now I was only ever looking at the heavens. I knew nothing of the earth, nothing at all. I was a feeble idealist. From now on, I'd become a child of the earth, and crawl that earth like a beast rather than waste my time gazing at the stars.

However, despite his wish to reform himself both as a man and a writer and to produce more realistic works from the basis of a more realistic outlook, and despite various proclamations to this effect in writings such as the preface to his novel 'Flowers of the Field' (No no Hana, June 1901) and 'Blunt Depiction' (Rokotsu naru Byōsha, February 1904), he was unable for some years to establish himself as a writer in this new vein. Many of his works from 1901 to 1907 were mere plagiarisms of Maupassant (or other Western writers), and were generally considered incongruous and bizarre relative to his earlier literature and the rest of the literature of the day.

Maupassant was not the only influence acting upon him during the early years of the 1900's, and amongst others Nietzsche, Sudermann, and Hauptmann were especially significant. His most successful work of the period, 'The End of Jūemon' (Jūemon no Saigo, May 1902, in 'The Quilt and Other Stories'), was, despite obvious elements from Zola, essentially based upon the theme and message of Sudermann's 'Katzensteg' (Cat's Bridge, to which Katai refers in 'The Little House in the Suburbs'), which in turn echoed the views of Nietzsche — that society had lost touch with the natural individual. However, while 'Jūemon''s relative success helped Katai financially, and promoted his name to a certain extent, it did not establish him in the top league of writers, and was moreover still considered rather bizarre. Had he been able to follow it fairly quickly with another substantial work or two it may have been a different matter, but as it turned out it was to be another five years before he really became known as a major writer. During that time he was to spend several months in Manchuria (1904), covering the Russo-Japanese War as a correspondent for Hakubunkan, and this experience of life's brutality was to develop further his realistic view and to make him more determined than ever to produce a blunt 'no holds barred' type of literature.

A further highly significant experience was the visit of a private pupil, Okada Michiyo, between January 1904 and January 1906. She was, ironically, an admirer of his earlier sentimental-type works, and had contacted him in the summer of 1903 to ask him to accept her as his pupil. He had just read Hauptmann's 'Einsame Menschen' (Lonely People), depicting a similar sort of situation in which a vivacious young girl student (Anna Mahr) visits the protagonist's (Johannes Vockerat) dull home (Katai too finding married life very dull by this stage), and, partly out of a wish to parallel the protagonist's experiences — a personality trait discussed in more detail in the following section of this introduction — he eventually allowed the girl to come to Tōkyō. What followed is described in almost slavishly authentic detail in 'The Quilt' (Futon) of September 1907, so suffice to say here that he was excited by her both spiritually and physically, but was unable to bring himself to 'consummate' that relationship. The experience did, however, enable him to write in 'The Quilt' the sort of blunt work he had been trying to achieve for several years, simply by cathartically writing about his immoral but arguably natural feelings for her. By this stage he was also driven to such relatively desperate lengths by the success of his friends Tōson and Doppo, which filled him with a sense of being left behind and with a desire to write a 'make or break' work. His feelings are described in the famous chapter 'My Own Anna Mahr':

> I alone felt left behind. ... I still hadn't written anything substantial... [I was] frustrated and determined to write something. I was filled with a mixture of despair and impatience ... I had to give it everything I'd got... Just at that time I was profoundly influenced by Gerhart Hauptmann's 'Einsame Menschen'. I felt that Vockerat's loneliness was my own. In addition I had to break away from my previous pattern and take some new direction with regard to my family and work. Fortunately I had profited from my extensive reading of foreign literature... I felt that in the ideology of people such as Tolstoi, Ibsen, Strindberg, and Nietzsche I could clearly see fin-de-siecle suffering. I too wanted to tread that path of suffering... I wanted to try revealing things that might even break me if I were to reveal them ... I decided to write about my own Anna Mahr.

'The Quilt' of September 1907 turned out to be an epoch-making work, as discussed earlier in this introduction. It not only rocketed Katai overnight into the top division of writers, but it was seen as heralding a new era in Japanese literature and even society in general, an era in which the individual could at least raise the possibility of defying social convention. Certainly it was seen as establishing a new genre, that of the 'I' novel. The genre was not new in that it was autobiographical — a feature of Japanese literature from as early as the tenth century — but in the exhaustive extent of its ruthless self-exposure and its concern with truth rather than prevailing standards of morality. Katai was accordingly hailed as a pioneer, and as brave to boot.

Of course, as discussed earlier, from Katai's point of view, writing 'The Quilt' was not just the relatively simple matter of conveying to the public his views on individualism and its relationship to social convention, since it clearly also reflected his own personality trait of paralleling Western literature, was largely cathartic, and was born of make or break desperation. But it *was* successful in many respects, and, for better or for worse, Katai was to follow it over the next few years with similar exhaustive and often distressing exposées of various members of his family and friends, as in 'Life' (Sei — see 'When I Wrote 'Life'') of 1908, 'Wife' (Tsuma) of 1908-9, and 'Relations' (En) of 1910. (The last work is considered especially interesting as a sort of sequel to 'The Quilt', in that it treats Katai's adoption of Okada Michiyo as his own daughter in January 1909, following her disinheritance by her own family.) And thus, especially when reinforced by the similar 'I' novels of Tōson's that were to follow, was the character of Japanese naturalism established, and thus was Katai established as its pioneer and leader. He himself, it should be noted, was not entirely happy with the genre, feeling it to be too inclined towards subjectivity, and in the same period 1907-10 wrote a considerable number of works that could not be called 'I' novels. Chief amongst these were 'One Soldier' (Ippeisotsu, in 'The Quilt and Other Stories') of 1908, depicting in almost callously impersonal terms the death of a soldier in the Russo-Japanese War, and the extremely popular 'Country Teacher' (Inaka Kyōshi) of 1909 (see the chapter 'Country Teacher' and my translation of the novel [UP Hawaii 1984]). It is always important to bear in mind that, despite Katai's inevitable linking with the 'I' novel and the type of naturalism represented by the genre, it is these two non-'I' novel works, 'One Soldier' and 'Country Teacher', that are considered his best works in terms of technique and popularity respectively.

Though Katai was not just a naturalist, it is true that his heyday could be considered as roughly corresponding to the heyday of naturalism, namely the period 1907-1910. Beyond that point in time, basic elements of Katai's approach to literature underwent a change, partly perhaps for pragmatic reasons connected with the Treason Incident discussed earlier, but more significantly as a result of changes in his outlook on life. While he refers in 'Crisis at Forty' to such things as general boredom and disillusionment, other major reasons for his depression are, unfortunately, not touched upon in 'Thirty Years in Tōkyō'. Put briefly, the whole business revolves around his fatal attraction to a geisha named Iida Yone. He met Iida in the summer of 1907 and, benefiting from his new confidence around that time, succeeded in developing a physical relationship with her. For him, she was the classic 'femme fatale', and she dominated his thoughts to a quite extraordinary extent. She, on the other hand, was by no means as smitten with Katai as he was with her, continuing to see other clients, and he became obsessed with attempting to secure her love for himself alone. He was caused such torment by this unbalanced relationship with her that his vision became narrowed onto the theme of the distress caused to individuals (notably himself) in their relations with the other sex, and from about 1911 on (when she appeared to be favouring another particular client) he wrote innumerable works, mostly autobiographical, on this topic. They were almost without exception received as monumentally boring by the reading public and even by his close literary friends, and were a major cause of his decline in popularity and for one unfortunate direction taken by the 'I' novel. (The assertion made by some Western critics that the Japanese reading public never find 'I' novels boring is simply not true in the case of many of Katai's post-1911 works.)

Adding to the unpopularity of these works was the fact that their treatment of male-female relations was bound up with an increasingly obscure view of nature, society, and the individual. Again put briefly, in his early romantic period in the 1890's, Katai had seen nature as an essentially benign force symbolised by bucolic beauty, and he had seen fate as an opposed cruel force. It was a naive view, but one that by its very simplicity gained a certain readership. After his contact at the turn of the century with Western writers and thinkers, especially Nietzsche, his view changed to one wherein nature had in effect been distorted by society and its agent morality, whose conventions man often interpreted incorrectly as fate. Though he had increasing reservations about this pro-natural individual, anti-societal view — reservations which can even be detected in 'The Quilt' if one probes deeply enough, in passages such as that in which man is referred to as a pawn at the mercy of an indifferent nature — it was nonetheless the view which, for the vast majority of the reading public of the day, characterised 'The Quilt' and Japanese naturalism. For them, it too was a simple and therefore appealing concept — the natural individual trying to be free, and artificial society trying to repress him with its weapon of moral convention. However, by about 1909/10 Katai's reservations about nature, which had started as early as his proper understanding of Maupassant in 1901 and had been fuelled by his exposure to the brutality of the Russo-Japanese War in 1904 and the cruel deaths of his brother Miyato in 1907 and his friends Doppo and Bizan in 1908, became very pronounced, and within a short time tied in with his obsession with Iida Yone to come to centre primarily on the arena of male-female relations. As works such as 'The Trap' (Wana) of October 1909 show, he had by this stage come to feel that nature was the prime force of the universe and that it was in fact responsible for everything in existence, including fate, including society and morality, including inter-sexual relations, and including life's suffering. In particular, this indifferent nature was concerned only with the survival of the species, to which end it brought mankind together in society in order to facilitate the meeting of the sexes and to which end it evolved the institution of marriage. Marriage was the best means of ensuring security for the future of the species, but — and here was the proof of the indifference — it was often injurious to the wishes of the individual. Over the next few years he developed the line of reasoning that although in one sense man the individual could be considered a more substantial entity than man the compliant social being, in nature's plan it seemed that there was no provision for such a free individual, except in the coldly comforting sense of serving to strengthen society by providing an enemy to it, and therefore to develop individuality was merely to invite disharmony, discomfort and distress. The main concern of mankind was to relate to the other sex, and the greater degree of individuality shown by the individuals in each relationship, the more troublesome that relationship would be. It was because he and Iida were such strong individuals that they could not make the sacrifices necessary for their relationship to be a smooth one. He could not change Iida, but he could improve matters by endeavouring to make himself into a less assertive and demanding individual. To this end he would undergo meditation, partly inspired by the similar experiences of the French writer Huysmans, and turn to religion, aided by his brother-in-law Ōta Gyokumei (since 1899, head priest at the Kenpuku Temple in Hanyū). There are a number of indirect references to this meditation in the final chapters of 'Thirty Years in Tōkyō', especially 'Six Months in an Old Temple', but it is not treated directly.

Katai's works after 'Thirty Years in Tōkyō', till about 1923, are almost all in the same obscure vein, a mixture of esoteric religious ideology (including a worship of time as nature's 'cleansing agent') and the search for harmony between individuals involved in sexual relationships, in the vast majority of cases using himself and Iida Yone as symbols of troubled relationships in general. In most of the works he appears to be writing for his own benefit, and it is questionable whether the average reader would have managed even the vaguest understanding of his concerns. Even researchers of Katai have shunned the daunting prospect of these later works, and I for one cannot foresee a study of them ever being undertaken by a Westerner.

Despite several periods of meditation and vague theoretical solutions to the distress he suffered in his obsession with Iida, he remained an unhappy man till 1923. In that year he finally did succeed in winning her devotion, not through any feats of convoluted religious reasoning but, ironically perhaps, through the age-old device of displaying gallantry. Specifically, he demonstrated considerable courage and heroism in searching for her in the aftermath of the Great Tōkyō Earthquake, finally fighting through burning ruins to rescue her in a river full of corpses. From that point on, till his death from cancer of the throat in May 1930, he wrote a number of admired works on historical figures, and continued to write of his relationship with Iida, but from a now different point of view. The most noted of these is 'One Hundred Nights' (Momoyo) of 1927.

b) *The man behind the career*

What sort of person emerges from the pages of 'Thirty Years in Tōkyō', and how does that personality relate to Katai's life and literature in general?

Though the work does not reveal all of Katai's personality traits — notable omissions being his increasing awe before nature and the full extent of his obsession with the opposite sex — 'Thirty Years in Tōkyō' is nevertheless rich in such material. Indeed, it is noted for containing one of the most extraordinary 'naked comments' to be found anywhere in Japanese literature, when, in 'Crisis at Forty', Katai compares himself with the recently bereaved Tōson:

> *My* children hadn't died. *My* wife hadn't died. I hadn't even had such a stimulus as that to make me start out into a new life. I cursed the banality, the monotony.
>
> And so, in that sense, I envied Shimazaki his trip to France. To have lost his beloved children, and his wife, must certainly have been a bitter blow, but on the other hand he was able to achieve a certain freedom as a result, and I felt that that was at any rate better than the banality and monotony of my own life.

To those who have read 'The Quilt' and certain other works of Katai's such a comment will come as no surprise, except perhaps in the extreme degree of its frankness, for in 'The Quilt' and elsewhere he has not infrequently expressed a fanciful notion to the effect that if his wife were to die (in childbirth or similar) it would leave him free to pursue possible relations with other women.

The statement above tells us a number of things: first, that he was not exactly enraptured by his wife; second, that he was far from being reserved or delicate when it came to discussing such matters; and third, that he was extremely self-centred. Each of these points has a bearing on his attitude to life and literature, and I think therefore that it is a fair way to lead into a discussion of his personality.

He married Risa, the sister of his poetry classmate Ōta Gyokumei, in February 1899, with almost no knowledge of the person he was contracting to spend his life with. This in itself is not necessarily uncommon in Japan, even today, but in Katai's case it seems to have had particularly unfortunate results. He had no physical knowledge of women prior to his marriage, and indeed had no girlfriend throughout his youth, yet, as 'Out in the Western Suburbs' and other chapters clearly illustrate, he was interested in girls to the point of spending whole afternoons trailing suitably attractive ones all around Tōkyō. He would envy those who could succeed in forming relationships with women, but seemed to lack the ability to even attempt to form them himself. As a result he would end up fantasising and masturbating, as he openly admits in works such as 'The Girl-Watcher' (Shōjobyō) of 1907 (in 'The Quilt and Other Stories'). In his early days he tended to attribute his lack of success to the fact that his family was poor and that therefore he was doomed to be considered unsuitable as a future partner by the family of whatever girl he was obsessed with at a given point in time. In fact, this was the very stuff of his early novels, such as 'The Young Poet'of 1893 referred to in 'Out in the Western Suburbs'. Many of his works would similarly feature a young man — clearly based on Katai himself — doomed to failure in love as a result of unbridgeable differences in social standing.

Yet, at the same time, the poverty of his family was clearly not the real reason for his failures. Nor could those failures necessarily be blamed on the hand of fate, as is also the case in many of his early works where one of the young couple-to-be obeys the call of duty or is whisked by 'inescapable' circumstances to some distant clime. The real reason is to be discerned in chapters such as 'K and T', where, by contrast with the assertive Doppo, Katai is made to look embarrassingly wimpish and naive. Katai tells us there that he was a worshipper of the concept of virginal beauty, feeling that virgins were "sacred things" and that "a virgin's purity was the most beautiful, the most perfect thing on earth." His reluctance to put himself in a position where he might actually destroy the very thing he worshipped is particularly clearly illustrated by the episode (in 'K and T') in which he accompanies Doppo to a nearby temple, presumably merely to gaze from a distance at the attractive girl Doppo has reported seeing there, and almost dies of apoplexy when Doppo starts making advances to the girl, eventually becoming both angry and afraid and forcing Doppo to stop:

> The girl was there as usual on the sunny verandah, bent over her sewing and revealing her pretty white neck...
>
> "Watch! I'll make her look this way!" said K [Kunikida].
>
> He gave a whistle.
>
> "Stop! Stop! For heaven's sake stop!"
>
> T [Tayama] stopped K from whistling again, a look of fear on his face.
>
> "What's wrong?"
>
> "Stop it! If you whistle again I'm going back!"
>
> T had started to walk off, so K refrained from whistling and merely grinned....

This failure to develop relationships with the other sex as a result of a reluctance to detract in the least way from the sacrosanct purity of virginity is in fact apparent in a number of Katai's early works. For example, in 'Forgotten Waters' (Wasuremizu) of 1896 the young male protagonist fails to declare his love to the girl of his heart's desires, and consequently loses her to another man, simply because "It was too beautiful a love." "I could not declare my feelings," he remarks, "because my love was not so base as that."

Though such stories usually contain a condemnation of a fate that is doubly cruel, firstly by endowing the protagonist with such abnormally pure feelings and secondly by allowing the development of circumstances not suited to those pure feelings, the reader is nonetheless invariably left wondering why on earth the protagonist didn't do something positive, and feeling that if he loses out in love then he only has himself to blame. The researcher, on the other hand, is left feeling that he has been given a glimpse of the writer at a deeper level than a protagonist merely bewailing the circumstances of 'fate', and that there is no doubt something waiting to be uncovered at an even deeper level still.

Why, then, should Katai have developed such a wimpish personality in his youth? Unfortunately the answer is not fully clear from 'Thirty Years in Tōkyō' alone, and one has to refer to other memoir-type works such as 'Things I have Done' (Watashi no Yatte Kita Koto, 1920) and 'Writing Novels', (Shōsetsu Sakuhō, 1909). It was, he tells us in such writings, because he was endowed with a highly-sexed nature but was at the same time raised in a puritanical family where non-marital sexual relationships were strongly discouraged, with the result that in classic over-compensation he distorted his sexual drives into extremes of idealisation. In 'Things I have Done' he writes "My need for women was certainly much greater than that felt by most men," while in 'Writing Novels' he writes "I was born and raised in a puritanical family.... The suppression of carnal desire was an important factor in making me descend into sentimentalism."

This stress led to an imbalance in his writing and indeed in his own personal life itself, and in both his works and his immediate consciousness he treated women (notably virgins) as shadowy, distant, vague creatures embodying an abstract concept of beauty and purity but at all times only to be viewed through a barrier of rose-pink haze, while at a deeper level he in fact had very basic carnal feelings towards them. He was, in his own words (from 'Things I have Done'), "not really as effeminate as my early works suggest. In fact, I was endlessly repressing sexual desire, and was a wolf in sheep's clothing." The change in his literature in 1907 was a direct result, he tells us (also 'Things I have Done') of "casting off the mask" and deciding to depict bluntly and honestly what really lay deep within him. Hence 'The Girl-Watcher', where the clearly Katai-based protagonist is killed when he is pushed from a crowded train while intently ogling some girl, can be seen — as Katai himself is said to have remarked — as the 'killing off' of the old, deceitfully timid Katai to open the way for the real, unmasked, (relatively) wolfish Katai to emerge with 'The Quilt'. The determination to follow this 'make or break' course is clearly revealed in 'My Own Anna Mahr', where he writes of his intention "to try revealing things that I had kept hidden and covered, things that might even break me if I were to reveal them." At the same time it is vitally important to appreciate that while the new, bold, decisive Katai of 1907 was responsible for the epoch-making decision to 'confess' his feelings towards his pupil, it is the old, wishy-washy Katai who is actually depicted in the work (set 1904-6). Hence the protagonist is, while not quite so naive as in his early works, still at times exasperatingly indecisive, and hence the sarcasm-filled gap deliberately left between Katai the author and Katai the protagonist. His meeting with his mistress-to-be Iida Yone in the summer of that year 1907 was also clearly a factor in his new attitude.

His problems regarding the other sex, which so plagued Katai's youth and beyond, explain in part a number of other things. For example, there is the intensity of his dependence upon his mother and subsequently — despite his belief in the strong individual — upon Iida Yone, and his intense feelings of rejection when these women not infrequently failed to return his affection. There is his obsession with the role of male-female relationships in the context of society, the context of the life of the individual, and the context of the universe in general. There is his tendency to introversion, self-pity, and in his early days exaggerated emotion and abnormal feelings such as a boyhood 'crush' on his elder sister Itsu. And, of course, it all helps explain the haste with which he married his friend's sister: for, through the very fact that she was the younger sister of a friend, he was able with relative ease to seize an opportunity for marriage and thence physical consummation of a legitimate and morally justifiable nature. As luck would have it, in terms of personality he and his new bride-cum-sexual outlet were soon to prove almost total opposites, she being happily old-fashioned and domesticated and the very sort of person whom Katai was to come to despise.

His contempt towards his old-fashioned wife was, as well as being a reflection of the torment he himself had suffered through old-fashioned puritanism, a reflection of his interest in Western literature and the Western way of life. His meek wife suffered in his esteem in direct proportion to his encounter with the strong women depicted in Western literature, such as Magda from Sudermann's 'Heimat' (Home), Nora from Ibsen's 'Doll's House', and Elena from Turgenev's 'On the Eve', all of which he cites in Chapter Three of 'The Quilt' as examples for modern Japanese women to follow. Compared with these women, and with modern-minded Japanese women like Okada Michiyo ('his own

Anna Mahr') or even just strong Japanese women like Iida Yone, his poor wife, "with her old-fashioned waddling walk and submissiveness" ('The Quilt'), didn't stand a chance. He preferred women strong enough to show the initiative that he himself found so elusive.

Katai's interest in Western literature went far beyond merely affecting his attitude towards his wife, and was so strong that it can unquestionably be thought of as a personality trait, and not simply a characteristic of his literary stand that occasionally spilled over into his personal life. Obviously, part of the reason that he was so strongly attracted to Western literature and ideology, and indeed so often threatened to reject or at least defy Japanese conventions, was that he felt cheated by Japanese society. His family had for generations, both on his father's and mother's sides, been warrior-retainers enjoying a quasi-noble status and various privileges. Suddenly, following the Restoration these privileges had been snatched from the family, causing poverty, a degree of humiliation, and, indirectly, leading to the death of his father. Like many scions of these former warrior families, he was left feeling a strange mixture of both pride and disillusionment in his heritage. This developed into a love-hate relationship with Japanese convention and with the Japanese State, wherein he vacillated between support for things Japanese and rejection of them in favour of the West, and often ended up pragmatically trying to obtain the best of both worlds. There are numerous examples in 'Thirty Years in Tōkyō' and in Katai's literature in general where he sweepingly condemns things Japanese and almost blindly advocates things Western, yet at the same time there are also numerous examples of how he is quite prepared to do things Japanese-style if it will help his cause. The early chapters of 'Thirty Years in Tōkyō' are good illustrations of this 'Japaneseness', describing his use of various family and fief connections to obtain employment and introductions and his readiness to use patrons to battle on his behalf (such as Emi Suiin in the early days of his career), while 'The Quilt' neatly reveals both sides at once, in his telling his pupil Yoshiko (Okada Michiyo) to abandon ridiculous old Japanese ways and become a Western-type free individual, yet virtually at one and the same time exploiting the role of Japanese-style guardian for his own ends (specifically to disrupt her affair with her boyfriend).

In Katai's attraction to Western literature one does not find merely a desire for exciting women or a disillusionment with Japanese traditions. There are certainly other factors, some obvious, some deeper and possibly requiring a psychologist's training to fully understand. The most obvious factor is that the pragmatist in Katai clearly saw Western literature as a means to survive — even perhaps to achieve success — in a world where he was otherwise relatively poorly equipped to compete.

Through poor eyesight and lack of funds he failed in early attempts to embark upon other careers (as touched upon in such chapters as 'Kōyō and Rohan'), and, as he tells us in 'Social Intercourse amongst Writers', he followed the path of literature because "I have no other ability, no other field I could enter, and so, self-indulgently, I have clung to [literary] art and somehow or other made it my life." But, as he also tells us, in 'Tōkyō Before the Electric Trains', he was, despite a certain prowess shown at school, not exactly ideally equipped for such a life: "Because my works weren't very good, because I was bad at socialising, and because I had a certain pretentiousness about me, I was always spoken badly of by literary people." Though the life of a writer was not necessarily admired in Japan, as discussed earlier in this introduction, the young Katai nevertheless envied successful writers such as Ozaki Kōyō and Kawakami Bizan. In 'Visiting Kōyō Sanjin' he writes:

> As I took my leave and came away I was filled on the one hand with a fired ambition, and on the other with gloomy thoughts about my own life-style. I had no cheerful upstairs rooms, no muslin cushions, no broad-beans, no latest publications: all I had was a desk in a dirty little room next to the toilet.

In 'The Room Upstairs' he even envies Bizan his being 'imprisoned' by publishers in order to complete a contracted work, to the point where Bizan has to tell him: "It's not exactly an honour, you know, writing in a situation like this!" Nevertheless, Katai is undeterred and continues "to imagine the free and easy life of a successful writer, which of course I still knew nothing of, and then to think about how particularly wretched my own humdrum 'stay-at-home' life was." And for the relatively untalented Katai, Western literature, to which he had been introduced at an early stage through his wealthy friend Nojima Kinpachirō (see 'Zola's Novels'), provided a path to success. It was still an area relatively unknown even to major writers of the day, and was therefore an area in which Katai could establish himself with relative ease. In 'Visiting Kōyō Sanjin', for example, he writes how he virtually talked on equal terms with Kōyō once the conversation turned to foreign literature, while in 'The Old Castle Ruins of Komoro' he makes the significantly pragmatic remark:

> At any rate, in those days we felt we had to study in earnest, and make plans for the future so as not to be tossed about by the waves of real life. Accordingly, we immersed ourselves in the study of foreign literature.

Elsewhere, he remarks that the literary world at the turn of the century was in a state of (stylistic) chaos, and in need of leadership, and that everyone seemed to feel that "There's nothing for it but to refer to

Western literature'' ('The Literary World in those Days'). Nor is it insignificant that Katai's 'heroes' in the world of Japanese literature were two men who did more than anyone else to introduce foreign literature, Mori Ōgai and Futabatei Shimei.

Katai's great admiration for Ōgai — his most respected hero of all — is also attributable to the fact that Ōgai was one of the few truly strong, arguably honest individuals in the Japanese literary world, having strength and courage enough to stick by his principles and having no need of the usual sycophantic acolytes. He writes in 'Ōgai Gyoshi at War' that ''I admired Ōgai more than anyone else,'' and ''I'd always liked Ōgai's individuality, and this frank, informed attitude of his impressed me greatly.'' The frankness and strength of individuality which Katai similarly encountered in Western writers, such as Ibsen, Nietzsche, and Tolstoi, was indeed another factor that drew him to Western literature and ideology. His earlier quoted famous statements on the ideology of the strong individual, especially the Nietzschean 'superman' (see 'Kōyō's Death' and 'The Second Floor of Maruzen'), make it clear how such ideology appealed to him on a deep and personal level. He also saw it as another pragmatic path to success, considering that the time was ripe for such a move. The Restoration had introduced a new life-style, but there was need for a new ideology to back up these external changes. Literature could act as a means of providing that new ideology, especially after the bastions of the old school like Kōyō were no longer present. And, as he writes in 'Brief Comments on Certain Writers', those who could not swim with the new ideological currents would be swept away. Though Katai may have lacked real ability in finer areas of literary expertise, he was certainly not lacking in the skills of survival, and his favourite weapons were his knowledge of Western literature and ideology, his Western-inspired belief in the strength of the self-aware individual, and his similar adherence to the Western-inspired view that honesty and bluntness stemming naturally from an individual's strength of inner conviction could give depth and meaning to literature. (In this last respect, one should not overlook the tenets of German naturalism which I touched upon earlier in this introduction and which Katai genuinely admired.) It is fair to say that bluntness was an attitude which suited Katai both on a personal and literary level, and gave him both real and artistic satisfaction. (In fact, contemporary critics such as Ikuta Chōkō termed Katai's unadorned approach 'the country bumpkin philosophy of stupidity', claiming with much contempt and no doubt considerable justification that since Katai lacked the ability to write either elaborately or carefully he had little free choice in arriving at a philosophy that revered blunt, 'just-as-it-is' depiction. The impressionistic dimension which Katai added to this approach from about 1908 on, whereby he ceased to pay any conscious attention to the details of whatever he was depicting and ended up producing material riddled with inconsistencies and errors of detail, as indeed is the case with 'Thirty Years in Tōkyō', could only be said to have invited even stronger criticism of this nature.)

A factor rather more difficult to assess in Katai's adoption of foreign literature was his actual parallelling of the lives and personalities that he found in Western literature, both amongst the writers themselves and amongst their literary creations. To an extent this may be attributed simply to his hero-worship of the strong individuals he found there, but, as suggested briefly earlier, it is also probably a manifestation of a deep-seated inferiority complex — possibly stemming from his lack of success with women — combined with his periodic disillusionment with and rejection of Japanese values. Certainly he suffered from what is popularly termed nowadays 'alienation of personality', especially from middle-age on, and seemed to feel a need to justify every major action or attitude by reference to a precedent somewhere in Western literature. In 'The Quilt', for example, we find him openly saying "I am Turgenev's 'superfluous man'," as well as lamenting the fact that, since Yoshiko/Michiyo has a boyfriend, he can no longer become a Johannes. In 'The End of Jūemon' we are told that the events discussed in the opening pages are like something from Turgenev's 'Sportsman's Diary'. In 'Thirty Years in Tōkyō', in 'My Own Anna Mahr', we find him saying how he wanted to tread the same path of suffering as Tolstoi, Ibsen, Strindberg, and Nietzsche. In later years, although it is only mentioned indirectly in 'Thirty Years in Tōkyō', he consistently parallels himself with Huysmans in his meditation in a religious institution, seeking an answer — like Huysmans — to the distress caused to individuals by male-female relationships. It also seems that the plagiarism of Western writers which Katai frequently resorted to in the early 1900's may not have been simply a pragmatic attempt to achieve instant success by questionable means — though that aim was certainly present — but at the same time a more complex desire to fuse his personality with that of a Western literary figure. To an extent Doppo could be said to have manifested the same sort of identity problems in his attitude towards Wordsworth, and it may be the case that Katai is merely, in this particular regard, an extreme example of a psychological phenomenon occurring among a number of Meiji writers — a phenomenon in which 'being influenced' led to 'seeking precedent' or to 'imitating', which in turn led to 'partly becoming' to the extent of a fusion of identities. In any event, it is a point that needs discussion beyond the limited scope of these pages, and it is mentioned here simply as background information to Katai's innumerable and often markedly esoteric references to Western literary figures — so esoteric at times that it is not possible to view them simply as examples of 'name-dropping' to impress the reader.

Finally, there is the question of Katai's self-centredness. I would go so far as to say that he was indeed 'selfish', and not merely 'self-centred'. To an extent it is an understandable characteristic in a person materially deprived during their youth, and no doubt it is a trait intensified by his difficulties in socialising, his introversion, and inferiority complexes relative to truly strong and successful people. It is therefore perhaps not surprising that a philosophy of self-aware individualism should appeal to him, but it is at the same time a sad fact that such ideology ended up developing his self-centredness into a cold and at times callous egoism. (It should be pointed out that at the time of the quotation given at the start of this section, 1913, Katai had himself recognised the lack of warmth in such a philosophy, but was still some time away from achieving a changed outlook through religion.)

The link between his individualism and his constantly evolving views on nature is also an interesting development. Having already discussed those views, and their evolution from a simple worship of physical nature to a belief in the superiority of the primally natural over the man-made and finally to a worship of nature as the ultimate force in the universe, I will not discuss them again here, but it should be borne in mind that his naturocentrism underlies many of the traits discussed in the last few pages, and that it too is an understandable characteristic in a simple man born and raised in an area of natural beauty and destined to be a pawn in the interplay of enormous forces.

Indeed, I find it convenient to think of Katai as a simple man tragically caught in the vortex of many strong and confusing forces, often pulling in opposed directions. He was caught between the old and the new, between Japan and the West, between morality and amorality, between acceptance and defiance, between fancy and reality, between artistic ideals and actual lack of talent, between the self and the universal, between the individual and the social, between woman as a source of appeal and woman as a source of rejection and misery, and between nature the friend and nature the foe. Though he undoubtedly had unpleasant aspects to his personality, I feel one that can understand that personality and even sympathise with it, and that one is indeed compelled to respect his ability to make the most of his limited skills.

As the chief memoirs of such a man, 'Thirty Years in Tōkyō' is a significant human document.

THIRTY YEARS IN TŌKYŌ[1]

by Tayama Katai
translated by Kenneth Henshall

In Those Days

In those days Tōkyō was a city of mud, of earth-walled houses and councillors' carriages and little street-stalls clustered round the bridges. It all seems like a dream to me now. With the exception of the Ginza, there was only one large Western-style building to be found in all the roads of Kyōbashi and Nihonbashi. It stood on the site of the present-day Niroku Newspaper offices in Sudachō, and belonged to the Xerez Company.[2] It had three storeys, and what looked like a wind gauge on the roof that used to spin round in the wind. I think they used to sell foreign foods, or something like that.

Mitsukoshi was still known as Echigoya. It was a large, irregularly shaped store with long shop-curtains whose white characters stood out against a black background. You could hear the clerks and shopboys inside calling out in a sort of rhythmic chant — "Hey, hey!" The streets

---

[1] The title, as indeed the idea for the work itself, is inspired by Alphonse Daudet's 'Thirty Years in Paris' ('Trente Ans de Paris'), 1888. The period is that from the 1880's to the 1910's.

[2] The Niroku Shinbun was founded in 1893 (ie. Meiji 26, from which it takes its name), and was known as the Niroku Shinpō ('Report') till 1904. It subsequently changed its name several times, including on two occasions back to 'Shinpō', before finally ceasing publication in 1940. Its offices stood in Tōrishinkokuchō 16 Banchi (present-day Sudachō 1 Chōme), in Kanda-ku, in a three-storey Western-style building as described below in the text. According to contemporary photographs and records it was the only such building in the area. It was formerly known as the Asahiya Building, Asahiya being a shop dealing in Western wines and spirits (see the later section 'The Asphalt Road'). There is, however, no mention of a 'Xerez Wine (Trading) Company' ('Keree Shōkai') in any of the official records of the Chiyoda Ward-Office or the Chiyoda Library, nor in any of the numerous local histories, architectural accounts, or foreigners' memoirs that I have consulted. In the later section 'The Asphalt Road' Katai refers to the Asahiya and "a place selling Xerez Wine (Keree-shu)" as though they are separate companies, and as there was categorically only one such building at the time we must assume that the Xerez Company was housed in the same building as the Asahiya and dealt in more or less the same merchandise. The problem is compounded by semantic difficulties: it is not absolutely certain that 'Keree' is intended to represent 'Xerez' (sherry), though this does seem the most likely interpretation, and it is remotely possible that it is a reference to some now-forgotten foreign entrepreneur named Kelly. It remains an intriguing mystery.

It should also be noted that Kyōbashi and Nihonbashi were 'ku' (wards) till 1947. From 1878 on Kyōbashi-ku included the Ginza area. However, Katai uses the terms very loosely, and the site of the elusive Xerez Company was in fact in Kanda-ku from 1878.

were narrow, and you could understand how it would have seemed to Loti's eyes like some dark, dirty and cramped oriental town.[3] At the end of the road to Sudachō there was a big, sunny open area that served as a firebreak. There were willows along the bank, and a stone arched bridge — one of the sights of Tōkyō in those days — just like you see in the old colour prints.[4]

"Only one tenpō, a real bargain!"[5]

I forget whether it was rice cake or sponge cake that they were selling, but anyway, whenever those bustling street-hawkers appeared, dressed in their Edo-style tradesman's livery and calling out their wares, women and children flocked out from the shops to buy from them. That one tenpō-sen cake sold really well. In those days I was an eleven year old errand-boy, and I often used to stand and stare enviously at people buying it.

What memories the tenpō-sen — that huge, oval coin — holds for me! In those days you could buy such a lot with just one of them. It was two rin short of a standard sen and was therefore used as a nickname for idiots and people who weren't quite all there, but in point of fact it was a very useful coin. One tenpō-sen was just the right amount for a helping of noodles, or beancurd, or raw salmon, or for the bathhouse. And every now and again people would give me one of those coins, with some remark like "Oh, the poor boy, in this cold! Let's at least give him a tenpō-sen."

Rickety old horse-coaches — the sort you don't see nowadays except right out in the country — used to pass by with horns blowing, on rainy days sending the mud flying high. I often used to race them. Sometimes

---

[3] Pierre Loti (1850-1923), a naval officer and writer referred to in more detail later in this same section. The visit in question was from July to September 1885.

[4] Meganebashi ('spectacle bridge'), spanned the Kandagawa and was built in 1873, replacing the Sujikaigomonbashi of 1676. European-style double-arched bridges had been built in Kyūshū as early as the seventeenth century, but were not seen in Tōkyō till after the Meiji Restoration of 1868. This particular bridge was the second one to be built in Tōkyō, and remained a 'spectacle bridge' till its replacement by a steel bridge in 1906. It is more commonly known as Manseibashi, though in its early days was also referred to as Yorozubashi, which, confusingly, is also the name of a separate bridge. From Katai's use of the term throughout the book it is clear that it applied to the general area as well as the specific bridge, and that it was used as a proper as well as common noun.

[5] Tenpō (or 'Tempō') is the year period 1830-1844. The Tenpō-sen — a sen being ten rin or one hundredth of a yen — was minted in 1835, but gradually lost its value. After the Meiji Restoration it was officially valued at eight rin, and was finally scrapped in 1891. To gain some idea of monetary values of the day it is worth noting that in 1886 the monthly salary of Katai's elder brother was fourteen yen (ie. fourteen hundred sen or fourteen thousand rin) and that this was considered lower than average. As a rough rule of thumb it could therefore be said that at the time Katai is describing one sen was approximately equivalent to one US dollar today.

I'd wait till the conductor had gone forward and then, thinking myself very clever, I'd snatch a free ride by leaning across his platform and keeping my legs up in the air. He'd always shout at me: "You wretched little boy!"

That wretched little boy always used to dawdle on his errands, too. I was forever stopping and gawping at something or other along the road. There were shops where lacquer was being stirred in huge pots, and picture book shops bedecked with colour prints, and shops with battledores for New Year's Eve, and in those days you could still see shopboys in front of the tsukudani shops on the main roads picking out leftover bits of fish and prawns with long chopsticks. I used to spend ages standing around at such places, pulling faces at the boys there.

I'm sure I must have been a very naughty little errand-boy. As I went about my daily errands, that invariably took me over the bridges of Kyōbashi and Nihonbashi, I'd usually be singing some popular song or other.[6] In those days there was a very popular song called 'Tekerettsunopa', and I'd go along singing "Riding together, with the hood up, tekerettsunopa."[7]

The girls went around with their hair done up in the Shimada-style, and wearing white dappled kimono and red aprons. I remember collars with hemp leaf patterns, too. The street lamps in those days were still oil, and it was interesting to see the lamplighters going around lighting them one by one. I used to race them.

Sometimes I'd go on errands round all the bookshops, carrying a notebook or pieces of paper listing all the things I had to get. I was apprenticed to the I- Book Company, which is still there now in Kyōbashi.[8] In those days there were still in existence such big and long-established bookshops as Suhara Mohē and Yamashiroya Sahē, and they'd have shopsigns in the form of square lanterns, and rows of thick boards with lists of books written on them. Of all the bookshops I used to visit, to

---

[6] The bridges of Kyōbashi and Nihonbashi — as opposed to the general areas — were both built in 1603 and subsequently rebuilt on numerous occasions. Kyōbashi, for example, was a stone bridge in 1875 and a steel bridge from 1929. They span the Kyōbashigawa and Nihonbashigawa respectively.

[7] 'Tekerettsunopa' appears to be a 'word' used for rhythmic purposes only. No native speaker consulted has been able to assign it any intrinsic meaning.

[8] The Yūrindō (or Iūrindō), a book publisher rather than bookseller (though the same term is applied to both), was located at the time in Minamitenmachō in Kyōbashi (till 1931). It was owned by the former samurai Anayama Tokutarō (dates unclear), who had connections with Katai's uncle Yokota Ryōta (1840-1917). The latter was employed as a steward by Okanoya Shigezane (1835-1919), a noted historian and Tōkyō-based vassal of Akimoto, Lord of Tatebayashi Fief. Katai gives a number of details of his apprenticeship in the course of the following chapters. It occupied approximately one year from February 1881.

present them with the various notes with my boss's orders on, today only one remains — moreover even busier than before — and that is Maruzen.[9]

All manner of food stalls were put up in the evening — sushi stalls, bean soup and rice cake stalls, boiled vegetables and hot saké stalls, noodle stalls, bean-jam and rice cake stalls — and they used to make me feel very hungry. You rarely come across it nowadays, but there was one particular dish which I was extremely fond of, especially on cold winter nights. It was called 'suiton', and was made from some type of wheat flour. The front of the suiton stalls would be packed with people standing around eating. The suiton lay piled in large bowls, with a warm and appetising steam rising from it, and it sold so fast that the boys working there hardly had chance to wash the bowls.

At the Western approach to Kyōbashi [Bridge] was a sight you wouldn't find anywhere in town nowadays — huge steaming pots of beef hash, with an aroma that couldn't fail to entice passers-by. Even people in the most elegant attire would stand there eating unashamedly.

As far as food was concerned, there were any number of stalls around most of the bridges. Thinking back on it, I'd say it wasn't much different from a Chinese town. You can still find the same sort of scene, for example, around Yingkou, Niuchuang, and Liaoyang. The liveliest places were the approaches to the bridges of Nihonbashi, Edobashi, and Aramebashi.[10] Beyond the sushi stalls, with their large canopies, and the sweet-saké stalls, with their gleaming brass cauldrons, you could see the riverside fishmarket, with its white walls standing out against the clear blue sky, and lighters and barges packed tightly together on the dark river.[11]

The location and composition of the fishmarket were the same as they are now, and I'd say that the buildings were the same too, but I seem to remember that the hustle and bustle, and the filth, were a lot greater in those days. I went in there once and got so caught up in the crush that I almost failed to get out again, and ended up on the verge of tears. After that experience I avoided going there again.

---

[9] Maruzen was founded in 1869 by Hayashi Yūteki (1837-1901), also known as Maruya Zenshichi. The company was originally known by the longer name Maruya Zenshichi-ten, changing to its present form of Maruzen in 1880. The other bookshops mentioned are obscure.

[10] The Edobashi, spanning the Nihonbashigawa, was a stone bridge between 1875-1900. The Aramebashi formerly spanned the Nishihoridomegawa in what is now Nihonbashihonchō 1 Chōme (Chūō-ku), but was pulled down following the filling in of the Nishihoridome in 1928.

[11] The fishmarket moved from its site near the Nihonbashi [Bridge] to its present site in Tsukiji (Chūō-ku) in 1923.

As for the approaches to the Ryōgokubashi [Bridge], by those days the sorts of things that Ishikawa Masamochi used to write about had largely disappeared, but nevertheless there were still a lot of sights to see.[12] There were peep-shows that drew in the customers with sentimental tunes, and monster snake shows, and shows featuring poor little dwarfs, and so on and so on, and each of them would be touting loudly.

As you went from Kyōbashi over the Edobashi [Bridge] towards Ryōgokubashi you came across a whole maze of narrow Edo-style alleyways. Finding it boring to keep going along the same old main roads I preferred to work my way through these intriguing alleys. Across the road in Kyōbashi was a narrow alley running between a main road and a medium sized road, and I'd often go along this alley, come out where it ended at the Internal Transport Company near Kaiunbashi [Bridge], with the tall building of the Daiichi Bank in view, and then head off towards Yoroibashi [Bridge].[13] It seemed like almost every day that I'd be going to the Hamachō and Yagenbori areas as well.[14] One thing I'll never forget is the large signboard of the Hōchisha Company, with the words 'Yūbin Hōchi Newspaper Company'.[15]

The Ginza hasn't changed all that much. Of course, the buildings have become bigger and grander, but in general it's the same as it was in those days. On the corner of Owarichō there used to be a bookshop called Hakubunsha, which later became the Usagiya Bookshop, but it has now disappeared.[16]

As an errand-boy I seemed to find myself going all over Tōkyō. At first I was accompanied by a senior boy, and pulled carts or carried piles of books as we went calling at the houses of clients or business connections. One winter's day, while out on one such errand, it suddenly started snowing heavily. I had a lot of heavy books on my back and the soft snow bothered me, sticking in lumps to my geta. I ended up falling over and eventually, helped by the clerk who was with me, going back in a rickshaw. I was just a young child, nine years and ten months old by the Western age system.[17] People were always telling me, "Don't try to do

---

[12] Ishikawa Masamochi (1753-1830), classicist and satirical poet.

[13] The Kaiunbashi Bridge formerly spanned the Kaedegawa in Kabutochō in Nihonbashi but was pulled down after the war. The bridge and the nearby Daiichi Bank building formed one of the sights of early Meiji Tōkyō.

[14] Yagenbori was a waterway in what is now Higashinihonbashi 2 Chōme, and was filled in in 1893.

[15] 'Yūbin Hōchi Shinbun', published June 1872-December 1894.

[16] Owarichō corresponds (from 1930) to present-day Ginza 5 and 6 Chōme. The Hakubunsha is unconnected with the Hakubunkan, the publishing concern for which Katai later worked and which is referred to extensively in later sections.

[17] As opposed to the Western system of increasing an individual's age with each birthday the traditional Japanese system accorded a child one year of age at birth and a subse-

too much — you're only little." I'd been brought to Tōkyō by my grandfather, and we'd come by river from a castle-town in the country, sleeping on rush mats in a cold boat.[18] At the time snow had lain in bright white patches along the banks of that long blue river, and there was even snow on the mats in the boat.

I went from my grandfather's care to my uncle's, then to that of a government official living near Sannoshita, who kindly arranged my employment, and finally ended up at that book company on the corner of Kyōbashi Road.[19] It was owned by a family of former samurai who had turned to commerce, and it mainly put out books on agriculture. I suppose the boss and his wife — I remember she had poor eyesight — are no longer with us in this world. I also heard later that their only son had died young, through illness. Their eldest child was a pretty girl of eighteen or nineteen, which would make her around fifty-four or five nowadays. We were only slightly acquainted so I doubt if she'd remember a little errand-boy like me even if I were to introduce myself.

Most of my time was spent carrying books round to clients' houses, but whenever I was in the company offices I used to sit for hours on end facing the shop-curtains of the Fūgetsudō, which is still there today.[20] Next door was a shop selling dried bonito, and next door to that was an establishment called Ōnishi Hakubotan.[21] On the corner opposite was a shop selling bags and pouches.

Not long ago I was talking to a certain lady who will be forty-nine this year.[22] "Really?" she said to me, "were you an errand-boy in those

---

quent year with each New Year. Thus a child born on New Year's Eve would be two years old the following day. Katai and many writers of his period tended to use a mixture of the two systems, resulting in considerable vagueness. For those born before 1872, when a calendrical change of some six weeks took place to adjust to the Western solar calendar, ages are especially imprecise. Katai was born on the thirteenth day of the twelfth month of the fourth year of Meiji, which is, precisely speaking, January 22nd 1872, and not December 13th 1871 as is commonly given. Theoretically, therefore, this incident took place in November 1881. In the later section 'Return to Tōkyō' Katai refers to his age at the time as eleven.

[18] Katai's (paternal) grandfather was Hoyata (1811-1888). The town is Katai's home town of Tatebayashi in Gunma Prefecture. Hoyata played a major role in Katai's early life after the death of his father Shōjūrō (b. 1838) in action in the Seinan Civil War in April 1877. (See too Note 681)

[19] The government official is the Okanoya Shigezane referred to in Note 8, who was also a government archivist. Sannoshita is the area at the foot of Sannōzaka (Sannō Hill), Nagatachō 2 Chōme, Chiyoda-ku. The uncle is Yokota Ryōta (also Note 8).

[20] Fūgetsudō is a famous confectionery shop still in existence today.

[21] There is an establishment of this name still in the Ginza today, selling kimono. However, it appears unconnected with the one mentioned here. The name, which means literally 'white peony', suggests that it dealt in either kimono or cosmetics.

[22] This lady is Kin (1869 - ?), the mother of Iida Yone (1889 - ?), the geisha who became Katai's mistress after 1907.

days!? Well what a surprise! But then, they do say your sins will find you out in the end! Our house was in Makichō in those days, and I knew the daughter of the place where you were very well.[23] We often went to nagauta classes together. If I remember right she was called Otama. The teacher's house was a few yards down a side street, on the right. I used to get up to some tricks in those days, I can tell you!'' She was very familiar with all sorts of things from those days, and we understood each other very well. She knew the song 'Tekerettsunopa' and about suiton. We also got round to talking about how cheerful the streets were on New Year's Eve with all the plants.

I asked her: ''Do you remember that big to-do when those dramatic news placards appeared in town, telling us the world would be destroyed on such-and-such a date?''

''Yes, that's right, there was an incident like that. My word, you do have a good memory! There were going to be floods on one day, then an earthquake on another day, and a tidal wave on another, and it was all shown in pictures on the placards.''

''Right.''

I thought back to that time. Even though such terrible, upsetting placards were being paraded around, the police didn't try to interfere. It shows just what a carefree, unrefined, unsophisticated city it was.

''And there was that noodleshop on the east corner of 4 Chōme. It's still there now, in fact.''

''Yes, that's right.''

''And at midnight on New Year's Eve the apprentices were always treated to noodles by their employers, and crowds of us were taken in tow to that shop. I remember it well. The streets were packed.''

''That shop's certainly been there a fair few years....''

It was the distant past. It seems like a dream. And yet, though the buildings have become grander and the roads bigger, you can still see old shops here and there, and to see them always fills me with thoughts of the past. That undeveloped old town, of earth-walled houses and rickety carriages and mud.....

Amongst the places I used to go to on errands there were two that were a particularly long way away. One was Count Yanagisawa's residence in Takanawa, and the other was the agricultural school in Komaba.[24] I

---

[23] The family owned a rice shop in Minamimakichō (present-day Yaesu 2 Chōme). The friendship between Kin and the daughter of Katai's employer was totally unconnected with his subsequent relationship with Kin's daughter Yone, and constituted one of those quirks of fate which were to obsess Katai in his later years.

[24] The Yanagisawa residence was the home of the descendants of Lord Yanagisawa Yoshiyasu (1658-1714). The Komaba school, founded in 1878, was the predecessor of the Tōkyō University Agricultural Studies Department, on the site of the present-day Faculty of Liberal Studies.

hated being sent to those places. I'd set off with a show of good spirits, but always lost heart at the distance involved. What really used to depress me was the great number of chōme in Takanawa and Aoyama. I'd watch for the number of each chōme written up along the way, but it got up to 8 Chōme, 9 Chōme, 10 Chōme! The agricultural school in Komaba was the furthest away of all.

But for all that, when I went down the hill in Miyamasu the surroundings took on a rural air, and there were thatched cottages and streams and bridges and waterwheels. I used to feel I'd gone back home, and was reminded of the thatched house in the country where my mother and grandparents were. I'd wipe away the tears as I walked along.

I can still clearly picture the huge grounds of the agricultural school. The school building stood all by itself in the middle of the grounds, looking rather lonely, and when I went inside the officials there would greet me with some remark like "Ah, the lad from the I- Book Company!" It was there that I saw for the first time such strange things as a stove. And, the officials gave me cakes.

When I went to Takanawa I used to enjoy looking at the sea and the steam train going along the coast. Having been brought up in the countryside I found such things fascinating. I'd gaze entranced at the sailboats and steamboats as they passed by under big white clouds that hovered like birds' wings. I'd be enchanted by the sight of the little steam train threading its way along the coast from the direction of Shinagawa, spilling out its grimy smoke. In those days there was only one railway line in Japan, and that was between Tōkyō and Yokohama.[25] And there were songs in fashion like the one that went:

> "The train's setting off — sai, sai,
> Leaving its smoke — sai, sai:
> Isn't it horrid, all this smoke! — sai, sai."

The train was still a novelty even for city dwellers. It was around this time that the Frenchman Pierre Loti came to Japan, and he really insulted the Tōkyō-Yokohama train — or rather, looked upon it with pity — and said, "A train, in Japan! A tiny little train! A rickety-rackety, bone-jarring little train!" But nevertheless, pathetic little train that it was, it did represent the first major enterprise of the Japanese government. I used to stand about twenty yards back from it, as though it were

[25] The Shinbashi-Yokohama line was opened in October 1872, but at the time referred to here (1881) there was in fact also a line operating between Kōbe and Kyōto (Kōbe-Ōsaka 1875, Ōsaka-Kyōto 1876). The full Shinbashi-Kōbe stretch was opened in July 1886.

some sort of monster, and stare as it went on its way surrounded by smoke and noise.

The long narrow street that ran from the rice cake shop near the Shinmei Shrine in Shiba to Rōgetsuchō was, even by Tōkyō standards, full of character and interesting people.[26] There was a large bookshop there called Yamanaka Something-or-other-hē, and I often went there on errands. I've lost count of the number of times I walked along that street in Rōgetsuchō, with all its second-hand bookshops. Compared with the dreary scenes of the main road in Kanasugi, where there was nothing to look at, it was a veritable whirlpool of variety.[27] There were food and drink stalls. There were colour print shops. There were rows of little bookshops. And it was along this narrow, bustling street that a little errand-boy went on his way, carrying a load of books.....

I'm always able to remember such scenes very clearly, perhaps because I was so young. I can remember the big, bleak fields of Satsumappara;[28] Okuyama in Asakusa where, instead of the rows of shops you find nowadays behind the Kannon Temple, there were interesting sights such as sand pictures and monkeys and sword displays; the temple-grounds of Nishihonganji, crowded from end to end with food and drink stalls and fortune-tellers and shows; the 'head washing spring' of the Sakurada retainers, near the moat down from the General Staff Headquarters[29]; narrow, cluttered Onari Street, running from Meganebashi right to Hirokōji in Ueno; [30] the crooked, narrow cuttings in Yushima......

But be that as it may, what was I thinking of in those days? Was I planning on becoming a merchant?

It's all so far, so very far in the past......

The House on the Riverbank

I crossed Takahashi [Bridge] in Fukagawa, turned left, and arrived in Daikumachi, where I opened the lattice-work door of a two-storey house

[26] Rōgetsuchō (often mistakenly read as 'Rogetsuchō' as a result of the commoner reading 'ro' for the first character, 'dew') corresponds to present-day Higashishinbashi 2 Chōme, Minato-ku. Shiba was a 'ku' from 1878 till 1947.

[27] Kanasugi is present-day Shiba 1 and 2 Chōme, Minato-ku.

[28] Satsumappara corresponds to the area of convergence of present-day Shiba 2,3,4,5 Chōme, Minato-ku.

[29] A reference to the assassination of Ii Naosuke (1815-1860), the pro-foreign prime minister, by Mito Clan retainers near Sakuradamon on March 3rd 1860.

[30] Onarimichi, literally 'street of honour', was used by nobles and dignitaries during the Edo period (1603-1868) on their way to and from Edo Castle. There were in fact several Onarimichi in Edo/Tōkyō, but this one was the principal one, and was one of the few streets actually referred to by name. See Note 4 for Meganebashi.

facing the Onagi River.[31] At the sound my little feet made on the floorboards my aunt came out with a look of surprise on her face.[32]

"Why, it's Roku!"[33]

My aunt — my mother's elder sister — was a kind lady, fond of the theatre. She'd lost her husband early on, and was living by herself doing needlework.

"What's the matter?"

I was carrying two salmon, having gone over that way on an errand for my boss of delivering year's end gifts. When she heard this my aunt seemed relieved, indeed sympathetic, and invited me inside where she proceeded to make a great fuss of me. Her needlework lay beside the hibachi, along with an illustrated rental book which she'd started to read. She was so fond of the theatre that she never missed a performance, and knew all about the talents of Danjūrō, Kikugorō, and earlier actors.[34] I wonder if it wasn't from this aunt, rather than my mother, that I inherited a taste for literature. She was kind-hearted and sensitive, and even in conversation her wrinkled old face would show great emotion. I'd often seen her in tears.

"There's nothing wrong with the theatre, but it does cost money, and rental books are cheaper," she would say, and avidly read the works of writers like Shunsui and Chikamatsu.[35] She loved to read for an hour or two before going to bed, after a whole day of sewing, and was forever caught up with some romance or tragic tale of a lovers' suicide. She also kept a shamisen in the house, and was very good at playing ballads on it.

In those days my aunt was, I suppose, in her mid forties. Legally she had a son and daughter, but they were not children she had given birth to herself. Her daughter continued to look after her for many years, but the son was a scoundrel who by those days had ceased to keep in touch.

In the same neighbourhood as my aunt's house there was a residence belonging to an old feudal lord, so a lot of former retainers lived there.

I can still picture the view of the Onagi River at sunset, from upstairs. There were boats, and creaking oars, and sails that cast shadows as big as houses across the rails. And early in the morning, even before the

---

[31] Daikumachi is present-day Shirakawa in Kōtō-ku (Fukagawa-ku till 1947). As this is south of the Takahashi [Bridge] over the Onagi River Katai presumably approached from the north, ie. from Ryōgokubashi.

[32] His mother's elder sister, Yamamura Hana (c. 1834-1886).

[33] Katai's real name was Roku(ya).

[34] Danjūrō is Ichikawa Danjūrō the Ninth (1838-1903). Kikugorō is Onoe Kikugorō the Fifth (1844-1903). Both were famous kabuki actors, both coincidentally dying in the same year.

[35] Tamenaga Shunsui (1790-1843), writer, and Chikamatsu Monzaemon (1653-1724), dramatist.

families living along the river were up and about, clam-boats would bob along in the current with their little oars, and you could hear cries of "Clams! Shelled clams!" From time to time customers would hail them, and then the little boats would make their way gently to the shore, piled high with a variety of clams. My aunt, too, often used to hail them, and take along a basket to carry the clams she bought.

In the afternoon a little steamboat used to pass Takahashi on its way from Kakigarachō to the Tone River. It held a lot of memories for me, did that steamboat. It was the boat on which we'd come up to Tōkyō.

Every time my mother or any of the rest of us travelled between Tōkyō and our home in the country we always stayed at my aunt's house by the river. My mother got on really well with her, and my aunt used to call her by the familiar form "Otetsu, Otetsu."[36]

In those days my elder brother was also in Tōkyō, studying, and on Sundays he too often used to visit our aunt. I remember her saying to me, "Minoru came to see me the other day, you know, but the funny thing is that he was wearing rain-clogs, even though it was fine weather!"[37]

Anyway, on that occasion I think we had a meal and she gave me some pocket-money, though I can't remember exactly. What I do remember is the kind old face of my aunt as she stood in the doorway, watching me go off into the cold with the two salmon. That dear, sensitive, old face, etched with the wrinkles of a turbulent age!

The Sound of Voices Reading

I went closer.

I could hear people reading inside. The building resembled the longhouse of an old-time feudal lord, and over the plaster-and-tile wall I could see little windows, covered in dust and bathed in the rays of the afternoon sun. There was a large signboard there, with the name 'Hōkō Private Academy'.[38]

Across the road was a big lotus tree which gave nice cool shade in summer, and some rickshawmen and labourers and passers-by were resting there.

The sound of voices reading!

---

[36] Katai's mother was Tayama Tetsu (1839-1899). The surname Tayama applies to her maiden name as well as married name, as she was a distant relative of his father's family.

[37] Katai's elder brother was Miyato (1865-1907) but was sometimes referred to as Minoru due to an alternative reading of the first character of his name.

[38] The Hōkō Gijuku was a classical studies academy founded by Nakamura Hōnan (dates unclear) in Hongōyumichō (present-day Hongō 1 and 2 Chōme, Bunkyō-ku).

I went up to the windows, feeling homesick. My elder brother was inside, studying.[39] However, I didn't want to embarrass him by revealing to everybody that his little brother was an errand-boy, so I didn't try to visit him openly. Poor, innocent, well-intentioned little me!

I hoped my brother might chance to come out. It would have been nice if he'd clapped me on the shoulder and given me a friendly greeting. The future of our family rested on his shoulders, and he was studying relentlessly. He had no money to buy geta, possessed only the clothes he stood in — and his hakama was ragged enough to start with — and was studying with true dedication. When I thought about his situation I realised, young as I was, that my own hardships weren't worth mentioning. On the other hand I was envious, even to the point of becoming upset, of the fact that my brother WAS studying.

I'd gone to that part of Hongō on an errand. I'd checked off the place-names along the way — Yumichō 3 Chōme .... Hōkō Private Academy.... But as I'd got nearer I'd almost decided not to go there. I didn't feel it was right to interrupt my brother's studying.

The sound of voices reading....

Suddenly the lattice-work door opened and someone came out. I moved away, flustered. It was a student wearing a tattered old hakama and carrying a thick walking-stick, just like my brother. He walked off, without paying any particular attention to me.

Again I thought to myself that it would've been nice if it had been my brother.

I didn't go back to the windows. Instead I went away, feeling very sad.

I remembered how, after being temporarily dismissed for misconduct, I had returned apologetically to the company where I worked.[40] On that occasion my brother had taken me to a back-street noodle shop and, with what little money he had, treated me to two bowls of fried fish and noodles. "You mustn't get up to those tricks again! Do you understand!?" he'd said to me. Now I felt the tears coming to my eyes. To stop myself from crying I picked up a stone lying in the street and hurled it away.

---

[39] Miyato entered the academy in 1880, supported by his relatively wealthy brother-in-law Ishii Osamu (1846-1925), a former retainer and the son of the noted historian Ishii Kakyū (1819-1900).

[40] Katai was suspended for a week as a result of persistent stealing, and given a good 'talking to' by Okanoya Shigezane. The date is not clear but was possibly May (1881). In any event, he continued to steal after his return to the company and was finally dismissed permanently early the following year. It is probable that the episode does not reveal any kleptomaniac tendencies in Katai — for which there is no subsequent evidence — but rather a deliberate attempt to terminate his career as an apprentice in order to return to school.

In those days there were any number of schools like my brother's, specialising in Chinese classics. There was Nakamura Keiu's Dōjinsha, and Mishima Chūshū's Nishō Institute, and there were a lot of students in those days who were forever making waves over some issue or other.[41] They used to pride themselves on going around dressed in rags with their hair in a mess, and particularly despised anything feminine. The Hōkō Private Academy had a good reputation for the reading of the Eight Poets of T'ang and Sung, and the teacher, Nakamura Ken — also known as Hōnan — had been an assistant lecturer at the Shōheikō.[42] I myself later met him on several occasions, but I don't know whether he's alive today or not.

Return to Tōkyō[43]

Our straw-thatched house in the country had only two rooms. Outside the kitchen, which was big and blackened with use, there was a well with walls of baked red clay. The well-bucket lay there upside down. The grass around the well grew thick in summer, and spilt water sparkled beautifully in the cool moonlight. Standing nearby was an old plum tree, which always produced gorgeous white blossoms.

I used to bask happily in the sunshine in the grassy fields around the old castle embankment, watching my kite fly through the air. I used to head off through the cutting behind our house to go dipping for tiddlers in the irrigation streams of the paddy-fields near the statue of Jizō. I used to dream about the future, letting my imagination run wild. I used to get carried away with fishing and pay attention to nothing except my rod and my creel, and get told off by my mother as a result. I used to wander through the town with my face covered in pimples. I used to get up to mischief in the primary school grounds. I used to be in love with the chief

---

[41] The Dōjinsha was founded by Nakamura Keiu (1832-1891), who was better known as the translator Nakamura Masanao, in 1873 in Koishikawa. It was noted for its English studies rather than its Chinese classics, according to most accounts. The Nishō Gakusha was founded in 1877 in Kōjimachi by the classics scholar Mishima Chūshū (1830-1919), and has been a private university since 1949.

[42] The Shōheikō was a well-known government school of Confucianist studies during the Edo period, in Yushima. The Eight Poets of T'ang and Sung were Han Yu, Liu Tsung-yuan, Ou-Yang Hsiu, Wang An-Shih, Tseng Kung, Su Hsun, Su Shih, and Su Che.

[43] The Tayama household returned to Tōkyō on July 14th 1886, following Miyato's appointment to a position in the Department of Historical Documents. Katai actually uses the word 'futatabi', meaning 'a second time', but this is inaccurate in his own case as, in addition to his apprenticeship, he had lived with his family in Tōkyō (Negishi) between March 1876-August 1877. The family had joined his father Shōjūrō, who had been serving in Tōkyō as a policeman from January 1875, but returned to Tatebayashi shortly after his death in the Seinan Civil War (April 1877, see too Note 18).

retainer's daughter, who was just coming of age. I used to blush and get flustered whenever I met her in the streets. I used to send poetry off to 'Eisaishinshi', the only magazine at the time for young amateur poets, and feel deliriously happy when it appeared in print.[44] I used to write terrible poems about the seasonal scenery of the marsh near the castle which, thinking to be really good, I would make up into little books like 'Miscellaneous Verses on the Four Seasons of Castle Marsh'.[45] Such was my life in our old home town. Now, suddenly, I had to go to Tōkyō again, this time with all the family.[46]

As a sixteen year old, Tōkyō seemed rather different to me than it had as an eleven year old. But compared with my brothers and sisters I was well acquainted with it. I knew my way around little streets and alleys that you wouldn't normally expect a teenager to know. Getting off the boat at Koamichō Boathouse I now went by rickshaw through places where I had often gone on foot in the past, such as Shianbashi and Oyajibashi.[47] On the way from Tokiwabashi to Kamakuragashi there was an old shop that sold peppers, with a large female doll on display. In the days when I was an errand-boy I often used to stare at it as I walked past, but now I saw it from a rickshaw.

I could see that now, in the Tōkyō of 1886, considerable changes had taken place relative to the Tōkyō of 1881. As we cut through from Takebashi to Hanzōmon even the pines of the Imperial Palace, reflected in the beautiful still waters of the moat, seemed somehow to have changed in their character and appearance. We were to live for a while in part of the residence of a certain feudal lord in an outlying area of Ushigome.[48] That year cholera was rife, and everywhere we went we heard talk about it.[49] There was an endless succession of stretchers heading for the quarantine hospital. It was impossible to eat fish or

---

[44] 'Eisaishinshi' (lit: The New Talent Magazine) was published by the Seishikaisha (later Eisaishinshisha) between March 1877 - June 1901.

[45] 'Jōnuma Shiji Zatsuei', a collection of poetry by Katai and a number of local friends which was put together into a little illustrated booklet, completed May 16th 1885.

[46] 'All the family' is not quite correct. Katai's elder sister Katsuyo (1868-1918) remained in Tatebayashi, having married a local weaver in March 1884.

[47] Shianbashi [Bridge] formerly spanned the Higashihoridomegawa in what is now Nihonbashikoamichō. The Higashihoridomegawa was filled in in 1949. Oyajibashi [Bridge] formerly spanned the same river, in what is now Nihonbashihonchō 1 Chōme.

[48] Ushigome was a large area of present-day Shinjuku, and was a 'ku' from 1878-1947. Katai and his family went to live in Ichigayatomihisachō. The house belonged to the Lord of Aizu (Fukushima) and had been vacant for some time. Miyato found the premises.

[49] One of the side-effects of the cholera epidemic was that people drank lemonade rather than water, with the result that lemonade producers could not cope with the demand. The Ōsaka Nippō Newspaper of July 2nd 1886 reported, for example, that a Kōbe company could not fill even one tenth of its orders despite working to maximum output.

anything like that. The whole city seemed full of yellow warning notices, and policemen standing guard. Going outside meant running the risk of falling victim to the cholera, and I remember being constantly in fear of this.

It was the time of the Security Measures, when a lot of prominent people were forced to leave Tōkyō, and the newspapers were full of the subject.[50] It was also a time when, despite the gradual development of the city, the outer suburbs were still quite rural, with woods and groves, and lonely little ponds hidden away in the grounds of some of the mansions. In the outer parts of Ushigome you could see foxes and raccoons every night. There were a number of places where you could see the same sort of scene, and experience the same sort of atmosphere, as that depicted in Nagai Kafū's story 'The Fox'.[51]

I learned poetry — both Chinese and Japanese — from my elder brother, and continued to contribute to 'Eisaishinshi'. But at two sen a time I couldn't afford to buy a copy every week, so every Saturday night I'd trek all the way to Yotsuya, to a picture book shop on the main road. If the magazine happened to be conveniently on display at the counter it was an easy matter to flick through and see if my work had been printed, but if, unfortunately, it happened to be back amongst all the picture books, it put me in a bit of a fix. There were not a few times that I was glared at by the shopkeeper as I left without buying the magazine I'd troubled him to get out for me.

Besides learning English at a little school in Banchō in Kōjimachi I also learned all sorts of things from the son of a former samurai, whose father was now working as an official in the Ministry of Internal Affairs.[52] He was attending the university preparatory school in Gojiingahara —

---

[50] In fact the Security Measures were enacted the following year, on Christmas Day (1887). Some five hundred and fifty persons opposed to the Government's stand on treaty revision were exiled from Tōkyō. The measures were repealed in June 1898.

[51] 'Kitsune', in the January 1909 issue of 'Chūgaku Sekai' (Middle School World), was an account of the suburban Tōkyō childhood of the novelist Nagai Kafū (1879-1959).

[52] Katai studied English at the Sokusei Gakkan (lit: 'The Intensive Academy'), a school specially for aspirants to the military college, in what is now Rokubanchō in Chiyoda-ku. (Banchō was divided into numbered sub-districts in 1929.) He withdrew from the school in April 1888 after failing the military medical on the grounds of poor eyesight. As a matter of some interest it is worth noting that Katai's teacher of English at the school, the nationalist Nishino Buntarō (1864-1889), was the assassin of the Minister of Education, Mori Arinori (1847-1889), on the day of the proclamation of the constitution (February 11th 1889). Although he dedicates a chapter to this day, Katai makes no mention of the assassination.

Katai's 'mentor' was Nojima Kinpachirō (1867-1915), son of Nojima Yoshiyuki (dates unclear, also known as Rinpachi), who was an old Tatebayashi friend of Katai's father Shōjūrō. The Ministry of Internal Affairs, which was abolished in 1947, was in Ōtemachi (in present-day Chiyoda-ku).

where the commercial college is nowadays — and was particularly good at English, being highly regarded at the school.[53] He was a classmate of Tokonami, and also knew people such as Ishibashi Shian and Yamada Bimyō.[54]

I used to set out from our part of Ushigome, go past the prison, head down the long road past the officers' college, and come out at Ichigaya Mitsuke.[55] Then, deliberately keeping to the embankment rather than the road, I could watch the shabbily dressed young men heading from the rear of the Shōkon Shrine towards Kudan.[56] There was a little park at the foot of Kudan Hill, and its green shade was the perfect place for my youthful reveries. That son of the Ministry of Internal Affairs official was called Nojima Kinpachirō. After giving up his studies halfway through he went on to lead a life of obscurity, largely serving in government positions in China and elsewhere. He finally made the rank of vice-consul, and died last year. In those days, however, he was living with his father in an official residence across from the Ministry of Internal Affairs, and it was to there that I went whenever I had any free time.

"Hey, shall we go out somewhere?"

Every time I went round there he'd invite me out. Being young I was much impressed by his frank, high-class, literary minded personality. Together we'd wander all around the streets of Tōkyō. We'd often walk around Kandabashi, with its unsightly jumble of boarding-houses and its unsavoury air; or along the road running past Nishikichō, where the Peers' School used to be, and out past the edge of Gojiingahara towards Hitotsubashi;[57] or along the road running from Kamakuragashi towards Imagawabashi. He often bought pencils and pens and ink at a little shop called Sankakudō on the corner of Ogawamachi, where a plump girl with fat cheeks used to work.

Although he had such a great penchant for literature, and was forever reading English novels and history books and biographies, he had no ap-

---

[53] Gojiingahara is now incorporated into Kandanishikichō. Kinpachirō enrolled at the school in September 1883.

[54] Tokonami Takejirō (1866-1935), politician; Ishibashi Shian (1867-1927), novelist; Yamada Bimyō (1868-1910), novelist and poet.

[55] The prison in Tomihisachō became the official Tōkyō Prison in 1903 but had existed as a prison for some years before that (it features on a map dated 1880). The officers' college was established in Ichigayahonmurachō in 1874, and moved to Zama City in Kanagawa Prefecture after the war.

[56] The Shōkon(sha) was the original name of the Yasukuni Jinja [Shrine], built in 1869. The name was officially changed to Yasukuni in 1879, but 'Shōkon(sha)' remained in popular speech for some years after. The 'shabbily dressed young men' are students from the forerunner of present-day Hōsei University, located behind the shrine.

[57] The Gakushūin (Peers' School) was established in 1877, was subsequently transferred to Toyojima-ku, and has been a university since 1949.

titude for classical studies, and could not write particularly well. In that respect he always rated himself inferior to me, since I was at least in the habit of writing poetry. He'd say things like, "If only I could write a bit better I'd have a go at literature myself. Say what you will, the profession of a writer is the most excellent and noble of all." He had so much up-to-the-minute knowledge about novelists and other writers that you wondered where on earth he obtained it. It may have been simply that he was living in the same atmosphere that nurtured Kōyō and Shian and Bizan.[58] He used to criticise Kōyō for studying Sanba at the preparatory school: "You know, you shouldn't study the likes of Sanba, like so many people are today.[59] There're any number of wonderful writers in the West, really excellent writers. From now on, people doing literature have absolutely got to read foreign works." He'd then proudly check off on his fingers the sort of authors he had in mind — "Dickens, Thackeray, Hugo, Dumas, Goethe....."

He also had splendid dreams about the harmonising of literature and politics, and often talked about Lord Beaconsfield.[60] "He becomes Speaker of the House, and then he becomes Prime Minister, and then he writes novels like that — marvellous!" He had lots of Lord Beaconsfield's works, and frequently talked to me about novels like 'Venetia' and 'Vivian Gray'. And he was always talking about recent publications such as 'Strange Encounters with Beautiful Women' and 'Plum Blossoms in the Snow'.[61]

It was just at that time that Sudō Nansui was publishing his serialised 'New-Look Beautiful Women' in the Kaishin Newspaper, and Nojima loved reading it for the depiction of the characters and atmosphere of Marquis Inoue's 'dance mania' period.[62] Saitō Ryokū was writing old-fashioned gesaku-type novels in the style of Kanagaki Robun, publishing

---

[58] Ozaki Kōyō (1867-1903), novelist; Kawakami Bizan (1869-1908), novelist.

[59] Shikitei Sanba (1776-1822), writer.

[60] Lord Beaconsfield was better known as Benjamin Disraeli (1804-1881). His novels included 'Vivian Gray' (1826, his first work) and 'Venetia' (1837).

[61] Respectively 'Kajin (no) Kigū' (published in no fewer than eight parts by Hakubundō between October 1885-October 1897) by Tōkai Sanshi (1852-1922), and 'Setchūbai' (1886, published in two parts by Bunkaidō in August and October) by Suehiro Tetchō (1849-1896). Both were so called 'political novels'.

[62] Sudō Nansui (1857-1920), a newspaper reporter and novelist, published his political novel 'Shinsō no Kajin' in the Kaishin Newspaper between September 30th-December 9th 1886. He had been instrumental in founding the newspaper, which ran between 1884-1893.

The Government Minister Inoue Kaoru (1835-1915) was instrumental in the organisation of dances for the entertainment of foreign dignitaries. These were held at the famous Rokumeikan [Hall], which was founded in 1883 in what is now Uchisaiwaichō in Chiyoda-ku expressly for this purpose. It survived in modified form till 1933.

them in the Konnichi Newspaper under the name Kōtō Midori.[63] "This writer's still only a novice, you know," Nojima said to me.

Chinese-style poetry, the Chinese classics, Japanese-style poetry, Lord Beaconsfield's novels, 'Strange Encounters with Beautiful Women', English, Bakin, Shunsui, the legend of Iwami Jūtarō, 'Eisaishinshi' — such were the varied things that occupied my sixteenth and seventeenth years.[64]

Nojima also used to take me to well-known restaurants. He was the first person to introduce me to Tenkin tenpura, and he also treated me to Nakagawa beef in Awajichō. He took me to Ryōgoku and treated me to Matsu sushi, and introduced me to Rengyoku noodles in Shinobazu.[65] And then he'd say: "There's a place in Azabu where you just have to try the noodles, otherwise you can't call yourself a noodle-lover. We absolutely must go there soon!"

He was an emotional person, and often wept when talking about his only sister, who had died through illness.[66] His amiable, old-fashioned, hard-working mother and his tall, stern, dogmatic father had both been friendly with my father, who had been killed in action, and I suppose they took pity on our fatherless household. Whenever I visited them I was treated like one of the family. And once, when I went there wearing old geta worn down at the heel, his mother said, "Rokuchan, we have an old pair here you can use," and swapped my geta for an old but still good pair of my friend's.

The Snow on the Day of the Constitutional Proclamation

There were a lot of public holidays in those days, on occasions such as the formal opening of parliament, but the only one I remember was the day of the constitutional proclamation, and the snow on that day.[67]

The previous day it had suddenly looked like we'd have snow, and sure enough, that evening it snowed so heavily that people stayed indoors.

"What a pity, on a memorable occasion like this!" my mother said.

---

[63] Saitō Ryokū (1867-1904), novelist and critic; Kanagaki Robun (1828-1894), writer. Gesaku (lit: 'frivolous works') were trivial lampoons. The 'Konnichi Shinbun', later known as the 'Miyako Shinbun', ran from September 1884-October 1942.

[64] Takizawa Bakin (1767-1848, also known as Kyokutei Bakin), writer. Iwami Jūtarō is a legendary sixteenth century hero who is said to have served Toyotomi Hideyoshi.

[65] Tenkin, Nakagawa, Matsu, and Rengyoku all appear to have been restaurants. Katai makes a further reference to Nakagawa — and a number of other establishments — in the later section 'A Man of Bygone Days'.

[66] Nojima Mura, who died of tuberculosis in May 1885, aged twenty-three.

[67] The first session of parliament was November 25th 1890. The constitutional proclamation was February 11th 1889 (see too Note 52).

Our family had by that time moved from the house in the outer suburbs, where we'd first stayed after coming up from the country, to N-machi.[68] My cousin, who had married my elder brother, had a bright, red ribbon in her hair, which was done up in the marumage style of a married woman.[69]

It was a three-roomed house — two-mat, six-mat, and four-and-a-half-mat.

Despite the heavy snow on the previous day it dawned crisp and clear, and although the roads were muddy there were a great many people heading downtown for the celebrations. Nihonbashi and Kyōbashi were where it was all supposed to be happening, with stalls and floats and geisha pageants and burlesques.

"Don't you want to go, Roku?"

My elder brother and mother both encouraged me to go, but at the time I was busy working on a piece of writing I'd started the previous evening, and replied that I couldn't be bothered. I spent the whole day cooped up in the house, while my elder brother headed off, with my younger brother, towards all the activity.[70]

There were also festivities being staged in our own neighbourhood, and I could hear the exciting sound of drums and street musicians coming from the various floats that had been put up, reverberating against the shōji of the room I was using. And cast gently across those same shōji were the shadows of plum blossoms and fresh green azalea leaves. The snow lay thick and white in the garden.

Ignoring all the raucous activity outside I sat quietly alone, facing the blank white paper on my desk, racking my brains to come up with some artistic inspiration.

My eyes shone out from my pale and serious face under all my long hair. From time to time I opened the shōji to look at the yellow narcissi blooming in the snow.

"You're not going, Rokuchan?"

My brother's wife came up to me. Outside, all was noise and bustle. The whole world seemed to have turned out. And just at that moment a local fancy-dress parade was about to pass down a nearby street, accompanied by some noisy musicians.

---

[68] The Tayamas moved to Nandomachi (in present-day Shinjuku-ku) in January 1889.

[69] In the same month as the move to Nandomachi, January 1889, Miyato married Yokota Tomi (1870-1891), the daughter of his uncle Yokota Ryōta (see Note 8). She died in giving birth to their first child in May 1891. Miyato remarried on two subsequent occasions but appears to have been fondest of Tomi out of his three wives.

[70] Katai's younger brother was Tomiya (1876-1938).

Our landlord's young daughters dashed out from behind our house to go and watch.[71]

It was so noisy, and so many people were going out to watch, that I too finally gave in. I put down my hesitant pen and went out into the mud and snow and afternoon sunshine.

All the local residents were there, watching the procession. I spotted one of the landlord's girls, a sixteen year old with her hair done up in the fashionable 'Chinese' style. I blushed.

The fancy dress parade went by. There was a man dressed up as a warrior, with two long swords, and a woman dressed up as a serving-maid, whose make-up was starting to come off, and ladies-in-waiting, and footmen, and so on and so on. In the front and rear of the parade came the boisterous musicians, with their flutes and drums and bells. Specks of mud spattered the hem of a man dressed up as a princess. The sun shone beautifully....

The Late 1880's

Travelling was quite awkward in those days, as there were only horse-drawn trams, and even then only on the main roads. To get around in Tōkyō you had to walk. Virtually every day I used to walk past the prison in Ushigome, past the officers' college, out onto Ichigaya Mitsuke, cut through the Shōkon Shrine in Kudan, and head off towards Kanda. Compared with today there were a lot of people walking about, and a lot of horse-drawn vehicles, and the top of the hill in Kudan was particularly busy.

In those days there was no bronze statue of Ōmura outside the Shōkon Shrine, nor the pair of stone lions brought back from China.[72] The huge iron torii was just in the process of being erected, and I remember seeing it lying in front of the shrine, looking absurdly large.[73] Then when it was

---

[71] The landlord was Sakada Masayuki (dates unclear), an official at the Treasury. Katai was particularly infatuated with one of his daughters, Kikuko (born c. 1873), who was the model for a number of his works and whom he describes in considerable detail in the later section 'Out in the Western Suburbs'.

[72] Ōmura Masujirō (1825-1869), Vice-Minister of the Army, was assassinated in 1869, and his statue, which was erected in the Yasukuni Jinja grounds in February 1893 and still stands today, was the first ever bronze statue of a Japanese person to be erected in Japan. The stone lions were seized at Hai-ch'eng in the 1894-5 Sino-Japanese War. There are at present two pairs of stone lions at the entrance to the Yasukuni Jinja grounds, a further pair having been placed there in 1966.

[73] There are at present two torii at the Yasukuni Jinja, the outer one (No. 1) of twenty-five metres and the inner one (No. 2) of fifteen metres. The outer one is of relatively recent construction, while the inner one — to which Katai is referring — was erected in July 1887 (some sources state 1886, but Yasukuni Jinja itself gives 1887). It was actually of bronze, not iron.

first put up my younger brother and I used to stop by on our way to and from the English language school we went to in Kanda, and press our cheeks against its cool iron, so pleasant in the heat of summer.[74]

About half way up the hill in Kudan, on the left-hand side, was a shop that sold birds. It's still there today, in fact. My brother and I often used to stop and stare in amazement at the various birds there. I remember the sun shining on cages of cockatoos and parrots and mynahs, and the aging shopkeeper sitting outside carefully grinding up their food in an earthen bowl. There were also white-eyes, and greenfinches, and skylarks, and cuckoos.

It was a long walk, so we always used to get hungry on the way back. When we had any money on us we'd find it impossible to avoid stopping at a cakeshop somewhere along the way, particularly one that sold bean jam buns. "Our trouble is that we give in too easily. It's true that we do have some money. But, today at least, let's try to go past without stopping to buy anything!" Despite such resolutions, when we actually came to the shop, we'd stop abruptly. In fact, the abruptness with which we stopped was quite extraordinary.

As we got nearer home our conversation was always the same:

"What do you think we've got for lunch today?"

"Bean curd."

"Bean curd? That's impossible. It's bound to be pickled vegetables."

"No, it'll be bean curd. There's no doubt about it!"

We always enjoyed it, even if it did turn out to be boiled or fried bean curd. Usually we crunched our way through the meal with a side-dish of pickled radish or red ginger.

Outside the Kobudera [Temple] they used to sell delicious crackers known as 'snow, moon, and flowers' — nature's perfection, in other words — and I used to look forward to going to the bathhouse with my elder brother and buying some on the way back.

I got to be quite strong on my legs in those days, and with the aid of a map I walked to most places in Tōkyō — places such as the Sengaku Temple in Takanawa, the park in Shiba, Shinmeimae, Ishikawajima, the residental areas of Tsukiji, and Higashi Hongan Temple.[75] And because I was writing poetry I often walked as well to local beauty spots such as Ueno, Asakusa, and Mukōjima.

---

[74] After his withdrawal from the Sokusei Gakkan in April 1888 Katai almost immediately enrolled in the Nippon Eigakukan (lit: 'Japanese Academy of English Studies'), which had been founded the previous year in Kandasarugakuchō.

[75] Shinmeimae is present-day Shibadaimon 1 Chōme; Ishikawajima is present-day Tsukuda(jima) in Chūō-ku. The names were officially changed in 1869 and 1872 respectively but lingered on in popular use.

I also loved to wander round second-hand bookshops. In those days there were any number of them throughout Tōkyō, just like the magazine shops today, and there were lots of collections of poetry and prose. I loved strolling round the shops in Ikenohata, and the narrow alleys of Rōgetsuchō in Shiba, and round Myōjinshita in Kanda and the hilly little streets of Yushima.[76] My elder brother was always telling me off for coming back with books I couldn't really afford, such as 'Chinese-style Verses by Accomplished Tōkyōites', and 'Chinese-style Verses by Thirty-six Tenpō Poets', and 'Chikugai's Chinese-style Verses of Twenty-eight Characters'.[77]

"If you're going to read Chinese-style poetry," said my brother, "you'd be better off reading stuff from the T'ang and Sung and Ming periods, rather than these modern Japanese poets." But, in my youthfulness, I found it easier to understand the Chinese-style poetry of Japanese writers than the Chinese poetry my brother was talking about.

I started writing Japanese-style poetry somewhat later than I did Chinese-style poetry and prose, but nevertheless there were a considerable number of Japanese poetry books in our house. The reason was that my father had been rather good at Japanese poetry, and in the early years of Meiji had even won honours in a New Year's Imperial Poetry Competition. Our bookcases contained lots of poetry anthologies such as 'The Inspired Collection' and 'The Common Collection'.[78]

Of all the places I used to walk around in those days — though they have now changed completely — I particularly remember Onari Street, the hilly cuttings in Yushima, the area around Manseibashi, Asakusa Kaminarimonmae, and Jinbōchō in Kanda. The narrow, jumbled slopes of those Yushima cuttings have now changed so much that they seem to belong to a different world. I remember how there used to be cluttered rows of second-hand bookshops and clothes shops there, that were always packed with people, and how they used to get covered in dust in the spring.

Onari Street was very narrow indeed, no more than five or six yards wide, so you can imagine just how much more crowded it was then than it is now. There were people and rickshaws and horse-drawn carts, and children would often get knocked down. And you can imagine the closeness and jumbled chaos of the shops there, with bean-soup and rice

---

[76] Myōjinshita is present-day Sotokanda 2 and 3 Chōme.

[77] Respectively 'Tōkyō Saijin Zekku' of 1875, edited by the poet Mori Shuntō (1819-1889); 'Tenpō Sanjūrokka Zekku' (Katai erroneously gives the title as 'Tenpō Sanjūrokka Shishū') of 1838, edited by Mikami Tsune (dates unclear); and 'Chikugai Nijūhachiji Shi' of 1858 by Fujii Chikugai (1807-1866, also known as Hiroshi).

[78] Respectively 'Reiyashū', compiled in 1806 by the poet Kiyohara Okaze (1743-1810); and 'Sōyashū', compiled c. 1816 by the poet Kimura Sadayoshi (1781-1846).

cake shops and sushi shops and bean jam bun shops and eel and rice shops all in the same row as second-hand bookshops and furniture shops and clothes shops.

It was also very busy around Meganebashi [Bridge]. I wonder if you could find anything quite like it anywhere in Tōkyō nowadays. The place was full of little shops and stalls and labourers and rickshawmen, and the public toilets were so incredibly in demand that you had to wait in a queue of half a dozen or more people. In those days there was still, despite all the development, something of the bustle of old Edo to be found.

The style of life in those days was symbolised by the fact that you could find Western-style buildings and purely Japanese-style buildings side by side in the same street. There were also cases of separate, distinct Edo-style and Western-style communities. Throughout Tōkyō I could see examples of the intertwining of these two elements, one developing, the other dying, one progressive, the other conservative.

In the Banchō area of Kōjimachi there were huge mansions belonging to high ranking government officials — the students of yesteryear — and carriages cutting a gallant dash on the wide flat roads. It was a time that saw the birth of official titles such as Councillor and Secretary and Minister, a time when society was overawed by the prestige of Prince Itō, then at its height.[79]

The Champions of a New Type of Literature

The English school I was attending in Kanda was founded by Hayashi Hōmei, the leading figure of the Liberal Party in those days, and his adviser was Hoshi Tōru.[80] Later it became Marquis Sasaki's son's school, and its name changed [from the Japanese Academy of English Studies] to the Meiji Academy.[81] Anyway, I studied English there for about three years.

Should I concentrate on classical studies? Should I concentrate on English? Or politics? Or law? At the time I was always at a loss as to what

---

[79] Itō Hirobumi (1841-1909), the leading political figure of the Meiji period, several times Prime Minister, and responsible for the drawing up of the constitution.

[80] The school is the Nippon Eigakukan discussed in Note 74. Hayashi Hōmei (1842-1921) was also known as Hayashi Yūzō. Hōshi Tōru (1850-1901) was a prominent Liberal politician.

[81] *Count* Sasaki Takayuki (1830-c.1907), from the same part of Japan (Kōchi) as Hayashi, took over the academy after Hayashi was expelled from Tōkyō under the Security Measures of December 25th 1887. Sasaki formed the Meijikai [Society] in June 1888, a patriotic society in support of the Emperor, and this accounts for the school's change of name to Meiji Gakkan. Later he was assisted by his son Takami.

to choose. I was always going round to N's study at their official residence.[82]

N advised me to do law and literature, and cited Lord Macaulay as an example. You can get an idea of the situation in those days from the very fact that Macaulay's 'History of England' and 'Biography of Pitt' were popular reading matter amongst young men.[83] It was also a fact that a great number of young men were very keen on law and politics. It was just at that time that Tokutomi Sohō came up to Tōkyō with a copy of his 'Japan in the Future', started the journal 'Kokumin no Tomo', and advocated democratism.[84]

'Kokumin no Tomo' had a yellow cover with a goddess holding a pen, and I'll never forget the first spring supplement, with a story by Yamada Bimyōsai that was illustrated with a picture of a naked woman.[85] I've forgotten the title, but it dealt with little-known facts about Emperor Antoku, and I was filled with surprise and admiration that such 'virgin soil' was being tilled in Japanese literature.[86] Dr. Tsubouchi's story 'Wife' was in the same issue.[87]

Dr. Tsubouchi's name had already achieved wide recognition a year or so before as a result of his 'Character of [Modern] Students', but as I didn't read such things as the Y Newspaper this was the first time that I myself came across his name.[88] But what struck me even more was Futabatei's translation 'Rendezvous', which had appeared a few copies

---

[82] Katai's chronology is a little confused at this point. Nojima left Tōkyō on April 7th 1888, ie. *before* Katai's enrolment at the school.

[83] Thomas Macaulay's (1800-1859) 'History of England' is well-known (five volumes, 1848-61 [last vol post.]), whereas the 'Biography of Pitt' is probably a reference to one of his many such articles contributed to the eighth edition of the Encyclopaedia Britannica (1853-60).

[84] Tokutomi Sohō (1863-1957), social, political, and literary critic. His 'Shōrai no Nihon' (October 1886) argued that Japan should, in order to develop, follow world trends of democratisation. He arrived in Tōkyō late in 1886, and founded the Minyūsha [Company] and its magazine 'Kokumin no Tomo' (The Nation's Friend, inspired by the American magazine 'The Nation'), which ran between February 1887-August 1899.

[85] Bimyōsai was an alternative pseudonym of Yamada Bimyō (see Note 54). His story 'Butterfly' ('Kochō') actually appeared in 'Kokumin no Tomo' in January 1889, and its famous illustration was by Watanabe Seitei (1851-1918).

[86] Emperor Antoku reigned from 1180-1185, and is believed to have drowned in Dannoura. Katai gives 'virgin soil' in English.

[87] 'Saikun' (January 1889, 'Kokumin no Tomo'), by Tsubouchi Shōyō (1859-1935), writer. Katai consistently uses the term 'hakase' (doctor) of Tsubouchi but strictly speaking he was only a 'gakushi' (BA) at the time, being awarded his doctorate some years later.

[88] Tsubouchi's 'Tōsei Shosei Katagi' (Katai gives just 'Shosei Katagi') was published in *seventeen* volumes — this type of fragmented publication being popular at the time — over seven months (June 1885-January 1886) by Banseidō. The reference to the Yomiuri Shinbun is connected with the fact that from 1887 Tsubouchi was in charge of the literary section of the paper.

earlier.[89] I had been brought up on unpolished Chinese and Japanese classics, so I was greatly impressed by the extraordinarily detailed depictive style. In fact, it was so unlike the style I was accustomed to that it threw me into confusion. But with such detailed depiction being a characteristic of Western literature, I felt that from now on Japanese writing had to follow the same lines. Henceforth, I read the magazines and newspapers carefully.

I always skipped classes on English conversation and grammar. I didn't think such things were important at all. Instead, I strolled casually around the streets of Jinbōchō and Ogawamachi, still wearing my classroom-sandals.

Fortunately for us impoverished students there was a bookshop in Ogawamachi, called Iroha, that rented out books. Nowadays there don't seem to be any such places where you can get hold of a book without actually having to buy it, but in those days, even if you didn't have the purchase price of a book, you could still obtain armfuls of them in this way. It was thanks to that bookshop that I was able to read new publications such as 'Garakuta Bunko', 'Shincho Hyakushu', and 'Kokumin no Tomo'.[90]

Kōyō Sanjin's 'Confessions' in the first issue of 'Shincho Hyakushu' also impressed me greatly.[91] Certainly the depictive style appealed to young men of the day. It also made me feel that it would not be impossible for someone like myself to produce the same sort of work. It seemed closer and fresher to me than remote Chinese-style writings, or traditional Japanese poetry, or esoteric English grammar. I was heartened too by the fact that the author was still a young man, no more than five or six years older than I myself was.

One of my friends and fellow contributors to 'Eisaishinshi', S, was also fond of literature and read the latest books and magazines.[92] Kindred spirits gathered at his house in Negishi to chat, so I too found myself heading there. S wrote Japanese poetry. Bad poetry. I often visited him on Sundays, heading through the Ueno woods. It was a large house beyond present-day Ikaho, with an annex.[93] S was always pleased to see

[89] Futabatei Shimei (1864-1909), translator, novelist. His 'Aibiki' (July-August 1888, 'Kokumin no Tomo') was a translation of a section of Turgenev's 'Sportsman's Diary'.

[90] 'Garakuta Bunko' (Bric-a-brac Bookcase) was the chief publishing outlet of the Genyūsha (Kenyūsha) school, and ran from May 1885-October 1889. 'Shincho Hyakushu' (A Hundred New Works) was published by Yoshioka Shoseki from April 1889-August 1891, and was associated with the 'progressive' literature of the day.

[91] Kōyō's 'Ninin Bikuni Irozange' (Katai gives just 'Irozange') (The Amorous Confessions of Two Nuns) appeared in April 1889. Kōyō Sanjin was one of Ozaki Kōyō's pseudonyms.

[92] Sakurai Toshiyuki (dates unclear).

[93] Ikaho was a restaurant.

me, and would treat me to dumplings at the Sawanoya in Imozaka. We put together a book called 'Raw Silk', and wrote a joint novel called 'Damask and Brocade'.[94]

As often as not we'd discuss the members of the Genyūsha [School], such as Kōyō, Bizan, Sazanami, Suiin, and Shian.[95] We also studied Aeba Kōson's 'Bamboo Cluster' and Kōda Rohan's 'Elegant Buddha', which appeared in the third volume of 'Shincho Hyakushu'.[96]

In opposition to the Genyūsha [School] were magazines such as Bimyō's 'Miyako no Hana' and 'Iratsume'.[97] We were filled with envy by Rohan's travelling from Yashū to the Kiso mountains with the fee he received for his 'Cluster of Dewdrops'.[98] "You can't deny that Rohan's got real talent!" we'd say. "The Genyūsha people couldn't write anything like 'Elegant Buddha'."

Our group, meanwhile, played verse-cards and so on.

Eventually O, I-, and T joined the group.[99] Yanagita Kunio was still only about fourteen or fifteen in those days, but he was an extraordinary genius, so S and I paid him a visit — that winter, if I remember right — at the house in Okachimachi in Shitaya where he was living with his elder brother Inoue Michiyasu, and made him a member of the group.[100]

---

[94] Respectively 'Seikenzōshi' and 'Ayanishiki', unpublished manuscripts written in 1890. The former was, like 'Miscellaneous Verses on the Four Seasons of Castle Marsh', actually made up into a booklet.

[95] The Genyūsha (lit: 'Friends of the Inkstone Society') is more commonly referred to nowadays as 'Kenyūsha', but it is clear from Katai's later use of the initial G that 'Genyūsha' was intended. It is also commonly referred to by some English-speaking critics as the neo-classical school. Iwaya Sazanami (1870-1933) was a poet and novelist who later became better-known as a writer of children's literature. Emi Suiin (1869-1934) was a novelist.

[96] Aeba Kōson (1855-1922) was an Edo-style novelist and critic. His 'Muratake' (Bamboo Cluster) was a twenty volume collection of sixty-eight of his works, published July 1889-December 1890 by Shunyōdō. The novelist Kōda Rohan's (1867-1947) 'Fūryūbutsu' (Elegant Buddha) was published on September 23rd 1889 in the *fifth* volume of 'Shincho Hyakushu'.

[97] 'Miyako no Hana' (Flower of the Capital), October 1888-June 1893, and 'Iratsume' (Young Woman), July 1887-June 1891. Bimyō was the chief writer for both magazines.

[98] Rohan's trip, from Tochigi Prefecture to Nagano Prefecture, took place in January 1889. 'Tsuyu Dandan' (Cluster of Dewdrops) was published in 'Miyako no Hana' from February-August, 1889. Rohan received payment for it, said to be fifty yen, in December 1888.

[99] O is Ōta Gyokumei (1871-1927), poet, novelist, and from 1899 resident priest at the Kenpuku Temple in Hanyū, Saitama (the setting for Katai's famous novel 'Country Teacher'). Also in 1899 he became Katai's brother-in-law following Katai's marriage to his younger sister Risa(ko), and therefore is a major figure in Katai's life. He first met Katai in spring 1890. I- is Ibusuki Kinshun (dates unclear), and T is Tsuchimoto Kōan (1871-1910).

[100] Yanagita Kunio (1875-1962), also known in his early days as Matsuoka Kunio, was one of Japan's best-known folklorists and poets, and one of Katai's closest friends. They

One of the unusual things about our group was that its members included a fortune-teller, Ōta Shunzan,[101] who was then in his early thirties. He had no interest in novels, and had only joined for the poetry. With his profession being so interesting S and I often called on him. He lived in an upstairs room of a house to the left of Onari Street in Kuromonchō. He'd face his clients there with a solemn expression, his divining-blocks and papers set out in a row, and tell their fortunes for five or ten sen. S and I joked about it. "It's funny, isn't it, to think that there are some people who actually believe what Shunzan tells them. I wonder if that means he's sometimes right?" S answered me with a laugh. "Even *I* can divine things," he said. "You just watch the next time we visit him. Just note what the first thing is that he tells his clients. He's bound to say, 'You're worried, aren't you!'. But of course they'll be worried — why else would anyone go to a fortune-teller!? THAT is the art of divination!"

Nevertheless, that young fortune-teller was an interesting person. His poetry was good, too. We once held a meeting upstairs there, when Sasaki Nobutsuna's father, Hirotsuna, attended.[102] S and O and Shunzan were all once pupils of Nobutsuna. In fact, I'm pretty sure that on that occasion Nobutsuna himself also came along.

We kept up our visits to him for at least three or four years. We'd call in, for example, on our way back from viewing the blossoms in Ueno, and for a laugh compose poems like:

"The fragrant cherries
Are in bloom in Ueno.
This year once again,
I viewed them without
A girl at my side."

A few years later Shunzan moved up to Hokkaidō, and I heard that he died a miserable death.[103] From time to time I've wished he were still alive. He once read my fortune, and told me, "The signs are good. As long as you put in the effort, you'll have a wonderful career. There's nothing to hold you back." I can still remember the look on his face.

met in spring 1890. Inoue Michiyasu (1866-1941) was Yanagita's second eldest brother, known as a poet but perhaps best remembered for his friendship with the major literary figure Mori Ōgai (1862-1922). The confusion of surnames stems from the system of adoption, which was extremely common in Meiji Japan. Technically speaking Yanagita was still Matsuoka till his marriage-cum-adoption into the Yanagita family in 1901. The S referred to here is Sakurai Toshiyuki.

[101] Ōta Shunzan (c.1858-1896) was no relation to Ōta Gyokumei.

[102] Sasaki Nobutsuna (1872-1963), poet and, like Yanagita, a child prodigy. His father Hirotsuna (1828-1891) was a renowned authority on classical literature.

[103] He moved to Hokkaidō in 1894 and died of illness in 1896.

Zola's Novels

I was always going into N's study, just like it was my own. I borrowed all sorts of books from him, and would go away with works by Victor Hugo, Alexandre Dumas, or Wilkie Collins, or Charles Dickens, which I would read in my own less than fully understanding way as part of my daily studies.

"You're amazing, the amount of reading you get through!"

It made me feel good to be praised like this. And so it was that, even on the rare occasions when N wasn't at home, I'd still go into his study and come out with some books. Then suddenly, one day, I was told off by his father:

"Who on earth do you think you are, going into someone else's study and taking books without saying anything?!!"

I was completely taken aback. I was also angry at having been told off like that. N's mother came along and smoothed things over, but I just hung my head and said nothing. I felt terribly sad.

N came back and explained matters on my behalf, but after that I just didn't want to go there again.

At the time it was the heyday of Émile Zola, but the English translations of his novels were still very few and far between in Japan. N, however, had two or three of them, such as 'Conquest of Plassans', 'Nana', and 'L'assommoir'.[104] He'd shown them to me but then put them away again. "This fellow's books are all the rage at the moment," he'd said, "but they're really dreadful. I think that at your age they'd do you more harm than good, so I'll put them aside for the future." And so, I didn't get to look at Zola's novels, much as I wanted to. I still remember how depressed I was.

A number of years later, in a second-hand bookshop in Jinbōchō, I came across 'Conquest of Plassans'.[105] By giving some desperate excuse to my mother I managed to get just enough money from her to enable me to buy it. But in those days I didn't really understand Zola's novels. I wondered just what it was that was supposed to be so interesting.

Kōyō and Rohan

The news that Kōyō Sanjin's 'Perfumed Pillow' and Rohan's 'Man with a Moustache' were to be serialised together in the Y Newspaper

---

[104] The mixture of French and English is as given by Katai.

[105] According to other statements by Katai this purchase must have taken place before May 1891 (see the later section 'Visiting Kōyō Sanjin').

created quite a stir.[106] It's no wonder the literary enthusiasts of the day were so surprised, since it meant that the leader of the realist school on the one hand and the leader of the idealist school on the other would be appearing in the same newspaper at the same time. The newspaper company itself also made a big thing of it, and put up illustrated advertisements on street corners.

I'm pretty certain it was around September.

Kōyō got on with his writing, while Rohan gave up after five or six episodes. Nevertheless, out of the two works it was Rohan's that was the more interesting and received the better reviews. All manner of gossip ensued. People were saying that Rohan was plagued by some worry. There was of course the business of that love affair involving Nakanishi Baika Dōjin.[107]

At this point in time Bimyōsai's prestige had fallen away quite considerably. He continued to write in 'Miyako no Hana', including major works like 'Strawberry Princess', but his reputation wasn't the best.[108] By contrast, the fluent writings of Kōyō were achieving ever greater popularity, and together with Rohan, who had achieved great success with 'Elegant Buddha', he was dominating the literary scene. That summer Rohan went off to Mount Akagi, but he also published the short story 'Sword' in the summer supplement of 'Kokumin no Tomo'.[109]

"Strike here — then you'll see just how well it can cut!"

This final sentence appealed greatly to the young men of the day. The depiction of the woman Oran was also highly praised by the critics.

The leading critic of the day was Ishibashi Ningetsu, followed by the sharp and sarcastic Shōjiki Shōdayū in 'Kokkai'.[110] Ōgai Gyoshi had

---

[106] Kōyō Sanjin's (one of the pseudonyms of Ozaki Kōyō) 'Kyara Makura' (Perfumed Pillow) was published in the Yomiuri between July 5th-September 23rd 1890. Rohan's 'Hige Otoko' (Man with a Moustache) ran in the same newspaper July 8th-July 18th 1890.

[107] Nakanishi Baika (Dōjin) (1866-1898), poet. He was also a notorious eccentric, hedonist, and one-time religious recluse, who died a lunatic under circumstances that are still not fully clear. (For many years he was believed to have died in 1891, but was in fact in a lunatic asylum for most of the 1890's.) It is remotely possible from Katai's phraseology that there was a homosexual affair between Baika and Rohan, but it is more likely a reference to Baika's unrequited love for Saitō Teru (dates unclear), who later became the sister-in-law of the famous poet Ueda Bin (1874-1916). As a close friend of Baika, Rohan was probably embroiled in the affair as the go-between typically found in Japanese romances.

[108] Bimyō's 'Ichigo Hime' (Strawberry Princess) appeared in 'Miyako no Hana' from July 1889 - May 1890.

[109] Rohan's 'Ikkōken' (Sword) appeared in 'Kokumin no Tomo' in August 1890. It is the story of a swordsmith's dedication to his craft, to the extent that at the conclusion of the story he offers his own body as a test for the sword's sharpness.

[110] Ishibashi Ningetsu (1865-1926), critic and novelist. Shōjiki Shōdayū was one of the pseudonyms of the critic and novelist Saitō Ryokū (see Note 63). 'Kokkai' (State) was published from November 1890-December 1895, by the Kokkaishinbunsha.

only just returned from Germany, and although he was not unknown he was still not really recognised as a writer and critic.[111]

Anyway, Kōyō continued alone with his 'Perfumed Pillow', writing fluently in the style of Saikaku.[112]

At the time, I was living in Nandomachi in Ushigome, and frequently passed through Kitamachi. I hadn't realised it at first, but S told me that Kōyō lived in Kitamachi.[113] I therefore kept a casual eye open as I walked through the area and, sure enough, one day I spotted a little gate between two tenements, leading to a house where I could clearly see, written in Kōyō's own Shoku Sanjin-style handwriting, the words 'Genyūsha: Ozaki Tokutarō'.[114]

"Ah, so this is where he lives!" I thought to myself in some excitement. The knowledge that this young man, who was only four or five years older than I, was the leading light in Japan's literary world, made me feel that I myself absolutely had to try doing something. I was envious, consumed with jealousy. I was fired with a youthful determination. Resolving to finish as soon as possible a novel I had just started writing, I hurried back home.

I was envious not only of Kōyō, but also of those around him, such as Sazanami, Bizan, and Suiin. At least they'd reached a starting point, whereas I....I myself....with my long hair and gloomy countenance...... The thought stirred me to action. "I SHALL make a name for myself. I SHALL become famous. I SHALL become an authority in the literary world. I'll show them all!"

Literary gossip was much more common in those days than it is now. "What's Kōyō up to?" "What's Rohan up to?" Comments like these were always cropping up in young people's conversation.

I was then in my early twenties. Four or five years had passed since my return to Tōkyō. I no longer contributed to 'Eisaishinshi', and I no

---

[111] Ōgai Gyoshi was one of the pseudonyms of Mori Ōgai (1862-1922), who was studying medicine in Germany from June 1884-September 1888. He presently established himself as a major authority in the literary world, especially as a translator and critic. He later became Surgeon-General.

[112] Ihara Saikaku (1642-1693), writer, was noted for his mixture of realism and ornateness of style.

[113] Katai's chronology is somewhat erroneous here. The Tayamas moved to Nandomachi in January 1889, but moved to (Ichigaya) Kōrachō (also in present-day Shinjuku-ku) on December 9th that same year (staying there till September 1893). Kōyō only lived in Kitamachi between March 1890-March 1891, when he moved to nearby Yokoderachō (where he remained for the rest of his life). Therefore, Katai left Nandomachi four months before Kōyō took up residence in Kitamachi. However, Kōrachō and Nandomachi were both situated to the west of Kitamachi and it is therefore likely that Katai passed through the latter area even after his move.

[114] Shoku Sanjin was the pseudonym of the satirical poet Ōta Nanpō (1749-1823); Ozaki Tokutarō was Kōyō's real name.

longer studied Chinese-style writings. After 'Confessions' and 'Elegant Buddha' I was strongly drawn towards this new Japanese literature. For the last year or so I'd been trying to write novels, slowly though it may have been.

With the revival of Chikamatsu and Saikaku bookshops such as Musashiya and Maruzen put out lots of little editions that you could buy for about ten sen, such as 'The Life of an Amorous Man' and 'The Life of an Amorous Woman'.[115] Books that I'd bought with my own money, such as 'Selected Poems by Sanyō', 'The Tower of Distant Thoughts: Selected Poems', and 'The Complete Works of Su-ton-p'o', were no longer any use to me, so I took them off to a second-hand bookshop and bought instead works by Chikamatsu and Saikaku.[116]

Although I was on the one hand passionate, strong, and tenacious, I was on the other timid and bashful, and always getting pushed into corners. That rather neatly describes my circumstances at the time. We were living in a little house with overhanging eaves and dark rooms, for which we paid about seven yen a month. Even living in a place like that it was difficult to make ends meet on my elder brother's salary, and we were in fairly desperate straits.[117] So you can imagine, by contrast, just how much better and brighter society at large seemed to me, and how I was always envious of others. Wherever I went, whatever I saw or heard, I always reacted. My heart leapt at the sight of huge mansions and thickly wooded gardens, or beautiful girls, or dashing carriages.

To cap it all my younger brother and I caught typhoid. This took place between the summer of 1891 and the following winter [sic].[118] At that

---

[115] Respectively 'Kōshoku Ichidai Otoko' (1682) and 'Kōshoku Ichidai Onna' (1686), both by Saikaku.

[116] Respectively 'Sanyō Shishō' (eight volumes, 1833) by the Chinese-style poet Rai Sanyō (1780-1832); 'Enshirō Shishō' (two volumes, 1837 and 1849) by the Chinese-style poet Hirose Nansō (1782-1856); and 'Sotōba Zenshū' (date unclear) by Su Shih (1036-1101), one of the Eight Poets of T'ang and Sung (see Note 42), known also as Su-ton-p'o and in Japanese as Soshoku or Sotōba.

[117] Miyato's salary at that stage was twenty yen per month. In addition, the Tayama household received a war-widow's pension of forty-six yen per annum, making a monthly total of just under twenty-four yen per month. (See also Note 5.) It is clear from these figures that Katai's poverty was not quite as desperate as he often makes out.

[118] It must in fact have been the summer of 1890 and the winter of 1890/1, with Katai probably coming down with the disease in February 1891 (and Tomiya presumably in summer 1890). The conclusive evidence for this dating is the reference Katai makes below to Miyato's wife, specifically to the troubled relationship between her and his mother in the same spring (ie. 1891) as he was lying in the sunshine recovering from his illness. As his sister-in-law Tomi died May 14th 1891 (see Note 69), his illness must have occurred before this point in time. (It is not possible to infer from the reference further below to his sister-in-law's sudden death that it is in fact Miyato's second wife, Kawamura Koto [born 1876], who was having the troubled relationship, as this marriage did not take place till 1894.) On the other hand, his illness must have taken place after

time we had moved from the house in Nandomachi, where the rent was too high, to a relative's house in Kōrachō.[119] That spring was the worst I've ever experienced. Lack of funds led to my withdrawal from the Japan Law School, which I'd just started going to with S.[120] In addition to that things were not going at all smoothly between my mother and elder brother and his wife, which upset me greatly. I'll never forget how I used to worry about the future as I lay in the sunshine on the verandah, recovering from my long illness. The house in Kōrachō only had two rooms, a six-mat with a hibachi and an eight-mat. My desk was in the larger room, by the window at the back, and it was there that I laboured so hard and dreamed my endless daydreams. The desk was up against the wall, and to the right was a shōji with a large pane of glass in it, through which I could look out onto the drab little garden. I was often reduced to tears there, tears of frustration that things weren't going as I hoped, tears over some girl or other, tears over my sister-in-law's sudden death, tears of envy towards those who had achieved an early success in life, tears of sadness over our poverty, tears over my own shortcomings..... To add to it all I was forever hearing my mother complaining: "How long's he going to keep on playing around, our Roku!? It'd be nice if he went out somewhere and brought back a few yen!"

Ōgai Gyoshi's 'Shigaramizōshi' came out in the latter part of 1891, and early the following year he published 'Dancing Girl' in 'Kokumin no Tomo'.[121] He then rapidly became a big name on the literary scene. I myself in those days was, as a student of literature, building up a better than average knowledge of what was going on overseas. I was greatly impressed by Ōgai's crisp, German-style criticism. I liked 'Letter Bearer', which he brought out after 'Dancing Girl'.[122] I also learned from 'Shigaramizōshi' that there were directions I could follow other than Kōyō and Rohan.

September 21st 1890, as this is the date of opening (as opposed to founding) of the Japan Law School which he states he had just started attending. Judging from a sudden cessation in his literary activity in February 1891, for some months, it seems likely that it was in that month that he contracted the disease. Subsequent chapters in this book reveal that he had recovered sufficiently by late May 1891 to go visiting Ozaki Kōyō and others.

[119] The relative was Ishii Osamu (see Note 39). The move was December 9th 1889.

[120] The Nippon Hōritsu Gakkō, the forerunner of the Law Faculty of Nihon University (in Kanda), was opened on September 21st 1890, though its actual founding appears to have taken place the previous year. S is Sakurai Toshiyuki.

[121] Katai is in error by two years in both cases. The first edition of the magazine 'Shigaramizōshi' (Tangled Tales) was October 25th 1889 (till August 1894), while 'Maihime' (Dancing Girl) appeared in 'Kokumin no Tomo' in January 1890.

[122] 'Fumizukai' (Letter Bearer) was published in January 1891 in 'Shincho Hyakushu'.

Literary gossip at that particular time was focussed on Kōyō's marriage. Kabashima Kikuko ..... chrysanthemums and red leaves.[123] She was very beautiful, and Kōyō was very much in love with her. People were saying that cushions had been made with chrysanthemums and red leaves on. It upset me to hear even things like that.

Visiting Kōyō Sanjin

It turned out that the great master received a letter from yet another student of literature — me. At the time Kōyō had just moved from Kitamachi to Yokoderachō, where he was to remain for the rest of his life. I had been plagued by worries and anxieties and eventually, with no other means of establishing myself on the literary scene, I resolved to write to him.

I don't remember what exactly I said but, like so many other literature students, I must have strung together a load of vacuous phrases. I still blush to think about it, and it depresses me to think just how desperate I was.

I received an immediate reply.

Perhaps, if circumstances had been different, he would simply have thrown my letter, too, straight into the wastepaper basket. However, as good fortune would have it, he had just formed — and financially guaranteed — an association to put out a magazine called 'Senshibankō', which was to carry works by his protégés.[124] And so upon receipt of my letter he sent me a set of the rules of the association, which was called the Seishunsha, and asked me to become a member.

How happy this made me in my despair! It even made me happy to think that the red letters over the rules were penned by Kōyō himself. Anyway, a day or two later I paid my first visit to him.

I wore a triple-crested haori of black calico and worn-down geta, and looked awfully nervous. I was shown through to an eight-mat drawing-room, next to a two-mat room near the door which was later occupied by the likes of Kyōka, Fūyō, and Shunyō.[125] The room looked down

[123] The marriage took place on March 21st 1891. The literal meaning of the pseudonym 'Kōyō' is 'red leaves', while 'kiku' usually means 'chrysanthemum'. The 'kiku' of Kabashima Kikuko, however, was written with different characters and meant 'eternal joy'. It is not clear whether this fact was not widely known or simply ignored.

[124] 'A Thousand Purples, Ten Thousand Crimsons', nine issues only from June 1891-April 1892.

[125] Izumi Kyōka (1873-1939), novelist; Oguri Fūyō (1875-1926), novelist; and Yanagawa Shunyō (1877-1918), novelist. In the work 'Modern Novels' ('Kindai no Shōsetsu', 1923) Katai states that Kyōka was actually in the room by the door when he visited Kōyō. However, Kyōka did not make his approach to Kōyō till October 1891, five months after Katai's visit. Fūyō's approach was also late in 1891, whereas Shunyō's was in 1895.

upon a little garden, below which I could see a cluster of houses. The lady who led me through was about fifty, and looked very elegant.

I was very excited.

I was also thrilled to see in the room a portable chest-of-drawers, obviously belonging to the new bride. That wasn't all. I could also imagine the new bride from the colourful array of dolls and clothes and mirror-stand and utensils. How wretched and miserable I myself seemed by comparison.

"Would you come upstairs please?"

It was the same elderly lady who had led me through to the drawing-room. The date was the 24th of May, fresh green leaves sparkled in the sunlight, and all the shōji were left open. I stood up, went out into the hallway and, in a six-mat room with a hibachi, next to the drawing-room, I spotted the young, beautiful, flower-like Kikuko. She had snow-white make-up on, and her gorgeous sparkling eyes were turned towards me. I was taken by surprise, and made a hasty bow.

It was a perfect picture, and I can still visualise it very clearly.

Upstairs there were two rooms, an eight-mat and a six-mat. The bright early summer sunlight was streaming in. There was a scroll hanging up with the character for 'long life' written on by Ichiroku Koji, to celebrate the wedding, and a sofa, various books scattered about, and some cushions.[126] Beyond these was Kōyō's desk, and sitting in front of it, next to a hibachi, was Kōyō himself.

"Come over here."

I went and sat on a bright red patterned muslin cushion in front of the hibachi. It was not a chrysanthemum and red leaf patterned cushion, as rumour had it. A tea-kettle, tea-cup, and other tea-utensils stood untidily nearby amongst books and the latest magazines, but the elderly lady who had shown me upstairs took them away to wash them.

My initial impression of Kōyō was a good one. He had a typical Tōkyōite manner of speech, lively and open, and didn't seem to look down upon me as a mere student of literature. He certainly put my nerves at ease. He talked about Saikaku, and Chikamatsu, and about a work he was writing for the Y Newspaper. This was 'The Mended Tea-cup' — in his 'Complete Works' under the title 'Tear-soaked Sleeves' — which was running to thirty or forty episodes and drawing considerable attention as it was said to feature Ōgai Gyoshi as the protagonist.[127]

---

[126] Ichiroku Koji (1834-1905), also known as Iwaya Ichiroku, calligrapher and poet.

[127] 'Yakitsugijawan' (The Mended Tea-cup) ran in the Yomiuri Shinbun from May 15th-June 25th 1891. It was included in his 'Complete Works' under the title 'Sodeshigure' (Tear-soaked Sleeves).

Talk then turned to foreign literature. I certainly must have seemed very forward to Kōyō. At first I hadn't said much, out of deference, but when we got onto foreign literature I gave my views on Hugo, on Dickens, on Thackeray, on Dumas, and even on German literature, which I had started to learn about through 'Shigaramizōshi'.

Kōyō stood up and took a foreign book down from his shelves. He handed it to me. It was Zola's 'Abbe Mouret's Transgression'.[128]

We started talking now about Zola.

"He's very popular at the moment," said Kōyō, "and you can see why from the detailed descriptions. It really is very detailed. He writes three or four pages just in describing a single room. You simply can't find anything like that in Japanese literature." He took up a nearby fan, opening it as he continued: "It's because he's very good at distinguishing between the overt and the covert. The plot itself is extremely simple — merely a priest becoming ill and then falling in love with an innocent girl — but the psychological depiction of the gradual process of his falling in love is very finely detailed. Japanese literature will have to follow suit."

So he had actually read Zola by that stage. Not to be outdone, I talked about 'Conquest of Plassans'.

Thinking about it now, it seems to me that Kōyō's realism developed from Sanba to Saikaku, and then in a leap to Zola. He was never without one of Zola's works at his side.

He tried to progress from Saikaku to Zola through 'Two Wives', 'Purple', and 'Much Feeling, Much Grief', in that order.[129]

I stayed there talking for about an hour, though I've mostly forgotten what was said. However, I do remember being greatly impressed by his luxurious life-style, his lordly magnanimity, and especially his beautiful wife Kikuko. While we were talking she brought in some boiled broad-beans, the first of the season and a rare treat.

As I took my leave and came away I was filled on the one hand with a fired ambition, and on the other with gloomy thoughts about my own life-style. I had no cheerful upstairs rooms, no muslin cushions, no broad-beans, no latest publications: all I had was a desk in a dirty little room next to the toilet. I also had a haiku, which Kōyō had just composed for me:

"A myriad threads,
Of scattered willow,
And flowing black hair."

---

[128] Given in English by Katai, who states in 'Modern Novels' that Kōyō was sent the work by a friend in America.

[129] Respectively 'Futari Nyōbō' (August 1891-January 1892, in 'Miyako no Hana'); 'Murasaki' (January 1st-26th 1894, Yomiuri Shinbun); and 'Tajō Takon' (February 26th 1896-December 9th 1896, Yomiuri Shinbun).

With Kōyō's introduction, the next day I visited Emi Suiin, who was more or less going to be looking after 'Senshibankō', at his temporary residence in Kitamachi — the place where Kōyō had written 'Perfumed Pillow' the previous year.

After that I often called on Kōyō, and I also remember Kyōka coming round to my humble home to collect the Seishunsha membership fee.[130] But for a busy person like Kōyō, visits from a pushy student like me got to become a nuisance, and eventually I was turned away. At that very time Kyōka and Fūyō were both busy writing in that little room by the door.

The Ueno Library

In those days the Ueno Library was still located behind the School of Fine Arts. It was an unforgettable part of my life. I used to walk there from Ushigome two or three times a week without fail.

I'd pay my five sen and go on upstairs to the reading-room, with its large glass windows and white curtains. The sunshine poured in, and you could see fresh green growth rustling outside. I used to spend the whole day beside those windows, reading books and dreaming my daydreams.

There were a lot of people reading there, but you'd get 'shushed' at the least murmur so it was always deathly quiet, with the occasional exception of the gentle sound of the supervisor's slippers as he went on his rounds.

I read all of Chikamatsu and Saikaku there, and of particular benefit to me was the introduction of foreign literature through Roka's translations, which appeared in number six type in 'Kokumin no Tomo'.[131] As I was still unable to obtain — or even get to read — very many foreign journals this was the only real means I had of finding out about foreign literature of which I was ignorant.

I was much impressed by a synopsis of Turgenev's 'Sportsman's Diary', especially by one of the stories, 'Woodsman'. Gradually I became familiar with the names of Russian authors such as Tolstoi, Dostoevski, and Gogol. In those days the two authorities on Russian literature were Futabatei Shimei and Saganoya Omuro, and I had in fact already met Saganoya on one occasion and heard various things about Russian literature from him.[132]

---

[130] The fee was ten sen, which was low enough to be called nominal.

[131] Tokutomi Roka (1868-1927), writer and translator, and younger brother of Tokutomi Sohō. Number six type is rather smaller than average.

[132] Saganoya Omuro (1863-1947), novelist and poet.

At the time there was an English translation of Tolstoi's 'War and Peace' in the library. Although I didn't understand any more than half of it I did at least read my way through it day by day.

I also read English critical works such as 'The Greatest Masters of Russian Literature'. The picture it had of Tolstoi showed him when he was still young. He was wearing a military uniform, from his Caucasus days.

There was one other reason I liked going to the library, and that was that I could always count on seeing the whiskered face of Kurokawa Yasuji (Takase Bun'en), a man some years my senior whom I liked a lot.[133]

Takase Bun'en! There's probably no-one nowadays who's heard the name, but to me it's a very dear old name indeed. The literary influence he had on me was unexpectedly profound.

He was always there whenever I went to the library, and I was always happy when I spotted his benign, whiskered, fatherly face amongst the crowd of readers. He too always looked pleased to see me, and used to take me straight off to the cafeteria to chat.

We always walked home together. He used to talk at length about philosophy and the classics, and this roused a great enthusiasm for research in me. He'd liked Dostoevski's 'Crime and Punishment' and Futabatei's 'Drifting Cloud'.[134] He was inclined towards the 'foreign literature school' rather than the Genyūsha, and when it came to criticism he was much sharper and more knowledgeable than people like Ningetsu and Ryokū. He was living in drab lodgings, leading a life just like Raskolnikov in 'Crime and Punishment'. Whenever I went to see him he always spoke without the least restraint about the literary scene of the day.

"Kōyō's a waste of time!" he'd say, getting quite worked up.

I don't know where he got his information from, but he was always fully informed about what was going on inside the literary scene. I learned all manner of literary gossip from him. At one time, writing in a magazine called 'Shinbundan', he waged quite a long war of words with Ōgai Gyoshi, who was then living in Sendagi.[135]

---

[133] Takase Bunen (Bun'en) (1864-1940), novelist and critic. Katai first met him in 1891.

[134] Futabatei's 'Ukigumo' (Drifting Cloud) was published in several parts. The first and second parts were published in June 1887 and February 1888 by Kinkōdō, the third part in the July and August 1889 issues of 'Miyako no Hana'. While still technically unfinished, it is considered the first psychologically realistic work in modern Japanese literature, and reflects Russian influence.

[135] 'Shinbundan' (New Literary World), published by Bungakukan, spans only four issues, between January-April 1896.

As far as novels were concerned he didn't write very much. His first work — I forget what it was called — appeared in 'Miyako no Hana', and later he had a book published by Shunyōdō, called 'Young Leaves'.[136] I was the first person to hear a reading of this book, and I was moved by the fascinating, oratorical manner in which he read it out to me. He also often gave me his critical opinions of things I wrote.

A complete loner, he spoke to no-one about his past or about his personal circumstances. I did hear that he had been a classmate of Matsuzaki Kuranosuke at a middle-school in Chiba, but he used to keep things very much in the dark and didn't even reveal his address to more than two or three people.[137] He kept changing his lodgings too, from Hongō to Ushigome to Koishikawa....

Whenever I went to see him he'd be sprawled out on a dirty, thin mattress. There was a little hibachi there, with cheap ground charcoal, and it was plain to see just how hard his life was. But he himself didn't seem in the least bothered. He'd give interesting and imaginative observations on life, with a serious expression hidden under his whiskers. And at the end of every year, without fail, he'd take himself off to some cheap lodging house in Asakusa or Senju. I've still got a whole pile of letters he sent me from such places.

His first recommendation was Futabatei Shimei, followed by Ōgai Gyoshi. Somewhat later he also recommended Ichiyō.[138]

"Hasegawa's marvellous.[139] Not content with Russian literature, he's now working on German literature. And he's studying Darwin, too. He truly is a fine man of letters."

He always sang Futabatei's praises.

To a young man like me he seemed a very strange person. I felt he was a real genius, and like one of those middle-aged students you find in Russian novels. Perhaps it was just that there weren't many people like that in Japan.

I don't know what he's doing nowadays. When Kawakami Bizan died he turned up unexpectedly at the wake, and said tearfully in front of the coffin: "THAT's why I told you not to get married and have children!"[140] Since that occasion, though, I've heard nothing of him.

---

[136] Bunen's first work was entitled 'Kairan' (Rolling Waves), and was published in 'Miyako no Hana' in 1890, while 'Wakaba' (Young Leaves) was published in January 1893, by Shunyōdō.

[137] Matsuzaki Kuranosuke (1865-1919), economist and doctor of law. His name became particularly well-known when, as Dean of the Tōkyō Commercial College, he became involved in a dispute with students and had to resign (February 1909).

[138] Higuchi Ichiyō (1872-1896), novelist and poetess.

[139] Hasegawa Tatsunosuke was the real name of Futabatei Shimei.

[140] Bizan took his own life on June 15th 1908 (see later section 'Bizan's Death').

Anyway, I spent three or four years in this way, going to the library. There were no electric trains in those days, and I used to plod home down the steps of the Tōshōgū Shrine, round Shinobazu Pond, and then through Hongō off to Ushigome. As I walked my head would be full of dreams and fancy, or else with the plot of some novel.

It's all in the past now, the dear old past.

The Road along the River

"I'm not going to concern myself with whether they're good or bad, or whether they sell or not. I'm simply going to make sure that I write two or three short stories a month!" I made my mind up.

At that time I walked every day along the narrow banks of the Tamagawa Waterway, which ran through Tsunohazushinchō in the outskirts of Shinjuku.[141] To earn a bit of money I worked till three o'clock every day copying out manuscripts at a historian's house, for which I got twenty sen a day.[142]

By then we'd moved to the Ōkido part of Yotsuya, from which I set out every morning, cutting at an angle past the Taisō Temple on the Shinjuku Road before following right along the pretty little Tamagawa.[143]

On check-up days I often encountered groups of horribly pale prostitutes coming towards me.[144]

When I crossed the Yamanote Line — a single track line in those days — at the level-crossing in Shinjuku the vista of the Tamagawa would open up before me like some beautiful water-colour.[145] There were fields

[141] Tsunohazushinchō corresponds to present-day Nishishinjuku 1-3 Chōme. The Tamagawa was a service-water course in the Yodobashi-Nishishinjuku area, not to be confused with several other Tamagawa (natural) rivers in the Tōkyō region. The time is 1893.

[142] The historian is Okanoya Shigezane (see Note 8).

[143] The Tayamas moved from Kōrachō to the corner of Naitōmachi (near present-day Yotsuya 4 Chōme) in September 1893, staying there till January 1896.

[144] Licensed prostitutes had to have regular medical checks. The prostitutes mentioned here would presumably be heading towards the health centre in Yotsuya.

[145] The history of Tōkyō's rail network is extremely complex, and establishing hard fact is made more difficult by popular terms that were often misleading or inaccurate. The Yamanote Line ('Yamanote' meaning literally 'suburban' but used particularly of Tōkyō's western suburbs), was opened from Shinagawa to Akabane in 1885. However, its correct name until 1905 was the Shinagawa Line. In 1905 the Toyojima Line was opened from Ikebukuro to Tabata, and the entire stretch down to Shinagawa became the Yamanote Line (a situation further confused by the fact that from Ikebukuro they are two separate lines). It is possible that Katai is using the term 'Yamanote' in the loose sense of 'suburban', but more likely he has simply applied the name in use at the time of writing (ie, 1917) rather than the correct name in 1893, the Shinagawa Line. There was in fact a second suburban line operating out of Shinjuku by 1893, the Kōbu Line, which was opened as far as Tachikawa in 1889. It is odd that Katai makes no mention of this.

of miscanthus, rustling in the breeze. There were oaks. There was a solitary, ancient-looking farmhouse beside the road up the hill. There were chestnuts. And there was the little stream, babbling on its ribbonlike way.

At one point it formed rapids, and foamed as it sped past.

In autumn the gently sloping banks were adorned with pampas-grass. There were a number of picturesque bridges, too.

Whenever I walked along the banks of the Tamagawa my mind would be full of creative thoughts. I was constantly struggling to come up with suitable material for short stories, and I'd be overjoyed one moment, down at heart the next.

"I've just got to write a masterpiece!" I'd keep telling myself every so often.

Sometimes, on my way back, I'd sit down in the miscanthus and watch the sun go down, my young cheeks blazing red in its setting rays.

I travelled this riverside road for at least three or four years. Meanwhile, the two or three stories I'd resolved to write every month piled up in the drawer of my desk. I got them out, at Otowa's suggestion, when the H Book Company decided to publish a cheap series of works called 'Meiji Library'.[146] If I remember correctly I ended up with a total of twenty-five yen for about half of them.[147]

"Twenty-five yen for three years' work! It's just not good enough! I simply cannot make a living as a writer." I remember having this depressing thought as I walked home with the fee.[148]

"I must do something," I thought to myself. "I'll have to change my approach. I'm twenty-five years old. I can't keep on living off my brother and mother for ever." Of course, it was one thing to think, and another thing to act. Anyway, I did at least think that I'd put the money to good use. I invited O, who was then doing literature at Waseda, and used it for a trip from Bōshū to Hakone and Atami.[149]

---

[146] Ōhashi Otowa (1869-1901). Formerly enjoying a modest reputation as the Genyūsha writer Watanabe Otowa, in 1893 he suddenly acquired great influence in the literary world by being adopted into the family of the owner of Hakubunkan, Ōhashi Sahei (1835-1901), to marry Sahei's daughter Tokiko (the marriage being 1895). The marriage was arranged by Ozaki Kōyō. The 'Meiji Bunko' ('Library') spanned fifteen issues, from September 1893-July 1894.

[147] Katai had three stories included in the series (actually less than a tenth of his output over the previous three years), of which the best-known is 'Sumidagawa no Aki' (Autumn along the River Sumida, in the fourth issue, December 1893).

[148] In actual fact twenty-five yen for three stories was not at all a bad fee. Katai has also omitted to mention that he was at the same time publishing quite regularly through other outlets, largely through the good offices of Emi Suiin. From November 1892 he had also been receiving fees for his works (see the later section 'My First Manuscript-Fee').

[149] O is Ōta Gyokumei. Bōshū is present-day Chiba Prefecture. Their trip was from December 25th 1893-January 4th 1894.

It was shortly before the war with China, a time when resentment over insults from foreign countries seemed to have reached a peak.

My First Translation

Maruzen's upstairs section was still small, and they didn't have the range of foreign books they do today. I'd go there from time to time, buy as many cheap books as possible, and order other books that I wanted. Turgenev's 'Fathers and Sons' and Daudet's 'Kings in Exile' were among the books I got there. One day, quite unexpectedly, I came across Tolstoi's 'Cossacks', selling for fifty sen in the Seaside Library series.[150] I read it and was extremely impressed.

Just at that time the first volume of Roan's translation of 'Crime and Punishment' had appeared, and was being discussed by all the critics.[151] I felt, though, that the work I had just read surpassed even the psychological depiction of Raskolnikov, and I said so to E.

One day not long afterwards he said to me:

"Why not try translating it? I hear it could go in H Company's series of translations."[152]

"Right. I will!"

I took the job on happily.

The series featured such works as 'Robinson Crusoe' and 'Don Quixote'. It was the time of the war with China, and I suppose the head of H Company was attracted by the term 'Cossacks', reasoning that this masterpiece of Tolstoi's dealt with the Cossack cavalry.[153] That would account for the company being prepared to accept the translation of an unknown literary novice.

Such things did not concern me. I was happy just to have the chance to translate such a fine work. That summer I went off with Yanagita to a temple in Nikkō, and it was there that I heard the news extras — 'Talks with China Break Down!'[154] When I got back I found that the big two-

[150] The Seaside Library was a pocket series published by George Munro, New York.

[151] Uchida Roan's (1868-1929) translation 'Tsumi to Batsu' appeared in two volumes in November 1892 and February 1893, from an English version.

[152] The 'Sekai Bunko' (World Library) series, fourteen volumes from February 1893-May 1894. E is Emi Suiin. H Company is Hakubunkan.

[153] Katai's translation, entitled 'Kossakku-hei' (The Cossack Troops), appeared in the eighth volume in September 1893. The Sino-Japanese War did not in fact start till the summer of 1894 (to spring 1895).

[154] Katai appears to have confused events that took place in separate years. His trip with Yanagita was in the summer of 1894, which is indeed the time when the Sino-Japanese War started. However, his translation was categorically published in September 189*3*.

storey house behind ours had just been put up for rent, so I took my desk over there and worked on the translation right through the summer.[155]

Of course, at the time, I was going to the historian's house to copy out manuscripts, so I could only work on the translation in the evenings and on Sundays. In addition to that my English still left a lot to be desired, and it was my first translation as well, so at first I felt I wasn't going to be able to do it.[156] But somehow or other I finally managed, after a fashion, to get through it.

For those reasons I'm sure it was a poor translation. Even the very text I was using had a lot of omissions, which didn't help.

I can still clearly remember working on the translation in that upstairs room. The afternoon sun would stream in through the window, and the insects were so noisy, and then, when the moon rose, its light would spill through the leaves of the thick growth in the garden. The lamp would be shining out from that upstairs room till late at night.

I pondered over Olenin's suffering, and Lukashka's life, and the feelings the old man Eroshka had towards nature. The strange life of the Caucasus merged with the dreams and anxieties of a young Oriental literary novice.

I finished it in three months. It covered more than six hundred sheets of paper.

I smartened it up and then, with E's letter of introduction, took it round to the H Company. It wasn't such a big book company in those days. It had moved from Honkokuchō to Honchō, but still had no editing office, and the boss, Shintarō, used to sit at a counter in the corner of the premises facing a back-street. He was still a young man in those days.[157]

As I had E's letter with me Shintarō took me over to his little spot at the counter for a discussion — a discussion with ME, a long-haired, sickly-looking literary novice who stared nervously at people!

An errand-boy brought over a book.

---

[155] It is not clear whether Katai rented the house or merely availed himself of its being empty. He refers to the entire house being for rent here, but later on mentions that he was using the upstairs only. It therefore seems unlikely that he actually did rent the house, at least in its entirety.

[156] It was his first *full* or professional translation, perhaps, but not his first ever translation. In 1890 he translated a section of 'Dream Life' by the American writer Ike Marvel (1822-1908, also known as D.G. Mitchell), and this was published — clearly stating it to be a translation — in three issues of 'Eisaishinshi' during June and July (1890), under the title 'Yūdachi' (Evening Showers). It was however a fairly inaccurate translation and Katai probably preferred to forget about it.

[157] Honkokuchō (more commonly read nowadays as Hongokuchō) and Honchō are both in Nihonbashi. Ōhashi Shintarō (1862-1944) was the son of Sahei the owner, but Katai's term 'boss' ('shujin') was a little flattering as Sahei in fact seemed to prefer Otowa to be groomed to take over as his successor. It was certainly Otowa who wielded the power in Hakubunkan, rather than Shintarō. (See Notes 146 and 584.)

Shintarō flicked through the numerous pages of my translation.

"There's quite a bit of detail about the Cossacks, I suppose?"

"Yes."

He opened the manuscript again. "The series isn't selling too well, and we're wondering what to do with it. So this translation of yours..... well, we DID request it so we WILL publish it, but.... I'm afraid we can only pay you thirty yen for it."

Six hundred sheets of translation, thirty yen. But I didn't complain. Soon I was hurrying away. Such was the birth of that dreadful translation of Tolstoi's 'Cossacks'.

The Troops Set Out (in the War with China)

It wasn't far from our house to the drill-ground in Aoyama, so I'd often go there in the evenings, alone, to watch the troops set out.

It was our first war with a foreign country, and although China wasn't a particularly strong opponent it was nonetheless a great power within Asia, and there was a lot of excitement in Tōkyō when the war began. The streets were constantly echoing with the cries of newsboys selling extras.

Now and again a column of gallant troops passed by, singing army songs.

Bayonets glistened in the sun.

The extras announced victories, and the streets were buried in a mass of Rising Sun flags. The picture-book shops — and there were still a lot of them in those days — were plastered with strongly coloured lithographs of Captain Matsuzaki's death, or else of a dead bugler with his bugle still at his lips.[158] A lot of new army songs were written, too.

Aoyama was linked by rail to Ōsaki, and the troops all set off from there, so the evening scenes at Aoyama were full of tension and sadness.

Rumour had it that dispersed troop landings had now commenced, and people in the city always seemed worried and distracted as they followed the war with a mixture of curiosity and emotion. This was true even of people who'd seen something of life, so you can imagine how tense a raw young man like me was.

I thought about the distant battlefields. I found myself constantly thinking about those who had gone off to that distant land across the sea, leaving their homes and families, about those compatriots who lost their

[158] The only record I can find of a war-hero named Matsuzaki is that of a Captain Matsuzaki Keitarō, who was killed in action in March 1905, in the *Russo*-Japanese War, or a Matsuzaki Yasuichi (born 1874), who was killed in April 1904 in the same war. Katai has possibly confused the names of heroes from the two wars.

lives out there in those lonely fields. I thought about war, and about peace, and about country scenes filled with artillery smoke. I thought I would like to go and see it all myself, too. There was the battle of A-san, the occupation of Kyong-song and In-chon, and the big engagement at Pyong-yang.

It was a bright moon that night, full and beautiful.

The ground at Aoyama was surrounded by a fence so I couldn't tell exactly what was going on inside, but the tumult and confusion was enough to convey to me a picture of the troops' departure. I could hear footsteps, and horses rearing, and I could see a black and white mixture of engine smoke rising constantly through the bluish light of the gas lamps before vanishing into the night.

I could hear an army song in the distance.

It sounded very sad, like the heart-rending funeral song of men going off to their death.

The train smoke was still rising through the lamplight.

Soon I could hear the train setting off, with a slow, heavy, hissing sound. Then came cheers of 'Banzai!', splitting the darkness.

I went home, filled with sadness.

But be that as it may, everywhere I went — town and countryside alike — I found excitement and enthusiasm and bravado. I heard cries of 'Banzai!' everywhere.

In the autumn that year I jouneyed along the coast road from Mito to Sendai, in my traveller's garb of straw hat, coat, and sandals. Even in the remotest village I saw Rising Sun flags fluttering in the breeze, marking another victory. People got together to farewell troops, and they drank to celebrate the victories — everything was connected with the war.

I can still picture the smoke around the arsenal. Of course, it wasn't as bad as the occasion of the war with Russia, but even so I remember the area around Suidōbashi and Koishikawa being blotted out with dreadful black and blue and white smoke.

> "Let me go to sea
> And die a watery death:
> Let me go to the hills
> ...."

Such was the spirit running through the entire Japanese nation.

What with the vicissitudes of the Restoration, and the collapse of the class system, and the ruination of the shizoku, there had long been a negative atmosphere in the nation, one of inability to do anything, and now the anti-foreign feeling that gushed forth during the war with China was a splendid thing to behold. There was still not the slightest sign of the argument that 'war was bad'.

The Author of 'Hide and Seek'

I don't know a great deal about Saitō Ryokū, but I did meet him on several occasions, and he also came to my house.

Ryokū, or Shōjiki Shōdayū, also used to be known as Kōtō Midori, and was from a family of retainers to the Tōdō Clan. He was said to have shown a very sharp mind right from his early childhood. After 'Hell of Oil' and 'Hide and Seek' he put out 'Shamisen at the Gate', writing a lot in newspapers, but then completely gave up novels and confined himself to bits and pieces of sharp, heavily sarcastic criticism.[159]

At that time he was despised as a gesaku writer, and thought of as a nuisance and a crank. Some writers even loathed him like some nasty little insect, and his very character was called into question. But where, after his passing, has one been able to find such sharp, sarcastic writing? Have we ever seen the like again of the perceptive criticism in 'Jumble Box'?[160]

With all the rumours I'd heard about him I didn't feel much like having anything to do with him at first, though I did admire his 'Hell of Oil'. I first met him at his lodgings in Yumichō in Hongō.[161]

The reason for our meeting was that he had suggested that, if I had any suitable piece of work, we should publish it under our joint names in a Hokkaidō newspaper. I've forgotten whether or not there was anybody acting as go-between, but anyway, that was how we came to meet.[162]

I know he must have been an unusual person, since my impression of him is still so strong. He criticised Bizan's 'Dark Tide', and told me with great authority that Bizan wouldn't have written what he had if he'd understood things a bit better.[163] He told me how the speech and narrative parts were unnatural, and how one had to write objectively, and so on and so on, but he didn't once bring up any philosophical or

---

[159] The three works are respectively 'Abura Jigoku', May 30th-June 23rd 1891, in 'Kokkai'; 'Kakurenbo', July 1891, in 'Bungaku Sekai'; 'Kadojamisen', July 26th-August 25th 1895, Yomiuri Shinbun.

[160] 'Midarebako', published May 1903, Hakubunkan, a miscellaneous collection of his writings.

[161] Ryokū lodged in Yumichō from 1895-1897. Precise dates are unclear.

[162] According to 'Modern Novels' there was indeed a go-between, the poet-critic Sassa Seisetsu (1872-1917).

[163] Bizan's 'Yamishio' was published from November 6th-December 29th 1895, in the Yomiuri Shinbun.

religious arguments. His conversation was always centred on literature and the real world.

I had an adaptation of a Zola novel, so I gave it the title 'Dawn of the Morning Moon' and published it in that Hokkaidō newspaper as a joint work with Ryokū.[164]

Contrary to rumour he was very precise when it came to money. He sent me the money regularly, as promised, in an envelope entrusted to some rickshawman.

He always liked to travel by rickshaw. He went everywhere that way, and often kept the rickshawman waiting for hours outside.

He never stopped criticising the Genyūsha and the university faction.

Even without actually reading what he wrote you could tell just by looking at him how deeply concerned he was with suffering between men and women, and how deeply he entered into his favourite works. He always looked depressed, and as though he was wrapped in thought about something. And he'd keep coming out with sarcastic comments in his conversation. I personally feel that Tokuda Shūkō lacks the bite of Shōdayū.[165]

---

[164] The work is titled 'Asazukuyo'. Other details remain unfortunately obscure, and indeed baffling. It is not found in the most exhaustive lists of works by Katai or Ryokū, and even a specialist in Hokkaidō newspapers has been unable to shed any light on the matter. In 'Modern Novels' Katai refers to it as covering some sixty issues, so it must have been a major work. The episode in itself illustrates a feature of the Meiji literary world that can hardly be called artistically desirable, or even honest. The patronage system was theoretically a means whereby great masters could offer practical advice to their pupils, and assist them in getting into print. However, as this episode reveals, it was on occasion extended to the point where established writers simply lent (sold?) their name to novices, even without so much as a single word of contribution to the work. Nor were the 'great masters' particularly fussy about who utilised their name, even if it was not one of their recognised pupils. Joint works of this period often smack of this sort of business, with the senior writer appearing to do very little — if any — work but nonetheless being involved in the fees. This system appears to have been allowed, however, by the reading public, who presumably turned a blind eye to bizarre combinations of writers and to the occasional work which was strangely incongruous with the literature of the writer in whose name it was published. Katai even managed to publish joint works with the great Ozaki Kōyō long after Kōyō had overtly rejected him as a pupil (eg. see Note 468). Background details are usually obscure.

[165] Tokuda was the early name of Chikamatsu Shūkō (1876-1944), novelist and critic. He changed his name to Chikamatsu — after Chikamatsu Monzaemon, whom he much admired — in 1911 to avoid being thought of as a pupil of the senior novelist Tokuda Shūsei (1872-1943). This rather sudden reference to Shūkō is presumably due to the fact that at the time of writing he was filling the same sort of critic's role as Ryokū had fifteen years earlier. His works include, for example, 'Bundan Mudabanashi' (Prattle of the Literary Scene) of 1910. As a matter of some interest it is worth noting that in 1931 Shūkō produced a work entitled 'Bundan Sanjūnen' (Thirty Years of the Literary Scene), which has something in common with this present work of Katai's. (See too the later section 'Hakuchō and Shūkō'.)

Ryokū came to our house one day, when we were living in Kikuichō in Ushigome. He was a senior figure in the literary world and I was a mere novice, so I was worried about how to entertain him. Unfortunately my friend N had also come, and he'd brought some beef and saké.[166] There was nothing I could do except ask Ryokū to join us. He didn't look as if anything was wrong, but he didn't touch any of the beef despite our constantly offering it him. Nor did he drink any saké. Nevertheless, far from taking an early leave he stayed talking for several hours. "Well, that was vintage Shōdayū," my friend said afterwards. "Full of sarcasm."

I once visited him in later years, when he was in Torigoe in Asakusa.[167] He was ill and had just been to see a doctor. He showed me a medicine bottle. "Look! The doctor's given me a number instead of a name!"

I didn't see him again after he went to Odawara, exept once when he came to the reception room at the H Company to ask me to put something he'd written in 'Taiheiyō', which I was editing at that time.[168] The woman who looked after him in his final years seemed to me to be very similar to the woman who looked after Heine in his final years, in Paris.[169] I still sometimes call to mind Shōdayū's gloomy face, plagued and exhausted by the discord between men and women.

---

[166] N is not Nojima Kinpachirō. The identity is not clear, but it is possibly the journalist and historian Nishimura Suimu (1879-1943). Katai lived in Kikuichō from January 1896 to September 1902.

[167] Ryokū lived here from December 1902-May 1903. However, as Katai says below that he did not visit him after his going to Odawara (1901), it is possible that he is referring here to 1899, when Ryokū lived in Mukōyanagiwaramachi (present-day Higashikanda 3 Chōme), which was approximately half a mile from Torigoe. Ryokū's illness, which is referred to below as having developed prior to the visit, was detected in 1898.

[168] Ryokū was in Odawara, near Hakone, from April 1901 till December 1902. Katai joined the Hakubunkan Company in September 1899 (to December 1912), and his duties included the editing of the magazine 'Taiheiyō' (The Pacific), a weekly magazine first issued in January 1900. Technically the magazine changed name in December 1902, to 'Jitsugyō: Sekai: Taiheiyō' (Business: The World: The Pacific), which would mean that Ryokū's visit to him as 'Taiheiyō' editor could only, strictly speaking (unless Ryokū made a special trip to Tōkyō), have taken place in December 1902. However, it was commonly known by its old name of 'Taiheiyō' even after the change of name right through till its cessation in July 1906.

[169] The woman who looked after Ryokū in his final years (he died of tuberculosis on April 13th 1904, having written his own obituary the previous day) was Kanezawa Take, a former maid who had cared for him during a visit he paid to an inn in Kanagawa in 1900. Heine (1797-1856) suffered from a spinal disease and was virtually bedridden from 1848 on. He was cared for by Eugénie Mirat, an almost illiterate sales assistant in a shoe shop whom he had met in 1834 and married in 1841.

My First Manuscript-Fee

Not long ago I got off the Yamanote Line at Nippori, to take part in a funeral procession after a bereavement in the O household.[170] Amongst the crowds getting on and off I caught sight of a familiar old face from the past, that of T F.[171] He looked very old, bent with age and with snow-white hair and deep wrinkles in his face. I called out to him and tried to attract his attention, but in all the crowd he didn't spot me and we passed each other by.

It gave me a rather strange feeling to realise that I probably wouldn't see him again. In his day he had been the chief editor of 'Miyako no Hana', had written the legend of the heroine Ofuji and lascivious short stories out of keeping with his age, and had been called 'Sensei' by everyone on the literary scene, including Rohan and Kōyō. He used to live in a side-street in Sarugakuchō. It was a nice house, comfortable but elegant. Everyone and anyone went there, from the great masters to complete novices. Countless manuscripts found their way to his desk, sent from far and wide with a hope of being published in 'Miyako no Hana', which in its day was the same prestigious journal that 'Chūō Kōron' is today.[172]

Bimyō was 'Miyako no Hana''s chief editor in name, but in practice it was T F who wielded the power. Through Emi Suiin's introduction I once sent a him rather poor short story. It left much to be desired, but Suiin was a good friend of T F and so, after I'd been asked to amend various parts of the manuscript, it scraped through and was published in the November issue of the magazine.[173]

Ichiyō's first work 'Fossil Wood' was published in the same issue, along with an introductory piece by her friend Kaho.[174] I heard that T F had commented that Ichiyō wrote like a man.

---

[170] Nippori is famous for its cemetery. O is not clear: Katai uses the initial for Ōgai, Oguri Fūyō, Ōta Gyokumei, and the Ōhashis, and of these the Ōhashi household would be the most likely contenders, though it is not Sahei (1901), Otowa (also 1901), or Shintarō (1944).

[171] T F is Fujimoto Tōin (dates unclear, but circa 1850-post 1913), novelist, and one-time editor of 'Miyako no Hana'. Katai's order of writing the initials is most unusual.

[172] 'Chūō Kōron' (Central Forum) was first published in August 1887, but did not establish a real reputation till some fifteen years later.

[173] The story was 'Shin Sakuragawa' (New Sakura River), published in the November and December 1892 issues.

[174] Ichiyō's 'Umoregi' (Fossil Wood) was not, strictly speaking, her first work (which was 'Yamizakura' [Night Cherry], March 1892) but her fourth. However, Katai may have been aware of this and may have been using the term loosely to mean 'first notable work' or 'first professional work'.

Miyake Kaho (1868-1943, also known by her real name of Tabe Tatsuko), was a poetess, novelist, and mentor to Ichiyō (they had attended the same school, with Kaho the senior by four years).

I visited T F's temporary residence in Sarugakuchō on a couple of occasions, and heard literary tales of the past that held little interest for a young man like me. He would still only have been in his mid-forties or so at the time. He looked a bit puzzled over my pen-name, 'Katai' — 'flower pouch' — and said that the 'tai' — 'pouch' — looked odd and rather common, and that if I insisted on a character with that meaning then I should use one read 'nō', which was far less mundane. If, on the other hand, I wanted to keep the sound 'tai', he suggested I use the 'tai' meaning 'hill'.[175] At least that had some meaning to it, he said. When my story was published in the magazine he did in fact use this 'tai' of his, without my permission. I was furious, but there was nothing I could do about it. When I complained to Emi he laughed. "It's a poor deal, all right!" he said. "It's one thing to correct a writer's work, but I've never heard of anyone correcting a writer's name!"

But as I said, it was too late to do anything about it.

I went to collect the manuscript-fee at the large reception room of the K Company, whose premises were located on the left of a side street to the west of Mitsukoshi.[176] After I'd been kept waiting a long time T F finally came and handed the money over to me in an envelope. It was seven yen fifty sen, representing thirty sen per page.[177]

That was the very first manuscript-fee I ever received. It was especially gratifying to me as it was the first money I'd earned from society as a result of entirely my own labours. And now my grubby little purse, which rarely contained more than a couple of yen, held almost eight yen!

I still clearly remember walking home along the long road that followed the moat towards Kudan, and feeling as proud of myself as if I'd become some literary giant.

Because the money represented something special I gave some to my younger brother and some to my mother, little as it was, and bought some eel and rice to take home to my elder brother and his wife.[178] I also

---

[175] When read 'Hanabukuro' rather than 'Katai' the name can mean 'flower-bud', which might have been more poetic, but Katai never intended it to mean anything other than 'flower pouch'. He took it from Ryūtei Tanehiko's work 'Yōshabako' (Writing-box, 1841), though it was actually read 'hanabukuro' there (still, however, with the meaning 'flower pouch'). He had started using it in March that year, and no-one really seems to know why. It certainly does seem a peculiarly silly name. If he had used the 'tai' meaning 'hill' as suggested by Fujimoto it would have fitted nicely with the fact that Katai's childhood home in Tatebayashi was very close to a renowned beauty spot called Azalea Hill. The name 'Flower Hill' might indeed have been called perfect, since Katai himself said that Azalea Hill was a source of poetic inspiration to him. However.....

[176] The K Company is Kinkōdō, the publishers of 'Miyako no Hana'.

[177] Ichiyō is said to have received eleven yen for her work, much to Katai's vexation.

[178] The last item is clearly erroneous, as Miyato's first wife, Tomi, had died in the previous year, and he did not remarry until 1894 — two years after the date of the incident depicted here.

sent some money off to my elder sister in the country, slipping a one yen note in with a letter to her. Before long I received a reply, thanking me. I still have her letter. "Thank you so much for the money you sent out of your first payment as a writer. I'm so pleased, not only for the money but also because your wishes have been fulfilled. I didn't want to waste it and have nothing left to show for it so I put a bit extra to it and bought a washtub. I really needed one......"

The Great Fire of Kanda

"It's a terrible fire. They say it's still burning," said the roundsman.

The previous night, which had been extremely windy, I'd heard firebells. I'd realised that there was a fire somewhere, but it had been too cold to go out and look. It turned out to be a truly huge fire, that had already reduced Kanda to ashes. It was now threatening to reach as far as Nihonbashi and Asakusa. The wind had dropped a little, but was still quite strong. Perhaps it was because of the fire, but the paper didn't come that morning. I finished breakfast and hurried off to look.

It was one day in March 1892.[179]

When I reached Kagurazaka I could see the whole area was in a state of anxiety. People were running about. "They say the fire crews are exhausted. There's nothing they can do," someone said. At Ushigome Mitsuke the crowds were even bigger. I hurried off up towards Kudan. My first thought was to gain a high vantage point.

The top of the embankment on Kudan Hill facing the moat was packed with people. From there I could see the aftermath of last night's fire. It was indeed an awful scene. The areas which the fire had passed through were just so much charred earth and smoke, while beyond them the fire had spread in several directions. I could see black smoke billowing across the horizon. "It's got to Nabechō now!" someone said. "It may even have reached the main road. Jikkendana looks threatened, too!"[180]

"It'd be some sight to see at night," said someone else, to which a voice answered:

"It was pretty enough last night, all right! Absolutely indescribable!"

I hurried down Kudan Hill, heading for Kamakuragashi. The area by the moat near the commercial college was crowded with onlookers and pumps and police and I couldn't get through, so I was forced to go

---

[179] The fire was actually April 9th-10th 1892. It destroyed over four thousand houses.

[180] Nabechō is present-day Kandakajichō 3 Chōme (unconnected with the word 'kaji' meaning 'fire'). Jikkendana is present-day Nihonbashihongokuchō.

through Marunouchi, past the printery, and come out at Tokiwabashi. I then headed towards Honchō. Everywhere it was the same terrible scene, the sort of scene that conjured up visions of the Meireki Fire, the so-called 'sleeve fire'.[181] Every house was the same — as soon as the fire became a real threat, the fire-resistant storehouses were secured, the baggage brought out from the house, the young and old removed to safety, then the firemen in their special clothing went in and out, manned the pumps, and climbed up on the roof to face the fire, totally absorbed in their task. Horrible black smoke billowed towards me. The sound of houses being burned, of things being destroyed, of people trying to stop it, of the westerly wind howling past the telegraph poles — everything merged into one sound, and it was as if some awful earthquake or tidal wave had struck. It was terrifying beyond description.

I went out onto the main road, and off to Jikkendana. North of Imagawabashi it was a mass of smoke and flame and people and pumps.[182] It was impossible to get through. I could hear some people yelling "It's got to Nabechō! It's got to the corner!"

It didn't look as if I could get across Imagawabashi [Bridge] so I crossed the next bridge along and just about managed to cut across the old Shōheibashi Road towards Mukōyanagiwara.[183] Everywhere there was noise and confusion and terror.

Fortunately the fire was put out just as it reached the main road.

For several days afterwards — indeed several weeks — the newspapers were full of the fire. You could read nothing but accounts of the fire and of people involved. Even the great fires of the past, such as the Maruyama Fire, the 'sleeve fire', were relived.[184]

Just at that time quite a long novel I had written was being published in the Kokumin Newspaper, but because of the fire no-one paid any at-

---

[181] This disastrous fire took place on January 18th-19th 1657, the third year of the Meireki period. The staggering figure of one hundred thousand people are said to have died in the flames, while thousands more, left without shelter, froze to death in a snowstorm two days later. The fire was believed to have started in the Honmyō Temple in the Maruyama part of Hongō, when burning sleeves forming part of a Buddhist rite were caught by the wind.

[182] Imagawabashi [Bridge] formerly spanned the Ryūkangawa, between present-day Kajichō 1 Chōme and Muromachi 4 Chōme, and was pulled down when the river was filled in during the Second World War.

[183] Mukōyanagiwara is present-day Higashikanda 3 Chōme.

[184] Though I have translated this sentence loosely, in Katai's favour, it should be noted that he actually treats the Maruyama fire and the 'sleeve fire' as two separate fires. (This is also true of the earlier reference.) There is no record of any major fire in Maruyama except the 'sleeve fire', however.

tention to it — just as I was starting to make a name for myself![185] Even my friends said nothing, although it appeared every Monday. I was very depressed about it, and complained to a friend, "No-one's taking the trouble to read it, they're so obsessed with the fire."

My younger brother, who was unconcerned about such things, went around nonchalantly singing some infantile song that had come into being thanks to the fire.

> "Clang, clang, the firebells go.
> The bricks of Kanda are tumbling down.
> Can't you get the pump to work?!
> It's burning right down, don't you know!"

The words were quite amusing, so eventually I too followed my brother's example, laughing as I sang.

The Park in Kudan[186]

The Shōkon Shrine in Kudan holds a lot of unforgettable memories for me. Ueno Park made a great impression on me, but still not to the extent of Kudan.

It first entered my life when I was about six.[187] I had an aunt living in nearby Fujimichō so, having come up to Tōkyō with my mother, I was forever being taken there to see the fountain and the golden carp.

Another bond between the shrine and myself, even in later years, was that my father's memorial tablet was there. He was killed on April 14th, and every spring my elder brother would take a day off work, don his formal hakama, and go there to pay his respects.

The shrine grounds were still quiet in those days. The cherry trees had only just been planted and were still small. The bronze statue of Ōmura stood all alone, except for the huge ungainly iron torii that towered overhead and looked completely out of place. I used to pass through the grounds morning and evening. Now I think back I can remember it all in great detail. Every day I'd walk along the stones at the foot of the wall to the left of the main building, sometimes with my younger brother, sometimes alone.

---

[185] The work referred to was 'Rakukason' (The Village of Falling Flowers — the reading 'Ochibana Mura' seems more natural, but 'Rakukason' is correct), which appeared in the Kokumin Shinbun from March 27th-June 19th 1892. It was, as a matter of interest, the first work for which Katai used the name 'Katai' (he had previously used a variety of names, but mostly the name 'Kotō Ken').

[186] The park intended here is not Kitanomaru Park but the grounds of the Yasukuni Jinja.

[187] See Note 43.

I always seemed to hear a voice within me: "You'll soon become famous! You HAVE to become famous!" As I walked along the stone steps I always thought about heroes and greatness. The spirit of my father, who had given his life for his country, seemed so close to me at that point.

I felt that the grounds were even more beautiful with the green of the new spring growth than at the time of the blossoms. I loved the way the new growth rustled in the dappled shadows, and how it looked in the wet, and I often used to stand there under my umbrella at the edge of the ornamental pond.

You can still see the same sort of scene there nowadays — young mothers with children on their backs, buying wheat-bread to throw into the pond so that all the goldfish and carp would come and nibble at it. "Look, there they are!" they say to their children, who look on in fascination.

The show-tents set up for the spring and autumn services also hold memories for me. "We're going to the Shōkon Shrine so can we have some money?" Nowadays it's my two boys who go there, but I was just the same when I was their age.

After I got a little older I used to like going out by myself at night to walk round the various illuminated stalls set up on the roadside, though these weren't proper shows as such. There were fortune-tellers, and people with acetylene lamps, and people who mended broken china by fusing the pieces under heat. They always had people gathered round their stalls, and I used to think that the very way in which they spoke was a type of art in itself. There'd also be someone singing sentimental love-songs, and someone — a student, perhaps — performing sword dances. I wonder what's become of such people nowadays? Where are they now? Such thoughts always make me ponder the endless flow of human life.

I remember the time the statue of Ōmura was erected, and the time when a fence was put round it. I remember the pair of stone lions being put there, after being seized at Hai-ch'eng in the war with China. I remember Yoshida Banka's large stone column being put up, inscribed with the name 'Yasukuni Shrine'.[188] I used to wander through the grounds towards the shrine, once an innocent youth, and once a promising young man full of ambition, and once a young man with a head full of beautiful visions and sentimental thoughts of love.

"When you go viewing the blossoms you should also note how the girls vary from place to place too. You can still view pretty girls at Ueno, but as you move from Asakusa to Mukōjima the quality drops right off, and

---

[188] The inscribed column was erected in September 1893. (See also Notes 72 and 73.)

they get really coarse. On the other hand there's Kudan. If your luck's in at Kudan you can view extremely beautiful, elegant, high-class girls. They're a very different type. And, it's nice and quiet there, without too much of a crowd. When it comes to quietly viewing blossoming beauty, you can't beat it." In the days when this sort of thing was said, I was growing up along with the cherry trees.

There were at least three or four girls that I used to dream about, as I sat on a bench in the park in Kudan. For the first year or so I dreamed about a tall, slim girl who was very good at the koto; next I dreamed about a cheerful, fair-complexioned girl from downtown, with her hair done in the 'gingko-leaf' style; then, from about the age of twenty, it was a bright-eyed, plump-cheeked girl with her thick hair swept back into a bun..... I also dreamed about my wife there, when she was a young woman.

However, my memories of the place relate only to that period. After starting out in life I rarely went there. The last time I remember going was when I was around twenty-six or seven, when I went there with Shimazaki.[189] We'd left together from his temporary lodgings in Daikonbatake, and I'd suggested we go for a walk while we talked.[190] We ended up there after walking right through the town talking about love and life and art. It was late spring, and there were beautiful late-blooming double-daffodils amongst all the fresh green. We could hear the frogs singing in the pond.

"Shall we have a rest, and something to drink?" Shimazaki suggested.

I wasn't in the habit of visiting tea-shops very often and was rather hesitant, but since Shimazaki had suggested it we did go to the teashop there and sat on a blanket-covered bench drinking tea and talking quietly. "Love's finished for the likes of me," said Shimazaki in a quiet, dejected tone.[191] "Spring's over!"

We left after about an hour. Shimazaki took ten sen from his purse and quietly left it on the blanket.

We still had things to talk about, so we went from there to the embankment in Banchō, then past Ichigaya Mitsuke onto the embankment of the

---

[189] Shimazaki Tōson (1872-1943), poet, novelist. Katai and Tōson first met in January 1896 (see the later section 'Our Group').

[190] Daikonbatake was a nickname for Yushimashinhanachō (present-day Yushima 2 Chōme in Bunkyō-ku). Tōson lived there from 1895 till August 1896. Katai first visited him there on April 17th 1896, with Ōta Gyokumei. The visit described here took place around April 27th.

[191] Tōson had a number of unhappy romances in his life, achieving considerable notoriety as a result. This particular comment may refer to his hapless involvement with Satō Sukeko, a pupil of his at the Meiji Jogakkō (Meiji Girls' School, where he first taught in 1892). The affair resulted in his temporary relinquishing of his appointment there.

moat near Yotsuya. We sat there looking out over the officers' college, the afternoon sun on our faces, talking about 'The Rendezvous', and Chikamatsu, and so on.[192]

Out in the Western Suburbs

The atmosphere in Ushigome, around Ichigaya, suited me to a T. We lived first in Nandomachi, then moved to Kōrachō, and then to Kikuichō and Haramachi.[193]

Even today, whenever I go out that way, the so-called 'suburban atmosphere' makes me feel very nostalgic. Young wives with their hair swept back in a bun, carrying children, and young men setting off for the office day after day, models of diligence — it's so very suburban.

Everywhere you sense the same sort of atmosphere — people starting out in life, new households with bright young wives to compensate for the numerous setbacks, lives full of ambition and expectation. This is all borne out by the shops selling cheap furniture, catering for the new households, and the shops selling cuts of beef, and the cheap Western-style restaurants. Such is the obvious character of Ushigome.

I used to wander all over the area. I'd be wearing a dirty old hakama and worn-down geta, and looking as if I had some nervous disorder, with my long hair parted in a peculiar way. Sometimes I'd wander around with my elder brother, and sometimes I'd go shopping with my mother. Sometimes, unknown to others, I'd wander about outside some girl's house, tormented by a secret love. Sometimes I'd buy baked potatoes. Sometimes I'd be walking around with a smug look on my face, dreaming of future greatness. Now I think back on it, I don't think there was a single street or corner where I couldn't be spotted at one time or another.

The first thing that struck me about Ushigome — I think it would strike anyone — was the Bishamon festivals.[194] They're still lively affairs, I understand, but I'm sure they can't be as lively as they were in those days. There weren't any trains then, which meant that people living in

---

[192] 'The Rendezvous' was first translated by Futabatei Shimei as 'Aibiki' in July-August 1888 (see Note 89). A revised translation by him was included in his work 'Katakoi' (Unanswered Love, a collection of translations of three of Turgenev's stories), which was published in October 1896 by Shunyōdō. It is possible that their talk about it may have been triggered by advance publicity of the revised translation.

[193] It should be appreciated that this list is far from complete and is in fact misleading. The three years spent in Tomihisachō, for example, are not mentioned, and contrary to the implication the Tayamas did not move directly from Kōrachō to Kikuichō but spent several intervening years in Naitōmachi.

[194] These festivals were held at the Bishamon(ten) Temple in Kagurazaka. The temple, which belongs to the Nichiren sect, is better known nowadays as the Zenkokuji. Bishamon(ten), or Vaisravans, is the god of treasure.

the suburbs invariably ended up walking along the main Kagarazuka road to get to the festivals.

Personally I didn't like the crowds so I didn't go myself all that often, but my brothers always did, without fail, every festival day. When we talk over old times my younger brother still laughs about how he'd always pester Mother for a sen or two every time a festival day came around, and how it was such a battle to actually get any money out of her. My elder brother was very fond of garden plants, and although he couldn't really afford it on his salary he always used to bring back some plants from the stalls there — azaleas, roses, fragrant olives, aronias, morning glories and so on depending on the season — and plant them out in the garden or on the verandah. In fact the large fragrant olive I have in my garden now is one of the plants he brought back one festival day.

The Bishamon Temple facing the Kagurazaka road is still as it was in those days, no different from the time they had monster snake shows there. The festival days continue to be busy, with crowds of young couples and students and workers, and there are still plant-stalls and floats as in the past.

The reason I'm so fond of that suburban atmosphere is that all those scenes are linked with my dreams. Those dreams of mine, my work, my early life, all seem in fact completely enmeshed with that atmosphere, with the fences and streets and gardens and shadows and sunshine.

"Roku, would you go and get some sweet-potatoes?"

I can still clearly remember my mother's voice, along with the afternoon sun that used to come flooding into the little six- and eight-mat roomed house.[195] "Baked potatoes again?" I'd say as I set off carrying a bag. I always went to a baked-potato shop on the Yamabushichō road, which is still there today. The potatoes there had sesame on them and were really nice, and very popular amongst the locals.

The old couple who ran the shop worked hard and saved a lot of money, so it was said. I also remember a rather plain girl who used to work there too.

Fish shops, noodle shops, saké shops — there's nothing that doesn't hold memories for me. People like my mother, or young women like my wife, would be there in the fish shops having their purchases cut up for them — flatfish, or bream, or spiky red gurnard, or mackerel, or squid, or shrimps.[196]

---

[195] This is presumably a reference to their house in Kōrachō, where they lived from December 1889 to September 1893. Yamabushichō referred to immediately below is very close to Kōrachō.

[196] The mention of his wife is rather misleading, as he did not in fact marry Risa till September 1899.

When we were living in Nandomachi I often used to pass through Nakachō.[197] There were three roads, going through Kitamachi, Minamichō, and Nakachō, but it was Nakachō that I remember best. The houses there were larger, and the gardens prettier. And in winter there was also a beautiful view of snow-capped Mount Fuji.

There were lots of attractive girls living in Nakachō. There was in particular the house of I-, who's now a major-general.[198] It was an elegant two-storey house, from which the exquisite notes of the koto cascaded like a string of perfect pearls spilling from the delicate white hands of his daughters. The truly fortunate might even catch a glimpse of these girls as they left the house.

I was so jealous of the young military men who could pay suit to such girls. By contrast, how wretched a poor literary novice like me must have seemed. "Someone who wastes his time writing novels just wouldn't stand a chance." Even people around me made such disparaging remarks to me.

The joy of playing cards on a cold New Year's night, sitting next to beautiful girls in a crowded room, watching the captivating sight of their delicate white hands peeling rich yellow mikan, getting bolder as the night draws on and saying the most outrageous things, and going home the next morning along crisp frosty lanes, and sleeping through the afternoon, with unwholesome visions of girls floating into your dreams.....

Our house in Nandomachi was just at the end of Nakachō. The landlord's daughter was a constant part of my dreams for a very long time, right until I met my wife.[199] The landlord, who was an official at the Treasury, was very fond of growing chrysanthemums, and he callled his daughter Kikuko — 'Chrysanthemum'. I wrote poems in my 'Versebook' like:

> "What memories they hold,
> The chrysanthemums
> Out there in my garden,
> Of that dear little hedge
> In old Ushigome."

and:

> "Even those chrysanthemums,
> In that dear girl's
> Sweet hedge,
> Fade and wither
> In the frost."

---

[197] That is, January-December 1889.
[198] I- is unclear.
[199] See Note 71 (and 196).

Later on she went to koto lessons in Banchō, and I often used to follow her. She'd go through Nandomachi to Jōrurizaka, then to the moat, then Ichigaya Mitsuke, then to her koto teacher's house in Sanbanchō. I'd follow her there, and then, while I waited for her to come out again, I'd read poetry in the cool shade of the trees up on the embankment at Ichigaya Mitsuke — which aren't there nowadays, by the way. I'd set off again as soon as I caught sight of her light blue parasol. What with her light brown satin obi, and her soft white arms next to it, you can imagine my feelings in those days of youthful passion. I'd like to meet her again. Indeed, for all I know I may well already have met her again, somewhere, without realising it. We'll both have changed so much that we wouldn't know each other unless we exchanged names. Such is this strange thing called life.

One of the works I wrote was called 'Young Poet'.[200] It wasn't my first work, and it was even quite well received in literary circles. The heroine of the work was Kikuko. Bizan read it and sent me a letter — the first I ever received from him — and a haiku:

> "A sweet little lily,
> In untrodden ground,
> At the base of a rock."

But of course I don't only remember things like that. I also remember walking round and about with my mother, to get my strength back after my illness. Yakimochizaka was just a narrow street in those days, with untidy rows of houses. Halfway up the slope there was a famous eel shop.

When I was getting over my illness I also used to go walking along the neighbouring Kōjizaka, supported by my mother. I remember falling down pathetically while trying to cross a little ditch. My mother was still young in those days.[201]

Beyond Yanagichō there were bamboo groves where the evening sun played softly. And beyond that, going towards Waseda, there were plum-trees and fields, and a lonely area where former shōgunal vassals lived out their ruined lives. Those suburbs were so lonely. You could hear foxes barking in the Waseda area, especially on snowy nights. I wrote a poem about it:

---

[200] 'Shōshijin', in the July 1893 issue of 'Kozakuraodoshi' (Cherry Braid, November 1892-July 1893).

[201] 'In those days' is presumably 1891, as he was recovering from his illness. His mother Tetsu was born in 1839 (died 1899), so by that time she was over fifty years old and hardly 'young'. His use of the term is presumably a reference to her sprightliness.

"Wasedamachi —
A part of the capital,
Yet on snowy nights,
You can often hear
The foxes bark."

The school at Waseda was still small, basically just two or three lonely-looking buildings standing in the middle of the fields.[202] There were some country cottages nearby, but nothing at all to suggest that the area would become as busy as it is today. There were only a few people walking about, and they were mostly dressed Japanese-style. O was one of them, wearing his shabby straw sandals.

You can't find them nowadays even in the outermost suburbs, and they were obviously a hangover from the old Edo days, but there used to be lots of rest-houses where you could buy tea and dumplings and sushi. People visiting temples always used to rest there. In the old days, when there were no trains or even rickshaws servicing the suburbs, people generally had to walk.[203] How the trains have wrecked the charm of the suburbs!

The Tsurumakichō part of Waseda was covered with ginger-fields, and Waseda Ginger was well-known in the vegetable markets. I often walked along the little lane through those fields, into the woods at the far end. Sometimes an old lady would come round, selling freshly pickled ginger from a basket.

In those days there were still woods around where you could go and think things over in peace and quiet. There were pine forests where red oleaster berries ripened without anyone knowing, and where mushrooms grew. In winter a cold wind would whistle through the trees. In the evening the trains on the one and only suburban line would echo far across the fields.

It was some four or five years later, when I was in my mid-twenties, that we went to live in Kikuichō.[204] The place had formerly been a lord's villa, and the garden must have been truly magnificent, with a splendid pond. However, nature had started to reclaim it, and the pond had become a patch of wet ground, and the rock-garden a mere hillock. The grounds were extensive, and the house we rented stood alone and

---

[202] The forerunner to Waseda University, the Tōkyō Senmon Gakkō (Tōkyō Specialist School), was founded in 1882. The name was changed to Waseda Daigaku in 1902. Katai's friend Ōta Gyokumei attended there.

[203] Contrary to popular belief rickshaws were not developed until 1869, and for many years after were largely confined to main centres.

[204] The move to Kikuichō was on January 27th 1896.

isolated. The quiet solitude appealed to me, so we ended up moving there from Yotsuya despite the objections of my mother and elder brother. The garden evoked endless daydreams in me.

The view from the little hillock beyond the wet ground was superb. On the far side you could see rows of alders, and hear carts passing along distant roads, echoing softly through the autumn air.[205]

I frequently went up to the top of the hill, sometimes alone, sometimes with friends. I don't think I'll ever again find such a look-out point. You could see things so clearly, such as the clouds drifting over the broad horizon, the distant range of green hills in Mejirodai, and the Edogawa [River] flowing below like a narrow ribbon.[206] The quiet autumn evenings were particularly pleasant. There was also the gentle rustling of the pampas grass that covered the hill.

I always took my friends there when they came visiting, as though it were something which belonged to me.

"What do you think?"

"It's fabulous! I didn't know there was a view like this around here," my friend would say, and then we'd sit there talking about poetry and novels. Then when they took their leave I'd always see them off from the top of the hill.

From up there I could see our house all in one glance, with its garden and well-bucket and my little study. And from our verandah you could see the afternoon sun playing on the face of anyone standing up there. Whenever I was out on a moonlit night I always tried, if possible, to return home via the alder wood and the hill.

When I got married my poetry teacher wrote a poem for me:[207]

"You and your wife
Will gaze fondly upon
The snow falling softly
On that gentle,
Welcoming hill."

How fond indeed I am of that gentle, welcoming hill.

My memories of people from the Meiji literary world are also connected with that hill. Doppo climbed it with me.[208] So did Bizan, and

[205] Though it is a rather academic point, I feel it is worth noting that this sentence, which occurs time and time again in Katai's literature, is almost a literal borrowing of a sentence in one of Futabatei's translations of Turgenev. He has said elsewhere that he was particularly impressed by the sentence.

[206] Mejirodai is in Hachiōji City.

[207] Katai's poetry teacher was Matsuura Tatsuo (1844-1909). See the following chapter for greater detail.

[208] Kunikida Doppo (1871-1908, real name Tetsuo), poet and novelist.

Chūgai, and Kōyō, and all experienced the view.[209] And it was on that hill that I discussed Turgenev's 'Rudin' with Fūyō, and that I often read writers like Zola and Daudet.[210]

There were a lot of Meiji writers living in suburban Ushigome. There was Dr. Tsubouchi living in Ōkubo, Kōyō Sanjin in Yokoderachō, Emi Suiin in Kitamachi, while Kawakami Bizan too moved from Tomisaka in Koishikawa to Kitayamabushichō in Ushigome.[211] In addition, Gotō Chūgai lived only a short distance from me in Bentenchō. So it was that the literary atmosphere in suburban Ushigome was a mixture of the Waseda group and the Genyūsha.

'Waseda Bungaku' and Ōgai Gyoshi's 'Shigaramizōshi' were mutually opposed.[212] The former favoured English literature, and Shakespeare in particular, while the latter favoured German literature, and the modernists. The healthy opposition between them was a rare sight in the literary world, but an even stranger sight was that of the Genyūsha, with its emphasis on creative writing, being positioned somewhere between the two.[213] There was often a spirit of alliance between the Waseda group and the Genyūsha, but Ōgai was opposed to this and always maintained an uncompromising position of independence. His unflagging attempt to make a clean sweep of the literary world had a great effect on young literature students of the day. From that time on, Ōgai disliked having protégés.

But in those days, when style was made so much of, to establish oneself as a creative writer there was little one could do but turn to the Genyūsha, who specialised in that sort of writing. Tsubouchi is said to have remarked to Kōyō, "You've got so many writers. I wish I had, but I haven't. It's because they can't polish their style enough at school." You can tell the difference between the groups in those days from this comment alone.

Anyway, Kōyō's works in the Y Newspaper were popular to an extent hard to conceive of nowadays. People could hardly wait to read him each morning, and were so disappointed when he took a day off. His works

---

209 Gotō Chūgai (1866-1938), novelist and critic.

210 'Rudin' was translated by Futabatei, as 'Ukikusa' (Floating Grass), and appeared April-October 1897 in 'Taiyō' (Sun, January 1895-February 1928, Hakubunkan).

211 Tomisaka is present-day Koishikawa 1-2 Chōme.

212 The history of the magazine 'Waseda Bungaku' (Waseda Literature) is quite complex, and it went through at least six distinct phases. Its first issue appeared in October 1891, its last in August 1959.

213 There is a conceptual overlap between 'creative writing' and 'fiction', both being rendered in Meiji Japanese by the same term 'sōsaku'.

included 'Purple', 'Red and White Poison Buns', and later on 'Much Feeling, Much Grief' and 'Golden Demon'.[214]

Amongst the early graduates of the literature department at Waseda there was Kaneko Chikusui in the first group, followed by Shimamura Hōgetsu and Gotō Chūgai in the second.[215] Whereas Kaneko and Shimamura remained in the Waseda camp, Gotō's thesis, by contrast, was on Kōyō, and he gradually moved towards the Genyūsha.[216] For that reason a lot of bright young Genyūsha writers were launched through 'Shincho Gekkan', for which he was one of the chief writers.[217]

In those days Shimamura wrote a good deal of fiction, including many excellent works. He generally tended to write in a concise Saikaku style rather than slavishly following a Western one. Works like his 'Waves of Marriage' were very well received.[218]

Uchida Fuchian also lived in Ushigome a lot of the time.[219] He came and went amongst the Sendagi group, and the Waseda group, and the Genyūsha, but he held his own particular views and tended to be kept at a respectful distance by all the groups. His 'How to Become a Man of Letters' was disliked by the Genyūsha in particular.[220]

In any event, the Ushigome suburbs hold unforgettable memories for me. Every road, every house, every blade of grass......

The Sunflower Hedge

My poetry teacher was Matsuura Tatsuo.[221] He was very firmly in the line of the Keien School, and was a pupil of Kagawa Kagetsune.[222] He

---

[214] 'Red and White Poison Buns' ('Kōhaku Dokumanjū) appeared in the Yomiuri between October-December 1891, and 'Golden Demon' ('Konjiki Yasha') periodically between January 1897-May 1902, also in the Yomiuri.

[215] The literature department at Waseda was established in 1890, with the first graduates appearing therefore in 1893.

Kaneko Chikusui (1870-1937), critic; Shimamura Hōgetsu (1871-1918), critic and novelist.

[216] Gotō Chūgai's thesis was actually entitled 'Bimyō, Kōyō, Rohan' (1894).

[217] 'New Publications Monthly', April 1897-May 1898. Actually, Shimamura Hōgetsu was a co-founder! Shimamura's graduation thesis (1894) was entitled 'On the Nature of Aesthetic Awareness' ('Shinbiteki Ishiki no Seishitsu o Ronzu').

[218] 'Meotonami', September 1897, 'Shincho Gekkan'.

[219] Fuchian was a pseudonym of Uchida Roan (see Note 151).

[220] 'Bungakusha to Naru Hō' (April 1894) was a sarcastic work making fun of the Genyūsha in particular. According to Roan, the necessary qualifications for a writer included being good-looking, lazy, dissipated, bigoted, argumentative, quasi-illiterate etc etc.

[221] Also known as Hagitsubo, 1844-1909. He was a friend of Ishii Kakyū and Okanoya Shigezane (see Notes 8 and 39).

[222] The Keien-ha was founded by Kagawa Kageki (1768-1843, also known as Kageshige). The school favoured simplicity and blunt honesty in depiction, rather than

didn't actually study under Kageki himself, but was a close associate of one of Kageki's best pupils in later years, Matsunami Yūzan (Sukeyuki).[223]

My teacher scorned fame, so apart from specialist poets there are few people today who know his name. However, I myself was greatly influenced both by his personality and his views on poetry.

In fact, I'd go so far as to say that much of the 'realistic tendency' in my work is derived from his views on poetry.[224] It was through poetry that I became so deeply involved in art.

In those days, Matsuura Sensei lived in Tamachi in Ushigome.[225] His house had a roofed gate, a storehouse with faded white walls, and a hedge crowned with sunflowers, which he had planted himself and which bloomed dazzling white in summer. I often went there with Yanagita Kunio, and Miyazaki Koshoshi and his late wife — who wrote that marvellous verse "Though I wake/From fitful dreams/The morning moon of autumn/Lingers still/At my window" — and S, and O.[226]

At that time Matsuura Sensei was still in his mid-forties, and spent every day working on historical research at the university, so it must have been a terrible nuisance for him to have young people like us constantly descending on him.[227] But he didn't show it in the least, and patiently carried on teaching.

"Poetry is not concerned with academically expounding, but with rhythmically expressing." Such is the basic tenet of the Keien School, and this is what Matsuura Sensei taught us so well, sometimes by reference to actual poetry, sometimes by argument.

Through his roofed gate was a dark, gloomy porch, with a step in it. Whenever we visited his home a girl — a relative of his — would come out here and greet us politely, to inform us whether he was in or not.

He received us in a large, ten-mat room.

---

concern with ideology and morality, and felt that the universal truths of nature were manifest in simple feeling. Kagetsune (1824-1865) was the son of Kageki, and was based in Kyōto.

[223] Sukeyuki is the commoner of these two names. He lived 1830-1906. To say he was one of Kageki's best pupils is probably something of an exaggeration, as he was clearly only thirteen at the same time of Kageki's death. He was also a pupil of Kagetsune in later years.

[224] 'Realistic tendency' is given in English by Katai.

[225] That is, Ichigayatamachi.

[226] Miyazaki Koshoshi (1864-1922), poet, novelist, and critic, married Hattori Mutsuko in May 1890. She died of illness on February 23rd 1902. (Koshoshi married again in July that year, to Toyojima Tatsu.)

S and O are Sakurai and Ōta (Gyokumei).

[227] He was working at the Department of Historical Documents (with Katai's brother Miyato) which was incorporated into the Imperial University (Teikoku Daigaku, now Tōkyō Daigaku) in December 1888.

We were very impudent and, without realising the depth of his knowledge and experience, would belabour him with naive and presumptuous views on art. Nevertheless he just patiently carried on teaching us what was necessary.

The collection of Matsuura Sensei's poetry was called 'An Old Lespedeza Branch'.[228] His poetry was a little stiff and classical and was more in the vein of Kageki and Tsurayuki than Naoyoshi.[229] As a result he tended to lack directness and spontaneity, which was a pity.

Unlike Naoyoshi he did not give free rein to his poetic sentiment but stuck steadily to the same approach in his search for the realm of mystery. In later years he penetrated deeply into that realm of other-worldliness known as 'yūgen'.[230]

"Waka and haiku are the same from the point of view of art. The first step is the content. The second is the expression. The third is nature — harmony with nature." In Matsuura Sensei's teaching I could clearly see the same basic tenets as in Arno Holz's 'thorough naturalism'.[231]

I can still clearly picture the inner-garden next to his room, planted with the seven flowers of autumn.[232] There was a verandah around it, and on the far side was an annex where his old mother lived. Of all the people I've known, I don't think there's anyone who has shown such filial piety towards their mother as did Matsuura Sensei.

"It's because we get on so well together by nature. Filial piety doesn't stem from conscious volition. It isn't something you can do consciously. I suppose you could call it part of that realm of mystery — that's to say, there's a profound bond between mother and son." His comment seems to me to have penetrated to the very heart of the matter.

When he died I went to his wake with Yanagita. It was many years later, when naturalism reigned supreme and when the dominant mood

---

[228] 'Hagi no Furueda', July 1905, private publication. He also had an earlier collection, 'Hagi no Shitaba' (Lower-leaves of Lespedeza, February 1894).

[229] Ki no Tsurayuki (872-945), a classical poet admired by Kageki; Kumagai Naoyoshi (1782-1862), a former pupil of Kageki's but noted for a relatively fresh and modern approach to poetry.

[230] 'Yūgen' is a term that is virtually impossible to translate. It includes such concepts as quietness, subtleness, beauty, elegance, and 'other-worldliness', and has been figuratively expressed as 'snow in a silver bowl'.

[231] 'Tetteishizenshugi' is a form of naturalism, developed in Germany, whereby the author seeks to reduce his subjectivity to a passive state, to become a medium that is then 'impressed' by the objects on which he focuses in order to reproduce them later with photographic and phonographic accuracy and without interposing his egoistic interpretation of those objects. Katai was greatly influenced by this form of naturalism, certainly more so than by Zola's analytical approach, and this has enormous bearing on the correct appreciation of the much maligned Japanese naturalism.

[232] Lespedeza, pampas-grass (eulalia), arrowroot, wild pink (dianthus), patrinia, eupatorium, morning glory.

was one of destroying falsehood and formalism. To people like me — 'free-thinkers' who desired freedom — things like wakes were old-fashioned and undesirable examples of form for form's sake.[233] Nevertheless I donned my hakama and attended Matsuura Sensei's wake, sitting there with my hands on my knees and not once dozing off. It was autumn, and the insects sang all night long.

From Matsuura Sensei I learned the wonder of other-worldliness and mysticism, the significance of experience, and the value of human character. I don't think he ever read any of my novels. Even if he had, he probably wouldn't have appreciated eighty or ninety percent of them. And yet, when I think about it, I can't help feeling that some seventy or eighty percent of my work has benefited from his personality and his views on poetry.

I was considerably influenced by writers senior to me such as Kōyō and Ōgai. I was also greatly influenced by the works of foreign writers such as Turgenev, Daudet, Zola, Maupassant, Flaubert, and Tolstoi. But influence from people in the flesh is always greater than from the written word. I am honoured to think that I am one of those fortunate enough to have received a part of Matsuura Sensei's spirit.

How dear to me is the memory of that sunflower hedge, of that garden, of those autumn flowers!

The Literary World in Those Days

The literary world in those days could more or less be divided into six groups, namely the Genyūsha, Waseda, Sendagi, Kokumin Bungaku, Negishi, and Jogaku Zasshi groups.[234] The Genyūsha and Waseda groups were the strongest, but the undercurrents tended to drift towards the Sendagi and Kokumin Bungaku groups.

The Negishi group included Rohan, Kōson, and Shiken.[235] They were linked partly to the Waseda group through Tsubouchi Shōyō, and partly to Ōgai's Sendagi group through Rohan, and, because they were essentially a social group concerned with pleasure rather than study, they tended to lack solidarity. Nevertheless the group had a rather interesting air about it. It included something of the old gesaku writer's attitude, and

---

[233] 'Free-thinker' is given in English by Katai.

[234] The Negishi group here should not be confused with the later (post-1898) similarly called group (Negishi-ha), which was more accurately named Negishi Tanka-Kai (Negishi Tanka Association) and which included poets such as Masaoka Shiki (1867-1902).

The 'Jogaku Zasshi' (Magazine for Ladies' Enlightenment) ran from July 1885-February 1904.

[235] Morita Shiken (1861-1897), translator and journalist.

the members seemed very interested in the theatre and in life at a rather vulgar level. They also liked travelling. When I remember how Kōson and Rohan argued and split up during a trip to Kiso it makes me realise that they too must have been young in those days.[236] Then they went on a trip to Myōgi with Takahashi Taika and others, and produced a joint travelogue to cover their expenses.[237] Miyazaki Sanmai was also connected with their group.[238]

However, a lot of young literature students disliked the attitude of the Negishi group. Indeed, I too wondered why Rohan had joined a group like that.

Even the cantankerous Saitō Ryokū, who might have been expected to join the group, had too much pride to do so. Nevertheless he got on well with Rohan, and seemed to respect him. It was perhaps in connection with this — or perhaps it was some other reason — that in later years he associated himself with Ōgai Gyoshi.[239]

When Ōgai put out 'Dancing Girl' people made criticisms to the effect that it was horribly foreign and seemed more like a translation, but his strength and scholarship easily quelled at once any such criticism from the small fry. Everyone bowed before the sincerity of his arguments. Even Dr. Tsubouchi was put on the defensive, so naturally the haughty Kōyō Sanjin had also to acknowledge him. Nevertheless, it seemed that Kōyō regarded Ōgai as a major enemy, and made use of the fact that his own pupil Sazanami Sanjin had studied German literature by attacking Ōgai's comments should even the least little chink appear in them.[240] But Sazanami's knowledge of things German was no match at all for Ōgai, and it was invariably Sazanami who ended up being torn to shreds.

Ōgai particularly hated the flippant, dandyish attitude of the Genyūsha, and the way in which they tried to avoid issues with some silly comment or other whenever they were in the firing-line, and he attacked them all the more for it. But for all that he did acknowledge Kōyō's talent and skill with the pen, and remarked, "I read 'that magazine' because of 'that one patch of purple'." 'That one patch of purple' was Kōyō, and 'that magazine' was 'Edo Murasaki', one of the publishing vehicles of the Genyūsha.[241] On looking through 'Shigaramizōshi' the most obvious

[236] It should be noted that there was in fact twelve years' difference in their ages (born 1855 and 1867 respectively), and that Kōson was hardly young in terms of years (though Katai is presumably implying immaturity). Kōson and Rohan met around 1890.

[237] Takahashi Taika (1863-?), novelist, writer of children's literature.

[238] Miyazaki Sanmai (1859-1919), novelist.

[239] In fact, Ōgai, Ryokū, and Rohan regularly wrote joint criticims from 1896 on in the magazine which succeeded 'Shigaramizōshi', 'Mesamashigusa' (Eye-opener, January 1896-February 1902).

[240] Sazanami Sanjin was a pseudonym of Iwaya Sazanami.

[241] 'Edo Murasaki' (Edo Purple), June-December 1890, twelve issues only.

hostility seems to have been the war of words between Ōgai and Shibanosono.[242]

Ōgai waged war on all fronts, and a single blow in any one quarter was often enough to destroy his various enemies. His arguments ranged with undiminished authority from painting and drama to sculpture and even elocution. When you read his works today they don't seem particularly astonishing, but in those days of retarded ideology and puerile criticism he seemed like a snarling wolf among a pack of sheep. So it was that serious students of literature all turned respectfully to 'Shigaramizōshi'.

Indeed, it wasn't just young literary aspirants, but established writers as well who liked to read it. Translations of his like 'Fossil Wood' and 'Impromptu Poet' stimulated enormous change in the literary world.[243]

His volume 'Collection of Bubbles' is, in my opinion, a particularly good commemorative anthology of those days.[244] Of course, it's not his own work but a collection of translations. Nevertheless, what a breath of fresh air those translations instilled in a literary world dominated by Kōyō and the Genyūsha!

Translations of foreign literature, which had started with Futabatei's 'Rendezvous', continued in force with Ōgai's 'Evil Karma', 'Waves of the Floating World', and 'Fossil Wood'.[245] Through them we learned that there were new paths to follow other than Kōson and Rohan and Kōyō.

On the other hand there was Dr. Tsubouchi at Waseda, but his platform was English literature, especially Shakespeare, and to young

---

[242] Yamada Shibanosono (also read Shibanoen) (1860-?), novelist and admirer of Kōyō's literature.

[243] Respectively 'Umoregi' (not to be confused with Ichiyō's work of the same title), a translation of 'The Story of a Genius' ('Die Geschichte eines Genies') by the Czechoslovakian-born authoress Ossip Schubin, in 'Shigaramizōshi' from April 1890-April 1892; and 'Sokkyō Shijin', a translation from the German version of Hans Christian Anderson's 'Improvisatoren', in 'Shigaramizōshi' and its successor 'Mesamashigusa' from 1892-1901.

[244] 'Minawashū', July 1892, Shunyōdō. Despite Katai's comment below it does contain some original works by Ōgai, three to be exact (and sixteen translations including the two works above).

[245] Futabatei's 'Aibiki' was generally accepted as the first *accurate* translation, but translation of fiction had been going on since that of Bulwer-Lytton's 'Ernest Maltravers' in 1878 (by Oda [Niwa] Junichirō [1851-1919], as 'Karyū Shunwa' [A Spring Tale of Flowers and Willows]), while non-fiction had been translated as early as 1871 (Samuel Smiles' 'Self-Help', translated as 'Saikoku Risshihen' [Biographies of Self-Made Men of Western Countries] by Nakamura Masanao [see Note 41]).

'Evil Karma' ('Akuinnen'), a translation of Kleist's 'Engagement in St. Domingo' ('Verlobung in St. Domingo'), appeared in 'Kokumin no Tomo' April-July 1890; 'Waves of the Floating World' ('Ukiyo no Nami'), a translation of Adolf Stern's 'Flood of Life' ('Flut des Lebens'), appeared in 'Kokumin no Tomo' August-October 1890. Both works were also included in 'Collection of Bubbles'.

literature students attracted to the ideology of recent continental literature it seemed very dull and insipid and inarticulate. It was totally impossible to look for perceptive modern awareness in recent English literature.

Apart from these two trends represented by Ōgai and Shōyō there was another group concerned with foreign ideology, a group that had gone its own way from the start. It was the 'Kokumin Bungaku' group, formed around 'Kokumin no Tomo' and the Kokumin Newspaper. If anything it tended towards England and Christianity, but because its concern was essentially with ideology it seemed somehow more modern than Waseda's English literature. You could tell the progressive nature of the group by the fact that 'Rendezvous' and 'Evil Karma' were published in 'Kokumin no Tomo'.

The Kokumin Bungaku group was of course led at first by Tokutomi Sohō, but as he gradually moved towards politics his younger brother Roka took over, followed by Miyazaki Koshoshi, Yamaji Aizan, Saganoya, and then Kunikida Doppo.[246]

It was certain Christian members from this group who founded 'Jogaku Zasshi'. Iwamoto Zenji was the main figure.[247] But, not satisfied with that Christian faction, the 'Bungakukai' group evolved as a separate entity.[248] They favoured purely English literature, in the tradition of such figures as Shakespeare, Keats, Byron, and Shelley.[249] Their ranks included Tenchi, Tokuboku, Shūkotsu, Tōkoku, and Tōson.[250]

This group was naturally considerably removed from the Genyūsha, though of course in later years certain of them did ally themselves with Kōyō.[251] It was also far removed from the Kokumin Bungaku group and the Sendagi group, and naturally had nothing to do with the Waseda group either. When Tōson put out his first novel, 'Seed of Verse', in 'Shinshōsetsu', the then champion of the new novelists, Izumi Kyōka,

---

[246] Yamaji Aizan (1864-1917), reporter, popular historian.

[247] Iwamoto Zenji (1863-1942, also read as Yoshiharu), critic and educationist. He founded Meiji Jogakkō, where Tōson taught (see Note 191).

[248] 'Bungakukai' (World of Literature, sometimes read 'Bungakkai'), ran from January 1893-January 1898. Its first four issues were published by the Jogaku Zasshi-sha.

[249] Sic. The fact that Katai treats Shakespeare and the three poets as somehow representing the same type of literature is probably indicative of his cavalier treatment of English literature rather than carelessness of expression.

[250] Hoshino Tenchi (1862-1950), novelist and critic; Hirata Tokuboku (1873-1943), essayist; Togawa Shūkotsu (1870-1939), essayist; Kitamura Tōkoku (1868-1894), poet,critic, and major figure in the romantic movement.

[251] Probably a reference to Togawa Shūkotsu, who later joined the Yomiuri Newspaper with which Kōyō was closely associated, and to a lesser extent Hirata Tokuboku.

made some remark about it like "Is that what he calls a novel?!"[252] It certainly makes you realise just how strong the Genyūsha were.

In any event, such was the disordered state of the literary world in those days. To add to it, style was considered more important than content. Everyone made remarks like "Ah, I see he's finally started to learn to write," or "It's horribly foreign, this style of his." For all this concern with style, there was still no standardisation. There were various types of 'genbun'itchi' and 'gazokusetchū', and then there was the Shiken-style, the Kōson-style, the Saikaku-style, the Chikamatsu-style, and so on and so on.[253] Writers like Kōyō seemed deliberately to change their style with each work. "Well, genbun'itchi's one thing, I suppose, but it's got no flavour to it. It just doesn't give you any sense of satisfaction for your effort," he said.

I also remember that in Chūgai's novels there was a style that was neither genbun'itchi nor gazokusetchū.

The fact that Ichiyō, with all her talent, wrote in such a cramped style is a good illustration of the lack of stylistic standardisation in those days.

You can also gauge the lack of standardisation by looking through Ōgai Gyoshi's translations. There's a considerable stylistic difference between 'Fossil Wood' and 'Evil Karma', for example. Then there is 'Flood', which is a perfect example of genbun'itchi, whereas 'Impromptu Poet' is an example of Ōgai's own particular stiff style.[254]

But, amidst all this 'Sturm und Drang' it's a fact that there was one focal point which promised standardisation. What was it? The answer is the view that everyone seemed to hold, that "There's nothing for it but to refer to Western literature."

I can't help feeling now that Kōyō's 'Much Feeling, Much Grief' and Ōgai's 'Impromptu Poet' were indicative of what was to follow.

And certain of the works of Kosugi Tengai and Oguri Fūyō were heading straight in the direction of the style you see nowadays.[255]

But, for all Ōgai's display of fighting spirit, the domain of creative writing remained under Kōyō's lordship. When it came to creative fiction, Ōgai simply couldn't compete with the Genyūsha. To add to the situation Rohan, who had once ranked alongside Kōyō, virtually aban-

[252] Tōson's 'Utatane' appeared in the November 1896 issue of 'Shinshōsetsu' (The New Novel, January 1889-November 1926).

[253] 'Genbun'itchi' is 'the unification of spoken and written language'. Writers generally acknowledged as helping to develop this include Futabatei (who wrote 'to be' as 'da'), Bimyō ('desu'), and Kōyō ('de aru'). 'Gazokusetchū' meant literally 'a mixture of elegant and common', and was considered somewhat more classical than 'genbun'itchi'. It is represented by much of Ichiyō's literature.

[254] 'Flood' ('Kōzui', October 1889-March 1890, 'Shigaramizōshi'), was a translation of a German version ('Sturmflut') of Bret Harte's 'Highwater Mark'.

[255] Kosugi Tengai (1865-1952), novelist.

doned writing, and rarely put pen to paper to produce a novel.[256] And as for Saitō Ryokū, he was fine when it was a matter of argument, but when it came to writing, all he could produce was stuff like 'Shamisen at the Gate'. Novels like Koshoshi's 'Illusion' could hardly be called good, either.[257]

Kōyō, Bizan, Ryūrō — those were the big names of the day.[258]

But then, after the war with China, new developments suddenly occurred in the literary world. Magazines proliferated — 'Taiyō', 'Bungei Kurabu', and 'Teikoku Bungaku' all appeared that year [of 1895].[259] New writers like Tengai, Fūyō, Chūgai, Kyōka, Shunyō, and Shūsei rose to prominence.

Kōyō said at the time: "These so-called new writers are all people from my camp. They're my young retainers." However, you can read between the lines that Kōyō was starting to feel pressured by these new developments. 'Shigaramizōshi', too, changed to 'Mesamashigusa' as the big names started to front up against the new writers.

In the field of criticism, too, new names like Chogyū and Keigetsu appeared.[260]

The period I'm talking about would be about 1895/6 to 1898/9.

It's interesting to consider 'Mesamashigusa' in the light of all these developments. Not content with Rohan and Ryokū, Ōgai even brought Shiken and Kōyō into his group.[261] The many criticisms they did, under such names as 'Favouritism' and 'Abuse', are extremely interesting phenomena from a literary point of view. The usual targets of these criticisms were writers like Chogyū and Keigetsu. The magazine also put out 'On Ichiyō's Career' and similar features.[262]

The Big Names at the Time

The literary world has seen few joint criticisms like those in 'Mesamashigusa'.

On the one hand they were full of wit and sarcasm and humour, and on the other they revealed incredibly precise and even pedantic research.

---

[256] The period 1889-1892 was commonly known as the 'Kōro Jidai' (The Kōyō-Rohan Age).

[257] 'Maboroshi', June 1892, Shunyōdō.

[258] Hirotsu Ryūrō (1861-1928), novelist.

[259] 'Bungei Kurabu' (Literature Club), January 1895-January 1933, Hakubunkan; 'Teikoku Bungaku' (Imperial Literature), January 1895-January 1920.

[260] Takayama Chogyū (1871-1902), critic famous for his championing of Nietzsche; Ōmachi Keigetsu (1869-1925), poet and critic.

[261] It should be borne in mind that Morita Shiken died in 1897 (November 14th).

[262] Higuchi Ichiyō died November 23rd 1896, aged twenty-four. Ōgai, Rohan, and Ryokū were all admirers of her literature.

Much of the criticism seemed rather like the words of maligned people fighting back in their turn.

The clever witticisms came largely from Ryokū and Rohan, who were no doubt getting things off their chest.

The new writers of the day left a lot to be desired with regard to their knowledge, scholarship, and writing. They were riddled with weak points, and easy prey for anyone.

Keigetsu was ridiculed for misreading the title of Ryokū's 'Deva King's Pestle' — 'Kongōsho' — as 'Kongōkine'.[263] Actually, 'Deva King's Pestle' was a clever work. I don't think anyone nowadays could write such witty stuff.

All the new writers tended to receive abuse, and I in particular had the most dreadful things said about me. But when I look back at it nowadays I can see that not all the criticism was mere abuse just for the sake of it. There were some extremely useful points made, useful to me even today. This was especially true of the comments made by Ryokū, Rohan, and Ōgai.

However, in those days I was young and didn't realise this. I couldn't have been expected to. And so, when I met people I'd say things like, "I can't stand it any longer. They just abuse people!" I hated seeing the latest issue of 'Mesamashigusa' in the shop front. I wanted to read it on the one hand, and didn't want to on the other. But of course I had to read it in the end, and would stand there at the shop reading only the worst bits about myself, go red in the face, and then storm off. Even now I can just picture that poor, miserable, literary novice.

In the same January that the first issue of 'Mesamashigusa' appeared, the New Year supplement of 'Kokumin no Tomo' featured 'Parting Ways' by Higuchi Ichiyō and 'Legend of Biwa' by Izumi Kyōka, the champion of the new writers.[264] The 'Kokumin no Tomo' supplements were considered the 'hallmark' of status as a major writer, rather like the 'Chūō Kōron' is nowadays. I remember being terribly jealous about the good reception of 'Parting Ways'.

At that point in time the 'Bungakukai' writers were loath to write for no fee, and ended up publishing their work in various other magazines. Shūkotsu became a critic for the Y Newspaper. Tokuboku sent his work to 'Teikoku Bungaku'. Shimazaki turned from poetry to prose, and published his first story, 'Seed of Verse', [in 'Shinshōsetsu'].

---

[263] 'Kongōsho' appeared in the literary criticism section of 'Mesamashigusa', from its first issue in January 1896.

[264] Respectively 'Wakaremichi' and 'Biwa Den'.

The Reception-Room of the H Publishing Company

To my knowledge alone the reception-room of the H Company changed on three occasions. At first it was an eight-mat room immediately above the business section. It was then changed to a small six-mat room further inside, where there was a collotype picture depicting numerous lovers' trysts on a moonlit spring night. The next location was an eight-mat room next to the editing department.

"It pains me to say it, but I finally had to go along to that company. I needed the money. There was nothing else I could do."

These were the words of Koshoshi, who in those days was writing a critical column for 'Kokumin no Tomo' under the name of Sanmenrō Shujin [sic], in which he always attacked the weaker works of the Genyūsha.[265]

It certainly wasn't just Koshoshi who was obliged to make such admissions. We all had to. We were all obliged to suffer the anguish of trying to sell our work, and the shame of having to throw ourselves on the mercy of magazine editors.

Fashionable new writers like Kyōka and Fūyō didn't have to worry, but people like me, who got bad reviews, always had to prostrate ourselves before editors whenever we ran out of money. When it came to selling our work we couldn't keep on bothering our friends and seniors forever.

In those days Otowa from the Genyūsha had married into the family that owned the H company, so he had a great deal of influence.[266] He had a new house in Tosakichō, and Kyōka moved in there after leaving Kōyō's house.[267] Otowa made a favourite of him and Ichiyō, the rising stars.

I also visited his house from time to time.

He had had his fair share of bitter experiences and was to that extent a very understanding man, but at the same time he had a free and easy, non-commital, rather denigrating sort of attitude, and straightforward people like me always ended up taking offence. I didn't want to visit him, but I was obliged to, so you can imagine how ashamed I felt.

But for all that I must say that Otowa helped me along in life. It was thanks to him that my 'Inner Reaches of the Nikkō Mountains' appeared

---

[265] Koshoshi's pseudonym was actually 'Hachimenrō', ie. 'eight-sided tower' as opposed to 'three-sided tower'. Katai gives 'Hachimenrō' later in the book. It is remotely possible that Koshoshi did at some early stage have a pseudonym 'Sanmenrō'.

[266] See Note 146. Otowa's position in the literary world is treated in some detail in Katai's novel 'Inaka Kyōshi' (Country Teacher, 1909).

[267] Tosakichō is present-day Koishikawa 3-4 Chōme and Hakusan 2 Chōme. Kyōka lived there from February 1895-May 1896.

in 'Taiyō', and that I was able to establish myself as a passing fair travelogue writer.[268] As far as my novels were concerned he had the same opinion as Kōyō, that they were worthless. He always criticised them as exotic and wishy-washy and naive, and told me that I was hopeless as a novelist and should concentrate instead on travelogues. He'd always buy my travelogues. I'm sure it was true that, from his point of view, my novels really did not amount to anything, and that bothered me not a little.[269]

It was at this time that I wrote 'Flowers of the Field'.[270] It was quite a long novel, getting on for a hundred and seventy pages. When I took it along to H's reception-room Otowa rolled it up and said: "It's just too long. If it was only twenty or thirty pages we might be able to do something with it, but.... Anyway, I'll have a word with the chief editor. It's not up to me alone."

Some six months later they sent me the manuscript back.

I can still clearly picture myself sitting there all alone in that reception-room, waiting for Otowa or some other staff member. All sorts of people used to visit that room, too. I met Saigiku Sanjin there, and Sanmai Dōjin.[271] I also met Rohan, and Ryūrō. At the time, Ryūrō was at the height of his popularity, and often wrote the lead story in 'Bungei Kurabu'. He mostly used to write in some prostitute's room in Yoshiwara, and would send along a messenger to collect his manuscript-fee.

"He's still there, you know, in THAT place...." Otowa would say with a laugh. Even by the standards of the day Ryūrō was known as a prolific writer, who could turn out fifty or sixty pages a night.

[268] 'Nikkōyama no Oku', January 5th-February 5th, 1896.

[269] Despite Katai's negative comments regarding the reception of his novels, Hakubunkan did in fact publish a considerable number of them, especially in its magazine 'Bungei Kurabu'.

[270] 'No no Hana' finally appeared in June 1901, in shortened form and published by Shinseisha. Its preface (dated May 27th) is famous for its advocacy of blunt depiction, and it is often seen as one of the first voices of naturalism in Japan. The work itself, on the other hand, is typical early Katai, sentimental and fanciful, and the contrast between preface and work is commonly seen as having set back Katai's career and the cause of naturalism by several years, despite Katai's rather clumsy statement in his preface that it (the preface) should not be seen as being in any way connected with the work itself. This statement is again commonly regarded as mere 'whitewashing'. However, it is clear from this sentence in 'Tōkyō no Sanjūnen' that Katai's statement was sincere. Even allowing for a memory lapse of several years, it is clear from the evidence below (that Hakubunkan rejected the manuscript after keeping it six months) that at the very latest the work must have been written by late 1900, which is before Katai encountered the complete works of Maupassant and underwent a major change in his approach to literature (May 1901, see the later section 'The Second Floor of Maruzen'). In other words, 'No no Hana' is old Katai, whereas its preface is the post-Maupassant Katai.

[271] Saigiku Sanjin (1832-1902, also known as Jōno Saigiku or Sansantei Arindo), gesaku writer; Sanmai Dōjin is the pseudonym of Miyazaki Sanmai (see Note 238).

In those days there were only two publishing companies that bought novels, H and S.[272] K, which had put out 'Miyako no Hana', was no longer interested in literary works at that particular time.[273]

Otowa's half-lifetime was short, but for those three or four years after marrying into the Ōhashi family it was spectacular.[274] In the days when he went by his old name of Watanabe he was merely known as just another writer, but after he took the name Ōhashi everyone would call on him at his home. Rohan was one of those who went to see him there.

Kōyō was certainly closer to the S Company than the H, and didn't get on well with the latter. Nevertheless he didn't criticise his pupils and friends for associating with the H Company.

I think, on reading Kōyō's novels, that he had a fairly good grasp of the psychology of men and women in their relations with one another. You can see this from his views at the core of 'Golden Demon', and that section in 'Three Wives', and Sumi Ryūnosuke's anguish in 'Much Feeling, Much Grief'.[275] Isn't it true to say that Ryūnosuke's anguish is not due to his being separated from his wife as such, but from a woman? Likewise that it is a separation born of life, not of death? At least, I think it's only natural to view it like that.

And as for 'Golden Demon', I wonder just who was the model for that widely appealing heroine Omiya? Similarly, who, I wonder, was the model for Kan'ichi? I did glean a few bits of information through N and O, but there's no need for me to discuss that here.[276]

The writers in those days — at least the ones who made any money — led quite a life of merry-making. It was the heyday of the Kōyōkan in Shiba, and Kōyō and N and S often went there for a bit of entertainment.[277]

---

[272] That is, Hakubunkan and Shunyōdō.

[273] Kinkōdō. They ceased publishing 'Miyako no Hana' in June 1893.

[274] Actually it was either eight years or six years, depending on what date one takes for Otowa's marriage (see Note 146). This sort of vagueness is not entirely Katai's fault. Rather like the imprecisions over ages and names, there is considerable imprecision in general with regard to dates of marriage where the groom is adopted into the bride's family, with a lag of three or four years between adoption and formal marriage ceremony being quite common. It will be seen from the notes to the later section 'Little House in the Suburbs' that this situation also applied in the case of Yanagita Kunio.

[275] 'Three Wives' ('Sannin Tsuma'), in two parts, March 6th-May 11th 1892, and July 5th-November 4th 1892, Yomiuri Shinbun.

[276] One of the models for 'Golden Demon' was rumoured to be Iwaya Sazanami, who was in love with a waitress at the Kōyōkan [Restaurant] (see below). His love was unrequited. N and O are not clear, but O could possibly be either Oguri Fūyō or Ōhashi Otowa, while N seems likely to be Nakamura Kasō (see below).

[277] The Kōyōkan was a well-known restaurant and reception centre. ('Kōyō' featured commonly in restaurant names and should not be associated specifically with Ozaki Kōyō.) S is Sazanami, while N is probably Nakamura Kasō (1867-1899), a Genyūsha writer who was one of Kōyō's regular companions in the early-mid 1890's.

If they read Kōyō's later diaries anyone can learn about his frequenting the demimonde of the Yanagibashi district.

Otowa, after his marriage, was greatly interested for a time in photography. Or it may be truer to say that photography was imposed upon him, since he was friendly in those days with Ponta no Kashima and in later years also struck up a close relationship with the renowned Mitsumura Risō.[278] There are still old geishas in the Yanagibashi and Mukōjima districts who remember the name Otowa.

Remodelling the City

At that time Tōkyō was in the middle of being remodelled.

From the beginning of the Meiji era it was gradually rebuilt as the new capital of the Japanese Empire. The number of earth-walled houses dwindled daily, to be replaced by Western-style buildings. The rebuilding of the main roads of Nihonbashi was much talked about, and comments appeared in the newspapers like, "I think they're making it all too Western. Surely the old Japanese-style earth-walled houses would give the capital more charm?"

But the demands of the new city kept on growing. Onari Street grew bigger as you watched it, and the main roads became much wider. What with the reconstruction of the bridges and the removal of the firebreaks and the improvement of the narrow streets, a bit more of the Edo of old was destroyed with each passing day.

Work on the water supply system was quite a nuisance. I remember how the streets of suburban Ushigome, where I lived, were completely dug up and became a quagmire of mud that was impossible to pass through even in the highest clogs. The narrow streets of Tamachi, where my poetry teacher lived, were particularly dreadful.

"It's an absolute sea of mud!"

"All thanks to the roadworks!" he'd say.

Iron water pipes lay all over the place, and mud covered labourers lit bonfires to huddle round on cold mornings. It was around that time that the 'water-pipe incident' took place.[279]

---

[278] Ponta no Kashima is unclear but seems almost certain to be the name of a geisha. The comment about photography being imposed upon him is probably a reference to the fact that at the time photography was a rather 'trendy' pastime/profession, so much so that it was virtually a patron's duty to be photographed with his favourite geisha in innumerable settings. Mitsumura Risō (dates unclear) was a professional photographer (later based in Kōbe) who in 1904 accompanied Katai to the Russo-Japanese War as a member of Hakubunkan's photography team.

[279] The 'water-pipe incident' was a scandal involving the supply of inferior quality pipes by the Nippon Chūtetsu Company, leading to the arrest on October 31st 1895 of the company president, Hamano Shigeru, and several public officials.

Of the five great metropolitan bridges it was Shinōhashi that remained in its original wooden state the longest. How I miss those days when all five of them — Umayabashi, Azumabashi, Ryōgokubashi, Shinōhashi, and Eitaibashi — were old-style, Edo-style wooden bridges.[280] When I think, as a further example, that there are said to be hardly any old-style covered boats left in Tōkyō nowadays, I realise just how much the city has changed over the years.

In particular my old friends from the country seem to have felt this. My friend T, who did poetry with S and O and who returned to his home in Kagoshima around 1892, came up to Tōkyō again after many years' absence and told me how he had wandered round the streets, unable to recognise old landmarks.[281] "It's all changed! Around by Meganebashi (— what memories that word holds! —) I just couldn't find any trace of the old days. There's something of those days left round by the military training place, but round by Sudachō it's just like a different world. And how Onari Street has changed, and Asakusa! There's nothing left of the old narrow streets, with their special atmosphere. I'm sure the literary world must have changed a lot too, so much so that I couldn't begin to understand what's what. I really have become a complete rustic!"

I myself had not fully appreciated the extent of the changes time had wrought, having been in the midst of them and therefore used to them.

I had once gone every year to look at the blossoms in Ueno and Mukōjima. Both those places had changed greatly relative to the old days. In Ueno, there was no longer any commemorative black temple-gate.[282] A main road was built alongside the Tōshōgū Shrine. The trees suffered more and more pollution, and started dying off. There weren't as many birds about as when I used to go to Negishi as a child. The library expanded. Mukōjima and its blossoms suffered even greater change. Thanks to the grime of numerous factories and to the hordes of people trampling daily along the embankment the cherries got worse every year, and even the area around Kototoi, which once used to be known as a 'tunnel of flowers', was completely spoiled. Everything had changed.

New words, too, came into being. Beancurd vendors now went round ringing bells. Clog-menders went round beating drums. We only think things novel when they first appear, and soon become so familiar with them that we think they've been with us from long ago.

---

[280] All these bridges spanned the Sumidagawa, and were rebuilt respectively in 1893, 1887 (and again 1928), 1904, 1911, and 1897.

[281] T is Tsuchimoto Kōan (see Note 99), while S is Sakurai Toshiyuki (see Note 92) and O is Ōta Gyokumei. Tsuchimoto visited Katai in Tōkyō in July 1909, a year before he died of typhoid.

[282] At the Kan'eiji.

How Tōkyō has changed!

Our Group

My friendship with Shimazaki started from around that time. I think that, out of Kunikida and Shimazaki, it was Shimazaki that I met first, just.

It was following Tōkoku's death that I got to know the people associated with the 'Bungakukai' magazine.[283] I suppose it was a bond formed by youth. But I personally was not satisfied with the attitude of the 'Bungakukai' people. I wanted to write novels. I was convinced that novels were more important than drama and poetry.

That was why I joined the Genyūsha group — rather than the Sendagi group that I so admired — although they did not recognise my novels. But on the other hand I also felt that the Genyūsha's attitude was not capable of producing a new type of novel suited to the future. In addition to that I didn't feel at all at home with the free and easy, 'man of the world'-type character of the Genyūsha people. But even so, if people like Kyōka and Fūyō and Shunyō had shown some appreciation of me I might have stuck with them. However, they tended to treat me like a stranger and to keep me at a distance. I came in for some pretty nasty remarks as a result of not being accepted as one of Kōyō's pupils. Occasionally I'd be the victim of groundless suspicions, such as that Kōyō may have told Otowa to stop buying my manuscripts. And so it was that I gradually moved away from the Genyūsha towards a different group.

The agent of my coming into contact with the 'Bungakukai' people was a letter of condolence that I sent to the magazine on the occasion of Tōkoku's death. Also, Yanagita had a cousin called Nakagawa who was friendly with the chief editor of the magazine, Hoshino Tenchi, and his younger brother Sekiei.[284] So it was that I gradually started contributing manuscripts to the 'Bungakukai' magazine. In those days, it seemed that the 'Bungakukai' people no longer felt it was worthwhile writing manuscripts for no fee.

It was at the 'Bungakukai''s New Year Party, held in a room at the Ikaho in Negishi, that I met Shimazaki, Baba, Hirata, Ueda, and Togawa.[285] It was a long narrow room alongside the railway line, and it

---

[283] Tōkoku took his own life on May 16th 1894. He had been the central figure of the 'Bungakukai' group.

[284] Yanagita's cousin was Nakagawa Kyōjirō (dates unclear), doctor and publisher. Tenchi's younger brother was Hoshino Sekiei (1869-1924), an architect who appears to have written only *one* story.

[285] The party took place in January 1896. Baba Kochō (1869-1940), translator, poet, and essayist; Ueda Bin (1874-1916), poet, translator, critic.

rattled and shook each time a train passed. I heard a lot of big talk there, the spirited talk of young men. Ueda Bin, with his red face and gold buttons, surprised me with remarks like "Ōgai's translations are full of mistakes. One of these days I'll check them all out!" I'm fairly certain that it was Shimazaki and Baba that I went back with, walking along the far side of Ikenohata towards the Hongō road. Shimazaki was a pale, quiet, pleasant enough young man. As we walked along he gave his opinions of the short stories I'd published in 'Bungakukai'.

Baba and I parted with Shimazaki at Shinhanachō, then walked for ages along the Hongō road. Compared with Shimazaki Baba was a cheerful, high-spirited young man. If I remember correctly, on that occasion he talked about Kyōka's novels.

The 'Bungakukai' people were inclined towards English literature, which didn't appeal to me, but at the same time I could see that they knew more about foreign literature than people like me did. Hirata was a student at higher normal-school, and Togawa was taking an elective course at university. Both were good at English. Hirata was in lodgings in Yushima, and was reading works like George Eliot's 'Silas Marner'. I lent him such works as Daudet's 'Sapho'.

I'm sure it was through my introduction that Yanagita first visited Shimazaki at his place in Daikonbatake, but because he lived nearby he ended up socialising with him more than I did myself. Yanagita would often go and call on him, wearing his white-striped hakama and with an excited look on his face, and they would talk about poetry and love and religion.

On the other hand, through Miyazaki Koshoshi I myself got to know Kunikida. Kunikida had just split up with that Onobu, and was living in a house on top of a hill in suburban Shibuya.[286] I'd heard about him before from Koshoshi, was interested in his love affair, and admired his fresh, vivid style of writing. I called on him one day, unannounced, when I went to visit Koshoshi at his temporary lodgings in Dōgenzaka.

The House on the Hill[287]

It was the end of November and a balmy autumn day, typical of the Tōkyō suburbs, with chrysanthemums blooming beautifully in the rural

[286] Sasaki Nobuko (1878-1949) married Doppo on November 11th 1895 after a storybook whirlwind romance that involved a virtual elopement and the defiance of Nobuko's parents. The marriage was finally brought about by the mediation of Tokutomi Sohō. However, Nobuko left Doppo in a rather abrupt fashion on April 12th 1896, with the divorce following on April 24th. She bore his child, Urako, in January the following year, but the child was registered in the Sasaki family. See the following chapter for details of Katai's visit to Doppo.

[287] Kunikida's (rented) house in Kamishibuya Udagawachō (present-day Shibuyamachi). He lived there from September 1896-April 1897.

hedges.[288] Ōta Gyokumei and I visited Barenya, the travel lodge where Koshoshi was staying, but unfortunately he was out and no-one knew when he would be back. We did think about going back home, but then I suggested to Gyokumei: "What say we call on Kunikida? He lives around here, so I understand. Koshoshi's bound to have spoken about us to him, so it's not as though we're total strangers. I'm sure he won't mind." Gyokumei agreed, and I led the way.

We went along the Shibuya road till we came out in some fields, where the main road to Komaba followed a curving course along a wood of oaks. Beyond, we could see the Nogawa [River] winding its way through the paddy-fields.[289] Nearer us, on its lower reaches, a waterwheel was turning busily. The horizon was vividly clear, and we could see the gentle range of hills in Musashi Plain, with their characteristic woods. We crossed over an earthern bridge next to the waterwheel, and walked on past fields of tea and giant radish.

"Isn't there a house of a Kunikida somewhere around here?" we asked a couple of times.

"What's he do?"

"I think he's living alone."[290]

"A student?"

"That's right."

"In that case, I think it's a little house up on the top of that hill there, beyond the dairy."

Finally someone told us where his house was.

We walked on a bit, past the dairy with its half-dozen lazy-looking cows, and then I caught sight of a little house on top of the thickly wooded, autumn mantled hill, bathed in the late afternoon sunshine. "Ah, that's it! That's the house!"

Then when we walked on a bit further we came across a little gate that led down to another little house, lower down the slope than the one we were heading for. We went there first, wondering if that might not perhaps be Kunikida's house, but a woman in her mid-twenties appeared, hair all dishevelled, and pointed to the house in the sunshine on top of the hill. "THAT's Kunikida's house!"

---

[288] The visit actually took place around the 12th of the month.

[289] The Nogawa flows through the southern part of Setagaya-ku, and would probably have been visible. However, the waterwheel he refers to below is almost certainly not on the lower reaches of the Nogawa but on the Furukawa, so it is possible that Katai has mistaken the name of the river from the start.

[290] Sic. Actually, as Katai himself makes clear later, he was living with his younger brother. The term 'alone' ('hitori de') presumably refers to his being without a wife or parents.

The narrow lane climbed gently up the hill amidst grassy banks and bright red leaves, and chrysanthemums standing out vividly against black soil, and fresh green vegetable fields — then suddenly we realised that someone was standing outside the house watching us. He was a young man, slim and debonair with a pale complexion.

"Does Kunikida live here?"

"I am Kunikida."

When we told him who we were it seemed that he had indeed already heard about us, and he gave us a hearty welcome. "Come in, come in! This is a pleasant surprise!" He too seemed to appreciate the pleasure of company on an autumn day.

"So Koshoshi wasn't in? I wonder where he's gone? He *should* have been in. Perhaps he's gone back to see his little sister." Although it was the first time we'd met we had things in common and spoke freely and in familiar fashion as though we'd known each other for ten years.

"This is a nice place."

"Not bad at all, is it! Just right for young poetry-lovers like us. Yamaji found it for me. It's ideal, living alone like this. Everyone who comes here thinks it's marvellous."

"It really is a nice place."

"You can certainly feel that it's Musashi Plain. Moonlit nights are just incredible!"

I was immediately taken by Kunikida's soft, sad eyes and his flowing, sincere words. "No wonder he writes in such a fresh style," I thought to myself.

His younger brother Hokuto was around 18 or 19 at that time — a ruddy-faced, handsome young man — and as we talked he listened quietly, sitting on the verandah or else wandering around in the garden with a walking-stick.[291] There was a grapevine trellis in front of the verandah, and we could also see, through the red leaves and young trees on the slope, the woods and hills and waterwheels of Shibuya.

The house comprised a six-mat room with a two-mat room next to it and a kitchen beyond, and it looked very much like the sort of place a Tōkyō merchant would build for his retirement. There was a bookshelf in a corner of the room, with works by Wordsworth, Carlyle, Emerson, and Tolstoi, and — if I remember correctly — a little alabaster figurine of Goethe. Copies of 'Kokumin no Tomo' and 'Jogaku Zasshi' lay on the lacquered papier-mâché desk.

It was in this lonely house on the hill that he was recovering from the wounds of his affair with Onobu.

---

[291] Kunikida Shūji (1878-1931, also known as Hokuto), journalist.

I've forgotten what we spoke about on that occasion, but I do know that we talked openly and understood each other well. We no doubt talked about Turgenev, and Tolstoi, and the poetry of Heine and Wordsworth. In those days Gyokumei was particularly active in the sphere of poetry, along with Koshoshi and Saganoya, so when it came to talking about poetry I'm sure he found Doppo even more of a kindred spirit than me. We were so engrossed in our conversation that the day drew to a close without our realising it.

When we went to take our leave Kunikida urged us to stay:

"Please stay a bit longer. You don't mind, do you?"

He continued:

"We're having rice curry, so have some with us."

He went off into the kitchen.

The woman from the house further down the slope prepared his meals for him. I've forgotten her name but I think she was married to a carpenter called Iso, and had come there with him after seeing out her term of service as a prostitute in Shinjuku.[292]

"The rice is ready now so you've got no excuse for not staying," said Doppo as he came back from the kitchen.

I'll never forget that scene — how we tipped rice onto a large plate, crudely mixed in curry powder, and then gobbled it up with a spoon.[293]

"It's nice, very nice!" we said as we ate.

The moon was bright when Gyokumei and I set out on the way back. As we hurried off towards Shibuya Station we talked about what a nice fellow Kunikida was, and how he was refreshingly frank and open.

After that we often went up to that house on the hill. With the passing of time a firm friendship developed between us. Sometimes I would stay at his house, and sometimes Kunikida would visit my house in Kikuichō. I was also drawn to his house by the marvellous view.

I went there with Yanagita, as well.

I have many memories associated with that house on the hill. When I visited him there Kunikida would go out onto the verandah and yell down to the nearby dairy for a pint or so of fresh milk. We'd then pour this into teacups, put in coffee, and have a real treat.

Sometimes Kunikida would be out when I visited, and I would wait there for him for an hour or two. One rainy day in early winter, when he was out, I caught sight of a book there that I wanted to read —

---

[292] Iso Hajime (dates unclear) is the husband's name. He was also caretaker of the house Doppo was renting.

[293] Sic. Obviously an unusual method of preparing curry. Note too the unusual method of preparing coffee mentioned below. It is not clear whether these were standard methods at the time.

Futabatei's 'Unanswered Love' — and spent the whole day sprawled out there quietly reading.[294] The next day I sent him a letter: "Yesterday you weren't there, but 'Unanswered Love' was, so I spent a quiet afternoon in your house reading it. I thought about all sorts of things. It was a memorable day."

Beyond the hill there was, unlike nowadays, much to remind one of old Musashi Plain, such as woods and hills and thickets. Kunikida and I often went walking there, past an old pond hidden away in the woods, along hilly lanes echoing with the sound of carts, through fields of miscanthus and pampas grass rustling in the breeze, with snow-capped Mount Fuji looming picturesquely in the evening air, and past solitary pines standing out on the moor, or across bridges spanning the railway line. Always we talked of life, and art, and love, and nature. We talked too of the sad affair with Onobu. I wrote about that in a later novel, called 'After the Parting'.[295]

Apart from Koshoshi, others who went to that house included Yamaji Aizan. He's still there in Shibuya, in the same house, which was not far at all from Kunikida's.[296] Aizan often went visiting with his eldest daughter, who was about seven or eight and whose name escapes me.[297] He was just as fat and bulky in those days, too. I remember on one occasion how he told us, with some amusement: "Children make the most fascinating observations, you know. On our way here, walking into the wind, this one of mine complained that the wind was lifting up her kimono! Now can you imagine us making the same observation?!" (And now, Aizan too is dead!)

It looked as if Kunikida was influenced by Gyokumei and Yanagita and Koshoshi, for from about that time on he started writing the poetry

---

[294] Futabatei's 'Katakoi' was published by Shunyōdō in October 1896. It contained three translations of works by Turgenev, namely revised translations of 'Aibiki' (Rendezvous, first published July-August 1888, 'Kokumin no Tomo') and 'Meguriai' (Chance Encounter, first published October 1888-January 1889, 'Miyako no Hana', and now retitled 'Kigū' [also 'Chance Encounter']), and 'Katakoi' itself, which was a translation of 'Asya'.

[295] 'Wakarete Kara', April 1912, 'Chūō Kōron'.

[296] From 1896 till his death in 1917 Yamaji was based at — though often absent from for extended periods — his house in what is now Hirō in Shibuya. He did in fact die in March 1917, three months before 'Tōkyō no Sanjūnen' was published but clearly after the manuscript was written. Katai's rather clumsy insertion at the end of this paragraph should be noted.

[297] His eldest daughter Yayoi was born March 28th 1894 (he did not marry till February 1893, to Tajima Tane [1873-1931]), and as Doppo only lived at the house in question till April 1897 she could not have been 'seven or eight' even by Japanese age standards.

that appeared in his 'Doppo Recitation'.[298] The poems 'Living Free with Nature', 'Snow on Distant Peaks', 'Old Man', and 'This Day Last Year' were all written in that house on the hill.[299]

I also remember hearing there a special recitation of the poem 'Spring has Come, Winter has Gone' just after it was written.[300]

Kunikida lived there in that house on the hill from the end of summer till our trip to Nikkō the following year. I'm sure that those six months or so were an influential and unforgettable time for him, too. His 'Musashi Plain' contains many references to red leaves, and autumn showers, and winter winds, and falling leaves, and morning mists, and frosts, and these are all impressions from that house on the hill.[301]

I'm now going to quote a letter I received from Kunikida the following spring, just before we went to Nikkō. It's written on Kokumin Newspaper manuscript paper.

"Shall we really go to Nikkō, then? It'll be wonderful to spend the spring there quietly together, with all the mist and water, putting into words these intense feelings of mine. The only thing I'm worried about is the state of our finances — but then, as you say, it shouldn't cost too much to live there. I'm sure the head of the temple isn't an avaricious type, and if we're careful we'll probably get by on sixteen yen a month between us — I hope.

"The only other thing that bothers me is giving up the cherry blossoms here. During the cold winter nights, with the wind whistling through the tree-tops, I've been looking forward very much to seeing spring arrive in the garden. I'm sure that, anxious as you are to be off, you will appreciate my feelings. The plum blossoms out in the garden have started to look a little ragged after the rain we've had these last few days. On the other hand, it won't be long at all till the cherries are in bloom. The twelfth of April is not only the day the cherries in Kudan are due to fall,

---

[298] 'Doppo Gin' was Doppo's contribution to the joint collection 'Jojōshi' (Lyric Poetry), published in April 1897 by Minyūsha. The other contributors were Katai, Ōta Gyokumei, Yanagita Kunio, Miyazaki Koshoshi, and Saganoya Omuro. This 'Doppo Gin' should not be confused with Doppo's poem of the same title published in August 1895 in the Kokumin Newspaper.

[299] Respectively 'Sanrin ni Jiyū Zonsu', 'Enzansetsu' (actually the first line of the poem correctly titled 'Mori ni Hairu' [On Entering the Woods]), 'Okina' (actually the first line of the poem correctly titled 'Kokyō no Okina ni Atau' [Addressed to an Old Man at Home]), and 'Kozo no Kyō' (lit: This Day Last Year, whereas the correct title is actually 'Kozo no Ima' [This Time Last Year]).

[300] Katai gives 'Haru ya Kishi, Fuyu ya Nogareshi', whereas the correct title is 'Haru Kitaru, Fuyu Yuku'.

[301] The anthology 'Musashi No' was published by Minyūsha in March 1901, while the specific work '[Ima no] Musashi No' ([Present-day] Musashi Plain: the 'Present-day'/'Ima no' is often omitted) was published January-February 1898 in 'Kokumin no Tomo'.

it's also the day my wife left me. It'll be sad to greet that day here in the capital, but nevertheless I'm waiting anxiously for it to dawn, much as it will upset me. Won't it be really nice to spend the Tōkyō spring in Tōkyō, and then greet the Nikkō spring in Nikkō![302]

"Today I was expecting Matsuoka (Yanagita Kunio) to come, and was waiting for him since morning. But it seems as though this rain has dampened even HIS spirits, seeing as he didn't turn up. To calm myself as I was waiting I smoked a lot of cigarettes, but I'm not used to them and I made myself dizzy. I went out into the garden for some fresh air, despite the rain, and spent the rest of the day gazing up at the clouds racing by overhead. It's now evening. I've left the rain-shutters open, and I can hear the wind roaring through the trees over to the west. The drops from the eaves are getting blown about as they fall. I've got 'Shigaramizōshi' on my desk, and I've also got 'Two Nights' open.[303]

"'Two Nights' is an excellent work. That girl in it has made ME fall in love with her too — in fact I'd give my life for her. I really do mean it, for love is truly a moving thing. The love affair puts me in mind very much of my own experience. And how that seems like a dream, like something a long way away! Love appears like a rainbow in the pitch darkness of human life, and then, just like a rainbow, fades away. Your wish is to see this rainbow, and my wish is to weave once again those vanished colours in the dark sky of life. But it's a vain hope. The evening before last I visited that captain's house again.[304] The sky was mainly clear overhead, the stars were sparkling over to the west, and I went on my way with my head full of thoughts.[305] My stomach had been playing up since morning, and I set out thinking a walk would do me good. There was a bonfire amongst the trees, and rainclouds over on the western horizon were blotting out Fuji. It seemed as melancholy as late autumn, although it was early spring. That section of the wood where we

---

[302] That is, since Nikkō is north of Tōkyō the cherry blossoms which symbolise spring open slightly later. The 'cherry blossom front' moves on average at approximately half a mile an hour.

[303] 'Futayo' is one of the translations appearing in Ōgai's 'Minawashū' (see Note 244), being a partial translation of 'Zwei Nächte' (Two Nights) by Friedrich Hackländer.

[304] A Captain Satō (born c. 1848), an engineer whom Doppo had met on board the Chiyoda in October 1894 while serving as a correspondent during the Sino-Japanese War. He is mentioned only briefly in Doppo's diary and remains a rather mysterious figure, which is unfortunate in view of Doppo's feelings for his daughter Hanako (see below). One thing that is clear from Doppo's diary is that the 'again' in this sentence is a reference to the fact that on March 12th, ie. some thirteen days before the visit described here, Doppo visited Satō to get his pistol repaired.

[305] Sic. 'East' seems more logical, especially in view of the clouds mentioned below. The entire geography of this passage is extremely difficult to follow, especially the reference to the hills.

listened to the sound of leaves falling in the rain last autumn, savouring the loneliness, has now been entirely chopped down, and reduced to a plain of white-topped stumps.

"When I looked from the top of the hill I could see that the rain-shutters of that house had still not been closed, and I could see the white of the shōji. They too were half open, and I could see the blackness by contrast of the room within. I went down the hill, up the other hill, and arrived at their gate. When I went in through it and trod on the boards my footsteps echoed right through the house, and the dog came out barking, but I didn't pay any attention to it as it always does that. Once in the garden I could see that the shutters had by now been closed, and I could see a bright light shining inside the two shōji at the entrance. Who do you think heard my footsteps and came to open the door? It was dear Hanako!

"How can I express with my humble pen the happiness of those next two hours? Her father, the captain, is fifty years old but nevertheless he talked and joked with me with not the least reserve. And she sat beside him, laughing all the time too. We talked about my stomach trouble, and I was given some hot wrapped salt.[306] I forgot the cares I was brooding about.

"The love I have for that girl is more fleeting than dreams, more transitory even than that in 'Two Nights'. I'm told that she will soon be placed in the care of her aunt, while her father goes to live with my friend Mizukami.[307] It will be difficult for me to see her again. Dear, sweet girl, here's hoping that you find happiness in the future. The count in 'Two Nights' received three passionate kisses, but I have yet to receive such reward. Nor do I expect I will in the future, either.

The evening of March Twenty-seventh,

To Rokuya,

From Tetsuo."

It saddens me to read this letter from the past. I can so clearly picture that house on the hill, so inseparably connected with the picture of Kunikida — sad, sincere, innocent, lonely, noble Kunikida. The life we imagined in those days was so different in so many ways from real life, but we were at least absolutely correct in agreeing that, at the end of it all, life would be swallowed by the flow of time.

[306] This was slipped inside one's clothing and used as a body warmer, especially by those with stomach ailments.

[307] There is a brief mention in Doppo's diary of a Mizukami Umehiko ('Mizukami' rather than the more common reading 'Minakami' appears correct). Further details are unclear, except that he seems to have been involved in some rift with his wife late in 1896.

It was 1896 [sic], and on the twentieth of April that year we left behind the blossoms of Asukayama and went to stay at the S Temple in Nikkō.[308] We stayed there a month or so and returned to Tōkyō at the beginning of June. Kunikida's brother Hokuto had shut up the house on the hill, so Kunikida had to go into lodgings in Banchō in Kōjimachi, near the Nishō Academy.[309] He stayed there for six months, or possibly longer.[310] There was a painter's widow living next door, with a lot of daughters, and Kunikida fell in love again, with the eldest who was in her early twenties.[311]

She is his present widow.

He often told me about the affair. He wrote a poem when they parted at Kichijōji Station, he having gone to see her off to Hachiōji:[312]

> "You're heading west
> And I'm heading east;
> And as we part here,
> On this country route,
> A wintry shower falls."

I wonder what's happened now to that dear little house on the hill? I dare say it's disappeared without trace. Along with the woods, and the grassy fields, and the thickets, and that dear old pond......

K and T[313]

K and T always went for a walk together in the evening. K had a walking-stick. It was made of bamboo root, and had a bit of a story behind it. The story of how he bought it in the Ginza can seem, depending on how you interpret it, rather like amorous prattle. T, however, having sympathy for K's sad affair and never himself having had such an experience, always listened with a serious expression on his face. He still didn't really understand K's love-story.

---

[308] Clearly it was 1897, not 1896. Asukayama is in Oji in Kita-ku, ie. en route to Nikkō. The S Temple is the Shōsonin (Shōson'in).

[309] In actual fact Hokuto had argued with Iso the caretaker and was obliged to move. See Note 41 for details of the Nishō Academy.

[310] He was in fact there till September that year.

[311] Enomoto Haru(ko) (1879-1962). They married in August the following year. Haruko later became a writer of some note. At the time she was clearly not yet in her early twenties.

[312] Kichijōji is in Musashino City.

[313] Originally written as a separate work and published in the Hakubunkan magazine 'Bunshō Sekai' (World of Writing, March 1906-December 1920) in January 1917, ie. five months before 'Tōkyō no Sanjūnen'. It was included in the original version of the latter but was omitted from most subsequent editions. K is Kunikida, T Tayama.

From time to time T wondered just how much truth there was to it. K's story-telling was done cleverly, buoyantly, crisply, and he always managed to get people absorbed right away in whatever he was talking about. Whenever any group of their friends got together K always became the centre of conversation and directed proceedings. T, who would be beside him listening, found it interesting at first, but ended up disliking the way K would get carried away and start playing to the audience. "He's off again, spellbinding his audience — I suppose that's how he gets the girls!" T would think to himself.

Nevertheless, T did admire K's sincere and pure and open feelings. He also admired a lot of the things K said. K had deep and particular beliefs on such matters as religion, and life, and love, and death. "It's because he's a Christian that he can talk so sweetly on such matters," T would say disparagingly, but for all that he admired him nonetheless.

"I've got none of your sort of egoism. Why don't you just open up a bit more to others, and be a bit more straightforward? And you're always going on about world-weariness and pessimism, but if you really dislike the world that much why don't you take yourself off into the hills and become a priest or something?!" K would often say such things to T, but, unlike K, T simply did not have the sort of character that would enable him to open up to others. Unlike K, who spoke frankly and simply and with an outgoing cheerfulness, T was gloomy and melancholy, full of sadness and despair that he couldn't bring to the surface, and was quiet and brooding.

They were both the same age, twenty-six.

"Isn't it incredible?! Don't you just feel the incredible vastness of life?! Here we are, you and I, in the middle of these mountains, on an evening like this, on the banks of foaming mountain rapids.....and look, there's a thatched cottage over there, with a light at the window! Even in a place like this, you can find human life!" K was very excited as he spoke. "I was lost for words to describe it when I was in Hokkaidō, too, surrounded by all that nature.[314] The miners were living in mountains just like this, men and women. They had their tragedies, and their comedies, just like anywhere else. But beyond lay wilderness, forests that had never seen man's axe, primeval mists. And there was I, alone in all this life. No, I wasn't alone — I was in the presence of God. I couldn't help feeling this. I'll never forget going to Utashinai, to have a look at that land that was going to be cleared. Just like now there was a house with a light

[314] He went to Utashinai, on the Sorachigawa [River], on September 16th 1895, looking for a plot of land on which he could literally build a life with Sasaki Nobuko. However, he returned to Tōkyō on the 28th of that month upon learning of her mother's opposition to the planned marriage.

on, surrounded by solitude. There was a white evening mist over the ground, but the sky was clear, and the moonlight bright as day. My mind was full of thoughts as I walked around there, alone. I became acutely aware of how terrible city life is, and how you can't live a proper life unless it's in the heart of nature. I was so keen to move there, with the girl I loved, taking all my ambitions with me too. When I left Nobu at Shiobara and went to Hokkaidō I was burning with youthful enthusiasm....'' — his speech faltered — ''...but now it's all over. My dreams have melted away like so much frost!''[315]

T had already heard that story from K many times before, how he had fallen passionately in love with Onobu and finally managed to marry her despite her parents' opposition, how he had returned from Hokkaidō and how they had spent those six wonderful months together on the G coast.[316] K and Onobu had now split up, but her memory never left him for a moment. Many a time he'd spend hours sitting quietly in a chair, hands clasped behind his head, staring into space.

It was all strange to T. Having still not tasted the forbidden fruit himself, he could only imagine, and not really know, just how bitter or how sweet it was. Moreover, he could not condone K's having selfishly dragged the girl off with him.[317] T wanted girls — virgins — to stay sacred things, untouched. For him, a virgin's purity was the most beautiful, the most perfect thing on earth. He couldn't believe that a marriage founded on such deep feeling could end up as it had now, after less than a year. He didn't WANT to believe it.

''How could it have ended like that?'' he was always asking.

''I don't know myself, so it's hardly surprising YOU don't!'' K would snap back. And then he would let out a deep sigh. ''Everything's finished, it's all history now,'' he would say, and tears would glisten in his eyes.

K and T walked for half an hour or so long along the riverbank and then headed back.[318] Even at night, the white spray from the river was clearly visible.

''It's incredible. It really gets to you!''

''It certainly does.''

---

[315] Before Doppo set out for Hokkaidō on September 16th he and Nobuko had spent four days at Shiobara, some hundred miles north of Tōkyō, in what was virtually an elopement. Nobuko's father, however, followed them there.

[316] The G is not clear. They lived in Zushi in Kanagawa, in a farmer's house that was rented out as resort accommodation, known as the Yanagiwa-ya. G is possibly a reference to Gokurakujizaka, a slope giving access to the beach in nearby Kamakura.

[317] In 'Modern Novels' Katai states that he and Doppo virtually came to blows over this.

[318] The river is the Daiyagawa.

T often called in to K's room before going to bed.

K's room was also upstairs, facing the river that raced past the temple tossing spray high into the air. The sound of the river seemed to fill the room.

K went to bed late and got up late. T, on the other hand, went to bed early and got up early. On one typical occasion T went into K's room.

"Are you going to bed now?" asked K.

"Yes."

"But it's still early! It's only ten o'clock. I was just thinking of getting down to writing a couple of poems to send off to the K Company."[319]

Scattered on K's desk was K Company manuscript paper, and a knife, and a pen, and an inkpot, and magazines, and books. 'Heine's Poem' [sic][320] lay there open. K showed him the poem he had started to compose, asked him what he thought of it, and then took it back and recited it.

From time to time they'd discuss the literary scene. The frivolous attitude of the G-sha was a target for their scorn.[321] K would also make remarks like, "Yes, I definitely will. To commemorate this visit, I definitely WILL write my first work. I've been thinking about it all day. I suppose it seems to you as though I just waste time, going for walks and the like, but in fact it's all work nonetheless." This was a reference to the fact that T was plugging away diligently every day at a long and hopeless novel that he wouldn't be able to get anyone to publish anyway. T got a little upset at the way K lounged around every day, going for walks or sitting in his chair and all the while thinking this to be work.

"He'll never produce anything, loafing around like that!" T would say to himself derisively. T managed to get two or three short works published, and of course they were pulled to bits by the joint critics in 'Ms-gusa', the authority of the day.[322]

Talk about 'Ms-gusa' often featured in their conversation. T was strongly opposed to the magazine, but K would appraise it in a relatively balanced fashion. "O is marvellous, though.[323] There's no-one

---

[319] The Kokumin group, which included the Minyūsha.

[320] Given thus in English by Katai. It is not clear whether this is a misprint or an error in Katai's English. A misprint seems likely.

[321] That is, the Genyūsha.

[322] Apart from Katai's contribution to 'Jojōshi' (which was published while they were at the temple: see Note 298), 'Wagakage' (My Shadow), he produced two works in the late May issue of 'Kokumin no Tomo', 'Nogawa no Kishi' (The Banks of the Nogawa) and 'Kokoro no Hana' (Flowers of the Heart), 'Kohan Zatsugin' (Random Lakeside Recitations) in the early May issue of the same magazine, and 'Haru no Nikkōyama' (The Hills of Nikkō in Spring) in the June issue of 'Taiyō'.

'Ms-gusa' is 'Mesamashigusa' (see Note 239).

[323] Mori Ōgai.

nowadays who can match the extent of his knowledge. I prefer him to Dr. T.[324] But what about S?![325] He's always nit-picking and thinking he's wonderful. What can you do with a cantankerous, carping attitude like that? People like him are just gesaku writers. W's just the same.[326] But R's a bit better."[327] T couldn't accept this view. As far as he was concerned 'Ms-gusa' was a group of cowardly established writers who trampled underfoot new growth that had just started to bud. He got particularly upset that some of the new writers were left unscathed, whereas others, like himself, were vilified. Whenever an issue came out T would stand hesitantly in front of the book-stall, not wanting to read it yet obliged to do so, and would then, with a mixture of trepidation and anger, flick through quickly and note to his mortification how dreadfully he was abused.

A, a university graduate in charge of the Y Newspaper's critical column at the time, was also frequently attacked by K and T.[328]

K would say things like: "He only writes things in tune with the reactions of the major writers. He's thoroughly disgusting. Big help, isn't it — this is good, or this is bad, and Petrarca did this, or Dante did that! I'm sick of hearing things like that. He should put an end to that pretty-pretty writing and pedantic research of his — enough's enough!" Then, getting angry, he'd say things like: "There're just too many petty-minded people around on the literary scene nowadays, and all they can do is meddle in other people's business and say uncalled-for things. That's why they're all so warped!" T would then join him in condemning the literary world of the day.

There were four rooms upstairs. One was K's room, and the room next to it was the dining-room, with a cheap hibachi that had a tin ash-pan. Next to that was T's room, and on the left of that was a room with

---

[324] Tsubouchi Shōyō.

[325] Saitō Ryokū.

[326] W is not clear, but in view of Doppo's rather old-fashioned habit of writing 'o' as 'wo' (as in 'wotome' for 'maiden') it could possibly be (W)Ozaki Kōyō. In 'Modern Novels' Katai refers to Doppo's lack of respect for Kōyō.

[327] Kōda Rohan.

[328] In Chapter Nineteen of 'Modern Novels' Katai makes a passing reference to "...Togawa Shūkotsu, who was at the time in charge of the Yomiuri's critical column." The time was the late 1890's and in view of the similarity of terminology it seems almost certain that 'A' is Togawa (see Note 250). He graduated from the Meiji Gakuin in 1891, and entered the Imperial University in 1895, though he did not graduate from here till 1898. The references below to Dante and Petrarca virtually confirm that it is Togawa, who was well-informed on Italian literature and history. However, the 'A' remains a mystery. It is possibly a reference to an unlisted pseudonym, but is more likely used rather like 'Mr. X' in English. (Katai uses 'A' like this in other works, but it is extremely confusing here.)

three beds, for foreigners who went there every summer to escape the heat. Both K's room and T's room had direct access to this bedroom.[329]

K was delighted when he saw the beds. "Oh, this is marvellous! Beds, with springs! What luxury-living! We must see the priest right away about getting permission to use them." Compared with T, K had class, and liked Western-style things. Anyway, they each used the bed nearest their own room, leaving a spare bed in the middle.

"This is marvellous!" said K again the first time they lay on them.

T started writing a long novel of several hundred pages, and when he grew weary he would take a midday rest on his bed. Then his mind would dwell on tasting that still untouched forbidden fruit. He was always going on about purity and the sanctity of love, but in his mind he would be thinking unwholesome thoughts about sweet pleasures and beautiful necklines and delicate flesh. "What, dozing again?!" K would say with a grin as he came into the bedroom, having heard T in there.

K never took midday naps. While T was dozing he usually went for a walk. With his stick, that he'd bought in the Ginza with Onobu..... And at night he always stayed up two or three hours later than T. T had his dreams and fantasies and impure thoughts, while K was never able to sleep without thinking of Onobu, who had left him the previous spring. K's pillow was surrounded by tangled memories from that sweet half-year, which he relived each night in his mind. And then, intruding into that beautiful and delicate web of bitter-sweet memories, would come the insistent, bestial sound of T's snores. K would sigh.

Sometimes tears stained his pillow. One day, amongst a collection of poems that T had, he came across a poem that ran:

> "Awake in the night,
> Longing for love,
> With the sound of tears
> Falling on my pillow:
> But no-one hears."

He was very moved, feeling that it described his own situation, and recited it over and over again. He'd remember it in the loneliness of the night, when on some occasions he stayed awake right through until the bells no longer rang to indicate the hour of night.

He could hear an unknown bird singing all night long.

---

[329] Katai's description may not be the clearest. Given the difficulty when one does not use a diagram, it is probably clearer to say that the upstairs floor contained four equal-sized rooms. Looked at from the front, ie. the river, Kunikida's room was front left, the dining room was front right, Tayama's room was rear right, and the bedroom was rear left. Every room had access to its two adjacent rooms. The stairs were outside, to the right of the dining room.

Once, in a conversation with some of the young priests at the temple, someone happened to mention the night-bird peculiar to that mountain area. "Ah, that's it!" said K. "That's the bird I hear, with that very loud and clear call. Yes that's it all right."

K was always woken up by T. And after waking up he always stayed in bed for a while. T would be waiting impatiently for him at the hibachi. By that time the breakfast soup — which an old lady brought from downstairs — would be ready, and so would the rice, and the kettle would be boiling furiously on the fire. Out in the garden the sun would be shining bright and cheerful onto the verandah.

When K got up he went straight away down the stairs, which were out through the room with the hibachi, and across to the bathhouse next to the huge kitchen. He'd wash his face in the clear, icy water flowing from the bamboo pipe, part his hair neatly, and then clatter energetically back up the stairs.

"I couldn't get to sleep last night. I was awake till two."

He'd sit himself down opposite T with some such remark. T played mother, K played father.

The fragrant aroma of hot tea, the smell of the breakfast soup, an array of teacups and rice-bowls and pickles and plates and dishes.... T would pick up his chopsticks impatiently, while K would carry on quietly drinking his tea.

Usually K would talk about some dream he'd had the previous night. He was a young man who dreamed the most extraordinary dreams. He'd have dreams of goldfish and women all mixed up, dreams of becoming famous, dreams of Hokkaidō, and always Onobu would be involved. He even had a dream in which he stabbed Onobu with a short sword. "It was THAT sword," he said, "the one that old man gave me. I stabbed her, and thought she was dead, but she kept on laughing and asking me to stab her again. There was no blood. It was just a dream, after all." He stood up and took out from its sheath the short sword he always had with him, staring at it. It was given to him as a keepsake by an ill-fated old man who had known people like Takasugi Shinsaku.[330] K would often take it out and stare quietly at it. It was an excellent, razor-sharp sword, some two and a half feet long in its red leather sheath. Sometimes K even took it with him on his walks.

T laughed too when K told him about his dream of the zoo moving house. "What a bizarre dream!" he said, as K recounted the details: "It wasn't an ordinary train, for people. The carriages were all open-topped.

---

[330] Takasugi Shinsaku (1839-1867), a Chōshū Clan samurai prominent in the anti-foreign movement of the late Edo period.

Now that's interesting, isn't it! The monkeys and tigers and bears were all riding happily together. And I remember seeing the elephant's huge trunk. The birds were neatly in their cages, too. And they all passed by, in a long line. What a weird dream!''

After breakfast they talked for a while and then T went off to his room. K stayed sitting there alone next to the hibachi, staring at the hills outside.

Before moving upstairs they had first of all put their desks in the walkway encircling the main building of the temple, and this had been their base for several days. The old priest — a man in his mid-fifties — had noticed the location which the young pair had chosen to establish themselves in.[331] ''Ahem, ahem'' — it was a habit of his to keep clearing his throat — ''I see you appear to have found a place for yourselves. It might be all right for you, for a while. If there's anything you need, please don't hesitate to let me know, T. I'm very busy with temple business at the moment, I'm afraid, but I hope to be able to look after you a bit better before too long.'' From time to time he came along to their desks to find out what they were doing. ''Oh you're writing for a newspaper? These manuscripts are going to be published in that newspaper?.....That's quite something!'' He'd then go off to the priest's quarters, dressed in his priest's robes. When he heard about K's once having been a Christian he remarked, in very cheerful fashion: ''There's nothing at all wrong with Christian priests.... I've no objections to them.... Religions are all the same, they all have the same spirit to them. Putting your hands together to Buddha is no different from the Christian amen. No, I've no objections at all.''

T and K knew that the old priest liked his saké, so they'd brought along a cask of Sawa no Tsuru for him as a present from Tōkyō.[332] The large round package had been something of a nuisance on the train, but when they saw the look of delight on the priest's face they both felt it was worth the trouble. T had also brought along a tap for the cask. ''My word, you've even brought a tap! It really is very kind of you, and I'm very grateful,'' he said, as he broke into a hearty laugh. T had been friends with him for some time, and K too took to him immediately.

''He's a decent old sort!'' said K cheerfully, thinking to himself that it would be by no means unpleasant if they stayed there for rather a long time.

K also found the spartan life of a mountain temple rather refreshing. To recover from the terrible wounds he had received from Onobu he had

[331] The old priest was a Sugawara Saneharu (dates unclear).

[332] Sawa no Tsuru is a well-known brand of saké.

spent some six months in Kyōto and then a similar period in the suburbs of Tōkyō.[333] In the latter case he had been living with his brother, but he had still been terribly lonely. Some evenings he'd be convinced that Onobu would come back to him in tears, to plead for forgiveness. He'd get up and open the rain-shutters to see, even when it was only the wind rattling them. Sometimes he'd work himself up into a dreadful state of rage and desperation, and even talk about how he'd never recover from his misery and how the only thing to do was to go and kill that fickle woman and then turn the sword on himself. It was at times like this that his friendship with T was strengthened. Indeed, it was through this tragic love-affair of his that he and T became such good friends. T wasn't particularly bent on playing the role of comforter, but nevertheless he was able to go some way towards alleviating the pain of K's wounds. K also found the literature-centred life of a poverty-stricken young man rather appealing. He too had reached a point in his life when he had to try out his talents. It was in order to settle himself down and think quietly that he had agreed to go with T to that mountain temple.

As soon as they arrived they bought food and other necessities. They bought sugar, cake, and — first and foremost — dried bonito. If they had nothing else to eat with their rice, they could always cut up some dried bonito. And so it was that upon the day of their arrival they had gone into town and bought a dried bonito that was, by the standards of impoverished young writers, large and expensive. They gloated to themselves that now they needn't worry about anything else to go with their rice. Leading a life of luxury and abundance had its good points, but so too did a life of frugality — at least, as students of literature, K and T were able to view things in such a way. "It'll be interesting to see just how cheaply we can manage to live," they told each other, and decided to write down all their expenses in the ruled notebook that T had brought along. K, who had read people like Carlyle and Emerson, came out with the English expression 'Plain living, high thinking'.[334] He was fond of reading Wordsworth, and Matthew Arnold's Wordsworth selection never left his side.

T, on the other hand, was never without his collection of Heine's poetry, which was strange for a believer in the holiness of love. That is to say, it was strange that his favourite reading should be the poetry of a man who lived out his final years in Paris in the company of a 'fallen' woman, a poet of poignancy and irony, a poet closer to the Devil than to God, a poet of carnal passion. But then, he was probably unable to

---

[333] In fact, Doppo was only in Kyōto from June 4th-August 26th, 1896.
[334] Given in English.

appreciate the poet's darker side, and was attracted merely by the pearl-like verses of love. So it was that, there in that little mountain temple, the curious mixing occurred of that Rydal poet on the one hand, extolling peaceful nature, and the fiery passion on the other of a poet consumed with sexual desire. K read Wordsworth to T. T read Heine to K.

The life of the old priest, whose lot it was to be in such a situation, was also rather interesting. It was not without reason that K and T thought highly of him. Until his early thirties he had tasted to the full life's sorrows and bitternesses, and its pleasures and pains. He had then experienced a religious awakening, had gone off in the company of his predecessor at the temple, who just happened to have gone preaching in that part of the country, and had then undergone numerous ascetic experiences. He had suffered the 'austerity of the winter peaks' — said to be one of the severest of the penances — and gone through the 'offering of flowers', as well as spending three hard years living alone in the Hall of Buddha. Even now he still refrained from eating meat.

The day after their arrival the bonito, which they been so careful to buy, went missing. They couldn't find it anywhere, and could only conclude that a cat had taken it. "Yes," said K, "now I come to think about it I do remember seeing a big stray around here, only a short while ago." T had also seen it somewhere around. They both gave a wry smile, and then K collapsed in a fit of laughter. The next time they bought bonito they made a point of buying two small fillets, which for safety's sake they hid away separately in their desk drawers. One day T caught sight of the stray cat and chased it off, with a few stones to help it on its way. They laughed when they talked about it.

When the old priest opened the saké they'd brought he invited them to join him, and served up some noodles too. There was a little hearth there, surrounded by a variety of battered old utensils. He took the saké-pourer out from the kettle and offered some to the young pair, neither of whom were strong drinkers.

"Well if you've got a sweet tooth we can provide something for that too!" he said with a grin, flapping his sleeves and bringing out some red and white beanjam buns, still wrapped, which he had received at a memorial service. "Ah, this is more my sort of thing," said K as he took one.

Just then, without so much as an 'Excuse me', a wrinkled old lady in her sixties came in, wearing dirty breeches and looking the epitome of naturalness, primitiveness, simplicity, and unpretentiousness, and shovelled up some burnt embers. "They're still warm," said the priest, and took the kettle from the centre of the hearth so that she could empty the shovelful of embers there. "The people from Ishimachi came," she said as she emptied her shovel. "Did you meet them?"

"The people from Ishimachi?" queried the priest, suddenly looking up with an expression of concentration on his face. "That would be Hattori's lot. Yes, I did meet them."

"Oh, you did? Well, that's all right, then. They were asking where you were." She gave an indescribable, wrinkly grin as she spoke, and then took her bent old frame off to the kitchen. She was the old lady who was cooking for K and T.

K had made the occasional remark like 'She's a pleasant old lady," and "I just can't understand anything she says." Having been born in the Chūgoku region [sic], in the west of Japan, it was hardly surprising that K had difficulty understanding unadulterated slang from the Tōhoku region, in the north-east of the country.[335] In fact, neither K nor T had ever before encountered such a truly rustic old lady.

"And yet," said K, "even an old lady like that has the same blood, the same heart as we ourselves."

"It really makes you think about living beings, about primitive beings unaffected by civilisation," replied T. "I've never seen even a sculpture of anything quite like her."

"That's very true. That face is indescribable. I'd like to show it to a sculptor. Those deep wrinkles are marvellous. And the way she smiles! It's all so unaffected. I get the impression that she's like that not because she doesn't know what worry is, but because she's had SO MUCH worry. I'd love to have a sculpture of her. But sculptors nowadays are just hopeless!"

With this remark K went on to talk about a sculptor that he knew.

"I've just been talking to that old lady," said K one day.

"Where?"

"She was out behind the temple, weeding. She really is a strange old lady, the sort you might expect to read about in some myth. She's also got a quite sense of humour, you know."

"Oh?"

"She calls the priest 'the old bonze', and makes fun of the way he clears his throat. She's a lively old soul all right!"

"Really?"

"It's a pity I can't properly understand what she says. I'm sure it'd be fascinating if I could, but unfortunately I still can't make out more

---

[335] In view of the close friendship between Katai and Doppo it is quite astonishing that Katai should make a mistake about Doppo's birthplace. Doppo was actually born in Chiba Prefecture, though he did live in western Japan from the age of four to fifteen.

than half.... She says she's sixty-five, but she's certainly tough for her age."

T had been to the temple a couple of times before, so he already knew something about the old lady. She'd been born in a village a few miles from town, and her family had once been wealthy tailors. However, her mother had led a wanton life and ruined the family. T told K about it. He also told him about her daughter, who was married to a carpenter in the nearby village of R and who came to chat with the old lady from time to time. "She kept saying her daughter was coming," said T, "and I was wondering what she'd be like, but she turned out to be an old lady too, in her forties!" K laughed.

One night, when the moon was irresistible, K and T went off for a walk. It was now the height of spring in the hills. Even the flowers in the dark cryptomeria woods were bathed in light. As they walked along they talked earnestly about life, and love, and religion, and faith. T was always stirred by K's emotive words, and moved by the sincerity of his feelings, even though he did at times think that he was getting too carried away by K's eloquence. K brought up such issues as the Sermon on the Mount from the Bible.

K's emotions were always fundamentally governed by his sadness at parting with his wife, but T still didn't fully understand this. T's idea of relations between men and women did not extend to the physical, and whenever the conversation turned to this aspect he looked away, feeling as if his own sacred purity had been defiled.

They walked as far as the bridge on the edge of town. The river tumbling down to the plain was lit up beautifully by the moonlight. Two foreigners walking by became an unusual poetic inspiration to them, and they recited some poems they had written.

Eventually they headed back to the temple, while discussing such things as the impoverished music teacher in Tolstoi's 'Lucerne'. The evening dew glistened beautifully on the evergreen trees in the temple garden. The moonlight had still not reached down to the river where it flowed through the deep ravine at the base of the cliff. They made their way towards the kitchen door.

Although the moon was bright the shōji of the kitchen door glowed a rich red through the relative darkness of the thickly wooded garden, thanks to the fire burning inside. K pointed to the shōji.

"Look!"

Silhouetted against the shōji they could see the old woman, hair dishevelled like a broomhead and clearly muttering something to herself. She was busy attending to the fire in the kitchen hearth, as usual.

"It makes her look just like some dreadful old witch!" laughed K. "You'd run a mile if you came across her in the middle of the night in some lonely mountain hut!"

T laughed too as he looked at the silhouette.

They went in and up to the hearth where the old woman was sitting. "Oh dear, oh dear me..." she said, looking up, her wrinkled face reddened by the firelight.

"What's the matter?" asked T.

"Oh dear, oh dear me," she said again, her voice full of emotion. "When you come back, T, you make me feel as if my young lad's come back to me. If only he COULD come back, like you have. But it's no good wishing, he's in the ground now!" Tears rolled down her wrinkled old face.

"What's happened?"

"It's just that I remembered my young lad, the one in the ground. He was just the same age as you."

"He's dead, then?"

"Yes, dead and gone. He went to Y and became a policeman, and he had a sword, and he was so dashing..... He came to see me last winter, but he won't be coming again. Not now he's in the ground.....Oh dear, oh dear, oh dear...."

"Did he die of illness?"

"It was all so sudden, of something called pneumonia. I didn't even have a chance to see him. I did so much want to see him for a last time, but there was no chance, it was so quick. I think of him whenever I see you."

"You've still got your eldest?"

"Oh, Jinroku's hopeless. It was my young lad I was looking to depend on! Oh dear, dear, dear...."

She threw some sticks on the fire, which blazed up. Steam rose from something bubbling in the big pot hanging on the hook.

"It's soy bean. The old bonze asked me to get it ready."

"Oh, beans?!" K grinned.

They took some embers upstairs, lit the lamp, and sat talking across the hibachi. The more they thought about it, the vaster human life seemed to them....the stranger.... the sadder.... particularly for young people like them, who were setting out to take their places in that life. They talked on. They talked about Turgenev's novels, about Stern's Eric, about Symond's 'Italian Journey', and still they had more to talk about.[336] "To think that an old lady like that is here in the mountains,

[336] Eric is the protagonist of Ōgai's 1890 translation of Stern, 'Ukiyo no Nami' (see Note 245). Symond's 'Italian Journey' is possibly a reference to his 'Sketches in Italy and Greece' (1874).

thinking about her dead son, weeping tears into the ashes of the hearth,'' said K, almost overcome with emotion. And then there were people like the old priest, sleeping soundly after his saké. And there were young people like K and T, sleepless in the moonlight. There were people voyaging across distant seas, standing lonely on some deck. There were people like Rudin, who had forsaken love and its torments. There were people like the talented Gesa, who went insane after a broken love affair[337].......K rested his head in his hands, pondering the question of human life, his bright young eyes glistening moistly. T sat in silence, a sad expression on his face. They sat opposite each other like this for some considerable time.

The moon shone brightly out in the garden.

T was writing in his diary.

''The river that flows ceaselessly past the temple will eventually reach the sea, the vast sea, the sea of life..... But what of me, of my being? The eternal sound of flowing water.... It will still be here in ten years, a hundred years, a thousand years. We will die, and our children will die, and our children's children will die, but it will still be there, flowing on and making the same sound. Who could possibly realise this without realising the vastness of life?''

But such sentimental, emotional, youthful observations were not all that the diary contained. There were also train fares, and expenses, and a drawing of the old lady. That little book also contained, inside its yellow covers, a number of poems, and ideas for novels arranged in sections such as 'young love', 'dogs and people', and 'short swords'. T was in the process of writing a long novel about a young man's disappointment in love. The luckless young man was a painter, and to heal his wounds he took himself off to a lakeside cottage near his home town, his mind full of a mixture of thoughts of creativity on the one hand and the girl on the other. The diary contained considerably detailed ideas about the last part. Sometimes T took his diary to his seat by the hibachi, and read out his ideas or his poems to K. But when K tried to take a look at the diary he quickly drew it back out of his reach. Under no circumstances would he show it to K.

K, for his part, kept a very long diary, which was entitled 'The A- Diary'.[338] He had written two or three volumes of this diary even

---

[337] Gesa is the protagonist of Ōgai's 1890 translation of Schubin, 'Umoregi' (see Note 243).

[338] 'Azamukazaru no Ki' (Honest Diary). The fullest version of this work was published after Doppo's death by Sakura Shobō (two parts, October 1908 and January 1909), but parts were published variously from March 1895 on. The diary started from February 3rd 1893.

before he'd gone to live in the Tōkyō suburbs. Thought followed thought, anguish followed anguish. There was virtually nothing he had seen or felt which did not appear in those pages. He often showed it to T.

The entries concerning his love affair, and his disappointment in it, were particularly detailed. "No, you mustn't look at that bit!" he would say, and cover up a bit that T had started to read.

Whereas T's diary was full of nothing but fancy, K's diary was full of painful facts and sad records. There were always a couple of volumes of this diary on K's desk, along with poetry collections and novels. He went through them to try and find material for that first work that he wanted to write, and they brought back memories of the past. Much of his time was spent in musing over the bitter-sweet facts of love that the diary contained. "It's all over now. It's all history," he'd keep telling himself.

K wrote in his diary:

"An old lady thinking about her son, an old priest sleeping off his saké, two young men, and outside, as always, the river flowing through the gorge..... My suffering in love is now a thing of the past. My having wanted to kill her and then myself too is now a thing of the past. Everything's in the past. I am now here alone in this room. It's a fact that I am here, a definite fact of existence. But who knows where I'll be tomorrow, or next year? My friend's already asleep, and that unknown bird is singing away, to comfort me in the night."

He put down his pen, lost in thought. The lamp shone bright on his cheeks, flushed with the blood of youth. The sword lay at his side.

"Do you ALWAYS have a debate after meals?!"

The priest spoke with a deliberate seriousness. They all had to laugh.

"Debates are very good things, you know," answered K with a grin.

"I suppose it does look a bit funny." T was grinning too.

They did indeed always talk about something or other after their meals. The talk would become a discussion, and then develop into a heated exchange of views. They were always discussing big issues like love, and religion, and literature, and death.

"If that's all the guts you've got you'd be better off killing yourself. Go on! Kill yourself! Right now, in front of me! There's a sword right here!"

K would get really worked up.

"When I die.... When I die...." T was struggling to get his words out. "When I die, I'll die by myself! I won't need your help! You should worry about yourself, and not about me. Say what you like, I've still got my chastity. I haven't had it despoiled like you!" T wasn't going to be beaten.

Before they'd moved upstairs, while they were still encamped down on the walkway, their discussions had not been so heated. After their move, however, it became a common occurrence. K didn't agree at all with T's views, which were full of pessimism and chastity. Or rather, it would be truer to say that he felt a duty to shatter such fanciful views. T, meanwhile, disliked K's familiarity with life's impurity, with impure female flesh. It would have been better if K hadn't made so much of those less than praiseworthy experiences, but at the least excuse he trotted them out with a superior air. T always got upset over K's line of argument, which was that things were facts because he himself had experienced them, and that because they were facts they were also truths. T always asserted: "You can't judge MY experiences in terms of YOUR experiences. I have my own experiences. They're MY experiences, that I alone experience!"

K tried to imagine what facts did form the basis for T's thoughts and theories. He also got impatient with T, T with his conventional way of thinking, T with whom he could not discuss with real frankness the torments he had suffered in love or over female flesh. K did wonder if T wasn't in love with that niece of his, with whom it would be impossible for him to form a relationship.[339] T often read him poems he had written about her. K had also seen her in T's house. She was light in complexion, with full cheeks.

"Thoughts only become factual truths when put into practice. Why don't you try putting them into practice? Why don't you try it and see what happens? At least some truths would result from it." K was always giving this sort of advice to T. It wasn't that T didn't understand his point, and it wasn't that he didn't believe the bit about truths, it was just that he always maintained that he wanted to act more prudently, more earnestly than K when it came to putting things into practice.

"Do you mean to say that my affair wasn't in earnest?! If that's what you mean, then say so! How on earth can it have been anything other than in earnest, when I've even contemplated death over it?!" K was indignant.

The priest sometimes overheard these artless confrontations between the two young men, and feared that things were getting out of hand and developing into a real argument. He'd go out into the garden to see what was happening. But they'd soon be laughing again. "Oh, it's not an

[339] Ai(ko), born 1877, was the eldest daughter of Katai's eldest sister Itsu (1858-1883, who married the Ishii Osamu of Note 39). In May 1895 she had married Momiyama Takeshirō (b. 1866), a naval paymaster, and had moved with him to Yokusuka in Kanagawa Prefecture. Aiko was frequently the model for early works of Katai's, and Katai's admitted unconsummated love for her forms an interesting contrast (to which Katai himself has referred in other memoirs) with Tōson's love for his niece Komako (see notes to later section 'Crisis at Forty').

argument at all. They're having a debate!'' he'd say knowingly to himself.

''It must look a bit funny.''

K always seemed to remember this remark with amusement whenever they started their discussions.

''Isn't it terrible! The priest's convinced we behave like this just to help digest our meals! And all the time we're actually having serious discussions about life and love....''

''True,'' said T, who was laughing too.

It was raining. They had their umbrellas up, and were walking past a long line of stone statues of Jizō.

The mountain torrent was tumbling along beside them with awesome force, seething as it raced over jumbled rocks. Amongst the clumps of grass on the far bank red wild-azaleas and yellow wild-roses were displaying their spring attire.

To reach that spot they had crossed a bridge, passed through a little mountain hamlet, and then gone past a house with a tub outside full of large red sprays of the azaleas.

Every now and again they had stopped along the way to gaze at the picturesque mountain stream with its foaming white spray and deep blue eddies. ''Incredible!'' they kept saying to each other. Presently they came to the rows of stone statues.

Some had parts of the head missing, others were lacking the entire upper part of the body. Some had no nose, others had no hands. All were weatherbeaten, and covered with dark green moss.

One statue was particularly striking. It sat there with a quiet composure, arms folded.

''I can't believe it's only stone,'' said K, looking deeply moved. ''No, I can't believe it's only stone, with no flesh or blood. I'm sure there has to be human blood flowing through it. There just has to be.''

He noticed that T was silent.

''It's the shape of mankind,'' he continued, ''of thousands of years of mankind, of countless generations of mankind. We must look upon it as man's very embodiment, formed from a vast accumulation of suffering and torment, of anguish over love and death and life. It's the shape of man from the distant past, and of man in the present, and of man in the far-off future. It is the symbol of mankind.''

''True,'' said T with a pensive look on his face.

''Don't you just feel the vastness of human life? Here we have stones in the shape of man. With moss on them. With rain falling on them, the rain of eternity. With infinite raindrops trickling down their heads, and off their noses.'' They walked on, looking at each statue in turn. ''They've all borne the same burden of life as we ourselves. They've all suffered in the same way. When you really think about it, it leaves you at a loss for words.''

T was forced to agree with him. It was true that he often argued with K — he was a different person, so he necessarily had different opinions — but in this particular observation of K's he couldn't help feeling a chord being struck deep within him.

''True. We soon live out our mortal lives, and then we end up like these stones, as part of man's history. It makes you realise just how pathetic our petty interests and squabbles are.''

''Indeed. When you think along those lines you can sense deep down the flow of life. What we call death isn't really death, and what we call life isn't really life. Even our very act of walking here has a definite significance. They say that all men are brothers, and that is so very true, regardless of time and place. We're all part of the same mankind.''

As he spoke K seemed overcome by his emotions, and fondled the rain-soaked head of one of the statues.

''I have these intense feelings inside me,'' said K as they walked on. ''I talked about them to Onobu, but she didn't understand at all. That was a great pity. I suppose some of it was my fault, but whatever the case, it upsets me a lot to think about it.''

T said nothing. They walked on in silence. The rain streamed down. Raindrops pattered down onto their umbrellas as they passed beneath the trees.

T was sitting by the hearth talking with the old lady when K came back grinning from one of his walks, brandishing his walking-stick as usual.

Every time he went for a walk K would come back with some tale or other to tell. There'd be an account of all the girls he'd seen at a local sewing-instructress' house, or of how he'd spotted the cook of the N Hotel standing in the shadow of the hotel wall chatting up some girl in her early twenties, or of a cleverly made model of a waterwheel he'd seen by the little stream outside the hut where the rickshawmen gathered.[340] K certainly seemed to find the town of N as full of interest as that town of S in distant Kyūshū, where he once used to live.[341]

K came and sat next to them, and spoke to the old lady.

''Do you know that girl at the S Temple?''[342]

---

[340] The N Hotel is the Nikkō Hotel.

[341] N is Nikkō, S is Saeki (Saiki) in Oita Prefecture, Kyūshū. Doppo taught in Saeki from September 1893-August 1894.

[342] The Shakadō [Temple].

"The S Temple?" She thought for a moment. "Ah yes, I know the girl you mean."

"Well, who is she?"

"Why on earth do you ask?! She's the schoolteacher's daughter."

"Not the caretaker's?"

"No, the caretaker's somewhere else. It's the schoolteacher who's living there. He's renting it."

K had just visited a temple famous for the grave of a loyal retainer who had followed his lord in death. Behind the temple was a house with a nice sunny verandah, where a girl of about nineteen or twenty was sitting sewing. She had her hair done up in the popular teenage 'momoware' style, and a nice white neck. She was sitting there quietly, bent over her sewing. K had gone forwards a few steps as if to take a closer look at the weeping cherry that was in blossom there, and she had looked up in surprise at the sound of his footsteps. She'd blushed as she looked towards him. She was exceptionally beautiful.

Even a little incident like that was a source of interest to the young men. From then on K often said, as he was about to set off grinning on one of his walks, "I might just perhaps head towards the S Temple." And the old lady would retort, also with a grin on her face, "He wouldn't be so keen on all these walks if it wasn't for the girls along the way!"

Apparently, the third time he went there the girl deliberately put on her geta, came down from the verandah, and walked a few steps towards him, smiling. "It looks as though things are all set for a tailor-made romance," said K to T. "Now prepare yourself, because you're going to have to play the part of one of those soldiers in Maupassant's 'Little Soldiers'."[343]

These stories of K's rather started to worry T, who rarely went for a walk of late and spent his time instead working steadily away at his long novel. It may just have been because he was paying particular attention to them, but it seemed to him that K's walks were increasing in frequency. There were not a few times when he went into K's room only to find that he was out somewhere.

---

[343] 'Little Soldiers' ('Shōheisotsu') was Katai's translation of Maupassant's 1885 work 'Deux Soldats' (Two Soldiers), in which a young soldier kills himself after realising that his friend and fellow soldier has won the heart of the girl they were both courting. Katai translated the story in February 1898 — the first full translation into Japanese of a Maupassant work — but did not publish it as he was not satisfied with his own standard of translating. The honour of the first published Maupassant translation therefore went to Doppo, who published 'Itokuzu' (A Piece of String, 'La Ficelle') in the March 1898 issue of 'Kokumin no Tomo'. Both works came from the English translation 'The Odd Number' (see Note 350).

"It's rather interesting isn't it! Someone like you, who's already suffered disappointment in love, going off on walks to see a girl like that. It'd make a good short story." T would say such things to K in a light-hearted way, but actually he did have a dark suspicion, with K being K, that he might really have succeeded in winning the girl's affections and that he might be up to something. T sensed a dark, ugly spectre pass close by his heart.

"That's why it's hopeless. That's why he's neglecting his writing. He goes on about writing his first work, but we've been here three weeks now and he's still not been able to produce anything.[344] When you get too caught up in real life you lose your artistic inspiration." It was by telling himself such things that T, who was plugging away laboriously to the point where he was starting to grow weary of it all, was able to derive some measure of cold comfort. It depressed him to think that K's good looks were so attractive to women.

K was dozing, his hands clasped behind his head, looking worn out by all his troubles. T was thinking about how gloomy everything was in his own life. Back in Tōkyō was his brother's distressing household, where never a day passed without some unpleasant incident or other. What with the clashes between his brother and mother, and between his brother's wife and his mother, it was all too depressing to describe properly to anyone else.[345] It seemed particularly miserable when contrasted with the warm relationships in K's family. K had certainly never witnessed such ugly scenes in HIS family.

K was forever making comments that revealed the warmth and peacefulness of his family, such as "He's pretty good, my father," or "My brother and I often used to tease Mother just to see how she'd react," or "My brother's a really nice fellow, completely open and unaffected." It may have been embellished somewhat by his clever way with words, but nevertheless it was a fact that K's family were very different from T's miserable lot. T was so envious, so jealous of K's pleasant family situation, and indeed of the very circumstances permitting such

---

[344] As discussed earlier 'first work' is a rather vague term, meaning in this context 'first recognised prose work'. Doppo finished the manuscript of 'Gen Oji' (Old Man Gen) on May 17th, twenty-six days after their arrival at the temple. It was eventually published in August in Hakubunkan's 'Bungei Kurabu'.

[345] After losing his first wife Tomi in 1891 Miyato married Kawamura Koto (born 1876) in 1894. However, his mother Tetsu appears to have disliked Koto from the start. In March 1897 (just a month before Katai's trip to Nikkō) Koto had fallen asleep while breast-feeding their week-old son and had smothered the child to death. Tetsu was quick to seize the opportunity, to get Miyato to divorce Koto. The divorce took less than a month to obtain. (Miyato married for the third and final time in 1899, to Nagasaka Toshi [b. 1872].)

a happy situation in the first place. He went on to think about the arrogant faces of the authorities in the literary world, the detestable duplicity of the critics, the bad reviews his own works received, and in particular the annoying fact that certain new writers were, despite being the same age as T himself, pulling away right ahead of him and making a name for themselves. Chastity and art! These were the things he clung to.

On one occasion K invited a reluctant T for a walk. K felt like cheering him up a little, as he always seemed to be cooped up indoors looking out of sorts. Of late K had started to worry about T's health, and had even refrained from saying anything too nasty in their after-dinner discussions.

K had been to the barber's and was looking neat and spruce. T, by contrast, had deliberately and rather perversely let his hair grow long, and had also gone without shaving. The only thing sparkling about his miserable face was his sharp, staring eyes. "At least I LOOK like a writer!" he said to himself as he looked in the mirror.

It was no easy matter at all for K to get the extremely reluctant T to accompany him to the S Temple, but eventually he succeeded.

It was quiet there, and they could hear the birds singing. The weeping cherry was at the peak of its blossom, and looked like a mound of snow. The girl was there as usual on the sunny verandah, bent over her sewing and revealing her pretty white neck. A nightdress, with a red muslin collar, was out there drying.

"Watch! I'll make her look this way."

K gave a whistle.

"Stop! Stop! For heaven's sake stop!"

T stopped K from whistling again, a look of fear on his face.

"What's wrong?!"

"Stop it! If you whistle again I'm going back!"

T had started to walk off, so K refrained from whistling and merely grinned, with an expression as if to say "Stubborn so-and-so!"

K didn't feel any particular need to react when he saw that T had something of the air of a new writer about him, as well as a pride of sorts. He merely thought to himself that, although he hadn't produced anything yet, and although T was giving him looks of contempt as a result, he would soon give T a real surprise and show him what he was really capable of. "It's a waste of time writing long novels that'll never amount to anything," K reasoned.

"That womaniser!" was T's opinion of K. "That cantankerous boor!" was K's opinion of T.

It was now more than a month since they'd arrived at the temple. An old lady had already come round selling bracken from the hills, while red azaleas coloured the gorge in front of the temple. Following the priest's lead they had decided that a few cups of saké after their evening meal might be quite a nice thing, and had ordered a three-pint bottle from the local dealer, which they left by the hibachi. K would sometimes wave it around and make some cheerful remark like "There's still enough left for us to enjoy ourselves!". Nevertheless, it only took a tiny amount to send them soundly off to sleep with bright red faces.

"When we turn to drink, you can be our teacher," they said to the priest, telling him about their acquisition. The priest couldn't help laughing.

Hanging prominently from one of the beams in the temple was a votive tablet written in gratitude by a dignitary who had, in former humble times, been in the temple's care for a couple of years. "We're soon going to be famous, you know," K remarked to the priest, "and then it won't be a matter of a votive tablet like that. We'll become great benefactors, and build you a new main hall, won't we T!" "Of course!" replied the priest, sipping his saké. "I took that for granted."

From time to time they added up the expenses entered in the ruled notebook. Those that K had paid for were indicated by a triangle. "So if I give you twenty-five sen we'll be even, won't we?" said K, taking the money from his purse and counting it out with a flourish. "It's been cheap, hasn't it! Only just over two yen!"

K toyed with his purse, turning it inside out. "You know, this purse has seen thousands of coins come and go." It had brought back memories of Onobu. He had bought it when in her company in the Ginza, and had taken it with him when they went to Shiobara, and when he'd gone off to the forests of Hokkaidō thinking of her.

A couple of money orders arrived, for both K and T. K's was from the K Newspaper Company, and T's from the H Book Company.

"Hey," said K to T, "I'll give you one yen out of this. It's for those poems — I sent three off. Incredible, isn't it! Our masterpieces going for one yen each!"

T's money order was the manuscript-fee for a travelogue that he had recently written.[346] He received thirty sen per page. K got very upset over this. "It's disgraceful, compared with what the big names get! One yen thirty sen per page, or even two yen per page — that's what people like Kōyō and Rohan get! And as for R, writing that pathetic cow's drivel for the masses, in a Yoshiwara brothel[347] ..as for people like him

[346] 'The Hills of Nikkō in Spring' (see Note 322).
[347] Hirotsu Ryūrō.

getting one yen fifty sen per page, while we only get thirty sen... well, it's making fools of us! H Company won't pay me any more than twenty-five sen per page, but in the future, if they won't give me at least forty, then I won't sell!"

"Never mind the manuscript-fee," said T.

"But we have to mind! We can't just leave things as they are! We pour our very blood into the works we write. It's infinitely superior to the stuff the big names churn out late at night!" K was really in a rage. He had in fact managed to write that first work, which was some thirty pages. Two nights ago he had read it out to T. T liked some bits, and disliked others. K, who flattered himself that it was a masterpiece, couldn't understand T's reservations. The next day he had sent it off to O at the H Book Company.[348] "If YOUR manuscripts fetch thirty sen a page, I'll be most upset if I don't get at least forty for MINE!" he'd said to T, who was a little put out by the remark. "*I* don't write for money! I wouldn't like to think of novels in such pecuniary terms," T told himself, and plugged away at his long, long novel.

About every other day the old lady prepared a bath for them in the bathhouse downstairs. "The bath's ready when you are!" she'd inform them, coming into their rooms in her baggy old breeches.

"Hey, T, you go in first!" K would yell from his room.

To get to the bathhouse they went down the steps leading down from the verandah outside the room with the hibachi. Beside the bath was a square tank, which was always full of clear water trickling from the bamboo pipe. T and K both felt relaxed in the bath. Sometimes, when they were feeling particularly amicable, they went in together. The view from the bath was marvellous, with the green slopes of the mountain in front of the temple dotted with red azaleas. On rainy days, grey and white clouds seemed to form eddies as they floated upwards. It was a great pleasure for K and T to gaze at these scenes from the bath, so if the old lady forgot to prepare the bath K would promptly remind her.

After his bath K always combed his hair neatly. He kept a comb, a brush, pomade, and a little mirror in the drawer of the hibachi. T hadn't got a moustache yet, but K had a splendid one, which he kept tugging.

Whenever they talked about foreign literature, names like Tolstoi, Turgenev, Dostoevski, Zola, and Alphonse Daudet invariably cropped up. K particularly liked Turgenev. He had a copy of the English translation of 'Smoke', which was hard to obtain in those days, and was always talking about Irina. Most of all he liked Turgenev's approach to nature, especially as seen in parts of 'Sportsman's Diary', but he also liked

[348] That is, Otowa at Hakubunkan.

reading 'Smoke' for the reason that Irina's love affair was similar to his own affair with Onobu. "Women are all the same," he'd say. "They really are exactly like that. The 'smoke' part's marvellous." Of the final section, describing Irina's life with another man, he commented: "It may look as though it's there merely to pad out the novel, but in fact it's not padding at all. It's a very important part. It's human life — vast, incomprehensible human life." His comparison of the lives of Blonski and Levin in 'Anna Karenina' impressed T considerably. K was especially full of praise for the translation of 'Acia', which had come out while he was living in the Tōkyō suburbs.[349]

T also liked Russian literature, but tended to prefer French.

By those days a few people had started to talk about Maupassant, and T was very fond of a collection of his short stories which he had borrowed from M at the university.[350] It did however appear that that particular collection had selected, from amongst the great number of short stories by Maupassant, only those which made for wholesome reading. Accordingly T knew nothing of Maupassant's preoccupation with the tragic side of the affairs of men and women. He knew nothing of Maupassant's irony, and thought of him as a writer like Turgenev and Daudet, who wrote only of beautiful things. When they'd first arrived there he'd gone into town and discovered a shop selling second-hand Western books. The shop also sold magazines, so he'd gone in not expecting anything at all — in fact almost with an air of contempt — but to his amazement he spotted the name 'Maupassant'. He'd taken the book down from the shelves. It was 'Pierre et Jean'.[351] His heart raced. It was the last place on earth he'd expected to find anything like that.

"How much?" he asked the shopkeeper. "One yen fifty sen," came the reply. T didn't have enough money to buy it. Reluctantly he'd put it back.

T just couldn't get the name 'Maupassant' out of his mind. He brought it up at the least excuse. He even had a dream about buying the book and bringing it happily back with him. He visualised the name 'Maupassant' written in Japanese script. K wasn't as enthusiastic. In

[349] Katai gives 'Acia' in English but it is more commonly romanised from the Russian as 'Asya'. The translation is that by Futabatei (see Note 294).

[350] It is clear from the later section 'The Second Floor of Maruzen' that Katai obtained the work ('The Odd Number', thirteen stories translated by J. Sturges, published by Harper Bros., New York, 1889) from Ueda Bin, then at the Imperial University. The 'M' is therefore almost certainly a printing error resulting perhaps from a badly handwritten 'U'. Some editors of later versions of Tōkyō no Sanjūnen' have gone so far as to change the text to read 'U'. However, it is always remotely possible that Katai obtained the work not directly from Ueda but through Yanagita (Matsuoka) Kunio, who was also at university at the time.

[351] Given in French, though it was an English translation.

fact, not being familiar with such newly introduced Western writers, he made fun of T's desperation, punning on Maupassant's name. "Mōpassan? What's this 'Mō, bāsan'? You do keep going on about the old lady!"[352] Whenever he went for a walk to town T always looked in the bookshop. "It's still there! I do hope no-one buys it. If only they hang on to it till I get some money!"

"Was the object of your desires still there?" K would ask when he got back.

And when K himself came back from town, the first thing T would ask him would be "Is it still there?"

"Yes, yes, still there."

"I do hope they don't sell it."

"Don't worry. No-one would buy a book like that."

Nevertheless T did worry. He never spoke without mentioning Maupassant.

It was the day he received his travelogue fee from the H Book Company. It wasn't much of a fee, but nevertheless T's first thought was to use it to buy that book. He cashed the order at the main post-office in the centre of town, then hurried off to the bookshop. It was with a wildly beating heart that he bought the book.

It was a typical French-style book with a yellow cover, and still in good condition. It looked as though some foreigner had left it there on an excursion. T spotted an English-looking name written at the front.

"I've bought it! I've bought it!"

He went into K's room and waved the book under his nose.

"So, you finally got to buy it?!"

K grinned, and took a look at it. His attention was caught by a picture it had of a man and woman kissing. "This is nice. It brings back memories."

T really did seem to treat the book as if it were his girlfriend, and never let it out of his sight. When he wasn't writing, he was sure to be reading it, at his desk, or by the hibachi, or outside on the sunny lawn.

"Is it interesting?" K asked him.

"Very. The psychological depiction's excellent."

But despite his words T was unable to derive from the work the same pleasure as when he had read those wholesome short stories. Not knowing anything about relationships between men and women he failed to understand the terrible suffering of Pierre and Jean. Relationships both spiritual and physical, women's deceitfulness towards men, the life of a coquette, two men with one woman, or one woman with two men — how

[352] 'Mō' means 'now' and 'bāsan' means 'old lady'.

could T be expected to understand such things? Even K may have been unable to understand them. And yet, T would make remarks to K such as "It's very interesting indeed. It's a masterpiece."

K did finally sell his first work, for twenty-five sen a page. It may well have sold because it was a convenient magazine length. No doubt too the editor thought it was interestingly different from the stereotyped works of the G-sha. "So I ended up with twenty-five sen a page after all! Disgraceful! I'll have to say something to them about this!" But despite such remarks K looked rather pleased, since he had been worried whether he'd be able to sell the work at all.

T listened with some amusement.

A few days later T also received a small money order, for some juvenile thing he'd written. It was the end of the month so they used it to pay their various bills — though these were of no great consequence — at the saké shop, rice shop, and charcoal shop. They did discuss a little present for the priest, too. "We should get him something when we leave," said K, "and that won't be for a few weeks yet." T agreed.

K still paid for some things, T for others. T punctiliously recorded even the smallest item of expenditure in his notebook and ensured that everything balanced out just so, which K thought to be just too much trouble.[353] "What's it matter, a few sen?!" he'd say. "But accounts are accounts!" T would reply.

Their total expenses came to four yen eighty-five sen, which meant that for the month they had each spent two yen forty-two sen five rin. "It's been ridiculously cheap!" said K with a chuckle. "It's as though we've come here expressly to save money. We've got money to spare!"

So it was that they started talking about going to Lake T and U Spa.[354] T had been there a number of times before, but K was new to the area and had never travelled to any such spots.

"If we're careful with the money it shouldn't cost us too much," said K enthusiastically. "It's about fifteen miles to Lake T, so we can walk there. Then we've got to have lunch — and that won't be too expensive if we avoid the sort of places the sedan set go to — and then we can continue walking.[355] All we have to pay for is accommodation. Let's go!"

---

[353] Though this must actually have happened, Tayama's 'punctilious recording' is totally contrary to his general lack of attention to detail. Without being unkind to Katai, it might be said that it was only in matters financial that he was 'punctilious'.

[354] Lake Chūzenji (Tyūzenzi) and Yumoto (Umoto) Onsen, about fifteen and eighteen miles respectively to the west of Nikkō.

[355] Those who were not walking would mostly be in sedan chairs, as rickshaws were rare (see Note 203). There were also a few bicycles and horses.

T too wanted to go, but he also wanted to get on with the novel he was writing.

It was afternoon. K and T were standing in the temple garden.

In front of them lay nature in all its vastness, full of beautiful colours and delicate, intricate variety. They often gazed out at those rugged hills, but today the view seemed exceptionally good. Perhaps it was because of the clouds, or the action of the sunlight streaming through the air. Overhead were patches of the blue sky of early summer, and clouds floating up from the hills in a variety of shapes, sometimes like smoke, sometimes like fabulous monsters, or islands in a sea. As the sunshine played on these drifting shapes it created an atmosphere of extraordinary freshness.

"What a vast thing nature is!"

K seemed overcome by emotion.

The clouds changed with infinite variety, and the sunlight too was in constant movement.

"No human being could ever produce a single one of these scenes," said K. "Compared with nature, man is quite pathetic. He just can't compete."

"True."

"Hey, what's that cloud over there — that bright bit? It's Mount N, isn't it? And isn't that the foot of Mount O?"[356]

K had been staring at the hills. Suddenly he seemed unable to refrain any longer from going for a closer look at the storehouse of nature's beauty there. "Well?! Why don't we go tomorrow?!"

"Hmmm...."

"You can write your novel when we get back, can't you?! Let's go!"

"It would be nice to go....."

"So let's do it, and not just talk about it. If we dither about we'll end up frittering away the money we've saved. Come on, let's go!"

"I wonder if we should. After all....."

"Well, I'VE decided to go! I'm setting off tomorrow!"

T fell in line. They prepared to face up to that vast and beautiful nature.

When he heard of their plans the priest made some vinegared rice-rolls for them, wrapped in bamboo. He also took down from the wall a favourite gourd which he'd bought at a night-market in Kyōto, when he'd gone there sightseeing, and sorted out a pourer as well. K asked him

---

[356] Mounts Nantai(san) and Omanago(san).

what he was doing. "When you go into the hills," he replied, "this is a must. It tastes completely different, you know, and it's no trouble for you to take something like this along. I've still gots lots of that saké left that you brought from Tōkyō, so please do take this with you." The priest insisted that they took the gourd, full of saké, and also wrapped up a cup for them.

Presently K stood in the doorway in straw sandals and leggings, dangling the gourd from his shoulder. He was waiting for T to finish getting ready. The priest and the old lady were there too.

"I look like a complete boozer!" said K.

The priest grinned. "Don't make such a fuss! You'll find it makes your trip a lot more enjoyable."

The saké sloshed around in the gourd as they walked. They were both full of the joy of life. In their minds there were now none of the gloomy thoughts there had been when K had stared at his sword late at night and wondered whether he should choose life or death, or when T, plagued by terrible spiritual and physical torments, had also on one occasion contemplated doing away with himself. Now, they were as happy as larks.

The first time they opened the priest's gourd was when they were sitting on the rocks at the W Falls Gorge, which was a little gloomy though not entirely shut off from the pleasant sunshine.[357] With much rustling K took out from his pocket the saké cup, which the priest had wrapped in paper, and handed it to T. "This is unusual," he said, and poured some saké from the gourd. However, they only drank one or two cupfuls. The gorge was full of red and white and yellow, the colours of the wild-azaleas and wild-roses and perillas.[358]

Everywhere along their route they were struck by the appearance of nature. Around midday they climbed the steep slope of F from the N Teashop and headed up to the flat expanse of O.[359] The white birches and beeches made K think of Hokkaidō, and nature, and Onobu. By the time they reached the awesome sight of the famed K Falls he looked decidedly ill, in a state of considerable distress.[360] In those days there was no safety-fence at the top of the falls. Countless cryptic youthful thoughts

---

[357] (W)Urami-no-taki [Falls].

[358] Katai appears to have mistaken his plants here. 'Mukona' (lit: 'bridegroom-flower') is an edible plant of the perilla family and blooms in autumn, not spring. The strange name derives from a legend in which a bridegroom from the capital married a country girl and was given nothing to eat but this plant.

[359] F is Fudōzaka, N Teashop is Nakano Chaya (lit: 'The Teashop along the Way'), O is Ōdaira.

[360] The Kegon Falls drop over three hundred feet from Lake Chūzenji at the head of the Daiyagawa. They are a famed tourist attraction.

had yet to be poured into the pool at their base.[361] K seemed drawn by the thrilling sight of the falls. "Hey, let's go to the edge," he said to T, forcing a path through the bamboo-grass and climbing down the little bank leading to the water's edge immediately above the drop.

"It's all right! We can get through!" he yelled back to T as he scrambled along clutching at branches and rocks.

They soon reached the mouth of the falls. They found a flat piece of ground between the rocks some three or four yards square, which they hadn't been able to see from a distance, and from here they could watch the water tumbling down with awesome force. "Incredible! If you went over the edge you'd get smashed to pieces in seconds!"

"Just one little effort is all it would take," said K. "This is the place to kill yourself!" It seemed as though the falls possessed some sort of mysterious power that was trying to lure him.

They got out the gourd again, and the vinegared rice-rolls. The saké flowed from the gourd into the cup. Fortunately they did not discuss death. Presently K took out from his pocket the proofs of their group's first poetry anthology.[362] One of the group had sent them from Tōkyō the previous day. K and T, both feeling a little merry after a couple of cups of saké, now recited the poems they had each contributed to the collection.

As they were about to set off K made a suggestion. "They say S of the 'Bungakukai' made an offering of Shakespeare at Ishiyamadera [Temple], so how about us sacrificing the proofs to the god of the falls, just to mark this occasion?"[363]

"Good idea!" said T.

As they threw the anthology into the falls they raised their hands in the air and yelled "Banzai!"

About an hour later they were walking along a winding road that every now and again offered glimpses of the mirror-like lake between the trees. To their young eyes everything seemed beautiful and attractive. They couldn't even pass a humble fisherman's cottage without making something out of it. They likened it to the scene in that work by their senior,

---

[361] Kegon Falls were, even by those days, famous for suicides (especially double 'love-suicides'), but shortly after the scene depicted here, in June 1903, an eighteen year old student named Fujimura Misao threw himself to his death after leaving carved in a tree-trunk a cryptic message indicating his disturbed state of mind. Fujimura was a student at an extremely prestigious institution, the Number One High School, and his death resulted in Kegon Falls becoming the favoured spot for intellectual suicides (Katai refers to this 'fashion' in his 1909 novel 'Country Teacher'). It is still a popular spot for suicides, with people travelling for hundreds of miles to kill themselves there. Ceremonies are held regularly to pray for the peace of the victims' souls.

[362] That is, 'Jojōshi' (see Note 298).

[363] Shimazaki Tōson is S; Ishiyamadera is in Ōtsu, Shiga Prefecture, near Lake Biwa.

Doctor O, and gave the cottage the name 'Hansel's House'.[364] They peopled it in their mind's eye with characters such as the mad Bavarian king and the ill-fated beautiful young woman. "So now we've established the location of the house of Hansel the fisherman," said K, pointing.

They trudged on, heads down, eyes fixed and staring.....K's mind was no doubt full of painful memories of Onobu, and he gradually fell silent, hardly saying a word by the time they reached the area of the R Falls.[365] He just plodded along with his head down. Presently they came to some open fields.

The spas deep in the mountains had only been open for a few days, and there were some here and there that still had their protective layer of rushes from the previous autumn. T and K went to the N Inn.[366]

It was still winter in that part of the mountains. There was no fresh greenery to be seen, and from a distance the woods of white birch seemed as if shrouded in white mist. The mountain cold was piercing. K, who had spent the last few miles wrapped silently in his memories, now spoke at last.

"It's still winter, isn't it! Spring's only got as far as the foothills."

However, the large vase in the alcove of the room at the inn contained some beautiful mountain rhododendrons. K stared at the delicate red flowers and remarked, with considerable feeling, "Marvellous, aren't they, these alpine flowers!"

"We still haven't got any hot water in this part of the building, so I'm afraid it'll mean a bit of a walk for you...." The clerk led them to an annex. They had already changed into padded yukata. The annex was for the exclusive use of foreigners during the summer, and there was a long gloomy corridor there and rooms with easy-chairs and wicker-chairs in them.

The clerk opened a door to the bathhouse, right at the back of the annex. They saw a room full of white steam.

"Oh, this is marvellous, marvellous! Just the thing you'd expect in a mountain spa!" K took off his yukata and, appearing to feel the cold, plunged into the hot bath.

Their relationship had had its share of ups and downs, but at that particular moment they felt nothing but friendship for each other. K looked upon T as his one real friend, and T looked upon K as a valued and

---

[364] The work is Ōgai's 'Utakata no Ki' (Record of a Bubble, August 1890, 'Shigaramizōshi'), which is set in Germany and treats a tragic love-affair. Hansel the fisherman is one of the characters in the work, as are the Bavarian king and the young woman mentioned below.

[365] Ryūzu-no-taki.

[366] The Nankan Inn.

respectworthy friend. They talked about this and that as they washed each other's backs as if they were brothers. Once again they talked about the vastness of nature, just as they had along the road. "It's lonely here, isn't it!" said K. "It makes you feel as if you've gone back into prehistoric times. It's so quiet — nothing but the sound of the water."

He strained his ears.

He was sprawled out with his head resting against the side of the bath, relaxing in the warm water. "Aah, this makes you forget everything — about the world, about literature, about the lot!"

"True," chimed in T.

T was the first to get up from the bath. He put on his padded yukata and walked out into the corridor. The door to one of the foreigners' rooms was open, so he casually went in. There was a table, wicker-chair, and a wall print, and on the table were two or three foreign novels, no doubt left there by some foreign guest after he'd finished reading them. T picked them up. They were by popular English novelists such as Anthony Hope, and Zangwell [sic], and William Black.[367]

K had just come out of the bath too, so T called him. "I'm in here!" K came into the room, his cheeks warmly flushed.

"Ah, a foreigner's room! So this is the sort of thing they stay in, is it?" He looked around. "What are those books? Novels some foreigner's left behind?"

"Look! This is the sort of thing they're reading. It seems that wherever you go you always find people reading this sort of mass-appeal stuff."

K flicked through one of the books. "What's this? A detective story?"

"Anthony Hope's not too bad, I suppose, but on the whole modern English literature's hopeless. It's out of touch with the ideology of the Continent, that's why."

K changed the subject. "But just think. These foreigners come even to mountain resorts like this! And while they're here they think about their homes and families. It's just like us going somewhere like the mountains of Switzerland." Then he added suddenly: "Hey, T! Why not really go?!"

"That'd be nice, wouldn't it!"

"If we did we could meet Daudet, and Zola, and Tolstoi — no, wait a moment, Daudet's dead, isn't he?![368] If only Turgenev were still alive.

[367] Katai gives these names in English. It is actually Zangwill, not Zangwell (Israel Zangwill, 1864-1926).

[368] Actually Daudet died December 13th 1897, more than six months later! His illness lasted for thirteen years, and he may well have been verging on death in May 1897, but it is more than likely that Katai has made an error of memory and that Doppo actually made this remark on a later occasion, or else phrased it differently.

I'd have done anything to get the chance to meet him."

"I'd still like to go, anyway."

"And we could meet women just like Irina and Marianna. They say that in places like Germany getting married and whatever costs a lot of money, so the Japanese studying over there always tend to do well with the girls. But by all accounts, if they *do* get engaged over there it can cause problems when they get back here."[369]

They went from one empty room to another. There was a large mirror in one of the rooms, and they looked at themselves in it — K with his flushed face and T with his unshaven, square-cut features. In one of the other rooms there was a visitors' book, with foreign names in it. T flicked through it. "There're a lot of American and English names, and some German, but it doesn't look as though any Russian or French people have been here," he said rather disconsolately.

They were surprised to see a thick mist outside, which had closed in without their realising. They both agreed, as they walked back to their room upstairs, that it was a very Russian-looking scene.

They had a little saké, and started another of their discussions. At one stage their voices were raised quite excitedly.

"Let's end the discussion! I'm going to the bath again," said K, leaving the room. T stayed behind, feeling very lonely.

He could hear a young woman reading aloud in the next room. However, he was too tired to be able to pay much attention, and fell soundly asleep.

When they got up the next morning T motioned with his chin towards the next room. "Did you know about next door? There's a girl there. She was reading something till late last night, and I heard her mention Kōyō and Rohan. It's a bit embarrassing to think that OUR discussion might have been heard next door."

"Who's she with?"

"Relax — I think it's only her mother! It sounds like her mother's come here for her health and that she's come with her. From her voice I'd say she was in her early twenties."

"Hmmm...."

"I'm pretty sure it was something of Kōyō's she was reading. Anyway, she was reading it till quite late."

From then on T paid particular attention to the next room, but didn't manage to catch sight of the girl.

---

[369] Marianna is a major female character in Turgenev's 'Virgin Soil', while Irina is, as Doppo discussed earlier, the heroine of 'Smoke'. It should be noted that 'Smoke' is set in Baden and not Russia. The comments about Japanese people having post-engagement problems is almost certainly a reference to Mori Ōgai's affair, as described in part in his 'Maihime' of 1890.

That morning, too, there was a slight mist about, and the area was very quiet. They could see the still, dark blue water of Lake U.[370]

K went off to the bath again, towel in hand, saying it was for a final time. When he came back to the room the first thing he said was: "She was there — the girl from next door! I got a really good look!" He told T how she'd followed him into the bath with her mother, hunching up her fair-skinned body. K also mentioned how he'd passed the time of day with her mother.

The Buds of New Ideology

The literature that had centred on Kōyō gradually felt the pressures of a new age, and new movements arose on all quarters. This started around 1895/6, and from that point on, till his death five or six years later, Kōyō waged constant war against these new movements.

If I remember correctly, the first group to show an anti-G-sha tendency was the Kokumin Bungaku group. Then there was Ōgai Gyoshi in Sendagi, who was advocating something that indirectly fostered anti-G-sha feelings in young people. In order to put Kōyō down the 'Kokumin no Tomo' critic, Hachimenrō Shujin, deliberately heaped excessive praise on Kawakami Bizan from Kōyō's own group.[371] There was also a strong spirit of opposition to the old authorities noticeable amongst the young Imperial University graduates. Takayama Chogyū was the most prominent of them in this respect.

The G-sha's power was still quite strong, though. Kōyō himself refrained from writing very much, but the group still had considerable solidarity, and there were also many young writers in the Sōsha — composed entirely of Kōyō's pupils — who were very talented although they may have lacked education.[372] So, all things considered, the world of fiction was still the domain of the G-sha. Chūgai's group over at Waseda was also, in the final analysis, under the control of the G-sha.

But naturally the new ideology and movements fostered by modern-minded senior writers like Ōgai and Futabatei could not be satisfied with the half-hearted, semi-frivolous literature of the G-sha. Through Germany and France new currents of thought from continental Europe came surging onto the shores of this remote Far Eastern island.

---

[370] Lake (Y)Uno(ko).

[371] Hachimenrō Shujin was a pseudonym of Miyazaki Koshoshi. Bizan was technically a Genyūsha member but gradually became opposed to Kōyō.

[372] 'Sōsha' (lit: The Sea-weed Group) was a group of Kōyō's younger pupils. Its four main figures were Yanagawa Shunyō, Izumi Kyōka, Oguri Fūyō, and Tokuda Shūsei. None of these four was a university graduate.

With his indomitable fighting spirit and his scholarship and reading Ōgai was ten or twenty years ahead of Kōyō. How Lermontov's Pechorin thrilled young students of literature![373] Even now, when you look through 'Moongrass' and 'Shade-grass', you can appreciate just how far behind the G-sha's literature was.[374] Sōsha writers too, like Fūyō and Shūsei, were given many new pointers by Ōgai's translations. Even the least influenced of these writers, Izumi Kyōka, wrote his 'Teriha Farce' with admiration for 'Impromptu Poet'.[375]

I can well imagine how Kōyō must have suffered admidst all these surging new movements. He was no longer the same writer as of old, when he had written 'Confessions' and 'Red and White Poison Buns'. He read Zola, and Dickens, and popular English novelists, and constantly tried to strike a new note.

For this reason he put everything he could into 'Much Feeling, Much Grief'. He had considerable faith in it, too. You can tell this from the advertisements for the work, which he wrote himself.

Kōyō may have been a tactician, or he may not — I'm not sure. But it's a fact that he naturally set up a defence against the pressures of these new movements. Apart from Chūgai, there's evidence that he tried to bring people like Ichiyō into his camp. He also tried to hold sway over two or three 'Bungakukai' people, such as Tokuboku and Shūkotsu. The latter is a particularly good illustration of this.

Takayama Chogyū, with his talent and learning and writing ability, not only took on Ōgai but also revealed his opposition to the G-sha, so Kōyō tried to ally himself with Chogyū's enemy Ueda Bin. This too is an undeniable fact.

While still a young man Ueda Bin even criticised Ōgai's translations, saying they were full of errors, and he was certainly quite a genius, as well as being well versed in foreign literature and an elegant stylist. Some people thought him pretentious, and it's also true that he was not entirely in tune with the new currents of thought, but nevertheless it was he and Chogyū who, albeit in opposition, ranked as the two leading lights of the

---

[373] Pechorin is the main character of Lermontov's 'A Hero of Our Times'. Like Lermontov himself, who was killed in a duel at the age of twenty-seven, Pechorin is considered to be a romantic but complex figure embodying the mal-de-siècle felt by young men. The work was translated serially by Ōgai's younger sister Koganei Kimiko (1870-1956) in 'Shigaramizōshi' between October 1892-June 1894, under the title 'Yūsen Ki' (Account of a Spa), and then later published in Ōgai's collection of translations and essays 'Kagegusa' (Shade-grass, May 1897, Shunyōdō).

[374] 'Tsukigusa' (Moongrass) was a collection of Ōgai's critical writings published over the previous few years, published by Shunyōdō in December 1896. For 'Kagegusa' see note above.

[375] 'Teriha Kyōgen', November 14th-December 23rd, 1896.

Imperial University. In my opinion, Bin may have been the better critic and translator, as well as the better poet.

The fact that Ueda and two or three of the 'Bungakukai' people did side with Kōyō to some extent was due to their having certain things in common, namely a liking for old Edo, and for emotional literature, and an admiration of sorts for Kōyō's depiction of women.

At the time, other G-sha members were not really making any positive progress. Ryūrō got carried away by his fame and over-produced. Suiin wasn't really applying himself. Sazanami Sanjin, for all his intelligence, was confining himself to juvenile literature. Bizan alone was writing seriously, but he too felt pressured by the new movements and was unable to express himself fully in his writings. Just like Kōyō, these other G-sha members too were struggling in the face of the new trends.

It was the young members of the Sōsha who were the ones to show spirit. Kyōka produced 'Yushima Pilgrimage' and 'Sage of Mount Kōya', Fūyō produced 'Seventeen, Eighteen', Shūsei set to work on his 'Where the Clouds Go', and Shunyō successfully came out with sound, detailed, depiction of the family.[376]

Kōyō's Death

While on the one hand the news of Kōyō's incurable illness filled the young writers of the day with sadness, on the other hand it also brought a certain sense of freedom to the new movements.[377] The literary scene changed as if by unspoken agreement.

It was a terrible verdict, one that drew everyone's sympathy. Naturally Kōyō himself must have been bitterly grief-stricken at having to leave the world with so many ambitions left unfulfilled.

After falling ill he went to Chōshi, and then stayed for some time at Narutō, as well as in his sick-bed at the university hospital.[378] He had been caused suffering by facing up to love, and now he had to suffer in facing up to death.

At the time, the 'Mesamashigusa' group of major writers, who had tried desperately to take on the newcomers, had more or less disbanded, either through weariness or through a realisation of their helplessness.[379] If I remember correctly Ryokū had gone off to Odawara. Rohan was vir-

[376] Respectively 'Yushima Mōde' (December 1899, Shunyōdō), 'Kōya Hijiri' (February 1900, 'Shinshōsetsu'), 'Jūshichihachi' (August 1897, 'Shincho Gekkan'), and 'Kumo no Yukue' (August 28th-November 30th, 1900, Yomiuri Shinbun).

[377] Kōyō's stomach cancer was confirmed in March 1903, at the Imperial University Hospital. The illness had started to debilitate him from the summer of 1899.

[378] Kōyō went to Narutō (Chiba Prefecture, not far from Chōshi) in June 1902.

[379] The magazine continued till February 1902.

tually silent. Ōgai too was doing little except for his long, ongoing translation of 'Impromptu Poet'. Shiken was confining his activities to the sensationalist newspaper 'Yorozu Chōhō'.[380]

In the year prior to his death Kōyō wrote a lot of letters and literary bits and pieces expressing his thoughts on dying. These writings are still in existence today. In the April or May of that year I went to the university hospital to visit him but, because only relatives and close friends and associates could see him, I was finally unable to meet him again.

By that time I had married, so too had Shimazaki, and Kunikida too for a second time, and we were all building new family lives.[381] Shimazaki had gone off to Komoro. Our other young colleagues too had all entered fully into the complex maelstrom of life.

> "Increase the dose
> Of morphine, please:
> There's a moon tonight."

Kōyō wrote that verse as autumn moved on, and with the final words:

> "If I have to die,
> Then at least it's pleasant to go
> While the autumn dew's still moist"

he died on the 30th of October 1903.

I will never forget how I felt at the time. His death was a very emotional affair for me. I was living in Kohinatadaimachi in Koishikawa, and the night I heard that his condition was critical it was raining softly.[382] I didn't sleep at all that night, I had so many thoughts on my mind.

He was the master writer of his generation, a man who held sway over almost the entire Meiji world of letters. He had numerous followers, who flocked daily to attend him at his house, and he had a beautiful wife. For such a man, so blessed with worldly honours, to die so young of an incurable illness — to die moreover while talking of serving his country through literature, and saying that even if he had seven lives he'd always

---

[380] Katai's chronology is a little in error here. While Ryokū's stay in Odawara and Ōgai's continuing with 'Sokkyō Shijin' can, like the termination of 'Mesamashigusa', be applied to 1902, and while it is true that Morita Shiken was a staff member of the 'Yorozu Morning Report' (sometimes incorrectly read 'Manchōhō') from 1896, Shiken did in fact die of typhoid on November 14th 1897.

[381] Katai's marriage to Ōta Gyokumei's sister Risa(ko) (born 1880) took place in February 1899; Tōson's marriage to Hata Fuyu(ko) (1878-1910) took place in April 1899; Doppo's marriage to Enomoto Haru(ko) (1879-1962) took place in August 1898.

[382] Actually, from October 15th 1903 his correct address was Suidōchō in Kohinata. He had moved there from Haramachi in Ushigome.

be a man of letters — it necessarily created a profound and moving impression amongst us young writers.[383]

I didn't attend the full wake, but I did express my respects for some three hours, surrounded by numerous followers and colleagues of his. The funeral took place on a fine late autumn day, and the narrow road by his house in Yokoderachō was so packed with rickshaws and carriages and people and flowers that it was almost impossible to move. The coffin was carried from Kagurazaka along the edge of the outer moat to Ichigaya and Yotsuya Mitsuke, and then to the cemetery in Aoyama. It still moves me even today to remember how Dr. Tsubouchi collapsed during the service.

His grave was down a slight slope to the left of the main roadway through the cemetery in the Kōgaichō direction.[384] The narrow little paths there running crosswise were filled with men of letters, who stood watching the bearers fill in the grave after the coffin had been lowered. Hōitsuan said something very heart-rending, and wept.[385]

At the time, deep within me, individualism was awakening. Through the medium of foreign literature I had been profoundly influenced by the belief that we are lone individuals in the universe and that communal living is a compromise, and by naturalistic ideology, new ideology that tried to suppress standardised grief. As I stood in attendance at Kōyō's funeral I thought to myself: "This splendid ceremony, this public sympathy, this grief based on a sense of duty and humanity, this sorrow shown by friends and colleagues and pupils alike — I wonder how it would all look in the light of new ideology? Isn't the ceremony simply a display of old morality? Rather than a grand service like this, wouldn't it be nicer and more meaningful for Kōyō's own sake if he were seen off from the world by two or three really sincere friends? In a world where new ideology reigned there would be none of this strength of formalism and obligation. I wonder if Kōyō will be the last writer to have such a splendid funeral, as if he were some great lord or noble? We have been caught up for too long with such stereotyped ideas as friends' sympathy and pupils' duty. We have been too bound up with standardised morality. From now on we must live our lives as our own individual selves!" Tears streamed from my eyes as these thoughts passed through my mind.

---

[383] Kōyō's statement about seven lives is a reference to the famous dying words of General Kusunoki Masashige (1294-1336), who gave his life fighting for Emperor Godaigo and said that he would do the same even if he had seven lives.

[384] The area around present-day Minamiaoyama 6 and 7 Chōme and Nishiazabu 2 and 4 Chōme, to the southwest of the cemetery.

[385] Hara Hōitsuan (1866-1904), novelist, critic, translator. Hōitsuan was himself dead less than a year later, dying in a lunatic asylum in August 1904.

On many subsequent occasions I went alone to Kōyō's grave. On one of those occasions I placed some wild chrysanthemums there that I'd picked along the way. I could hear the sound of gunfire from the practice-range at the nearby barracks. A lonely white cloud drifted by in the clear autumn sky.

The Second Floor of Maruzen

It was thanks to the upstairs section of Maruzen that the surging currents of thought of nineteenth century continental Europe broke relentlessly through onto the shores of this remote Far Eastern island.

It was a small and gloomy section. The attendant, who had a limp and was very pale, had a ready smile. The shelves were thick with dust, and the literature books were put away behind the glass with a mixture of science books and guide-books. Nonetheless it was here that one came across the masterpieces that shook Europe. Of course, it wasn't that the company had ordered them through any appreciation of their literary value; rather, it had merely decided to try stocking a few such books on the basis of their being talked about a lot, just like some bookshops in remote country towns try stocking a few books from the capital on the basis of advertisements.

So what sort of people read these works, and what were their reactions? Did they think nothing in particular, and just put them away on their bookshelves? Or did they throw them into the wastepaper-basket? In fact the seed of truth in these works — the seed of truth at the very heart of mankind — was not something that could, in the final analysis, be thrown away and forgotten. It was impossible to bury such things as Zola's forceful naturalism, Ibsen's profoundly symbolic view of life, Nietzsche's lion-like roars, Tolstoi's blood and flesh, the nihilism of 'Fathers and Sons', or Heyse's research on the female sex. It is difficult to say exactly when it happened, but nevertheless it is a fact that that seed was sown in the virgin soil of this remote Far Eastern island.

You'd encounter some young man walking along the streets of Marunouchi in the vicinity of the Palace, clutching the copy of 'Fathers and Sons' that he'd ordered some time before and looking as if he'd just met his sweetheart. You'd see some other young man spotting a copy of 'Anna Karenina' on the second-floor shelves at Maruzen and emptying his month's allowance from his purse to buy it with a look of delight on his face. The favourite reading matter of such young men included Alphonse Daudet, with his cheerful sympathy, Pierre Loti, with his impressionism, and, among American writers, the short works of the Californian poet Bret Harte, who wrote about life in the mines.

Balzac was also popular. Young literature students were often to be seen with cheap copies of 'Père Goriot' or 'Eugénie Grandet'.

When it came to German writers people like Paul Heyse and Gottfried Keller were amongst those read. Nietzsche and Ibsen were introduced a little later, but by the time of Kōyō's death names like Hauptmann and Sudermann too were on the lips of young writers.[386]

The arrival of the great waves of European thought was an interesting phenomenon. It was a grand sight to see such things as Nietzsche's fire, and Ibsen's defiance, and Tolstoi's 'self', and Zola's analytical approach enter into the midst of a set national character formed by three thousand years of insularity — a calm little world of chivalry and Confucianism, Buddhism and superstition, duty and humanity, humiliating self-sacrifice and forbearance, compromise and social etiquette. Of course, it is hard to say to just what extent these new things were understood, or whether they were introduced correctly and without distortion in the first place. But at any rate it is a fact that they did arrive, full of fearsome energy and might, upon the Japanese literary world, which had nothing but Chikamatsu and Saikaku. Young people were all attracted to the new arrivals.

In those days I often went searching for such books with Yanagita Kunio. With great excitement we searched out advertisements appended to magazines, and catalogues appended to books. And then, with money we could scarce afford, we ordered these rare books from Maruzen.

I had first learned Maupassant's name through the short story collection 'The Odd Number', which was in Ueda Bin's possession.[387] Then later I bought 'Pierre et Jean' at that Western bookstore in Nikkō. However, in those days, no-one knew what sort of a writer Maupassant really was, nor his position in the literary world.[388] And because that collection

---

[386] Nietzsche was introduced in 1897 by the critic Hasegawa Tenkei (1876-1940), but was particularly strongly advocated by Takayama Chogyū in the years 1901-2 (Chogyū died of illness on December 24th 1902). Ibsen (sometimes treated with the Germans due to his long residence there) had been introduced in name as early as November 1892 by Tsubouchi Shōyō, while 'Doll's House' was translated in 1893. However, like Nietzsche, his 'golden age' in the world of Japanese literature is felt to have been the first decade of the twentieth century. Hauptmann was introduced by the critic Tobari Chikufū (1873-1955) in October 1900, while Sudermann was being read and discussed by Katai, Yanagita, and others by early 1901 at the latest.

[387] See Note 350.

[388] This is something of an exaggeration by Katai. Tōson, for example, had as early as March 1892 translated an English critique of both Zola and Maupassant which unmistakably treated Maupassant as a very different writer from the sweet romantic Katai had first imagined him to be (Tōson's translation is entitled 'Shōsetsu no Jissai-ha o Ronzu' [On the 'Actuality' School of the Novel], in 'Jogaku Zasshi'). While it is true that Tōson's personal knowledge of Maupassant's literature was limited, it is hard to believe that he and Katai had not discussed such things as that critique at some point

contained only wholesome stories I for one thought of him simply as a writer of sweet love-stories. But of course there was more to Maupassant than that. I came to realise that he was a writer very different from the likes of Daudet.

One day I went upstairs at Maruzen. As usual, I looked through the large catalogue. Suddenly I noticed a cheap series edition of Maupassant's short stories, in some ten or twelve volumes.[389] I was thrilled, and ordered it straight away with no thought to the cost.

I'll never forget the day it arrived. It was around the 10th of May, 1903 [sic].[390] By that time I had joined Hakubunkan, and was editing 'Taiheiyō'. It was raining that day. When they told me over the telephone that it had arrived I was so excited I couldn't wait to go and collect it. But, I had no money. It was only a matter of seven or eight yen, but I simply didn't have it. On the other hand, I couldn't bear to have to wait till the end of the month. In desperation I went to the head of the publishing section, U, and pleaded successfully for a loan of ten yen against a work I was in the process of writing, 'How to Write Elegantly'.[391] I got the money, and set off through the rain to Maruzen.

It was a cheap, rough series, but how happy it made me. I also felt so pleased with myself that I was the first person in Japan to read those dozen volumes. I patted them and caressed them.

To add to my happiness I discovered that the edition contained a very large number of short stories. I couldn't cut open the leaves quickly enough, and read avidly.

How amazed I was by those dozen volumes of stories. I had been deeply moved by Zola's 'Therèse Raquen' [sic] some time before, but my amazement over these stories brooked no comparison.[392] I felt as though I had been struck over the head with a club. My way of thinking was turned completely topsy-turvy. I felt that I had seen a profounder view of life than in the stories of Daudet and Coppée and Turgenev.

---

following their meeting in January 1896. Similarly, it is hard to believe that extremely well-informed and intelligent critics like Ueda Bin could have been so ignorant, especially with Bin's detailed knowledge of French literature.

[389] The After Dinner Series, eleven volumes, translated by R. Whitling, and published by Mathieson, London, 1900.

[390] This is a classic illustration of Katai's appalling memory and lack of attention to detail. It was categorically 1901! In other writings Katai has given the date correctly as 1901, but also incorrectly as 1900. See also note below.

[391] U is Uchiyama Masayuki (dates unclear). 'How to Write Elegantly' (Bibun Sakuhō) was actually written in November 1906! The work Katai was writing at the time, and which he intends here, was 'Zoku Nansenḥokuba' (Sequel to By Boat to the South and on Horse to the North, June 1901).

[392] Given thus by Katai but the correct spelling is 'Raquin'.

"That light touch of his is superb. I wish I could write something like it," Kōyō once said of one of Maupassant's works. His style was referred to as "clear and concise" in Ōgai Gyoshi's 'New Theories on Aesthetics'.[393] Ueda Bin spoke of him simply as a bright artistic writer. But how was Maupassant really? How was the Maupassant who now lay open before me?

It may have been that I had arrived at just the right sort of turning-point in my attitude to life.[394] But at any rate, I was overwhelmed by those books of short stories. I couldn't put them down even for a moment, and went so far as to put books in my pocket and take them to work with me. I'd read them in my work-breaks, and in rickshaws, and in bed. What dedication!

I soon lent a couple of volumes to Yanagita. "They're horrible!" he said. "There are some good stories here, but a lot of really horrible ones too. So that's the sort of writer he is!?"

"But don't you find them interesting?"

"Well, I suppose you could say that, but he's just too much for me."

"I see."

I thought about the difference between Maupassant and Daudet. I'd read Pierre Loti's 'Iceland Fisherman' quite recently, and I compared him too with Maupassant. I could see clear differences — between a writer who described incidents, and a writer who depicted psychology; between a writer who had limits, and a writer who didn't; between a romantic writer, and a realistic writer. Something deep within me responded immediately to this Maupassant, something hidden away, something restless, fermenting. I wrote in an essay at the time: "Up till now I was only ever looking at the heavens. I knew nothing of the earth, nothing at all. I was a feeble idealist. From now on, I'll become a child of the earth, and crawl the earth like a beast rather than waste my time gazing at the stars."[395]

After reading Maupassant I came to better understand Saikaku too — but in a completely different sense from that intended by Kōyō, Rohan, and Kangetsu.[396]

---

[393] 'Shinbi Shinsetsu', February 1898-September 1899, 'Mesamashigusa'.

[394] That is, having married in February 1899, lost his mother in August 1899, and started his first serious employment in September 1899, as well as becoming a father in February 1901, Katai was no longer the naive young man of the 1880's and 1890's, and needed a new philosophy to support his changed outlook on life. This explains what might otherwise be termed an over-reaction to Maupassant.

[395] 'Ten to Chi' (Heaven and Earth, March 1902, 'Taiheiyō') is probably the work intended here, as it contains very similar lines.

[396] Awashima Kangetsu (1859-1926), poet, novelist, essayist.

The Little House in the Suburbs

One afternoon in early spring I left the office and went on the Yamanote Line past Shinagawa and round to Shibuya, where I got off.

It was just after four o'clock. I went out from the station onto the Miyamasu road, then turned left down a road that I had been told about. It was a lonely country road. The frost had thawed, and my heels sank deep into the mud. I tried to tread carefully, avoiding the worst patches.

When I look out at that area from the train nowadays I see that it's full of houses and little factory-chimneys pouring out smoke, but in those days it was still a lonely suburban area, with hardly any houses even except for the occasional thatched cottage. Since a month or two previously Yanagita had been renting a room in a farmhouse there, and commuting to his office.[397]

He was still called Matsuoka, and it was just after it had been settled that he would marry into the Yanagita family.[398] His wife-to-be was then eighteen or nineteen, and was still going to Ochanomizu.[399]

The cloth-wrapped bundle I was carrying contained some books I had just picked up from Maruzen, having ordered them some time before. They were Hauptmann's 'Sunken Bell', Sudermann's 'Cat's Bridge', and Ibsen's 'Little Eyolf'. I may also have had one of Bjornson's novels of the mountains.

The house that Yanagita was staying in lay along that muddy road, in the shade of a large zelkova tree.

"Is — in?" I asked.

Fortunately he was in, and I went in through the verandah. The scene struck me as very lonely and rustic, with the weak afternoon sunshine slanting onto the bamboo grove, the fields of pale plum blossom, and vegetable fields seared reddish-brown by the frost.

"Nice place," I said to him.

"Not bad, I suppose."

---

[397] After graduating from the Law Faculty of the Imperial University he started work in the agricultural section of the Ministry of Agriculture and Commerce, and lectured at Waseda University on agricultural administration. From 1902 he worked in the Cabinet Legislation Bureau, as well as continuing to lecture at various universities. He moved to the house in Aoyama, described here, on January 18th 1901, before moving to the Yanagita house in May that year. The time of Katai's visit described here must therefore be February or March 1901.

[398] The date of the adoption and formal name-change was May 1901, but the date of the marriage itself was April 1904.

[399] His wife was Yanagita Taka (born May 1886) who was clearly not eighteen or nineteen at the time but fourteen or fifteen (or sixteen by the old Japanese counting system). Ochanomizu was a women's higher normal-school, founded in 1874. It has been a university since 1949.

Yanagita's face loomed pale through the cold evening air — Yanagita the poet who, in his 'Along Country Lanes', had sung of love before 'Young Leaves' appeared.[400] "There're still a lot of plum blossoms up on the hill. It's marvellous. I really find it bracing and invigorating here, especially when I'm alone at night."

I could see a large lamp with a silver-coloured base, a vermilion desk, and bookshelves, and some large colourful cushions. They all looked like things he'd brought from the Yanagita family's house.

I took my books out.

"Ah, so they've arrived! When did they come?"

"Today. I've just picked them up."

He looked over the splendid new cover of 'Sunken Bell', and remarked, "It's a nice-looking book. I can sense the new ideology in it."

Then he picked up 'Cat's Bridge'.

"This looks good too. I'd like to read them all, right now!"

We were both deeply attracted to the new ideology. Yanagita and I were always talking about Ibsen, and Nietzsche, and Daudet, and Turgenev. We couldn't carry on as we were. We couldn't carry on dilly-dallying. We had to do something to emerge as the champions of a new society. We talked over and over again about such things. And our conversation always included talk of young men in the hills of Norway, and girls living by fiords, and impoverished farmers in the Steppes, and washerwomen on the banks of the Seine in Paris.

"They say 'Iceland Fisherman' is Loti's best work," said Yanagita.

"Oh?"

"So Ueda was saying."

"The romanticism's interesting."

"And the way he writes is interesting, too — looking down on the world and writing about frozen seas one minute and the war in South China the next. And I really think that part where the girl's waiting for the fishermen to return to port is wonderful."

Yanagita was put in mind of the sea off Chōshi.

We had a nice meal that evening and talked till late. Yanagita asked me to stay the night, but my young wife was waiting back home for me, so I went back on the last Yamanote Line train to Shinjuku, where I changed trains.[401] I was living at the time in Haramachi 3 Chōme in Ushigome.[402]

---

[400] Yanagita's 'Nobe no Yukiki' was his contribution to 'Jojōshi', predating Tōson's 'Wakanashū' of August 1897 (Shunyōdō) by some four months. The comparison between the two poets is hard to understand, however.

[401] His wife had given birth to their first child, a daughter Reiko, on February 1st.

[402] In early 1901 he was actually living in Kikuichō. He lived in Haramachi from September 11th 1902-October 15th 1903.

After that I visited this 'country retreat' of Yanagita's on several occasions. Yanagita gave his opinion of Regina's story, which I'd lent him.[403] He felt that the bit about the snow falling on Christmas night was wonderful, and also admired the last section, which he felt was full of the spirit of the modern novel. I remember how we discussed this.

One day we held a poetry meeting there. My poetry teacher attended, and so too did Yanagita's future mother-in-law.[404] The plum blossoms were truly splendid. The fields were a sea of blossom. One of the poems I read out went as follows:

> "What should I do
> About this sadness of mine,
> On an evening like this,
> Full of the whiteness
> Of flowering plum?"

Ōgai Gyoshi at War

The first time I met Ōgai was the occasion of the war with Russia, when our Second Army was setting out from Ujina.[405] We met in a room in a large inn in Ōtemachi in Hiroshima.

I can still picture clearly all the activity that was going on at the time in Hiroshima. There were cavalry troops, and infantry troops, and artillery troops, and artillery carriages. Everyone was on edge, always making a fuss and getting impatient about something or other. There was a confused atmosphere of parting sorrow, and patriotism, and thoughts of glory, and apprehension.

I had gone to Hiroshima with the Second Army as a member of a proposed photographic team. I was also hoping to serve as a war-correspondent.[406] My young mind was naturally both excited and apprehensive about the war.

Our party set itself up in a cramped room in a dirty little inn just in front and to the left of Motoyasubashi [Bridge], and we waited there ex-

---

[403] Regina is the heroine of Sudermann's 'Cat's Bridge'.

[404] It is odd that Katai has used the term 'my' and not 'our', since both he and Yanagita were pupils of Matsuura. There is no evidence that Katai is referring to any other teacher.

[405] Ujina is in the immediate vicinity of Hiroshima.

[406] Katai was in charge of the private team of eight persons sent by Hakubunkan, which included Otowa's friend Mitsumura Risō (see Note 278). Katai left Tōkyō on March 23rd (1904), not returning till September 20th. There is no evidence that he was active as a photographer, but his work 'Dai Ni Gun Jūsei Nikki' (Diary of the Second Army at War) was published by Hakubunkan in January 1905.

pecting the departure order to arrive any day.[407] Having put our applications in we just couldn't bear to be left there in silence like that, so we were forever going to the Second Army Command Headquarters trying to follow up connections. The Vice-Chief of General Staff was Yui Mitsue, now a lieutenant-general but in those days a major.[408] We often got told off at HQ.

"You lot are a real nuisance! Can't you just wait quietly?!" we'd get told, or else we'd get threatened with some remark like "I've no idea if we can take you along or not. Just who vouched for you anyway?"

Ōgai was then head of the medical corps, and staying in an inn in Ōtemachi called Naganuma. Every time I saw the flag of the Second Army Medical Corps, with its white characters on a black background, I wished I could meet him. But even majors had no time for me, so I didn't hold out much hope of meeting someone with the rank of general.

But I was so desperately keen to meet him that one morning I made up my mind and went along there with a name-card.

"The General, is it?" asked a soldier on duty — an orderly, by all appearances — as he compared my name-card with my strange apparel. "One moment, please."

He went out of the room.

"This way, please," he said as he came back, and led me through to the verandah. "The General's upstairs."

I felt grateful to literature. I wasn't much of a name as a writer, but nevertheless, even though it was a time when majors rarely deigned to see me, here was the head of the medical corps apparently quite willing to do so!

It was thanks to literature.

I admired Ōgai more than anyone else, though I didn't always admit it, and had profited greatly from his writings, so I had been very keen to meet him for some time. But in those days Ōgai seemed to have got fed up with the literary world, and had stopped 'Mesamashigusa' and more or less stopped writing too. Especially after going to the army division in Kokura he started using terms like 'the literary world of the scions and mignons'.[409] Furthermore, along with Ueda Bin, he seemed to be looking rather favourably upon Yosano Tekkan's 'Myōjō', which rather

---

[407] Motoyasubashi spanned the Motoyasugawa, about half a mile from Ōtemachi. The team was in Hiroshima for about a month, finally setting sail on April 21st (arriving on the Liaotung Paeninsula on May 5th).

[408] Dates unclear.

[409] Kokura is in north Kyūshū. Ōgai went there in June 1899, returning to Tōkyō in March 1902.

put me off visiting him since it was a magazine that often said nasty things about me.[410]

"Well, come in," he said. "You're Katai, then?"

I was thrilled to hear him address me in such familiar fashion.

I'd always liked Ōgai's individuality, and this frank, informal attitude of his impressed me greatly.

"There in that huge bright room — it was some fifteen or sixteen mats in area — and surrounded by uniforms and bags and swords we talked about the war and about literature. "Which writers apart from yourself are going to the war?" asked Ōgai. "Kuroda from the 'Nichinichi', you say? Hmm, who's this Kuroda, I wonder?"[411] He looked pensive.

I took my leave after half an hour or so, not wishing to hold him up too much, and we talked of meeting again at the front.

However, I visited Ōgai again before we got to the front, in his cabin on board ship as we were crossing. This time the atmosphere was far more relaxed, and we talked about foreign literature. We talked about Hauptmann's 'Poor Heinrich', and Maeterlinck's optimism, and D'Annunzio. We knew we were in Korean waters — though not exactly what part of the coast — as we were advancing with lights out just in case we happened to encounter the enemy. The cigarettes Ōgai was smoking had a very pleasant aroma. He offered me one.

After that I thought to myself that, even if I didn't get to meet him again, I would still be able to draw great strength from the mere knowledge that he was there with me in that same Second Army. It always comforted me just to pass his door, which had 'Second Army Medical Corps' written on it in katakana rather than characters in case there might be enemy spies about.[412]

The plains of the Liaotung Paeninsula had little on them to see or eat, just the dirty houses of the inhabitants, with their cooking-pits full of rushes. Later on it did get gradually warmer and it was pleasant to see the plum trees and apricot trees blossoming amongst the mud walls, but when we landed it was nothing but a bleak scene of yellowish-brown earth and dust and a bitterly cold wind. When I read Ōgai's 'Verse Diary', which was published later, I can appreciate how he himself felt

---

[410] Yosano Tekkan (1873-1935), poet, founded 'Myōjō' (Venus) in April 1900. The magazine went through several distinct phases till its cessation in October 1949, its most famous period being from its founding until November 1908.

[411] Kuroda Kōshirō (dates unclear), journalist. The (Tōkyō) Nichinichi Shinbun ('Daily') was founded in 1872 and existed independently till 1911. It is now part of the Mainichi Shinbun.

[412] That is, Chinese and Korean people could understand the meaning of Japanese characters but not necessarily katakana. Katakana was the usual medium for army messages.

on those plains, thinking of his young wife whom he'd left behind in Tōkyō, along with his beloved new-born daughter.[413]

The beauty of Ōgai's wife was a talking-point in the literary world of the time so I did know something about her, albeit indirectly. I remember hearing Tamura Shōgyo say to someone at Hakubunkan, just after Ōgai's marriage: "That Ōgai took his wife to Asukayama, and he was fawning over her so much I couldn't bear to watch," and I felt angry at Tamura for saying such a thing.[414] And now Ōgai was living away from that beautiful wife of his, in those desolate Liaotung plains.

We set up our first base in a little village in the vicinity of Ch'e-chia-tun and Chuan-chiao-fang, not far from where we landed. On one occasion, when the commanding officers had gone off to see the fighting at Shih-san-li-t'ai, there was a big panic amongst those of us left behind in the village when there was a report — which turned out to be false — that the enemy were attacking. Ōgai said afterwards: "It wasn't anything serious at all — just some lunatic letting off a gun. But I do admit that for a time there was a bit of a flap and panic on, because if it HAD been an enemy attack, with the commanding officers away *I* might have had to take command!"

Whenever there was a battle, such as at Chin-chou and Te-li-shih, the medical corps was very busy, and Ōgai never had a moment's peace. After the battle at Te-li-shih we were based for a while in the village of Hsien-shan-tzu, which had a lot of shady trees and was quite a pretty village by the standards of the Liaotung Paeninsula. I remember there was another panic over an enemy attack in that village, too. After I got back to Japan I sent some poetry to Ōgai, who was still at the front, and in return he sent me a postcard with a 'poem' of his own:

"Hsien-shan-tzu,
Where I had such a good view
— Of your droppings!"

This was a reference to the fact that at the front, where almost everyone relieved themselves out in the fields, my favourite spot for answering nature's call was a field just behind the medical corps' headquarters. I had to laugh at the realisation that I had been spotted in the act.

I was with Ōgai at Kai-p'ing, and T'ai-shih-ch'iao, and Hai-ch'eng. One thing I won't ever forget is going down with fever at Ch'en-lou-tzu,

---

[413] Ōgai's 'Uta Nikki' was published in September 1907 by Shunyōdō. His (second) wife was Araki Shige. They had married in January 1902. The daughter, Mari (born January 7th 1903), became a writer of note.

[414] Tamura Shōgyo (1874-1948), novelist (in USA 1903-1909). For details of Asukayama (Park) see Note 308.

in Hai-ch'eng. I was quite a nuisance to the medics, but Ōgai kindly suggested I move into a bed in their headquarters, which I did. My fever was bad, and there were fears it might develop into typhoid. Ōgai came to my bedside to check my progress, and comforted me.

Before I fell ill I'd gone with some others from T'ai-shih-ch'iao to Ying-kou, for a bit of a break — I wrote about our returning from there in a short story called 'Death' — and in a corner of a general store there I spotted some foreign novels.[415] I bought a collection of short stories by Heinz Tovote and 'Bienchen' by Anatole France, and showed them to Ōgai when I got back to base.[416] "Oh, thanks," he said, spread a white blanket over a pile of stretcher-boards and, with a swish in his hand to keep away the flies, promptly sat down and read them.

So it is that Ōgai's 'Verse Diary' brings back many memories for me, and that I find it so interesting. I also find interesting the many poems about his wife and daughter, and when I think how he missed his home and family I can fully appreciate the bitterness of distant duty, having experienced the same pain myself. I remember composing a verse myself when we were in the Ta-shan-p'u area, which I wrote out on numerous fans:

> "How I wish
> I were at home,
> To go viewing the flowers
> With my sweet little wife:
> Such moonlit delicacy."

When I left Ōgai at Liaoyang to return home, he said to me: "You're lucky! I really envy you. I'VE got to keep heading in the opposite direction!" He smiled a sad smile as he spoke.

The Old Castle Ruins of Komoro

As soon as he got married Shimazaki went off to teach in Komoro in Shinshū, so we met only rarely and generally relied on letters to keep in touch.[417] I believe his years in Komoro were a terribly lonely period for

[415] 'Shi' was published in 'Taiyō' in January 1910.

[416] I can find no record of any work 'Bienchen' (which Katai gives in romanisation) or similar by Anatole France, at least in French or English. However, since Katai mentions the work along with that by the German writer Heinz Tovote (whose works would almost certainly be found only in the original German), since he showed them to the German specialist Ōgai, and since Katai himself had a basic knowledge of German, it seems likely that 'Bienchen' is a German translation of France's 'Abeille' (Bee) of 1883. (Bienechen/bienchen means 'little bee'.)

[417] Tōson left for Komoro (Nagano Prefecture) the same month as he married Hata Fuyu, April 1899. He taught at the Komoro Gijuku (Academy), and was in Komoro till April 1905.

him, and at the same time a period when art and life clashed. Although he was quite agitated deep down he remained quiet and calm on the outside, and I think it is quite clear that he was contemplating himself and human life in general. Even poems such as 'Evergreen Tree', 'Labour', and 'Harvest' show clearly how troubled he was.[418] However, his art was so powerful that it could not be destroyed by practical problems or worldly troubles or family demands. From the time of 'By the Old Castle of Komoro' on he tried his hand at writing novels.[419]

Shimazaki's name in those days may not have been particularly widely known, but it should be noted that it was unsullied. He certainly did not overproduce, and he was always scrupulous in his writing. As a result his works were always well received.

In those days Shimazaki and Kunikida had only met each other on a very limited number of occasions, and still did not understand each other. I think the first time they met was in my house in Ushigome, and neither gave much recognition to the other. Kunikida remarked that Shimazaki was too caught up with form.

At any rate, in those days we felt we had to study in earnest, and make plans for the future so as not to be tossed around by the waves of real life. Accordingly, we immersed ourselves in the study of foreign literature.

The literary world in those days had already grown weary of Ryūrō, and centred instead on Tengai and Fūyō. Tengai's realism was naturally considerably influenced by the modern age — the post-G-sha age — but unfortunately it lacked even the the substance of the 'Hototogisu' group and only barely progressed beyond the shallow realism of Ryūrō.[420] By

---

[418] 'Evergreen Tree' ('Tokiwagi') and 'Labour' (actually 'Songs of Labour', 'Rōdō Zatsuei') were published in 'Shinshōsetsu' in January 1900 and November 1899 respectively, and both were included in the collection 'Rakubaishū' (Fallen Plum Blossoms, August 1901, Shunyōdō). There is no poem entitled 'Harvest' ('Shūkaku') in Tōson's published literature, though there are two prose works with that title. One is a short story published in 'Bunshō Sekai' in October 1908 and is clearly not relevant. The other, from Section Seven of 'Chikumagawa no Suketchi' (Chikuma River Sketches, June 1911-August 1912, 'Chūgaku Sekai'), might loosely be called a 'prose poem' and is probably the work intended here. Though this work was not published till 1911, in a letter to Katai dated November 19th 1903 Tōson stated "I have still not been able to write the manuscript for 'Harvest'," indicating that he had intended to write it many years earlier (he is unlikely to have been referring to the short story as its setting is different). A less likely alternative is that both Katai and Tōson were referring to a third work of the same title which has been lost, unpublished, to posterity. However, Katai seems to assume public awareness of the work.

[419] 'Komoro naru Kojō no Hotori', April 1900, 'Myōjō, and later in 'Fallen Plum Blossoms'.

[420] The 'Hototogisu' magazine (Cuckoo) was first published in January 1897, and in its early days largely promoted a realistic form of haiku under its chief writer Masaoka Shiki (1867-1902).

comparison Fūyō, being in the direct line of the G-sha, wrote ornate texts with detailed observation, and appeared more penetratively naturalistic.

The world of poetry was dominated by the 'Myōjō' group, with their grotesque characteristics. Akiko's poetry was clearly idolised by young men of the day.[421] However, the 'Myōjō' group lacked the ability to write novels. Moreover, their knowledge of foreign literature was second-hand, and they also lacked the ability to study it for themselves.

There was a need for a new movement to come into being, but there was no-one who could produce anything suitable.

Yanagita and Kanbara and myself were in continual correspondence with Shimazaki.[422] Shimazaki too gradually started studying more foreign literature. It seems that he paid particular attention to Balzac. He also read D'Annunzio, Maupassant, Zola, Flaubert, and the Goncourts. Ibsen seems to have impressed him greatly, too. The letters we exchanged in those days are still in existence, and show clearly how much we aspired towards art of the future.

At the time, Shimazaki wrote such works as 'Straw Sandals', 'The Shadow of the Palm-Leaves', 'Old Man', and 'Old Maid'.[423] 'Old Man' already revealed the influence of Maupassant.

Shimazaki came to Tōkyō two or three times a year. Amongst his old 'Bungakukai' colleagues it seems to have been mostly Baba that he visited. He also came to my house, and often went to Yanagita's too. On one of the occasions when he came to Tōkyō, during the spring holidays, he and I went off to the Koganei-Mogusa area with Baba, Kanbara, and Osanai.[424] I'd hurt my leg and couldn't walk with them, so I went by rickshaw.[425] I remember it all so clearly, even today.

It was January 1904 — I know the date because it was the year the war with Russia started. It was also the year I wrote 'Blunt Depiction' for 'Taiyō'.[426] On a sudden impulse I visited Shimazaki up in the hills of Shinshū.

With the snowy prospect of Mount Asama before me I travelled across the Jōshū Plain, gradually nearing the Usui Pass. Everything was

---

[421] Yosano Akiko (1878-1942, known early on as Hō Akiko), poetess and wife of Tekkan (married autumn 1901). 'Grotesque' is given in English.

[422] Kanbara Ariake (1876-1952), poet.

[423] Respectively 'Wara Zōri' (November 1902, 'Myōjō'), 'Yashi no Hakage' (March 1904, 'Myōjō'), 'Oyaji' (January 1903, 'Shōtenchi'), and 'Rōjō' (June 1903, 'Taiyō').

[424] Osanai Kaoru (1881-1928), novelist, dramatist. Mogusa is in the area of Hino City.

[425] Katai burned his leg in December 1902 and was incapacitated for several months. The visit described here is therefore early 1903, and not to be confused with the 1904 visit (to Komoro) described below.

[426] 'Rokotsu naru Byōsha', February 1904.

beautiful, pleasant, fresh. Beyond Usui Pass it was a land of snow, with the sun sparkling beautifully on the surrounding hills.

I got off at Komoro Station and went along a quiet, frozen road towards Babaura. There was a bitter wind blowing, and the streams were half frozen over.

"Shimazaki's house?" I kept asking, and eventually arrived at a thatched cottage in what was virtually the middle of the fields. In front of the house was a frosty rape-field.

It was Shimazaki's house.

It was the house that Shimazaki wrote of in his later short story 'Servant', and the house where he wrote 'Water Colour Painter', warming his frozen ink with his breath.[427]

It makes me very sad to think that his cheerful wife and children are no longer in this world.[428]

What did we talk about on that occasion? We talked about Ibsen, and Bjornson, and Tolstoi, and Maupassant. We talked on into the night, the conversation unflagging. Hauptmann's 'Lonely People' was a particularly interesting source of discussion for us, as we were concerned about the problem of 'family'.

That night we slept under the kotatsu.

I was extremely keen to write something. I had to do something, something that would stand out. The problem was, however, that my confused thoughts and observations just wouldn't fit together.

The following morning we went up to the ruins of Komoro Castle. From there we could see, between the pines, the snowy range of hills sparkling in the sunlight. A train passed close by — the same train that Shimazaki had so often wished to return to Tōkyō on for good — puffing out its dreadful black smoke.

Shortly after I got back to Tōkyō the war broke out, and life became hectic. Everywhere you went you heard newsboys yelling "Extra! Extra!" My second son was born on the same day that enemy ships attacked the Tsugaru Strait.[429] The troubled waves of human life soon came surging into my own personal life.

---

[427] Respectively 'Hōkōnin' (August 1909, 'Shumi'), and 'Suisai Gaka' (January 1904, 'Shinshōsetsu').

[428] Tōson's wife Fuyu died in childbirth on August 6th 1910. By January 1904 Tōson had had two children born — a daughter Midori on May 3rd 1900 and another daughter Takako on March 31st 1902 — and both were to die in infancy, on June 12th 1906 and April 7th 1906 respectively. During Katai's visit Fuyu was pregnant with a third child, another daughter Nuiko born April 9th 1904, and she too died in infancy, on June 6th 1905. For further details on Tōson's children see notes to the later section 'Crisis at Forty'.

[429] Mizuho, born February 21st 1904.

When I went into the office Tsuboya said to me:[430]
"What about going off to the front? Are you game?"
"Of course I'll go!" I answered indignantly.
Kunikida, at that time, was in Sakuradahongōchō in Shiba, editing 'Kinji Gahō', while continuing at the same time to produce his short stories.[431]
Before long I set off for the war. Shimazaki wanted to go too, and soon after I left he came up to Tōkyō. However, he was unable to secure a suitable appointment and went back to the hills where, still wishing he could have gone off to the war, he started writing that long novel 'Broken Commandment'.[432]

Brief Comments on Certain Writers

I think that if Kōyō had lived for another ten years or so there would have been a considerable change in his writing. In terms of outward appearances there was considerable imitation in his works, while in terms of content there was considerable looseness. It was style that he most concerned himself with, but because the contents of his works lacked the compelling depth and richness of Saikaku his style and content ended up disjointed, with a lot of obsolete words. On the outside his works were beautiful brocade, but on the inside they were faded artificial flowers.

But that's hardly surprising. After all, he was still young, and though he did have some knowledge of the world that knowledge was definitely limited. That's why I wish he were still alive now.

In that sense, Doppo was a precocious genius. He always focused hard on the faded interior of Kōyō's work rather than the beautiful exterior, and was always critical. "There's no inner substance anywhere in Kōyō's literature. It's no good making things pretty on the outside if there's no life inside!"

The most profound of the Genyūsha writers was of course Ryūrō [sic].[433] He was followed by Bizan, who tried hard to get away from stereotyped style. In his 'Waterwheel' period Suiin published some fresh and original short stories.[434] He should have carried on writing. Unfortunately the literary world of the day was very ready to compromise and be diplomatic, and there was much factionalism, with a lot of writers

---

[430] Tsuboya Suisai (1862-1949), one-time editor at Hakubunkan and later a prominent local politician.

[431] Sakuradahongōchō is the area of present-day Nishishinbashi 1 Chōme and Shinbashi 1 Chōme. 'Kinji Gahō' (Modern Illustrated), March 1903-December 1907.

[432] 'Hakai', March 1906, private publication.

[433] In the previous section Katai referred to Ryūrō's 'shallow realism'.

[434] 'Mizuguruma', a short story collection published in August 1895.

happy to stay within the confines of their group. There were few writers with the independent spirit of Sendagi Sanbō.[435] In short, they were unable to believe deeply in themselves. I understand that this is what Ryūrō is saying even now.

Partly as a result of his being misled by common critical opinion as to its poignancy, Ryūrō's realism gradually lost its natural purity and started to include deliberate exaggeration. It lost its sparkle because he went on to leave too much to his skill with the pen, and his realism ended up as something concocted in his study. He also went on to use dialogue as a means of furthering the plot, when in fact the dialogue should have been given more importance and made more animated.

Suiin had a type of idealism about him that left him unsatisfied with realism. This led to a theatrical illogicality and incongruity. When it came to depicting scenes he was definitely some way ahead of his time, but spoiled things by his grandiose idealism, and ended up with a certain sort of stereotyping. He also gave too much importance to 'newspaper novels'. But in the case of both Ryūrō and Suiin I am convinced that if they had only believed less in society and more in themselves then they would not have been swept away, however fearsome the surge of new currents might have been. Unfortunately they could not transcend the 'group' and fix firmly onto the 'self'. One can say that the only person really aware of something beyond the 'group' was Bizan, who cut his own throat.

Of them all, it is Rohan who still remains a mystery. There are those who question his true significance as an artist from the point of view of training and erudition, but I am certainly not one of them. Doppo too had a lot of respect for Rohan, certainly more than for Kōyō. He was always making remarks like, "They say Rohan's finished, but he's not the sort of person to get pushed out by youngsters. One of these days he'll come up with something wonderful, something that'll take people's breath away." Nevertheless Rohan slipped up with 'Towering Waves'.[436] 'Slipped up' may not be quite the right term, but at any rate the work was a great disappointment, especially when so much had been expected of it. Then there was his poem 'Back from Retirement', which was laughed at by the young poets of the day.[437] But I still think there's more to Rohan than 'Nawa Nagatoshi'.[438] He certainly does remain a mystery.

---

[435] Sendagi Sanbō was a pseudonym of Mori Ōgai.

[436] 'Sora Utsu Nami' was an unfinished novel published serially in several phases in the Yomiuri Shinbun, from September 1903-May 1905.

[437] 'Shutsuro', a long lyric poem serialised in the Yomiuri Shinbun March-December 1904.

[438] 'Nawa Nagatoshi', titled after a fourteenth century nobleman, was a drama written in the summer of 1913 and first staged (at the Imperial Theatre) in October that year.

Self-understanding and new knowledge formed the basis of the movements of the new age. Those who underestimated this fact were all swept away — big figures, little figures, and whole groups of figures alike.

Tokutomi Roka is a good example of someone who, despite an old-fashioned and mundane way of thinking, was able to hold firm against the tide thanks to a relatively deep understanding of himself and to his not having ignored new knowledge. People like Koshoshi and Saganoya were all swept away because they had no faith in themselves.

In both their attitudes and their positions Sendagi Sanbō and Waseda's Dr. Shōyō were complete polar opposites. Sendagi Sanbō was thoroughly independent-minded. He was a true 'individual'. He never let himself be bothered by pupils and acolytes. It's very significant that his favourite heroine is Princess Iida from 'Letter Bearer'.[439] He only ever did what he wanted to do. He went alone along his own chosen path. He didn't worry about society or the world at large.

One very important point that literary critics absolutely should not overlook is that he wrote, in the introduction to Ibsen's 'Master Builder' and in the very midst of the new currents of thought, that the new age was passing noisily by around him.[440] He was able to elevate himself adroitly above the flow and gaze down upon it from the embankment, as it were. He never lost his 'self'. Nor did he ever omit to leave sufficient margin between himself and that flow before his gaze to enable him to appraise it. No-one could deny 'Subaru' has poured a rather different current into the present literary world.[441]Even now one can see about him the spirit of his 'Shigaramizōshi' days.

By comparison Waseda's Dr. Shōyō is merely the leader of a 'group'. He is certainly not an 'individual'. I've always seen him surrounded by people of one sort or another. And I've seen those people constantly squabbling amongst themselves, regardless of him. Moreover, although most of those people have received far more patronage and attention than those who look up to Sendagi Sanbō have, it is the latter who have injected more freshness and vitality into the literary world.

The well-known 'no ideals' dispute clearly shows the difference between them.[442] And I find it interesting that, whereas 'Shigaramizōshi'

[439] 'Fumizukai''s (for publishing details see Note 122) heroine Princess Iida is a rather sensitive, independent-minded, dignified, romantic figure.

[440] Ibsen's 'Solness the Master Builder' was translated by Chiba Kikukō (1870-1938) in July 1909, as 'Kenchikushi', and published by Ekifūsha. Ōgai wrote the introduction.

[441] 'The Pleiades', a literary magazine running from January 1909-December 1913, is commonly regarded as the successor to 'Myōjō', which ceased its first phase of publication in November 1908. Ōgai was a leading figure of the magazine.

[442] A long, drawn-out difference of opinion between Ōgai and Shōyō from the early 1890's on. Basically, Ōgai favoured writers taking a subjective, idealistic stance, while Shōyō was opposed to this.

ceased publication in a somewhat spectacular fashion, 'Waseda Bungaku' has continued through till today despite a complete change in its content and influence.

Then there was a magazine called 'Teikoku Bungaku'.[443] When I asked what had happened to it, and whether it was still being published or not, someone told me that it was indeed still in existence but that its content had changed completely.

'Teikoku Bungaku' was the journal of the young Tōkyō Imperial University graduates, and in its early days it was quite active. In the days of Chogyū, Keigetsu, and Ryūson (Ueda Bin) it was a magazine that was essential reading every month. It adopted an interesting stance opposed to both 'Waseda Bungaku' and to 'Shigaramizōshi''s successor 'Mesamashigusa'. Of course it had a number of talented writers, and a lot of critics in particular writing for it. Both Doppo and I frequently suffered abuse from them, and Doppo often got angry.

"What do they know about critisism?! As soon as they graduate they go off into the country and forget all they ever learned about literature!"

It was in fact true that there were any number of them who'd go off full of their own importance only to sink into oblivion after a year or two. Some did become respected scholars or language teachers, but there were very few who spent the rest of their life involved with literature. On the other hand it may just be an inevitable result of the direction taken by liberal studies at the university.

Amongst the 'Teikoku Bungaku' people it was Chogyū and Ueda Bin who were the most significant as far as we were concerned. Most people rated Chogyū's skill with a pen over that of Bin, but in my opinion it was Bin who made the greater contribution to literature. There is no particularly outstanding work in Chogyū's entire writings, whereas Bin wrote a great number of works that were fresh and excellent by the standards of the day and that appealed to young people. I believe he ranks second only to Sendagi Sanbō in terms of importing new knowledge. Unfortunately, however, Bin lacked the ability to put his ideas into practice. When it came to practice he was always hesitant and indecisive, and often played the role of onlooker.

In fact, I'm sure that amongst the opposition to naturalism it was Bin's views that were the freshest and the most significant. I was always taking issue with him. It was inevitable that we should clash. I particularly felt this when the magazine 'Geien' first appeared.[444]

---

[443] 'Imperial Literature', January 1895-January 1920.

[444] 'Field of Art', one issue in February 1902, then further monthly issues from January 1906-May 1907, published by Sakura Shobō. Bin was a leading figure in both cases.

'Myōjō' shone brightly thanks to Akiko's talent, but actually it owed a lot to Bin, especially to his translation 'The Sound of the Tide'.[445] It certainly was an excellent piece of work, especially by the standards of the day. But people like me followed a different direction. For me, literature had to be in closer touch with real life, and more thorough in its depiction. Rather than French literature I preferred the directness, the earnestness, and the simplicity of Russian literature.

Tōkyō before the Electric Trains

In those days there were still no electric trains in Tōkyō. Even the horse-drawn tramcars were confined to the main roads, and eighty or ninety percent of transport was necessarily based on the rickshaw.[446]

To get from Hakubunkan to my home in Haramachi or Wakamatsuchō I used to get in one of the rickshaws waiting at the corner of Honchō, go past the moat to the foot of Kudan Hill, up the hill in Iidamachi, and then head from Ushigome Mitsuke to Kagurazaka, where I got down from the rickshaw and walked the rest of the way home.

That journey held many associations for me. My mind was always busy as I went along, worrying about my family, about the future for my wife and children, and about my never making a name for myself in the literary world.[447]

Because my works weren't very good, because I was bad at socialising and was prone to make enemies quickly, and because I had a certain unpleasant pretentiousness about me, I was always spoken badly of by literary people. After 'Mesamashigusa' I had virtually come to expect abuse as a matter of course.

And because my salary was so bad I had to do extra work at home. To add to it all I tended to be a bit of a worrier about life. I couldn't put

---

[445] 'Kaichōon', published as a collection in October 1905 by Hongō Shoin, containing fifty-seven pieces by twenty-nine European poets, especially symbolist. It was the first major introduction of symbolist poetry, and many of the translations were first published in 'Myōjō' and helped the magazine to establish its reputation.

[446] It is peculiar that Katai again fails to mention the steam-trains. For example, the Kōbu Line (the present-day Chūō Main Line) ran from Shinjuku-Tachikawa from April 1889, from Shinjuku-Ushigome from October 1895, on to Iidamachi (Iidabashi) in 1896, and on to Ochanomizu in 1902. The Kōbu Line appears to have been the first line in Tōkyō to be electrified, in 1904, while the first electric train (tramcar) in Japan ran in Kyōto in 1895. (It should also be borne in mind that 'electric train' and 'electric tram' are represented by the same term in Japanese, and that differentiation is always problematic.)

[447] His first child, a daughter Reiko, was born on February 1st 1901; his second child, a son Senzō, was born on March 11th 1902; his third child, a second son Mizuho, was born on February 21st 1904. Later children were another daughter Chiyoko on March 9th 1908, and a third daughter Seiko on November 27th 1909.

art above and beyond life, like Kunikida could. As a result I ended up churning out a lot of 'pot boiler' works, which I was by no means proud of but which I could at least convert into cash. Whenever I had any money to spare I bought foreign books.

Even in those days Tōkyō had changed greatly from the time I had first arrived there. The remodelling of the city was about eighty percent completed, the underground water-supply had been laid down, and the streets made to look very attractive. Four or five years previously Hibiya Park had been created, and although at the time the trees there were very sparse and it didn't look very park-like, it was now a marvellous green park.[448] The day I decided to go off to the war I passed through there, and the plum blossoms looked beautiful against the sky.

A Group of Young Men

In the street behind the British Embassy in Banchō in Kōjimachi there was a little Western-style restaurant, standing all by itself. There were a lot of trees nearby, and looking out from the restaurant you could also see the red brick wall of the embassy and a gentle slope.

The name of the restaurant was written starkly in black against a pale painted background:

'Kairakutei — Western Cuisine'.

"The owner used to be a cook in the British Embassy, so the food's excellent," said Kanbara, who went ahead and arranged several of our meetings there.[449]

In those days Ariake was living in a house behind the military hospital in Hayabusachō. It was a period when, thanks to his 'Lonely Lament' and 'Ariake Collection', you could say that he dominated the world of poetry.[450] He was particularly fond of the type of poetry represented by the Rossettis, the Pre-Raphaelite School, and Swinburne. We often used to call on him in his house in Hayabusachō.

I went to the restaurant straight from my office, and went on upstairs. On opening the door I found Ariake there, who gave me a hearty welcome as always.

---

[448] The park was built in 1903, along German lines, and was the first Western-style park in Japan. As Katai is referring to the period early 1904 his chronology is clearly a little suspect.

[449] The first meeting there was held in January 1902, though the group had met before at members' houses.

[450] Respectively 'Dokugen Aika', his second poetry collection, published in May 1903, and the considerably later 'Ariake Shū', his fourth collection, published in January 1908. Katai may have intended Ariake's first collection, 'Young Blades of Grass' ('Kusawakaba'), which was published in January 1902.

"No-one else has come yet," he said, "but I'm sure they will. Kunikida will of course, and Yanagita said he'd call in on the way back from the office, and Ikuta also said he'd come."[451]

"What about Oguri?"

"He hasn't let me know, but I'm sure he'll come," he said confidently.

A short while later Ikuta arrived. He had a large mouth, which was always smiling, a cheerful disposition, and neatly groomed hair. Thanks to works such as 'Princess Fumiko' he earned quite a reputation as a new writer.[452]

"I saw your 'Genealogy of a Young Woman', you know![453] Typical woman-worship! No-one can match you, Tayama, when it comes to that sort of stuff!" He gave a hearty laugh.

The pale, diminutive, sprightly Oguri arrived next, followed by Kunikida with his dashing air, and finally by the tall, rather sober-looking Yanagita.

The conversation grew very lively around the table.

Kanbara laughed out loud. The talk turned to Oguri's 'Youth', which was running in the Y Newspaper.[454] Yanagita made a tongue-in-cheek remark about it to play up to Oguri: "You know, there's a woman of my acquaintance who looks forward very much to reading it every morning. In fact she makes things a bit awkward for me by asking me what's going to happen to Shigeru." Oguri rose to the bait, and suddenly became full of his own importance. At this, Ikuta chipped in with a comment: "Oguri's a very popular young man at the moment, so I suppose we've got to allow him a little bit of pride."

Kizan was a member of the Thursday Society but was also close to the G-sha and so was particularly friendly with Oguri.[455]

---

[451] Ikuta Kizan (1876-1945), novelist.

[452] 'Fumiko Hime' appeared in April 1906 in the Ōsaka Shinpō but was then banned. Again, the date of this work is incompatible with the period depicted, which is almost certainly before November 1904, when the group started to move to a different location (see notes to later section 'The Ryūdokai [Society]').

[453] Katai's 'Shōjo Fu' appeared in 'Bungei Kurabu' on January 1st 1904.

[454] 'Seishun', a long novel serialised in the Yomiuri Shinbun from March 15th 1905-November 12th 1906. Clearly, this work is unlikely to have been discussed in the same session as Katai's 'Shōjo Fu', and would almost definitely not have been discussed at this restaurant. Shigeru mentioned below is one of the characters of 'Youth'.

[455] Confusingly there appear to have been at least two 'Thursday Societies' (Mokuyōkai), the most famous being the one started by Natsume Sōseki in October 1906. The one referred to here is the group started by Iwaya Sazanami in approximately 1899, a group which included Nagai Kafū and Inoue Aa (1878-1923) and which published such magazines as 'Katsubundan' (The Living Literary World, November 1899-June 1901). Its meetings were held at Sazanami's house in Kōjimachimotozonochō (present-day Ichibanchō).

Yanagita favoured Izumi, which seemed to upset Oguri. "That Izumi! I can't stand his neo-romanticism! It's just a load of contrived fancy! Is Maeterlinck like that, Tayama?"

"Very different."

"Really? Well, I just can't stand that new sort of stuff!"

Kunikida, on the other hand, was busy making fun of Ikuta. Ikuta was laughing out loud. "Your works are worse than obscene! Of course it's only right they should be banned!" said Kunikida, at which even the easy going Ikuta ended up heatedly trying to defend himself.[456]

At this point several Western dishes were brought to the table. There was fried food, cutlets, raw cabbage, and suchlike.

"Not bad at all."

"Something different, that's for sure."

"And — " said Ariake with pride — "the setting's very good, as I'm sure you all agree. It's nice to be somewhere like this, a little out of the way. It's the sort of place you could find in Paris, don't you think?"

"Exactly" said Yanagita. "It's as though it's straight from the pages of Alphonse Daudet's memoirs."

Then Oguri remarked: "That novel of Sudermann's that K was writing about recently shows an interesting clash between old and new ways of thinking.[457] It's certainly an essential feature. Do you have the work, Tayama?"

"Yes I do."

"Then tell us about it."

As I was so bad at speaking I let Yanagita do the talking for me. Then afterwards the talk turned to poetry. We talked about people like Verhaeren, Verlaine, and Baudelaire, with the conversation centring on the translation of many such poets which Ueda had published in 'Myōjō' under the title 'The Sound of the Tide'. Ariake still didn't even possess any English translations of them!

The talk then turned to Turgenev, and on to Tolstoi, and Maupassant, and on to a discussion of the literary scene. The room was filled with Kunikida's cutting sarcasm, and Yanagita's indignant comments, and Ikuta's hearty laughter. The gas lamp cast a bright bluish-white light over the proceedings.

---

[456] Many of Ikuta's works were banned as a result of themes such as adultery, though they were almost all later than the period depicted here. Apart from the work 'Princess Fumiko' mentioned earlier, his better-known banned works include 'Vanity' ('Kyoei', November 1907, Ekifūsha), 'The City' ('Tokai', February 1908, 'Bungei Kurabu'), and 'Bird Entrails' ('Tori no Harawata', October 1907, 'Chūō Kōron').

[457] Katayama Kōson (1879-1933), a scholar of German literature, who wrote most of his articles on German literature (especially symbolist poets) after 1906. The work of Sudermann's is probably 'Cat's Bridge'.

Everyone was flushed with youthful vitality, and there was an air of limitless ambition.

Next moment, Ikuta was going on about his love-life — clearly not having learned his lesson — and was being made fun of by Kunikida. Yanagita, typically, was involved in an earnest discussion, with Oguri.

On the way back we talked about what a nice fellow Ikuta was, and how the meetings were always livelier when he was there. Ikuta and Oguri always went off together to see some woman or other.

We held three or four meetings there. It was the forerunner to the Ryūdokai [Society].[458]

Ueda Bin

Ueda Bin ranks second only to Ōgai Gyoshi with regard to the introduction of foreign literature to Japan. He was a talented, intelligent, refined man who wrote elegantly and who had something about him that made him stand head and shoulders above the common crowd.

In comparison with Chogyū it is Bin who stands the higher in pure literary terms. Chogyū had popular appeal and enthusiasm, but he was certainly not as knowledgeable as Bin when it came to foreign literature.

Bin was, however, often called affected and smug. Such criticism may have been brought on by his characteristic upper-class air. I think it unfortunate, though, that his true artistic potential was not realised as a result of his scholastic pursuits.[459]

The first time I met Ueda was, as I said earlier, at that New Year's Party of the 'Bungakukai' group [in 1896]. But we didn't have a particularly deep relationship afterwards, and would usually merely exchange greetings if and when we met.

Our relationship grew especially distant after he took up with the 'Myōjō' people. At that time 'Myōjō' was a very great influence on young men of letters and, by comparison with other magazines, was not bad at all. It influenced a lot of magazines in this country to include woodblock prints and to revise their format. However, I never got on well with Yosano from the start, right from the time of his 'East, West, North, South'.[460] Not that that means we had much to do with each

[458] Founded in November 1904. See later section 'The Ryūdokai [Society]'.

[459] After graduating from the English literature department of the Tōkyō Imperial University in July 1897 Bin spent almost the entire remainder of his life as a lecturer and professor of literature. His name is particularly linked with Tōkyō Imperial University (1903-1907), along with Sōseki and Arthur Lloyd, and Kyōto Imperial University (1908-1916).

[460] 'Tōzainanboku' was Tekkan's first poetry collection, published in July 1896 by Meiji Shoin.

other. We only met on two or three occasions and only knew each other by sight.

But naturally I had to admire Akiko's poetry. I even used to learn by heart — and recite — some of the poems from her 'Tangled Hair' and the collection that followed it.[461] There is no disputing that she was the leading woman writer after Ichiyō.

It's something of a miracle that 'Sound of the Tide' was put out in 'Myōjō'. Ueda was at least ten years ahead of the times, and 'Sound of the Tide' was certainly a dazzling event in the poetry world of the day.

He went from Keats and Shelley and Wordsworth to Rossetti and then in a sudden leap to Verhaeren. It's hardly surprising that the people on the poetry scene found it hard to take in.

Ueda disliked Zola. Amongst the naturalists it was Daudet whom he preferred. He did have a certain admiration for Maupassant, but only for his brighter artistic aspects, and he didn't go very deeply into his literature. It was the same with Russian literature — he avoided the gloom, and only liked the brighter parts. He very much belonged to the school of the fresh and the modern.[462]

In other words, he didn't like to go too deeply into anything gloomy, and even if he did concern himself with such a work it could only really appeal to him if it had some high-class artistry about it. I think this is why he was dissatisfied with the naturalist movement that arose after 1905/6.

I'm also told by one of his pupils that although he had the ability to talk about things he lacked the ability to put them into practice: "When he was telling people what to do he'd be really enthusiastic. 'Go ahead, do it!' he'd say. But then, for some reason or other, he'd become very aloof. I know he had his academic duties to occupy him, but I still feel there was something 'lukewarm' about him."

I think that's what so many people meant when they talked of his 'dilettantism'.

But for all that I'm sure that Ueda did always want, somehow or other, to realise his potential. Of course I do appreciate that in terms of our

---

[461] 'Midaregami' was published in August 1901 (Shinshisha). The collection that followed it was 'Ko-ōgi' (Little Fan, January 1904).

[462] Sic ("Akumade 'Bankin-ha' de, 'Seishin-ha' de atta"). This sentence seems totally incongruous, and moreover clashes somewhat with a later remark about Bin's penchant for the Edo period, as well as his remark in 'Buds of New Ideology'. I believe it is an awkward attempt on Katai's part to indicate Bin's being 'au courant', but only with those things that appealed to him. Katai's phraseology and chronology in this part of 'Tōkyō no Sanjūnen' seem exceptionally loose (eg. see the preceding and succeeding chapters).

ideologies and tendencies we were bound to be at odds, but even so he was certainly an enemy to be reckoned with.

In his Edo taste he shared common ground with Kōyō Sanjin. And his ornate style was shared with Oguri Fūyō. For the same reason it was Nagai Kafū with whom he had things in common later on. He always seemed set apart from the common, the base, and the vulgar.

He once put out a magazine called 'Geien'.[463] Morita and Ikuta Chōkō were amongst those who worked with him on that magazine, and it clearly reveals his views on art and literature.[464] Ikuta Chōkō's 'Essay on Oguri Fūyō' appeared in the magazine, but it was a singularly poor work, and the comparison between Fūyō's works and foreign literature makes one blush to read it nowadays.[465]

However, it was an undeniable fact that Ueda's artistic predilections made him an enemy to the naturalist movement that arose around 1905/6, and I felt that there would come a time when we would have to take up a more positive stance in opposition to him.

Sad to say, though, 'Geien' came to an end after only a year or so.

Naturally the views held by Ikuta Chōkō and Morita on naturalism are even today somewhat influenced by Ueda's views. I also think they have inherited something from 'Myōjō'.

The Room Upstairs

I was led to the room upstairs at the S Book Company.[466] The S Company had been a powerful force in the world of letters ever since Kōyō's days, and was well-known for its marvellous covers, its attractive frontispieces, and the quality of its paper. I was a young literary novice at the time, and I was going there to visit Kawakami Bizan, who was being 'detained' there as a result of being unable to finish his writing.[467]

If I remember correctly it was in early spring, in either February or March. I felt strangely business-like. I'd had a novel called 'Evening

---

[463] See Note 444.

[464] Morita Sōhei (1881-1949), novelist; Ikuta Chōkō (1882-1936), critic and novelist.

[465] 'Oguri Fūyō Ron', in the March 1906 issue.

[466] The Shunyōdō Company.

[467] Publishers often went to such lengths to ensure that authors (especially important ones) actually did complete contracted work. The practice still continues, and is known nowadays as 'canning' ('kanzume', as opposed to Katai's term 'toriko ni naru', 'become a captive'). Of course, publishers have no legal authority to detain writers. The writer has to agree to be 'detained', and then (nowadays) moves into a hotel near the publishing company, where he shares a room with a 'supervisor' appointed by the company. Few if any writers appear to have protested against the practice, no doubt welcoming the opportunity to get down some intensive writing, the notoriety, and the chance to avoid the possibility of more serious consequences over breach of contract.

Frost' serialised in some fifty or so issues of the Y Newspaper since about the previous November, and I was now hoping to get it put out as a book.[468]

"Hallo there."

Kawakami gave me a breezy greeting.

That sunny six-mat room was quite notorious, since not a few writers had ended up spending a week or two there after finding themselves unable to write. Hōitsuan and Shōdayū, for example, were two such victims. Such events were always the source of gossip. People like me, who had still to make a name for themselves, felt jealous of those writers who became 'detainees'.

"I see Bizan's 'in custody' again!" one of the G-sha people said.

And so it was that I visited Kawakami, partly indeed out of curiosity.

He was sitting at a rosewood desk, dressed very fashionably and looking rather princely. If I remember correctly it was the second half of 'Dark Tide' that he was being asked to write.[469]

"Are you able to write anything?" I asked.

"No, it's hopeless!"

"But you do seem to be writing something."

"Well, yes, I am putting pen to paper, but...."

He offered me a cushion. When he clapped his hands a girl brought some tea and cakes up from downstairs.

I talked about 'Evening Frost'.[470]

"I see," he said, putting his head on one side. "I hear things didn't go too well with the last young writer, so I don't quite know what to say...." He thought for a while. "But I'll see if I can put a word in. You know, you'll find before too long that book companies will be knocking on your door, to the point where you get fed up of it. It's just a question of being patient for a while."

I thanked him for any help he could provide, then added: "At least it's different here from being at home, in that you know you really

---

[468] 'Yūshimo' (Evening Frost) actually ran in the Yomiuri Shinbun March 21st-April 15th 1895, spanning some twenty issues only, and it was never subsequently published as a separate book. Katai appears to have confused his details with at least one other work, namely Bizan's 'Dark Tide' ('Yamishio'), which ran from November 6th-December 29th 1895 in the Yomiuri (some fifty issues), and possibly a further work 'Fuefuki River' ('Fuefukigawa' [near Kōfu]), a joint work by Katai and Kōyō which ran in the Yomiuri May 1st-July 17th 1895 and which *was* subsequently published in book form by Shunyōdō (December 1896).

[469] It was indeed 'Dark Tide' (see note above), but it should be noted that the work was never actually finished, despite its being put into book form by Shunyōdō (also in December 1896 and under the title 'Ajirogi' [Wickerwork]).

[470] That is, Katai is asking for Bizan to help him in getting the work accepted by Shunyōdō.

HAVE to write, so that must make it easier to come up with something."

"No, it's hopeless. There're too many distracting temptations. Friends keep coming, for instance, and asking me out for meals. And then there're all the interesting shows around here."

"Oh, I see. But I understand that quite a few people have been in your position, and have been made to write."

Kawakami laughed. "It's not exactly an honour, you know, writing in a situation like this!"

"Has Kōyō ever been in the same position?"

"No, not him. But it's true that lots of other people have."

That was about the extent of our conversation, and I took my leave after about an hour. I thought to myself how perfectly Kawakami's fashionable figure went with that book company room there in the entertainment district, and then I went on to think about the girls in the entertainment district, and the pleasures there. Does he write at night, I wondered. I supposed not. I imagined he went out somewhere. After all, there were lots of restaurants nearby. There were geishas too, and assignation-houses. I imagined the free and easy life of a successful writer, which of course I still knew nothing of, and then thought about how particularly wretched my own humdrum, 'stay-at-home' life was.

Even now, more than twenty years later, I get a strange feeling when I think that some writers became detainees in that upstairs room.

I mentioned it only recently when I was at the S Company. "Really?" they laughed. "Then it seems there's quite a history to the room. It's worth preserving!"

My own Anna Mahr[471]

Y K came to the reception-room at Hakubunkan and asked me to write a lead story for the September issue of 'Shinshōsetsu'. It was supposed to be about one hundred and twenty pages.[472]

It was two years after my return from the war, and one year after the fighting had ended.[473] Japan hadn't got any reparations, but society in

[471] Anna Mahr is the heroine of Hauptmann's 'Einsame Menschen' (Lonely People). She is a bright, vivacious, independent-minded student who provides a complete contrast with the rather dull, domesticated, old-fashioned Kitty, the wife of the protagonist Johannes Vockerat.

[472] Y K is *not* Yanagita Kunio, and seems likely to have been Yamagishi Kayō (1876-1945), a novelist who was very active 'behind the scenes' and often acted as middle-man in publisher-writer negotiations.

[473] As the date is spring or summer 1907, it is clearly 'three years' and 'two years' respectively (Katai returned in September 1904, while the war finished in September 1905).

general was full of high spirits as a result of the victory. In the literary world, Shimazaki's 'Broken Commandment' had come out and earned great praise, while Kunikida's 'Doppo Collection' had finally been recognised and was going into reprint.[474] "It looks like our time has finally come," laughed Kunikida.

I alone felt left behind. I'd gone off to the war, but I still hadn't written anything substantial. I knew how Shimazaki had left Komoro and worked stripped to the waist under that hot tin roof in the Ōkubo suburbs, and this made me all the more frustrated and determined to write something.[475] I was filled with a mixture of despair and impatience.

It was at this juncture that I received the request from 'Shinshōsetsu'.

"Right, let's see what I can do!" I said to myself determinedly.

I knew that this time I had to give it everything I'd got. While walking along the muddy roads of the newly developed suburbs on my way to and from the office I gave much anguished thought to coming up with a work.[476] But I kept rejecting ideas as somehow not being right.

Just at that time I was profoundly influenced by Gerhart Hauptmann's 'Einsame Menschen'. I felt that Vockerat's loneliness was my own. In addition I had to break away from my pattern to date and take some new direction with regard to my family and my work. Fortunately I had profited from my extensive reading of foreign literature — imperfect as it may have been — and in particular with regard to the new currents of thought in Europe. I felt that in the ideology of people such as Tolstoi, Ibsen, Strindberg, and Nietzsche I could clearly see fin-de-siècle suffering. I too wanted to tread that path of suffering. I wanted to fight valiantly against the world, and against myself. I wanted to try revealing things that I had kept hidden and covered, things that might even break me if I were to reveal them.

I decided to write about my own Anna Mahr, who had tormented me for some two or three years ever since that spring when the war with Russia broke out.[477]

---

[474] 'Doppo Shū' was published in July 1905, by Kinji Gahō-sha.

[475] After returning from Komoro on April 29th 1905 Tōson rented a house in Ōkubo (Shinjuku), and worked on the completion of 'Broken Commandment'. He had a little annex built on to the house to use as a study, and it had a cheap tin roof. He remained in Ōkubo till October 1906.

[476] On December 8th 1906 Katai had moved to his own house in the newly developed suburb of Yoyogi, in Sanyachō (present-day area of Yoyogi 4 and 5 Chōme and part of Kamizonochō). His daily route through the muddy fields to the station, as well as his anguish at the time, is described in detail in such works as 'Girl-watcher' ('Shōjo-byō' [lit: 'Ill over Girls'], May 1907, 'Taiyō').

[477] Okada Michiyo (1885-1968), later a writer of some note, who was a private pupil of Katai's from February 1904-January 1906. Katai was attracted to her both physically and spiritually.

In November the previous year I had had a new house built in suburban Yoyogi. I wanted to get my thoughts in order there, and settle down to some real work. I couldn't do anything about having to go to the office, but I hated being bothered by visitors even after getting home, especially visitors who just wanted to chat about trivia. I wanted to avoid that at all costs. And so, with that thought in mind, I had a detached house built out in the fields at the edge of town. It was an area of white morning frost, that often lingered on the roads right through the day, and an area where you could hear the sounds of the city in the distance, and the horn of the outer-suburban passenger coach. I enjoyed being able to spend uninterrupted hours in my study after getting home from the office.

My Anna Mahr was now back in her home town in the hills. I had visited her there the previous autumn, on my way back from a trip.[478] I still had a very clear picture of her in my mind. Should I write about her? If I did, I would have to realise that it would mean my abandoning completely my love for her. Should I then not write, and wait for some future occasion when that love might prosper?

I was in a quandary for some considerable time, but finally I was prompted to write the work by several factors, such as the time-limit on my promise to 'Shinshōsetsu', my position of having to write something decisive, and the appearance of new trends in the literary world.

It was late July. It had gradually got hotter, and the leaves of the parasol-tree in the garden rustled in the morning and evening breeze. The fresh greenery was now well advanced, and from time to time rain darkened the windows. On fine days the late-blooming azaleas were a dazzling red in the sunshine. I set up my desk in the drawing-room and started to write.

I got up early every morning and worked at my desk till about ten o'clock. Then I'd continue after getting back from the office, and the light shone brightly in the study [sic] till late at night. I finished the manuscript after about ten days.

I did feel that the work was not ineffective, but I wasn't expecting any really great response. I was also troubled by the thought that 'she' might read it. I felt embarrassed and awkward, and even after finishing the manuscript I didn't hand it over to 'Shinshōsetsu'.

The title was also a problem. 'Love and Love' would have been the best one, but there was already a work out by Tengai under that title and I didn't want to duplicate it.[479] Another couple of days passed as I wor-

[478] She lived in Jōgemachi in Hiroshima Prefecture (given misleadingly as Niimimachi in 'The Quilt'). Katai passed through the town at the end of October 1906.

[479] 'Koi to Koi'. Tengai's work by this title was published in June 1901 by Shunyōdō.

ried about the title. Then the chief writer of 'Shinshōsetsu', G, telephoned me at the office.[480]

"It's ready," I told him.

"You've put the character-readings in too?"

"Yes."

"And the title?"

"'The Quilt'." I ended up giving him a title I had come up with that morning on the way to work.

"'The Quilt'?" He seemed a little bewildered.

"The 'quilt' you sleep in."

"I see, 'Quilt'...... Right, well, I'll send someone over tomorrow to pick it up."

So it was that I was finally obliged to hand over the manuscript, which I duly did the next day.

The work appeared in 'Shinshōsetsu' in September and, oddly, caused a big stir. Oguri was the first to get in touch with me. "I feel I've now seen your true talent" was the comment he sent.[481] It was talked about here, there, and everywhere. Maeda, whose desk was next to mine at the office, said "I've read it, you know," and stared at me with a most extraordinary expression.[482] And that wasn't all. I soon received a sad, angry letter from the countryside, from my Anna Mahr.

I felt terribly sorry, and sent her a letter of apology.

The work became a talking-point in the literary world, and was called 'epoch-making' and 'the flesh and blood of naturalist doctrine'. 'Myōjō', which was rather inclined to the enemy camp, published a joint criticism that was a mixture of scorn and opposition.[483] 'Waseda Bungaku''s joint criticism was favourable. One of the more unusual criticisms was the abusive poem which Yoshii Isamu wrote in 'Myōjō', in Roman script.[484]

---

[480] Gotō Chūgai.

[481] Though this phrase is sometimes used in Japanese in a genuine sense, it is also used sarcastically, as is almost certainly the case here. Katai refers later (see 'Doppo's Death') to Oguri's constant ridiculing of him.

[482] Maeda Akira (1879-1961, also known as Kishirō), translator, critic, and Hakubunkan writer.

[483] This is not quite true. Not counting the poem discussed below, three out of four of the criticisms published in the October issue, including that by Tekkan, could be said to demonstrate grudging praise. The 'Myōjō' writers were opposed to the type of literature being developed by Katai, but nevertheless admired his frankness and courage.

[484] Yoshii Isamu (1886-1960), poet, dramatist, novelist, and major contributor to 'Myōjō'. The poem, which appeared in the October issue, was actually a joint work with Kitahara Hakushū (1885-1942), of which Yoshii's contribution was entitled, like Katai's work, 'The Quilt' ('Futon'). It is an attempt to ridicule the naturalists' 'banner waving', and includes a reference to Katai's 'sleep-dulled contribution' (ie. making a play on 'quilt').

Amongst my circle of friends, Yanagita gave a look as if to say "It wasn't necessary" but didn't actually utter a single word, while Ikuta Kizan said with a laugh that it was a bit on the sentimental side. I couldn't get any comment out of Shimazaki. Kunikida too said very little about it, but I do remember hearing him say at one Ryūdokai meeting, in reply to some criticism of it, words to the effect of "So what if it's sentimental?! That's the way Katai's love is, and even if it IS sentimental or whatever, it is at least plain and to the point!"

I forgot to mention that I did the proof-reading of 'The Quilt' in the priest's quarters at a temple in the hills of Nikkō.[485] I went there in the August with my young niece, to get away from the heat, and spent about a fortnight there.[486] I had intended to try and write something of 'Country Teacher', the material for which I had gathered two or three years before, but I ended up unable to write anything.[487]

When I started doing the proof-reading the young priest was very curious, and asked me to read it out to him.[488] So, I read part out to him and my niece.

Even nowadays he says things to me like, "It was a pity that you threw that manuscript away. It should have been put on one side. It was a real gem!"[489]

The Ryūdokai [Society]

The Ryūdokai took its name from the fact that its meetings were held at the Ryūdoken [Restaurant] in Ryūdochō in Azabu.[490]

The French cuisine there had a very good reputation, and the first people to go were a group of artists.[491] Unlike nowadays it was at the time a very small establishment, with just one or two rooms. There were a lot of Western-style paintings there, by people like Wada, Okada, Nakazawa, and Kume, and it was a nice, quiet place.[492]

---

[485] The Shōsonin, the same temple where he had stayed with Doppo in 1897.

[486] This niece is not Aiko (see Note 339). It has been suggested that it is Ōta Hideko (born 1902), the daughter of his brother-in-law Ōta Gyokumei, but in view of her age it is more likely to be one of the five daughters of Katsuyo (married 1884).

[487] See later section 'Country Teacher' and notes thereto.

[488] Sugawara Hidenobu (dates unclear).

[489] That is, after the novel had become so famous the handwritten manuscript would have become a valuable collector's item.

[490] Present-day Roppongi 7 Chōme, Minato-ku. The first meeting there was held November 22nd 1904.

[491] The Hakubakai (White Horse Society), from 1902. The central figure was the art critic Iwamura Tōru (1870-1917), who was keen to see a French-style café in Tōkyō.

[492] Respectively Wada Eisaku (1874-1959) (there is also a Western-style painter named Wada Sanzō [1883-1967], but Eisaku, who had illustrated the cover to 'Jojōshi' of 1897, seems the more likely), Okada Saburōsuke (1869-1939, who illustrated the fron-

Who of our group went there first? I think it was probably Kanbara Ariake, or else perhaps Hiratsuka Atsushi.[493] Anyway, I'm sure it was one of these two, and they then took Kunikida there.

The thing that most attracted us young men was not whether the food was actually good or not, but the fact that it was French. When we first held a meeting there I think Kanbara was the secretary, and that the name 'Inspired Spirit Society' was written on the menu.[494] We laughed as various dishes were brought out with names such as 'Kōyō's Coffin' and 'Myōjō's Akiko'.[495] Anyway, we gradually started holding our monthly or bi-monthly meetings there rather than at the restaurant behind the British Embassy.

First of all it was Kunikida who was the central figure of the group, but when Yanagita came he enthralled people with his characteristic eloquence, and talked about Paul Bourget's 'Pastel of Man' and 'Portrait of Women'.[496]

There was rivalry over some woman between Osanai and a 2nd lieutenant in the Reserves called Kojima — who was also active as a writer to some extent — and I remember Kojima turning on Osanai with a furious look on his face.[497] I can still picture clearly how Yanagita got very angry at this and leapt to Osanai's defence. "I've no idea what's been going on," he said, "but this is OUR meeting! It is NOT the place to bring up such matters!" Osanai blushed, looking as timid as a dove.

---

tispiece to Katai's 'Inaka Kyōshi' of 1909), Nakazawa Hiromitsu (1874-1964), and Kume Keiichirō (1886-1934). All of these painters were prominent as illustrators of literary works, especially 'Myōjō'.

[493] Hiratsuka Atsushi (1884-?), journalist.

[494] 'Fūkotsukai'. There is a story in circulation that the character for 'fū' (inspired) was accidentally replaced by a similar looking character 'bon' meaning 'mediocrity', with the result that the society had the name 'The Mister Average Society'.

[495] Some accounts of this meeting say that a dish of pork bones was called 'Kōyō's Bones' (which may or may not be the same as 'Kōyō's Coffin'), and that the names were thought up by an over-enthusiastic proprietor much to the embarrassment of most persons present. In any event the whole business seems in questionable taste. Possibly in an attempt to redeem this disrespect towards Kōyō, who was buried in nearby Aoyama Cemetery, the group henceforth held special commemorative meetings on each October 30th, the anniversary of his death.

[496] Katai gives these, in English, as two separate works, whereas Bourget's 'Pastels: Dix Portraits de Femmes' (1889) is one work (dealing only with women). He possibly intends as well the 'portraits' of men in 'Essais de Psychologie Contemporaine' (1882) and 'Nouveaux Essais de Psychologie Contemporaine' (1885).

[497] Kojima Shafū (c.1880-?), writer, who was stationed in the immediate vicinity of the Ryūdoken. One account of this incident has it that Kojima actually drew his sabre on Osanai, but in my opinion this is an exaggeration due to the ambiguous term 'kenmaku', which is the term used here by Katai and which can mean either 'to draw a sword' or, figuratively, 'to turn on someone in a rage'. The latter meaning seems the more likely, since Katai makes no specific mention of a sword being brought to the meeting as part of a uniform, etc.

Kojima was a big, fat man. He'd graduated from the School of Foreign Languages, was good at French, and liked Chateaubriand's 'René'.

Kunikida brought along Nakazawa Rinsen. He had works to his credit such as 'Wonderful Whiskers Collection', and we respected him as a critic.[498] He was a gentle, silent type, full of intense feeling but never showing it, and always with a smile on his face. Yanagita remarked, after being introduced to him, "He's a very pleasant fellow indeed. It's interesting that you can find people like that amongst engineers. There's something really nice about him."

The laughter of Iwano and Kanbara was a conspicuous feature of our society.[499] Both of them attended regularly.

"I hear that one of our own Ryūdokai members is soon to set off for France," said Kunikida. "We must make sure we give him a really good farewell party." Our enthusiasm for foreign literature was so intense that we necessarily thought along such lines.

Oguri also came. So too did Ikuta, with his booming laughter. Shimazaki came too, from about the time he put out 'Broken Commandment' after returning from Komoro, and afterwards — when Kunikida no longer came — he became a popular figure at our meetings.[500]

By then the Ryūdoken had changed to the modern Western-style building it is today, and the proprietress — who seemed like an ex-teahouse owner — had started to lavish so much attention on us. People were saying that naturalist literature was born at the Ryūdokai, so later on we had lots of reporters coming along, and meetings of twenty-five or more people were not uncommon.[501]

At that time people like Katagami, Maeda, and Yoshie also attended.[502] So too did Togawa Shūkotsu, and Egi Tasuku, the present-day politician and former Chief Cabinet Secretary.[503]

Shimazaki said at one later stage, with a laugh, "We were young in those days, weren't we! Fancy going all the way to Azabu!"

---

[498] Nakazawa Rinsen (1878-1920), engineer by profession, also noted as a critic, novelist, and translator. One of Doppo's closest friends. 'Binka Shū' (also translatable as 'Splendid Sideburns Collection'), May 1905. A collection of criticisms and translations.

[499] Iwano Hōmei (1873-1920), poet, novelist, critic.

[500] Kunikida's health started to deteriorate from the middle of 1905, and he frequently spent time out of Tōkyō in an attempt to recover. He was finally hospitalised in February 1908 (see following chapter).

[501] Chikamatsu Shūkō, for example, said that "Naturalism was born in the ashtrays of the Ryūdokai."

[502] Katagami Noboru (1884-1928), critic, and Yoshie Kogan (1880-1940, also known as Yoshie Takamatsu), poet and critic.

[503] Egi Tasuku (1873-1932).

The Ryūdokai gradually declined after we started holding large meetings in Yanagibashi.[504]

Doppo's Death

I'd get off at the station, walk through the old town — still with something left about it of the days when it was a relay-station — cross over the level-crossing, and come to a primary school surrounded by poplars. From there I could see a pine wood, and the white clouds around Mount Fuji sparkling in the cold air.

Many times did I walk along that winding road, through pines and fields, past elegant summer-houses and humble thatched cottages and fishermen's huts.

Kunikida had gone into the Nanko Hospital, in Chigasaki in Sagami, in February 1909 [sic].[505]

I was full of emotion as I walked along. Kunikida had finally had his talents recognised, stood at the very centre of the new trends, and had had his 'Doppo Collection' and 'Fate' reprinted several times.[506] And now he had contracted an incurable disease! Kunikida was my closest friend, so naturally I was deeply saddened. At the time, I was writing 'Life' in the Y Newspaper, and whenever I was a few issues in hand I visited him there in the hospital.[507]

I can still clearly remember the night I first visited him.[508] I wrote about it in 'Relations', and it is a scene I could depict over and over

---

[504] Yanagita Kunio in particular felt that by this stage the society had lost its original character, and on February 1st 1907 he founded the Ibsen Society (see later section by this title), with a dozen or so Ryūdokai members (who did not necessarily cease to attend Ryūdokai meetings afterwards). The Ryūdokai continued in some strength till March 1913, when a farewell party was held for Tōson, who was setting off for France. This is considered the last real meeting of the Ryūdokai, though it was resurrected, virtually in name only, by Iwano Hōmei and others in 1915 and survived theoretically till 1918.

[505] It was categorically 1908 (February 3rd), as Katai himself makes clear elsewhere. Sagami is present-day Kanagawa Prefecture.

[506] 'Unmei' (Fate), a collection of Doppo's stories published by Sakura Shobō in March 1906.

[507] 'Sei', April 13th-July 19th 1908, Yomiuri Shinbun.

[508] This date is invariably given as February 25th. However, the visit he made on February 25th was one where, unlike the situation described below, he spent the night at Chigasaki Inn, in the company of Oguri Fūyō and the artist Kosugi Misei (1881-1964). (Katai refers to this episode later in the chapter and gives the date as the end of March, but it can be proven to have taken place in February from a report of it in 'Bunshō Sekai' on March 15th, which clearly gives the date as February 25th.) On the other hand, his first visit as described here must have taken place after the 14th (February), as he refers to Kunikida's family staying there and they are known to have travelled down to Chigasaki on that date. The most likely explanation is that Katai has confused details from several visits, and that the visit he proceeds to describe was not in fact his first visit (especially in view of his reference to it too being in March).

again.[509] He was lying in bed in a separate room near the sea, and his wife and Okimi were taking it in turns to nurse him.[510] Okimi was his final lover. She was a nurse, and he had got to know her when she was nursing at his house in Shiba.[511] Regardless of what may have been said amongst friends I had from the start looked with approval upon the affair. Even though it may have involved a clash with his wife I think that the very fact that Okimi nursed him to the bitter end shows that she loved him very much. I feel that it gave an artistic coloration to his life to have attracted such a woman to him at his deathbed, after having been caused such distress by a woman like Onobu.

There was a westerly wind blowing at the time, and the sand was hitting against his windows with a fearsome force. There was a shelf against one wall, laden with medicine bottles, and some five or six feet in front of it was a hibachi. It was there that I sat talking with him.

Because our literature was being recognised as a result of the new trends, and because Kunikida had numerous acquaintances in journalism, his condition was constantly reported in the Tōkyō newspapers, and his name much talked of. Satō of Shinchōsha was planning just then to publish 'A Collection of Twenty-eight Writers' and to present it to the ailing Kunikida.[512]

Kunikida's flourishing name made a strong contrast with his wretched sickbed. But even at that sickbed we talked with unflagging enthusiasm about literature.

When it grew late I went to take my leave, but Kunikida asked me to stay. I myself wanted to stay too, so I got Okimi to show me to a nearby inn. She and I walked in silence along the hospital's long corridor. I wanted to ask her about the affair with Kunikida, but couldn't bring myself to speak about it. Compared with Kunikida's wife Okimi looked neat and elegant, and understandably attractive. There were lights at intervals along that long corridor.

---

[509] 'En', March-October, 1910, Mainichi Denpō. The description of the scene is much the same as the one given below, and does not clarify the date.

[510] Okui Kimi(ko) (1881-1909?) was a nurse who had first nursed Doppo's ailing father. She and Doppo became lovers after his father's death in January 1904. After Doppo's death she is reported to have returned home to Saga (Kyūshū) broken-hearted, and to have died the following year of unclear causes.

The system in most Japanese hospitals is different from that of most Western ones, in that the nursing is generally done by relatives and private nurses rather than nurses on the hospital staff.

[511] This is a reference to her nursing of his father. The house was in Sakuradahongō (present-day Nishishinbashi 1 Chōme/Shinbashi 1 Chōme, Minato-ku).

[512] Satō Giryō (1878-1951), publisher and founder of Shinchōsha in May 1904. 'Nijūhachinin Shū' was a collection of writings from twenty-eight of Doppo's literary colleagues, as a tribute to the dying man. It was edited by Katai and Fūyō and published by Shinchōsha on April 15th 1908.

"Just a moment, please," said Okimi as she searched for her shoes at the hospital door. She then led the way through the pines.

"Is it far?"

"No, we're almost there. There's a large inn about half a mile further on, called the T Inn, but the one we're going to now is quite small.[513] It's where hospital visitors often stay when it gets late."

The seaside air on a March evening, and the quiet pine wood with its occasional plum blossoms, struck me as extremely romantic.

"It's here," said Okimi as she pointed to an inn that was totally indistinguishable from the other thatched houses. This too filled me with poetic feelings.

"What an interesting inn!"

"Well, it only barely qualifies as an 'inn', but...." said Okimi as she went on ahead and announced that I wanted to stay. A young maid came out and led me through to a room. There was a moon that evening, and the moonlight wove patterns with the shadows of the pines. Beyond were the sand-dunes, and from beyond those I could hear the gentle sound of the waves. It was indeed a romantic scene. I had soy-boiled horse-mackerel and a bottle of saké. All night long I could hear gentle sounds filtering through the pines to my pillow.

Kunikida's wife had come with the children and rented a little three-roomed house amongst the pines directly opposite the inn where I stayed.[514] From there she went to the hospital to nurse her husband, taking turns with Okimi. There was a little swing at the edge of the pines, and I could see the sad sight of the boy and the girls playing on it.[515]

I could feel the tears welling within me at the sight of the boy, who was about six, taking a short-cut alone through the pines to visit his father in the hospital. It was also sad to see the girls, dressed in their muslin topcoats.

That pine wood near the hospital, and that stretch of coast, hold many memories for me. Sometimes I walked along there alone, sometimes in

[513] The T Inn is the Chigasakikan (Tigasakikan) [Inn].

[514] As discussed in Note 508, Doppo's wife and children came to stay in Chigasaki on February 14th. There were three children: Sada, a daughter born October 29th 1899 (died 1920); Torao, a son born January 5th 1902 and later a writer of some note (died 1970); and Midori, a daughter born June 18th 1904. (A further son, Tetsuji, was born after Doppo's death, on September 1st 1908. The pregnancy must have been confirmed while Doppo lay dying, and it is odd that Katai makes no mention of this 'life out of death' episode. It is particularly odd in view of the fact that it is a theme which was dominating his literature at that very time. In 'Life', for example, he deliberately brings forward by one year the date of his wife's first pregnancy to coincide with his mother's death, thus highlighting the counterbalance of life and death.)

[515] It is worth making the touching observation that the swing was made by Kimiko, as Doppo's children found no playmates in the area.

the company of friends. I wasn't sure if Mayama Seika genuinely worshipped Kunikida or whether he only wanted to use the ailing patient for publicity, but at any rate he was the first person to ask me to take him to visit Kunikida, which I did.[516] But afterwards he did visit Kunikida there on many occasions, and was most attentive.

At this point I have to go at some length into certain background details so that one can fully understand the happenings of this time, such as Nakamura Seiko wrote about in his 'Now They'll Dance'.[517] I think that, with the emergence of new trends at that time, Oguri was at pains to ensure that he didn't lose his position and influence, and that accordingly he felt it necessary to bring even the dying Kunikida into that sphere of influence. Whether Mayama knew that or not, or whether perhaps he himself felt the same way as Oguri, I know not, but they suddenly appeared on the scene and tried to displace even Kunikida's closest friends. This may also have stemmed from the fact that it was Shinchōsha that was publishing 'Collection of Twenty-eight Writers' and that Shinchōsha was at the time particularly close to the Totsukatō [Group].[518] Anyway, I later regretted having taken Mayama to see Kunikida.

In addition, I'm convinced that Oguri and Mayama were trying to get me into their group, too. I had known Oguri for some time on a personal level, but on a literary level I was very loath to call him a colleague. In his cheap witticisms and frivolous lampoons he had something about him left over from the Genyūsha, and I hated that flippant attitude of his towards even the dying Kunikida, to the effect that "That guy's not got much longer left, that's for sure!" I hated him for having written such frivolous nonsense, for example, even when it was meant to bring some comfort to a dying man.[519] Maeda got very angry over this, and it was

---

[516] Mayama Seika (1879-1948), novelist. The visit was May 2nd. The comment concerning publicity is partly a reference to the fact that between May 11th-June 23rd Seika published eight accounts of Doppo's condition in the Yomiuri, known collectively as 'Kunikida Doppo-shi no Byōjō o Hōzuru Sho' (A Report on the Condition of Kunikida Doppo).

[517] Nakamura Seiko (1884-1974), novelist. 'Karera wa Odoru' appeared in 'Taiyō', rather belatedly, in September 1916. It deals with the alleged frenzied attitude engendered in the naturalists by Doppo's death, and describes events on the night immediately following his death (which Katai also gives an account of later in this chapter).

[518] The Totsukatō centred on Fūyō, and took its name from Totsuka in Shinjuku, where he was living from July 1907. Its members were largely pupils of Fūyō, such as Mayama Seika and Nakamura Murao (1886-1949, novelist, not to be confused with Nakamura Seiko).

[519] This is presumably a reference to Fūyō's contribution to 'Collection of Twenty-eight Writers' (though it should not be forgotten that he was a co-editor of the work as well), a short story entitled 'Ryōen' (Cool Flames) which could be considered insulting to Doppo for the following reasons: first, it was unfinished; second, it was six years old, having first been published in 'Shinshōsetsu' in April 1902; third, it was in extremely

not without reason that, when we happened to be there at the same time as Iwano and Masamune visited, we didn't stay at the Chigasakikan [Inn] but all went off together to Kōzu — the reason being that at the time a lot of Totsukatō people were staying at the Chigasakikan.[520] One must not overlook either the contrast between Masamune and Mayama.[521]

Anyway, I hated the unpleasant way in which Oguri and Mayama made their presence felt. Moreover, Oguri used to mock me at the least opportunity. And to add to it all I was very occupied with writing 'Life', and my nerves were rather on edge as a result.

However, my memories of the Chigasakikan are not all unpleasant. One day I chanced to meet Oguri and Kosugi Misei, and we walked together along the beach to the Chigasakikan.[522] It was the end of March [sic] and still cold, most of the rooms were shut up, and it was a very lonely and gloomy corridor that we walked along.[523] I'll never forget the quiet, pleasant night I spent there on that occasion.

Unaware of these various goings-on, Kunikida was growing daily worse. People would bring him presents of Chikuyō eel, or beef fillet, and he would say things like, "I don't mind dying if I have to, but I would like to visit Shinbashi once again before I do."[524] And Mayama's 'The Latest on Doppo's Condition' kept appearing in the Y Newspaper.[525]

---

bad taste as an offering to a dying man in that it not only dealt with the death of a young husband but also voiced a view that it is not the deceased who should be pitied but his bereaved family, who are caused much suffering by his 'inconsiderate' (sic) death; fourth, artistically it was a very poor work, with the dialogue in particular being embarrassingly amateurish; and fifth, at a time when writers like Katai and Doppo were championing the individual its two main characters were shown — with no apparent criticism from the author — as mindless marionettes whose only aim in life was to serve the State. By contrast, Katai's contribution (as one example) was a short story — entitled 'Ippeisotsu' (One Soldier) — which, while perhaps unfortunate in one sense in that it dealt with a young man's death, was one that treated death in a serious, thought-provoking way that highlighted the question of individuality. It was also one of Katai's finest works from an artistic point of view, and one of his most recent (January 1st 1908, 'Waseda Bungaku').

[520] Masamune Hakuchō (1879-1962), novelist, critic, playwright. Kōzu is a coastal town about fifteen miles west of Chigasaki. The visit in question took place on May 23rd.

[521] Uno Kōji (1891-1961, critic and novelist), for example, later contrasted these two writers, both of whom were seen as rising stars, by a pun on the literal meaning of their pen-names, calling Hakuchō 'a white bird' and Seika 'a green fruit'.

[522] Kosugi Misei (1881-1964), also known as Kosugi Hōan, poet and painter. He illustrated 'Collection of Twenty-eight Writers', and his picture of Doppo on his deathbed is particularly well-known.

[523] See Note 508.

[524] Chikuyō was a restaurant famous for its eel dishes.

[525] See Note 516. Katai has slightly miswritten the title, giving 'Doppo-shi no Kinkyō o Hōzuru no Sho'.

There is a photograph of a large number of people clustered round Kunikida at the hospital door.[526] It's written about in 'Now They'll Dance' as well. On that occasion Maeda and I, wanting a photograph of Kunikida, specially arranged to go there with someone from Hakubunkan's photography section. However, both of us were upset over the business of the nonsensical writing, and went off to stay at Kōzu that evening. It was the following day that we went back there and that the photograph was taken.

Nakamura and Sōma spent that evening in the Chigasakikan.[527]

By then Kunikida's condition was very bad. He could hardly get out of bed, let alone walk, and had to be supported by Okimi and his wife. That photograph certainly holds many memories.

I went frequently to the hospital to see him, whenever I had got ahead with the 'Life' manuscript. Later on I endeavoured where possible to go alone, wishing to share with Kunikida my true feelings of sadness. In April the pine wood looked like an impressionist painting, as it was dotted with the colours of various flowers — the yellow of rape, the green of barley, the red of peach blossom.

At a fisherman's house along the road some gutted horse-mackerel lay spread out on a mat in the glorious spring sunshine.

There was a delicate haze over the sea, and white sails scudded quietly past Eboshi Rock.

"Terrible, isn't it!"

This was all I could ever find to say when Kunikida's wife turned to me in tears.

April became May, and May became June. A long rainy season set in. As I sat at my desk writing 'Life' I kept thinking of that cheerless hospital room on the coast.

I had had my share of arguments with Kunikida. There had been not a few times when I had thought things such as "The wretch! What a cheek he's got!" He was always pestering me with his manuscripts, too. Since I worked for Hakubunkan he was forever asking me "Just make sure everything's all right with this manuscript, will you?" But unfortunately the chief editor, Tsuboya, was a sworn enemy of Kunikida's as a result of something to do with local politics, and so whenever I took him any of Kunikida's manuscripts he always handed them back with some comment like "It's a waste of time if it's Kunikida's!"[528] I often got

---

[526] The photograph was taken on May 24th. Those appearing in it are, apart from Doppo himself, Katai, Maeda, Masamune, Hōmei, Nakamura Seiko, Fūyō, Kosugi Misei, Mayama Seika, Yoshie Kogan, and Sōma Gyofū (1883-1950, critic and poet).

[527] Sōma Gyofū (see note above).

[528] See Note 430.

caught between the two parties and ended up in an awkward position. But for all that Kunikida was a close and valued friend. Whenever we got together and talked, any conflicts were soon resolved. And yet, I now had to say goodbye to him forever.... The thought made me terribly sad, and I pictured him lying on his hospital bed, his face sunken and gray.

To add to it all, just at that time 'Life' was becoming difficult to write and constantly caused me trouble. As my name became more widely known my enemies increased too, and I had to keep up a spirited resistance against them. To lose a friend and ally at such a time was indeed depressing.

The rains cleared. My own Anna Mahr came back from the country and stayed once again in my house.[529] I had a lot of other personal business to attend to as well, after my elder brother's death the previous year.[530]

"I really must visit him again soon. It's very bad of me not to," I kept thinking to myself, but I was kept constantly busy by all my personal business. Then, one day, I received a postcard from Chigasaki, written by Kunikida himself. "I desperately want to see you again so please come at once," he wrote. I really did want to go to him that day — and if I had gone, then I would have been there at the end — but, I had only written one further day's episode of 'Life', so I decided to spend that evening writing two more episodes and then go early the following day. So that night I wrote till late, and it was after eleven when I got to bed. Then, in the middle of the night, there was a loud knocking at the front door. It was a telegram, which my wife took receipt of. It turned out to be a telegram informing me of Kunikida's death![531] I stood there in a daze, telling myself that I should have gone that same day.

I set off early in the morning. At Shinbashi Station I met up with Saitō Chōka's wife[532]. Kunikida's death had already been reported in the newspapers.

By the time I arrived at Chigasaki his body had already been taken to that house among the pines. There is no need for me to write here about the tears of his wife and Okimi. Kunikida's body was dreadfully emaciated, just skin and bones, and he had died with a peaceful look on his face, which was turned away.

---

[529] Okada Michiyo arrived back in Tōkyō in April, and stayed for a lot of the time with her brother (Sanemaro). Katai adopted her as his daughter not long afterwards, on January 14th 1909 (adoption annulled February 1917).

[530] Miyato had died of tuberculosis on November 9th 1907..

[531] Kunikida died at 8.40 p.m. on June 23rd.

[532] Kiyoko, wife of the journalist and novelist Saitō Chōka (1877-1950). The Saitōs were close friends of Doppo.

"You know, Tayama, I've been thinking deeply about death this morning. The difference between a short life and a long life is just the difference between fifty steps and a hundred steps. In fifty years from now you'll be gone from this world as well."

I remembered Kunikida's poignant words, spoken some time before in Ōkubo, and fell to thinking. His ill-fated life — a victim to love's torments and now a victim to such a death — struck me as a life befitting a poet, a life of colour and sadness.

The house was still quiet. The rain had just stopped and bright sunlight filtered through the pine trees, accompanied by the gentle sound of the sea. I was thankful that Mayama and Oguri were not there and that I could pay my respects to the departed Kunikida in quiet solitude. As I faced his coffin I composed a poem:

"The rain has stopped,
And drying in the sunlight
On the straw thatched eaves
Are white cocoons of silk,
As I mourn your death."

There was a time when I would never have believed that I would in fact be there, in that pine wood by the sea, mourning his death.

Tokutomi Sohō arrived. He had come as fast as he could after seeing the morning papers. His relationship with Kunikida could be called that of teacher to pupil. Kunikida was greatly indebted to him, and half his literary career was attributable to Sohō's good offices. Sohō had also helped him greatly in his affair with Onobu. I was so glad that Sohō had hurried there to pay his respects.

"So, it's all over. What must be, must be. He was a bit capricious at times, but there was a lot of good in him." Sohō went on to talk about the Kokumin Newspaper days.

Kunikida's wife and Okimi and Chōka's wife went out into the fields and gathered as many flowers as they could, which they then placed over Kunikida's body in the coffin.

Okimi's tears too fell into the coffin.

During the afternoon a great number of mourners arrived from Tōkyō. There could be but few occasions when so many mourners have gone to pay their respects to a person dying away from Tōkyō. The house was surrounded by writers and reporters. I myself was asked outside on several occasions to talk to reporters about Kunikida.

That evening we followed the coffin as it was taken to be burned at the Ropponshō Crematorium beyond the pines at Chigasaki.[533]

The scene that evening in the Chigasakikan has been described by Nakamura Seiko in his 'Now They'll Dance'. Why did I display such an unruly attitude?[534] It was because I was angry over the cloying insincerity of Oguri and Mayama. I was also upset by all the commotion that was going on. I am terribly, terribly sorry that I ever introduced Mayama to Kunikida. I am ashamed that I was led into a situation where I seemed to turn my back on sincere friends such as Nakazawa, Yanagita, Yoshie, and Nunami.[535] I just wanted to be alone to think about Kunikida.

"Well, at least Kunikida's not going to go unremembered," people were saying.

It was true. All the newspapers gave a lot of space to his death.

The new movements did indeed 'dance' a very lively tune upon his death.

Bizan's Death

Undoubtedly Bizan suffered from a persecution complex. Naturally, he also had problems in his day-to-day life. But it is certainly not for those reasons alone that he killed himself.[536]

Bizan's position in the literary world was made very difficult as a result of the new movements. His heyday was during Kōyō's later years, when he wrote works such as 'Dark Tide' and when Kōyō and Bizan were the two top writers to contend with. He came into contact with the new currents of thought at a fairly early stage, was the most modern-thinking of the Genyūsha people, and from that point on was in constant distress over literary matters. He had by that stage already started drawing closer to the 'Bungakukai' people. He knew Futabatei as well, and also associated with Takase Bun'en.

Bizan was always reading foreign literature. He read Balzac, Daudet, Zola, and even people like D'Annunzio. He abandoned 'Dark Tide' halfway through and went on a trip around Zushi and the Miura Paeninsula, saying that he was going to make a fresh start.[537] It was at this point

---

[533] Actually the Roppongi Crematorium, about two miles from the station. The procession left the house at 7.30 p.m., with the mourners then going at 10 p.m. for a commemorative meal at the Chigasakikan. Doppo's cremated remains were laid to rest in the Aoyama Cemetery on the 29th.

[534] He was reportedly drunk, belligerent, and virtually came to blows with Fūyō.

[535] Nunami Keion (1877-1927), poet.

[536] Bizan cut his own throat early in the morning of June 15th 1908, just eight days before Doppo's death. He was thirty-nine years old.

[537] The trip took place in the first half of 1897. He was based mostly at Emi Suiin's house near Zushi. His trip is described in the travelogue 'Futokoro no Nikki' (Pocket Diary, January 18th-March 9th, 1897, Yomiuri Shinbun).

in particular that he suffered with regard to his writing. He tried desperately to change his style, his approach — everything.

He felt very dissatisfied with the people he had associated with for many years, such as Kōyō, Suiin, Sazanami, Ryūrō, and Shian, and tried to break away from the old-style cheap witticisms and claptrap and fabrication and vulgarisms. Naturally this resulted in his moving away from the sphere of influence of the Genyūsha. Amongst the Genyūsha people it was Ryūrō who was treated as something of an outsider, then later on it was Bizan who received the same treatment.

By that stage Bizan was already established as a major writer. Therefore it was difficult for him to 'stoop' to mingle with the new up-and-coming writers. But on the other hand he was not really in a position where he could assume command of them from on high. He was trapped in 'no man's land' between the old and the new.

He was constantly struggling to develop a new style. Having returned from his trip to the Miura Paeninsula he moved into lodgings in the vicinity of Tsukudo in Ushigome and then moved again to Minamiyamabushichō, but he was simply unable to produce the type of work he wanted to and was increasingly troubled.[538] The fact that so many of his works around this time are unfinished reveals this clearly. In his day-to-day life, too, things were not going as he hoped. He now visited Kōyō on only the rarest occasions.

For some two years around that time I had a lot to do with Bizan. Of course, in those days he was my senior not only in years but also in terms of literary standing. I was then living in a little house in Kikuichō in Ushigome, near the woods. I was not yet married. Bizan stayed there with me on one occasion for about a week, telling me that domestic circumstances obliged him to 'keep on the move'. I remember talking to him about a work I was reading at the time. It was Lermontov's 'A Hero of our Times' — which I think I was reading in a cheap pocket edition — and I talked to him about the hero Pechorin's going off to Persia.

Bizan had a princely appearance and spoke in a quiet, refined, elegant manner. To think that that gentle outward appearance actually harboured such intense feelings!

"Oh, really?" he kept saying as I talked on. Even now, when my wife or someone says that, it brings back memories of Bizan.

My wife has always wondered how such a gentle person could do what he did.

---

[538] Upon his return to Tōkyō Bizan lodged with Nakamura Kasō (see Note 277) at the latter's house in Shinogawamachi, which is probably the address intended by Katai's 'Tsukudo'. Bizan moved frequently from that point, but was usually to be found in the Ushigome area not far from where Katai was living (till 1906).

Bizan moved from Minamiyamabushichō to Kitayamabushichō. There was a half-size scroll hanging there, with the words "A clap with one hand produces no sound."[539]

Whenever I visited him there he'd come to the door with red eyes.

"I just couldn't sleep last night."

Although he frequently stayed up late into the night he did not, for all that, produce very much. People were always making remarks like "I wonder what Bizan's doing?" and the implication behind such comments was that it was a mystery as to what exactly Bizan did do with his time if it wasn't writing.

Then Kōyō Sanjin died. New trends appeared in the literary world. There were many people who felt it was a slack period, and many adaptations of foreign literature came out, but all the time these new trends were gradually growing in strength, like sprouts from under the ground. Oguri Fūyō was one who seems to have suffered in the face of the new trends, but I think that Bizan suffered even more. He was desperate to open up some new path, and tried various experiments. Later on he also fraternised with Fūyō.

He was interested in such things as the tea ceremony and bonsai, particularly the former.

"*I* must get myself a wife too. I can't go on being single like this for ever," he said to me with a laugh some three of four years after I got married. But he found it difficult to get himself a wife. There was something about him which seemed to suggest that in the past he had had some terrible and painful experience with a woman.

Eventually he did get married though, to the woman who is now his widow.[540] My wife and I often used to call on the couple in their house in Minamiyamabushichō.[541] His wife was pretty, with a pale complexion, and she made one feel very relaxed. My wife in particular admired the warmth of their home.

Later on Bizan also attended regularly at Ryūdokai meetings. He completely abandoned any 'major writer' air and willingly associated with us younger writers in an endeavour to involve himself in the new trends. However, he could not succeed in abandoning his old literary approach, nor his old style.

After I moved to Yoyogi I rather lost touch with him. Whereas up until that point we had met at least two or three times a month, we now went two or three months without seeing each other.

---

[539] A well-known Zen statement. The meaning is that ears are not enough to understand what others are trying to say, and that one must also listen with one's heart.

[540] He married Satomi Shūko in August 1903.

[541] By all accounts he was living in Minamienokichō at the time. This is perhaps a slip of the pen by Katai, repeating the similar-sounding address he wrote earlier.

He was certainly lonely. Even though he had a group of followers, known as the Shunseisha, there was no-one amongst them who could give him strength or with whom he could really talk.[542] Presently 'Broken Commandment' was published, 'Doppo Collection' established a reputation, and people like Hakuchō and Seika appeared on the scene.

I only went once to the house in Tenjinchō where he killed himself. I went there to ask him if he'd spare one of his manuscripts for Kunikida's sake to put in 'Collection of Twenty-eight Writers', and he was very happy to oblige me.[543] There just happened to be a get-together there at the time, of his Shunseisha followers, and I joined them for a photograph.

And then, not long afterwards, came his death.....

I think I can understand what was going through his mind that morning. He had come to find it a nuisance to carry on living. His chronic persecution complex, his gentle personality that led him to 'bottle' everything up inside, and his tendency to give such importance to his literary standing — such were the causes of his terrible death.

The fifteenth of June — the anniversary of the company where I worked.[544] When I went into the office Ishibashi Shian said:[545]

"Bizan's gone and done it, with a razor...."

"What?!" I gasped in surprise.

"I've just been to see. He's done a really fine job, just here — " He pointed to his throat. "Apparently he got up very early this morning, when it was still dark, and his wife wondered what he was doing. Then she heard a groan, went to investigate, and found that he'd taken a razor to himself. I've just been told about it on the telephone."

I was terribly shocked. I thought about the loneliness of an artist. Is it not a fact that some artists are fated to suffer such tragedies, especially the sincerer they are? Why hadn't I visited him more often? Why hadn't I offered him companionship in his loneliness? These thoughts troubled me all through the anniversary meal.

After the meal was over I left immediately and called on Shimazaki in Shinkatamachi.[546] We talked about what had happened.

"Really? Is it true?!"

Shimazaki's voice too was trembling with shock.

---

[542] 'The Spring Star Society', more commonly known as the Shunsei*kai*, and not to be confused with Kōyō's Seishunsha (Youth Society).

[543] 'Yūdasuki' (Cotton Sleeve-cord), originally published in February 1906 in 'Waseda Bungaku'.

[544] It was the twenty-first anniversary of the Hakubunkan, which was founded by Ōhashi Sahei in June 1887.

[545] Shian joined Hakubunkan in 1901.

[546] Present-day Yanagibashi 1 Chōme, Taitō-ku.

We who follow the path of art are fated to face such tragedies from time to time. Love, and death, are always present in the world of art. Is it not true to say that it is through love and death that we are able to go beyond the mundane world and enter into a profound realm of mystery?

"It's certainly not just something that we can dismiss as being of no concern to us."

"Indeed not."

We sat in silence.

Takase Bun'en came to the wake, drunk. Ignoring the noisy chatter of the Genyūsha people he turned to the coffin and said tearfully, just as if he were speaking to a living person: "THAT's why I kept telling you not to get married! It's not the thing to do if you're an artist! YOU've got no problems, now that you're dead, but what about those left behind?!" I can still clearly remember Takase's words and attitude on that occasion.

When I Wrote 'Life'

I started writing 'Life' from the 1st March [sic] 1908.[547]

Four or five days earlier Shimazaki's 'Spring' had started appearing in the 'Asahi', so I realised I had to try all the harder.[548]

I knew that my literary position was at a critical point, in the sense that it was at an important yet dangerous stage. 'The Quilt' had created something of a literary sensation, and in the New Year I had put out 'One Soldier' and 'The House on the Bank', which had both received good reviews.[549] If I did not now put everything I could into my writing, who knows when such an opportunity might come my way again? Such were my thoughts at the time.

Most nights, when I got back from the office, I sat at my desk writing. It was cosy in the study, with the lamp lit.

I wrote the first few episodes.

The material for 'Life' was something I had had in mind for several years. It was about people around me, so I didn't need to use any imagination, but on the other hand it was, for that very reason, difficult

[547] 'Sei', an autobiographical work centring on Katai's mother, was published in the Yomiuri Shinbun from April 13th-July 19th 1908. At first reading it is possible to think that Katai's 'March 1st' is not an error but the date he started writing, as opposed to the date it appeared. However, it is clear from the following comparison with Tōson's work that he means 'writing' in the sense of 'publishing', and is in error by some six weeks.

[548] 'Haru' ran in the Tōkyō Asahi Shinbun from April 7th-August 19th (1908).

[549] Respectively 'Ippeisotsu', January 1st 1908, 'Waseda Bungaku', and 'Dote no Ie', also January 1st 1908, 'Chūō Kōron'. 'Ippeisotsu' is considered by many critics to be one of Katai's finest short works.

to write. I found it particularly difficult to write about my mother. But what else could I do? I resolved to write openly about everything.

The first set-back came with the illustrations. One would have expected the artist to read what I wrote every day, but whether he didn't have a brain, or whether he simply couldn't get a good grasp of the characters as a result of reading the work one section at a time, I don't know, but the characters he depicted every day were all different from what they should have been.[550] He depicted my mother, for example, in such a way that she could only come across as a cantankerous old woman who plagued her daughters-in-law. My elder brother was similarly wrongly depicted, and so too his wife, and Sennosuke.[551]

I was always afraid that the spirit of the work would not come across to readers as a result of these illustrations.

I hated looking at the paper every morning. I hated seeing the illustrations, I hated rereading what I had written, I hated seeing people with a copy of the paper on my way to the office, and I hated arriving at the office and seeing the expressions of the people in the editing-section, especially Maeda. If he started to say anything I'd cut him off curtly — "Let's drop it!"

I was also very upset by the defiant obstructiveness of those opposed to my type of literature, such as G and I- and H.[552] Nevertheless the

---

[550] The artist intended here is Kaburagi Kiyokata (1878-1972), who also illustrated Tōson's 'Broken Commandment' and was generally very highly regarded. Kaburagi should not be confused with the artist of the book version of 'Life', put out by Ekifūsha in November 1908, Hashimoto Kunisuke (1884-1953). Katai's attitude may be something of an over-reaction caused by lingering resentment towards illustrators, engendered in him by the inaccurate art-work which accompanied his 'Quilt' of the previous September. There is a crucial scene in 'The Quilt' where the protagonist (Tokio, who represents Katai) farewells his girl pupil (Yoshiko, representing Okada Michiyo) at the station. He is standing on the platform, wearing a brown felt trilby hat. Unknown to him Yoshiko's boyfriend is also there, behind him, and he too is wearing a brown felt trilby hat (though the reader has to piece together this information over the course of the preceding pages). When Yoshiko returns home she sends Tokio a letter in which she states that she will never forget that brown-hatted figure on the platform. Tokio is, of course, flattered to think that she means him, whereas the reader knows that there is very definitely room for doubt as to whom she is really intending. The scene clearly reveals a definite detachment of author from protagonist, in the sense that the author is subtly mocking the protagonist: that is, it is a clever form of self-ridicule. Appreciation of this is vital to a correct understanding of the work. However, the artist, Kobayashi Shōkichi (1877-1946), depicted Tokio *bareheaded*! The consequences of such an error are enormous, since readers often let pictures, if they are present, convey stronger impressions to them than the words themselves, and this is certainly part of the reason that 'The Quilt' was long misunderstood by the average reader (and not a few critics). The role of the illustrator is, I feel, a much neglected element of the study of literature.

[551] Sennosuke represents Katai himself.

[552] Though it is impossible to be certain, it seems probable that G is Gotō Chūgai, an arch-enemy of naturalism despite, paradoxically, his having been the editor of the magazine which published 'The Quilt', 'Shinshōsetsu' (he was editor from March 1900

reviews were quite favourable, and publishers who had once snubbed me now competed to call on me at my home and pay me transparent flattery.

As well as producing the right work I felt I had to show a bold front to society in general terms. Society is a sort of fashion that can end up overlooking people's worth. But at the same time, in another respect, I believe it can rouse the individual to greater efforts.

To add to it all, as misfortune would have it, just at that time there was the business of the S Company taking legal action over the copyright to 'The Quilt'.[553] I understand that it was a result of G considering me an upstart and wanting to put me in my place, but it was certainly a heavy blow to suffer just as I was labouring so hard over 'Life'. I was frequently being asked to the public prosecutor's office, and being questioned by Ohara, the district attorney.[554]

My position, however, did not allow me to give in before all these problems. I ignored the pain and wrote about the troubled family life of my mother and my elder brother and his wife. My mother's death seemed a constant source of anguish to me in my already distressed state.

I took note of Shimazaki's 'Spring', and read it without fail every morning. Critics were saying that it would not have wide appeal, but I thought that the impressionistic style was excellent. Shimazaki was certainly outperforming me. I cursed my faltering pen.

---

to January 1911: see too the following matter of the dispute over the copyright of 'The Quilt'). I- is possibly Izumi Kyōka or, more likely, Ikuta Chōkō. H is possibly the critic Higuchi Ryūkyō (1875-1929). All the above figures were actively writing anti-naturalist articles during 1908.

[553] The Shunyōdō Company, through Gotō Chūgai, tried to bring legal charges against Katai as a result of his 'Quilt', which was first published in Shunyōdō's magazine 'Shinshōsetsu' in September 1907, being included in Ekifūsha's 'Tayama Katai Collection' ('Tayama Katai Shū') of March 28th 1908. It is interesting that it was the author, and not Ekifūsha, who was the party accused of breach of copyright. The situation regarding copyright in late Meiji Japan was extremely vague: in theory, following the Publishing Regulations of 1875 it was the author who held copyright, but specific details were determined by case-by-case contracts with publishers. The contracts were usually deemed by all parties to exist for form's sake only, and in practice it was a gentlemen's agreement ('shinshi kyōtei') which prevailed. The gentlemen's agreement normally covered six months, in which the author agreed not to sell his work for republishing to any other company. Katai was, therefore, acting according to established custom when he agreed to Ekifūsha's publishing the work six months after its original publication. A district attorney was brought in at Shunyōdō's request and preliminary investigations were made. In the end no charges were laid, after it had been established that the fee which publishers paid to an author secured only their right to publish that author's work in a non-exclusive sense and did not convey eternal ownership of the work. To judge from a report in the Yomiuri of April 19th the incident resulted in bad publicity for Shunyōdō, and the general feeling seems to have been that the whole business stemmed from a grudge Gotō Chūgai had against Katai and naturalism. It might even be said that it won some unexpected sympathy for the naturalist cause.

[554] Ohara Naoshi (1877-1966), later a government minister.

Apparently Kunikida said, from his sickbed in Chigasaki, "They're both bad. I've never seen such sloppy works put out as newspaper novels!" From summer to autumn the previous year Kunikida too had tried his hand at a long novel, and had started on 'Hurricane'.[555] He'd given it up, however. Therefore I'm sure he made that remark because he himself wanted to write a long novel. For both Shimazaki and myself it was our first attempt at writing a long newspaper-novel. Moreover we were very keen to break away from the newspaper-novel stereotype. We refused to let our art be controlled by the demands of the newspapers. That is why we wrote the sort of works we did.

The material for 'Life' was causing me a great deal of anguish. Both my elder brother and his wife were still alive [sic], and I felt ashamed to subject them to analysis.[556] I was embarrassed that they would think "Ah, so that's the way he felt!" I also had to consider the feelings of my numerous relatives. The most painful thing of all for me was the open analysis of my mother. I had had such sympathy for her, such pity, and that made it so hard for me to write about her. I was made to appreciate in full what Maupassant meant by 'the agony of skinning'.[557]

While all this was going on Kunikida died. I took just three days off as a result, and somehow I managed to complete 'Life', my first long novel. It was night when I finished writing the last section, and I felt glad

---

[555] 'Bōfū', August 8th-28th, 1907, Nihon (Shinbun).

[556] This is an astonishing error. His elder brother Miyato died of tuberculosis on November 9th the previous year, and on April 1st (ie. a week before 'Life'), in 'Taiyō', Katai had even published a short story 'Elder Brother' ('Ani') specifically discussing his death! Normally one might have been able to dismiss it as a simple slip of the pen for an intended 'younger brother' (Tomiya, who *was* still alive), but Katai has also used for 'wife' a word meaning specifically 'elder brother's wife' ('aniyome'), so the error becomes twofold. The 'aniyome' is Miyato's third wife, Toshi (see Note 345).

It should also be pointed out that Katai's term 'analysis' ('kaibō', also translatable as 'dissection') is rather odd too, since in other writings he has stated that he generally avoids analysis in his works, preferring impressionism, and that 'Life' is a good example of a work containing no analysis. It is possible that he simply meant something like 'exposure', but he has not said this. See too the following note regarding 'skinning'.

[557] This is a reference to Maupassant's statement in his travelogue 'Sur l'Eau' (On the Water, 1888, not to be confused with his short story of the same title) that "The writer's pathological sensitivity makes him a man, as it were, skinned alive." The term 'skinned alive' was mistranslated into Japanese as 'skinning' ('kawahagi', specifically 'kawahagi no kutsū', 'the agony of skinning'), with the result that the emphasis switched from the writer being skinned to his subjects being skinned. That is, when this term is used in Japanese it usually means that the writer is not suffering agony as a result of his naked hypersensitivity, but the agony of guilt over his cruel dissection of his characters. In view of Katai's normal opposition to analysis it might seem possible to assume that he is using the term in its correct sense here, but, in the light of his earlier reference to 'analysis/dissection', it is more logical to assume that he is using it to mean the agony of guilt. Frankly, it is hard to know just what he does mean.

that I had finally put down a heavy burden that had seemed at times about to crush me.

'Life' evoked quite a lot of reaction. The criticisms ranged from good to bad, but the general view seemed to be that it wasn't too bad a work. Natsume Sōseki said it resembled "a dirty picture book of a back-street tenement."[558]

As soon as I finished writing it I went off on a trip to Kyūshū.

Myself and Travel.

I have been fond of travel for many years now. My first real trip was when I was eighteen, when I went back home to see my elder sister and then went on to Nikkō, using as funds some two yen fifty sen that I had saved up from pocket money given to me by my mother and aunt and uncle.[559]

There was a temple in Nikkō, the S temple, which had links with the old lord of our fief, and my elder brother arranged for me to stay there for a couple of nights.[560] My sister gave me a roll of home-woven cloth to hand over as a present in return for my being allowed to stay there.

I walked along the Nakasendō [Road] as far as my home town, and then continued to Nikkō, still on foot.[561] I did not take the train. I walked from Sano to Tochigi and then on to Kanuma, where I stayed the night. Then the following morning I continued along that lonely, cedar-lined route that the old imperial messengers had travelled, and arrived in Nikkō.

I stayed a couple of nights there. It was the start of my association with Nikkō. Then I headed through the heavy rain that was falling at the time and went from Chūzenji across the Asagata Pass to Akakura in Ashio, where I stayed at another temple to which I had a letter of introduction. From there I followed the banks of the Watarase River to Kiryū.

I have long enjoyed solitude. Whenever I've been troubled with worries I've always tried to dispel them through travel. And how travel has provided me with vitality, new experiences, freedom, and truth! Whenever I set out on a trip I always feel that I am my true self.

---

[558] Natsume Sōseki (1867-1916), novelist.

[559] The trip was in August 1889. He visited his sister Katsuyo (see Note 46).

[560] The Shōsonin, where he stayed with Doppo in 1897 and where he proofread 'The Quilt' in 1907. The lord of their fief, Tatebayashi Fief (fiefs were abolished in 1871), was Lord Akimoto. The Akimotos were based in Yamagata till about 1859, and took their retainers with them when they moved to Tatebayashi. (Hence Katai's various references to Yamagata being his traditional family home.)

[561] The Nakasendō (lit: Central Mountain Road) was one of the principal routes of old Japan, linking Kyōto and Edo (Tōkyō). It passed through what are now the prefectures of Saitama, Gunma, Nagano, Gifu, and Shiga.

Farmers, labourers, woodcutters, old women, young women — they have all been both my teachers and my friends. I've seen life's beauty, and I've seen its ugliness. I was able to learn about human relationships at an early stage.

I have an inexhaustible stock of memories — of quiet spas, of long avenues of pines, of sleeping wearily amidst fragrant camomiles, of lovely old stations lit up by the evening sun, of the sea on a beautifully clear morning — but of them all, I particularly remember a trip I made from Mito along the coast to Namie, then across the mountains to Fukushima, Sendai, and Morioka, and then over the Sengan Pass to Akita.[562] I was an inexperienced traveller at the time, and everything I saw seemed new and strange and marvellous. I took a pencil and a little notebook with me, in which I jotted down occasional poems and material for novels.

I still have that notebook. In amongst all the poems and observations and sketches I wrote my daily expenses — seventeen sen for lodgings, two sen for straw sandals, five sen for lunch, two sen for cakes, and so on. I used to think that I'd have to start economising if I spent more than thirty sen a day. I travelled around the Tōhoku district for about a month on twelve or thirteen yen.

Generally speaking the lodgings on the Iwaki coast were cheap, but beyond Morioka, as I went on to Akita, they suddenly rose to twenty-two or even twenty-five sen. Of course, I never used to leave a tip in those days.

I remember crossing the pass into a village called Obonai, with a lonely inn, and seeing the beautiful red leaves of that Kakunodate area. I had searched in vain to find somewhere to eat in the village before the pass, and had finally, after virtually begging in tears, been given some millet and rice, only for the lady to refuse the five sen coin I offered her.[563] I walked along munching apples in the Morioka area, and quinces in the Akita area. It was a very lonely night that I spent in Obonai:

> "A weary traveller,
> Sleeping peacefully
> At the foot of the mountains:
> A cold wind blows,
> And the fallen leaves scatter."

It was the time of the war with China, and flags bedecked the straw-thatched houses of that mountain village.

On my way back I went through Yamagata, visited my mother's old home town, admired Mount Gassan and the splendid scenery of

[562] This trip was in October 1894.
[563] The village before the pass was probably Harukiba.

Yamadera, and then visited my ancestors' graves at the Bongyō Temple in Tōkamachi [sic] in Yamagata City.[564] From there I proceeded to Kaminoyama, across Kaneyama Pass, through Shichigashuku, and arrived at Fukushima the next day, after seeing the 'wooden rock' in Watarase.[565]

My trip to the Bōsō Paeninsula was with O.[566] We went to Kisarazu, then Mount Kanō, on to Tateyama and Sunosaki, then turned back from Shirahama, crossed the sea to Uraga, went on to Yokosuka, and then on to Izu, crossing Hakone in the snow.

I first earned some recognition as a travelogue writer with my 'Inner Reaches of the Nikkō Mountains' in 'Taiyō', followed by 'Ill-fated Landscape', which was an account of tracing the Tamagawa [River] to its source.[567]

"Tayama's always going on about being 'ill-fated', but he's a bit too ready to use that word. He's yet to write anything that's truly about being 'ill-fated'." So said Kōyō Sanjin and Otowa, and it's true that I was rather presumptuous.[568]

I went to Nikkō on numerous occasions, but the three trips I remember best were when I went to Kuriyama, when I went exploring the inner hills with H, and when I went to look at the autumn leaves with my mother.[569] When I went to Kuriyama I went really deep into the hills, as far as Nikkōzawa and Kinunuma.

Travelling gave me all sorts of knowledge and inspiration. And the railways weren't developed then like they are nowadays, so in most cases I travelled on foot, covering some twenty to twenty-five miles a day.

In 1897, at the beginning of September, I went to the Atsumi Paeninsula in Mikawa, visited Tokoku's overgrown grave in Fukue, and spent about ten days in the little village of Iragozaki.[570] Yanagita happened to

[564] His mother's old home town was Takatama, a few miles north of Yamagata City. The Bongyōji [Temple] is actually in a suburb of Yamagata City called Mikkamachi (lit: Third Day Town) and not Tōkamachi (lit: Tenth Day Town). Katai has perhaps confused it with the relatively nearby town of Tōkamachi in Niigata Prefecture.

[565] Watarase (unconnected with the earlier Watarase River), Shichigashuku, and Kaneyama Pass are all on the road from Kaminoyama to Shiroishi, to the south of Mount Zao.

[566] With Ōta Gyokumei, January 1894.

[567] 'Nikkōyama no Oku', January 5th-February 5th, 1896, in 'Taiyō', and 'Fugū Sanzui', November 3rd 1896, 'Bungei Kurabu'.

[568] This is a reference to the young Katai's tendency to wallow in self-pity, even to the point of transferring epithets of misfortune. His circumstances were not quite as wretched as he made out, and those who knew this, especially those who had themselves been the victim of greater hardships, often took offence.

[569] H is Hasegawa Tenkei (1876-1940), critic.

[570] The trip actually took place in 1898, specifically two weeks from August 27th. Tokoku is Tsuboi Tokoku (?-1690), haiku poet and close friend of the renowned Matsuo Bashō (1644-1694, haiku poet). His grave is in the Chōonji [Temple].

be there at the same time, looking a typical aristocratic university student, and we travelled together by boat to Kamishima.[571] The scenery of Kamishima was so wonderful that even today I still keep wanting to go back there. At any rate, I am convinced that the raging Toba Channel offers some of the best coastal scenery in Japan.

Anyway, after about ten days we went across by boat from Fukue to Kamezaki on the Chita Paeninsula, and then went on by train to visit O in Isshinden in Ise.[572] It was the night of the old harvest moon festival, and the three of us went drinking at a local inn. I remember Yanagita getting completely drunk and reciting Heine's poetry. From there he continued on to Nara, while I made a very cheap trip from Nagoya to the Kiso Valley for virtually the price of a ticket back along the Tōkaidō Line.

Shimazaki and I still talk about that visit I paid him in Fukushima in the Kiso Valley.[573]

After getting married and starting a family I was unable to travel very much. And because I had to go to work during the week my only free day was Sunday. I used to sit staring out of the white-curtained window of the office facing the street, gazing up at the wide blue sky and longing for freedom like some caged bird.

However, some five or six years later I worked on the editing of 'A Geography of Japan', and so once again I was able to travel.[574] Of course, the way I travelled then was very different from how I had travelled in the days when I was a literary novice. This time I travelled by train, second-class, and wore Western-style clothes, and carried a large bag, and tipped maids, and even hired geishas. Rather than scenery I started to develop an interest in the particular atmosphere of places, in the people living there, and in distinctive characteristics. It was in this period that I got the material for such works as 'Girl from Nabari'.[575] In other words, I gradually started to experience for myself

---

[571] Yanagita had been staying there since July 20th, on his summer vacation, and had in fact invited Katai to join him.

[572] Ōta Gyokumei had been teaching English at the Takada Middle School (present-day Takada High School) in Isshinden since October 1897. They visited him on September 5th.

[573] September 7th 1898, according to Tōson's diary.

[574] 'Dai Nihon Chishi', published in ten volumes by Hakubunkan 1903-1915 (see following chapter).

[575] 'Nabari Otome', June 1st 1905, 'Bungei Kurabu'. (Nabari is in Mie Prefecture.) The story is a rather distorted account of an incident more factually reported in his later work 'Flowers of the Camellia' ('Tsubaki no Hana', May 1913). It appears from these two works that Katai had an extra-marital affair with the proprietress of an inn in the Nabari area, possibly early in 1903, and that this may have been his first experience of sex with anyone other than his wife. Hence his comments immediately below.

the sorts of things I had formerly only seen and heard about with envy. Accordingly I started to look upon those former exploratory trips as ridiculously immature. But on occasion I still resorted to my old habit of walking, and didn't find ten or twenty miles particularly troublesome.

My first trip to Kyūshū was when I went with a certain woman as far as Kyōto — parting with her in fact at Kōbe — and then went on into the hills of Hyūga and Ōsumi.[576] I climbed Mount Kirishima — with a labourer carrying my large bag — and spent three or four leisurely days in the area.

By comparison with the changes Tōkyō has seen over the last thirty years the countryside hasn't changed all that much, but nevertheless the spread of public transport has sometimes resulted in a second life for towns that were once on the decline, and similarly decline for towns that were once flourishing. The change of character brought about by the laying of a railroad is an interesting phenomenon. Transport has brought to all areas the equal diffusion of knowledge, the introduction of things new, and the gradual destruction of the atmosphere of old. Nowadays, whenever I go travelling, I endeavour to seek out quiet, old-fashioned towns.

Geographical Editing

I started helping with the editing of 'A Geography of Japan' in 1903.[577] Yamazaki Naokata and Satō Denzō were in charge of it, and as assistants there was myself, one young bachelor of arts, and one bachelor of science.[578] I am indebted to Yamazaki and Satō for teaching me a scientific approach to the study of geography.

The first base for our editing was a room in the O mansion.[579] It was a dark, cold, depressing room, and I always seemed to be on my own there. Whenever I got bored I'd put on my sandals and go for a stroll around the quiet garden.

---

[576] This trip is the one referred to at the end of the previous chapter. It took place from the end of July to the middle of August (1908). The 'certain woman' is his mistress Iida Yone (1889-?), a geisha with whom he had formed a relationship in the summer of 1907 and who remained his mistress till his death in 1930.

Hyūga and Ōsumi are present-day Miyazaki Prefecture and eastern Kagoshima Prefecture respectively.

[577] See Note 574.

[578] Yamazaki Naokata (1870-1929), and Satō Denzō (1870-1928) were both lecturers in geology and geography at the Imperial University, and both possessed doctorates. The bachelor of arts was Saitō Ryūzō (1875-1961), a history graduate of the Imperial University and later a noted art historian. The bachelor of science was Saigusa Senzaburō (dates unclear).

[579] The Ōhashi mansion, in Kamirokubanchō in Kōjimachi (present-day Sanbanchō), which was at the time in the hands of Shintarō.

Plum blossoms stood out like stars against the cold sky, and large cycads stood completely overwhelmed by dead grass.

The owner of the mansion often came into the room when I was there alone and made remarks like "It's no good being a novelist, you know. Just look at Kōyō's family — terrible, isn't it! You'd do better to go to the university lectures on geography, and do some serious studying." Academics were indeed greatly esteemed, whereas people like me, who chose to follow the path of literature, were looked down upon. "Yes, you're quite right," I would say in agreement, feeling doubly wretched that not only was I a humble employee but that I had also failed as yet to write a really good work. But a voice deep within me was saying, on behalf of the cause of literature, "Some day I'll show you!"

That quiet room was, in point of fact, a fine 'studio' for me.[580] I'd quickly get my geography work out of the way and read foreign novels which I'd brought with me. The new currents of thought coursing through the works of D'Annunzio and Ibsen and Bjornson and Hauptmann constantly filled that quiet room to overflowing.

Then at night the room — now brightly lit — saw a change of atmosphere, and there would be animated discussion about the earth's mantle, or about granite, or about some lake having originally been a maar, or about double-volcanoes.[581] Yamazaki had only recently returned from overseas and still had to establish a reputation. He was very refined, and always knocked twice before entering the room.

Yamazaki's manner of speech revealed youthful ambition, intelligence, and occasional sarcasm. He gave the impression of a scholar of great refinement. By contrast, Satō was a fat, greasy-complexioned fellow who was always grinning. He also always had a flushed face when he arrived, apparently having had a drink along the way.

It was actually Satō who appeared to be the greater scholar, but nevertheless I was always impressed with the knowledge of the talented Yamazaki. It seemed that there was nothing Yamazaki didn't know, particularly when it came to human geography. I learned a lot from him.

Yamazaki was also far from ignorant about literature. I remember showing him a book by Paul Bourget, and his remarking "Ah-ha, a psychological novel!"

He'd listen with interest when I talked about running a literary magazine, and about the literary world. And I for my part was very interested in what he had to say about his time in Germany, when he visited the poet Ganghofer in the Alps.[582] He also talked about the old

[580] 'Studio' is given in English by Katai.
[581] A maar is a type of volcano where no cone is formed.
[582] Yamazaki was studying in Germany from 1898-1900.

town of Bruges, which could be called the birthplace of modern Belgian poetry.

I also benefited greatly from the history talks of the bachelor of arts, Saitō Ryūzō.[583]

Doppo also visited that quiet studio on two or three occasions.

"This is a nice place! Are you always on your own here?"

"The geography teachers come along in the evening."

"But you're on your own during the day, then? That's nice. You can take things easy. I dare say you can even get on with your own private work."

"Well, of course, I can't actually do any writing of my own."

"Who cares about writing?!"

He sauntered out into the garden.

"This is a luxurious place, I must say!"

"But it's very quiet, you know. The boss goes off early every morning, and then there's just the family left behind, with hardly ever any visitors. It's quiet all day long."

"That's because he's still not established himself as a man of influence.[584] Anyway, it's a really luxurious place all the same."

He browsed through the various maps and geographical works scattered around the room.

"You must be learning a lot about travel, spending all your time looking at things like this. We should go on another trip, you know, just for a day or two."

When the war with Russia started I left off the editing work for a year or so, but got down to it again when I got back.

O's library was right next door. There weren't many geography or history books there, but nevertheless I often went in there looking for one thing or another.

Soon the new trends surged to the fore. By the time the fourth volume of 'Geography of Japan' appeared my 'Life' had already been published in the Y Newspaper.

My own Anna Mahr also visited me at that quiet studio.

---

[583] See Note 578.

[584] Shintarō was actually the third son of Sahei, and also appears to have ranked behind the adopted (and younger) Otowa in terms of inheritance. However, his two elder brothers died young, Otowa also died prematurely in June 1901, and so when Sahei also died in November that same year Shintarō suddenly found himself in charge of Hakubunkan. Although he had been working at his father's company since 1888, he appears to have had few connections, even by 1903 (the date of the scene depicted here), and relatively little interest in literature per se.

But presently the location of the editing base was changed to a factory in Koishikawa.[585]

The atmosphere there was entirely different from that at the O mansion. There was no nice Western-style food for lunch, and no eel and rice either. There were no cakes. The tea was awful, and the table I worked on was always covered with dust and grime.

"This is a fine demotion, I must say!" laughed Yamazaki. But I couldn't complain too bitterly as it was at least nearer my home.[586]

'A Geography of Japan' didn't sell too well and suffered an ever colder reception from the bookshops. As a result we too lost our enthusiasm, and didn't feel like putting very much effort into it. In addition, 'Bunshō Sekai' was started in 1906, and this took up a lot of my time.

We gradually met less and less frequently. Three times a week became twice, then once, and we often skipped that once-a-week meeting too.

Those weekly sessions were held on a Thursday, and Thursday seemed to come round very quickly. "Is it Koishikawa day again already?" I'd say to myself as I set off from the company offices. I'd spend a sleepy afternoon or a cold night there, amidst the noise from the factory steam-whistles, the roughness of the workers, the grime, and the horribly crudely-built surroundings. I spent a couple of weeks just picking out photographs, which was particularly boring.

"I can't stand Thursdays!" I was always grumbling.

My grumbles were not without reason. It was still a long way to my home in the suburbs, and I had to change trains, and by the time I got off at Y station most households had already gone to bed, and only the occasional lonely porch-light twinkled sadly in the darkness.[587] And when I got home I invariably found that my wife — who liked her sleep — had

---

[585] It was a room over a printery, specifically Koishikawa Kyōdō Insatsu, in Hisakatamachi (present-day Koishikawa 3-5 Chōme). Something is wrong, however, with the dates involved in this and the previous sentence. In the second chapter of 'The Quilt' Katai refers to writing a reply to Okada Michiyo from the room over the factory, and the reply can be factually verified as having been sent on August 25th 1903. This would mean that the change of location took place before August 25th 1903. However, in that case it would have been impossible for Okada Michiyo to visit him at the studio, as she did not arrive in Tōkyō till February 1904. The only explanations are that: a) Katai did not in fact write the reply from that room, but somewhere else, which means that the location given in 'The Quilt' is either an error or fiction; or b) that the change of location was a gradual 'overlapping' process and that Katai spent some time before the 'move' in the room over the factory and some time after the 'move' still working in the studio. The latter alternative seems the more likely. (There is also some evidence to suggest that the official date of the change of location was April 1905.)

[586] From October 6th-December 9th 1903 Katai lived in Suidō (Bunkyō-ku), having moved there from Haramachi. On December 9th 1903 he went to live in Wakamatsuchō (near Haramachi), and on June 27th 1905 he moved again to Yamabushichō in Shinjuku, staying there till his final move on December 8th 1906 to his own house in Yoyogi.

[587] That is, Yoyogi Station.

fallen asleep with the young baby still at her breast.[588] It was at this time that I got the material for my short story 'Vetch'.[589]

Desk

I try sitting at my desk in the study.

I take up my pen, set out my copy-paper, and prepare to start writing. I try putting down a few words. I don't like what I've written. I don't like the theme, and I can't muster any enthusiasm. I just don't think I'll be able to produce a satisfying work. The deadline is drawing near but I tell myself "It doesn't matter — take another day to think about it," and I get up from my desk, despite all the preparations, and go off into the living-room.

"Still nothing?" my wife asks.

"No, nothing!"

"Oh dear."

"I'll do it tonight, definitely."

I walk about on the sunny verandah, and amongst the trees in the garden. I idle away the time, always waiting for inspiration.....

I dread the arrival of the T magazine's editor.[590] He's bound to come. And then he'll adopt the attitude that he can't possibly wait any longer for me to hand over the manuscript. I'll say that it's because he's come a little earlier than I expected, but my words will contain a complex mixture of feelings. I write. I write something trivial. It gets published. It gets reviewed.... The thought makes me terribly depressed.

I now start to think that I'll never be able to write anything. I start getting frustrated and angry. I feel amazed that I've been able to write as much as I have. My material disintegrates. Things I had once thought interesting now seem trivial, a waste of time. I wonder how on earth I could ever have brought myself to write such stuff.

"It's hopeless, absolutely hopeless!"

---

[588] Presumably Chiyoko, his second daughter, who was born March 9th 1908.

[589] 'Genge' (September 1st 1911, 'Chūō Kōron') is an almost certainly fanciful short story depicting Katai himself travelling back to Yoyogi late one night and making passionate love on a patch of wayside grass with a mysterious young woman (at her instigation), who gets off the train at the same station and whom he has never seen before and never sees again.

[590] The 'Chūō Kōron' ('Tyūō Kōron'). The editor at the time was Takita Choin (1882-1925), a former pupil of Ueda Bin's. There is an expression (still occasionally heard today) "Takita Choin's rickshaw," which means 'a stroke of good fortune'. The expression derives from the fact that a visit from Choin, who invariably travelled around in a distinctive black lacquered rickshaw, was considered a blessing in view of the prestige of the magazine and Choin's reputation for giving opportunities to novice writers.

"You really can't write anything?"

My wife too looks worried as she asks.

"I must look like a caged tiger at the zoo, padding around like this."

"Yes, you do rather."

It looks as though my wife is suffering, too, as though she can't bear to watch me suffering. It's at such times that I get bad-tempered. I take my anger out on things. I yell at my wife. I yell at the children.

"Oh, how I hate it! I hate it! I hate writing novels!"

"Well, if you can't write, then that's all there is to it, as far as I can see." My wife will say things like this, but never anything like "Can't you just write enough to keep them satisfied, and stop all this nonsense?" That makes me feel all the worse.

At this point T arrives.

"I just can't do it," I tell him. "I think we'll have to give this one a miss."

"That's bad news. We were depending on it. If we don't get it we'll have a blank space left."

"I'm sorry, but I'm afraid I can't do anything about it."

"Well, I'll wait one more day," says T, and takes his leave.

I sit at my desk again. I end up hating to look at my pen and paper. I feel as if some sort of devil dwells in them, and inside me too.

My wife is worried and comes quietly to see how I'm getting on. She tries to look without letting me know she's there, in case I get angry. She goes away relieved when she sees me sitting there with pen in hand.

"Were you able to write anything?" she asks me later.

"No, nothing."

"But weren't you writing a while ago?!"

" — " I say nothing.

However, in the middle of the night I have an idea come to me, get up, and start writing. I'm able to write what I want. How satisfying! What a relief! What happiness! Before long I've managed to write two pages, then three, then four, then five.... I forget my earlier complaints about my terrible profession. I've rekindled the flames of old, the days when I was a young literary novice — the days when I wore my hair long and worked diligently in the dim lamplight. In those days there was no literary world, no T, no public, no anything. There was just paper, and pen, and feelings, all working together.[591]

---

[591] These are strange sentences. Presumably Katai means that in the early days he was able to write with relatively greater facility as he was not troubled by such practical issues, but he himself has made it clear that his youth was hardly troublefree.

Programme

There was a signboard at the entrance facing the road, with 'Doppo Remembrance Meeting' written on in large characters.[592] The public was already flocking in. There were people in Western-style suits, and people in formal haori and hakama, and young men in student attire....

I went in through a different entrance, one with stone steps.

When I opened the door of the room upstairs I saw that T, and N, and Y, and M and so on had already arrived. S was there too.[593]

I had to give a speech, which I'd never done before. I'd been told that it would be acceptable for me to read out something prepared beforehand, so I'd written five or six pages, but still didn't feel I could go through with it. I told this to T. "Oh dear, that could be a problem. We really do need you to say something — well, either you or S...." He looked over towards S, and asked him "Would YOU mind giving a speech?"

"Oh, I couldn't — not me!" S declined.

It looked like there was no way out for me, and that I would have to do it. It wasn't the audience that bothered me. They were strangers, and didn't worry me in any way. It was Doppo's many friends that I was concerned about. There were a lot of scandalmongers amongst them....

However, there was nothing I could do about it. I had to give the speech. When I went downstairs I saw that a lot of his friends were indeed there, busily folding programmes or doing similar little jobs.

There was O and Y S and K.[594] I could also see 'Mrs. I-' — his widow's younger sister — sitting there folding up some programmes.[595]

Mrs. I- is the heroine of Doppo's 'Third Parties'.[596] Before she married I-, when Doppo was living in Harajuku and she was in her late teens

---

[592] The meeting was held at the Young Men's Christian Association Building in Kandamidoshirochō, on the afternoon of June 30th 1908 (the day after the funeral service at Aoyama Cemetery).

[593] Tamura Sanji (1873-1939, also known as Kōtō), journalist, close friend of Doppo, and master of ceremonies on this occasion; Nunami Keion; Yanagita Kunio; Maeda Akira; and Shimazaki Tōson.

[594] O and K are Osanai Kaoru and Kosugi Misei, while Y S is (according to Maeda Akira) Yoshie Kogan.

[595] Details about Haruko's younger sister are surprisingly obscure. She was born about 1882 and married a journalist called Itō (again according to Maeda Akira), accounting for the initial 'I'. I have consulted a number of Doppo specialists and endeavoured to trace the Enomoto family records, as well as consulting Doppo's diary and trying to investigate her husband (similarly obscure), but I have been unable to establish even her name (presumably, from information Katai gives below, a name beginning with 'K' and one that was moreover quite well-known in its day).

[596] 'Daisansha', October 1903, 'Bungei Kurabu'. Actually, according to Doppo himself, the heroine of the story, Otsuru, is a composite of his sister-in-law and his own first wife Sasaki Nobuko.

and very attractive, we often used to find ourselves in her company.[597] Y used to remark how pretty she was, and how pleasant-natured she seemed.[598]

And from her point of view, I'm sure that Y himself, with his refined upper-class air, must have seemed very attractive. In those days I had already married, but Y was still single. Whenever the three of us — Y, she, and myself — found ourselves together she always looked embarrassed, and gave the impression of wanting to be with us but of trying hard not to be at the same time. "She's at that age where she's started taking an interest in the other sex, so you'll have to excuse her behaviour," said Doppo.

She married I-, who loved her very much, and was much talked of as the 'notorious Mrs. K-ko'. 'Third Parties' depicted the ups-and-downs of their marriage.

She'd attended Doppo's funeral, and the wake too. I hadn't really had chance to speak to her then, so I now made a point of going up to her.

"You're doing a fine job!" I said.

"I heard all about you, T!" she replied, without mincing words.

"About what?!"

"You may well say 'what?'! It's no good trying to cover it up, you know!"

"I've no idea what you're talking about...."

There were a lot of people about so she didn't make it fully clear what she meant, but nevertheless I was forced to take the defensive and didn't really know what to do.[599] Just then, fortunately, Y came along.

"This must take up so much of your valuable time," he said, turning on the charm.

Mrs. I- now suddenly became serious, indeed docile, as if a shining light had appeared before her, and she cast a surreptitious glance at Y's handsome face as she said to him:

"Thank you for all the trouble you've gone to."

"Not at all, not at all...." replied Y rather smugly.

A strange feeling suddenly came over me. "Just look at the two of them!" I said to myself. I thought it might make a good chapter in a novel, and I also felt rather ill at ease at the same time.

---

[597] Doppo lived in Harajuku (present-day Sendagaya 2-3 Chōme area) in the latter part of 1900.

[598] Y is still referring to Yanagita Kunio.

[599] Nor does Katai make it clear to the reader what she means. It is possibly some reference to the events occurring at the Chigasakikan (see Note 534), but it is more probably a reference to his relationship with Iida Yone or with Okada Michiyo.

It appeared that Y had not met Mrs. I- for some considerable time, either. He stood next to her with a rather nostalgic look on his face.

"It's been a long time!"

"It certainly has. You've changed a lot."

"And you...."

Y laughed. Mrs. I- blushed bright red.

"It must be five or six years!"

"Is it really?"

Mrs. I- now spoke in a gentle, bashful tone that was totally unlike the direct, assertive way in which she had spoken to me. I felt increasingly ill at ease, but continued to think that it was a very interesting scene. I just stood there, watching.

Just then Y S had to attend to some urgent business, and Y took his place helping to put the programmes together with the door-prize tickets (which were donated by the bookshops).[600] O had been handling the tickets, and now Mrs. I- said to him:

"Please let me take over from you — I'll do it....."

She took up his place.

I watched Y and Mrs. I- working together, the movements of their hands synchronising each time they placed the two items together. Mrs. I- was smiling happily. Y too looked very happy. The pile of programmes and tickets beside them grew gradually higher.

"There're a lot here," said Y, "I wonder if this many people will come?"

His neat, frock-coated figure as he stood there seemed to balance perfectly the seated figure of Mrs. I-.

I thought about Doppo. If I could have shown him this scene, I'm sure he would have said "How hilarious!" and had a good laugh.

'Country Teacher'[601]

Shortly after getting back from the war I visited O at his country temple.[602] Passing through the cemetery I happened to notice a fresh grave-marker, with the words 'Here lies Kobayashi Shūzō.[603] It looked as if the burial had only recently taken place, judging from the many flowers placed on the grave.

---

[600] Sic. It seems in extraordinary bad taste to offer door-prizes on such an occasion, but obviously was not thought of as such.

[601] The novel 'Inaka Kyōshi' was published on October 20th 1909 by Sakura Shobō.

[602] From May 1899 Ōta Gyokumei had been resident priest at the Kenpukuji [Temple] in Hanyū, Saitama Prefecture.

[603] The protagonist of 'Country Teacher', Hayashi Seizō, is based closely upon the real-life person Kobayashi Shūzō (1884-1904).

I went on into the temple, met O, and talked about the war. Then I suddenly remembered that grave.

"There's a grave here of a Kobayashi Shūzō. I'm sure I know the name. Wasn't he that young man who was lodging here a year or so ago?"

"Yes, that's him."

"When did he die?"

"Only very recently. It was only a day or so after the fall of Liaoyang."[604]

"That's sad. Illness, I suppose?"

"Tuberculosis."

"That really is a shame."

I'd met him a couple of times and could remember him, albeit vaguely. My first thought was that on that day when Liaoyang fell — that most glorious day in Japan's international history, a day when people were rejoicing in their tens of thousands — there was a young man dying a lonely death like this, without achieving anything and without even going off to fight in the war. I was filled with profound sadness over the hopes of this young man buried here in the countryside. I then pictured the graveyard scene in 'Fathers and Sons'. He was very different from Bazarov, but, nevertheless.....

I thought I'd try writing something dealing with the young men of Japan during the period 1901/2 - 1904/5. I also wanted to relate it to that glorious day in Japan's history. By a stroke of good fortune O possessed Kobayashi's diaries from his middle-school days, his primary school teaching days, and the year prior to his death. I promptly borrowed them and read through them.

I would probably have written 'Country Teacher' even without those diaries, but it is undeniable that they proved to be excellent material, particularly the diary for the year prior to his death.

These diaries may well represent Kobayashi's life-work. Within their pages I discovered not just one, but many young men buried along with their hopes in the countryside, many lonely souls passing into oblivion without achieving anything. I felt I had succeeded in grasping the essence of 'Country Teacher'.

The diary continued until the day before his death. Naturally it looks as though he wrote it in considerable distress while lying in his sickbed, and the writing is feeble, with large, clumsy characters. It brought tears

---

[604] Liaoyang fell on September 4th 1904, whereas the temple records show that Kobayashi died on the 22nd. However, Ōta was away at the time of Kobayashi's burial and may not have consulted his own temple's records to check the exact date.

to my eyes to see it. After all, isn't it a fact that his humble spirit, as he lay on his wretched sickbed thinking of his country's victory at Liaoyang, was still a part of the Japanese spirit in its entirety, that same spirit that won such international glory?

The setting, too, was close to my own home town, and I think that this helped me to understand his young spirit all the better. After I'd read his diaries he was no longer simply Kobayashi Shūzō — he was MY Kobayashi Shūzō. Wherever I went I felt he was alive beside me.

The scenes he had witnessed, the sights, his feelings — all were now mine. The hedges, the temple garden, the thawing roads, the horse-drawn coach — everywhere I could see a living Kobayashi.

Whenever I went to the town of H I always visited his grave.

His friends had already had a large headstone of natural rock erected. Here there was love, there were tears, there was an undying spirit, and here his pitifully moving patriotism as a Japanese citizen lived on, risen again. I picked some of the flowers blooming in the fields and made an offering of them.

One autumn day I gazed out from the temple over the broad expanse of fields. I saw the late afternoon sunshine slanting brightly through the yellowing rice, and the shadows of the scanty alders. I heard a cart passing by in the distance. At that moment I felt as if Kobayashi were there with me, watching the same evening sun over the fields, listening to the same distant cart.

"Life is a vast tapestry," I said sadly to myself.

I had heard the terrifying sound of gunfire at the front, and I had seen brutally slain corpses and the hell of battle, so I was particularly moved by these quiet scenes of nature. The contrast made me think deeply about human life and nature.

"How about taking me to Miroku?" I asked O one day.[605]

We chose a quiet autumn day, and went quietly along that same seven mile road that Kobayashi had travelled every day. The sun shone brightly over the fields, the autumn flowers were in bloom, the little stream flowed quietly along, and the woman at the noodle-shop on the corner was busy rolling out noodles.

First I visited the school where he had taught. I was shown the duty-room he'd stayed in, met his colleagues, including the principal, and was also shown the organ he'd played. It was after classes had finished, and some teachers and students were quietly throwing a ball about in the garden, just as they had in Kobayashi's time.

---

[605] Miroku is the little village on the outskirts of Hanyū where Kobayashi taught.

Nowadays the village of Miroku has become a busy place, but in those days it was very quiet and melancholy, with white smoke coiling lazily from the bathhouse chimney, and smoke from the farmers' rubbish-fires drifting across the fields by the Ogawa Inn standing at the waterside.

We had boiled vegetables at the inn, with some saké.

It was very funny how the principal had been afraid that my visit was some sort of detective investigation.

I also visited Kobayashi's parents' house. I wasn't able to tell them that I was writing a novel about their son, so I pretended I'd come to chat about pictures.[606] It was indeed the house where Kobayashi's deathbed had been laid.

After visiting the house my plans for the novel started to take shape. I could clearly visualise everything written in the diaries. I now decided to go along the road he had travelled daily to Miroku, this time from Gyōda.

I thought things over. I'd come to a fairly good understanding of Kobayashi as he was when staying at the temple, but I just couldn't seem to grasp his relationships with his friends. His middle-school diary contained a lot of fantasy, and I couldn't tell what exactly was true. Much of it was written in fun, as a sort of joke. Having resolved to depict young men of the period 1901/2 - 1904/5, I had to do a lot of research. The young men of that period were considerably different in type and character from the young men of my own youth. They were young men enthralled by 'Myōjō', young men who were half romantic, fanciful, who had still not arrived at the new ways of thinking, and I found it very difficult to depict them. I couldn't understand about his first love-affair, during his middle-school days, nor the love-affairs that followed, so for a long time I was unable to write.

Two years passed, then three.

I'd had the idea for 'Country Teacher' since before 'The Quilt', but even after finishing 'Life', and then 'Wife', I still couldn't get down to writing it.[607] I felt that the material was getting older and older, gradually mouldering away. Also, in an age full of new ideology, the tone of the work was too inclined towards the romantic and sentimental. I already felt that the tone of 'Life' and 'Wife' was falling away and becoming a bit 'sugary', and such a sentimental work as this could only make matters worse. As a result, I let another year or so slip by.

However, when I looked through those diaries again I felt I absolutely had to write. Their pages showed in clear detail the tragedy of a modern

---

[606] Kobayashi's father dealt in pictures — of questionable authenticity, according to Kobayashi himself.

[607] 'Tsuma' (Wife), October 14th 1908-February 14th 1909, Nihon (Shinbun).

young man of an age just past. And so I made up my mind to write and ignore all worldly considerations. I'd write it regardless of the fact that it might be romantic, and sentimental, and lacking in new ideology. Having made up my mind I then visited K — Kobayashi's friend K — in Ōzuka, and borrowed several letters from him, and then I went to Gyōda to see Ishijima.[608]

Ishijima was a very busy man but was nevertheless kind enough to show me all sorts of things. He took me to the former samurai residences, and to the ruins of the house Kobayashi used to live in.

On that occasion I also took a rickshaw to Kumagaya. It was then that I got the material for the depiction of the road alongside the watercourse. I also visited Hagiwara in the post-office there.[609] At that particular moment he was rather busy, so I waited for him at the Senshū Restaurant, which his family owned. Hagiwara is the second or third son of the family, and nowadays he is head of the post-office in H. That he is a very kind, responsible person is abundantly clear in the diaries. That day we had a wonderful meal at the restaurant, and I was able to learn all sorts of things about Kobayashi, as well as observing Hagiwara's personality.

I wanted to find out a bit more about the girls in Kobayashi's life, but everyone was very reticent about this matter. Moreover, I didn't have chance to meet any of the girls themselves. This was most unfortunate, but there was nothing I could do about it so I started writing regardless.

I commenced writing on the first or second of June. I felt very relaxed sitting there writing by the window, with the summer rain falling outside, and my pen was able to capture the gentle mood of the work. On the other hand, my life at that time was in many ways at an unsuitable stage for writing 'Country Teacher'. I had many worries, many anxieties, and was ill as well, often having to stop writing to go and lie down.

Nevertheless, by the end of August I was able to finish some two-thirds of the work. I then sent this off to Seki with a sigh of relief.[610]

After that I had to continue writing while having a good half of my time taken up with proof-reading. It seemed like every day that Seki and Shibata Ryūsei came around with their pressing demands. And of course, I still had to go to the office, and couldn't simply take time off when I wanted. The lamplight shone out onto the trees in the garden till late at night.

---

[608] K is Kano Masuji (Katō Ikuji in the novel), and Ishijima is Ishijima Ikutarō (pseudonym Ishijima Bizan), who appears in the novel as Ishikawa Kizan.

[609] Hagiwara Kisaburō (Ogyū Hidenosuke in the novel) worked at various times in both the Hanyū and Kumagaya post-offices, eventually becoming head of the Hanyū office.

[610] Seki Yosaburō (dates unclear) was a member of the Sakura Shobō staff, as was the novelist Shibata Ryūsei (1879-1913) mentioned below.

There was a considerable reaction to the work. I myself anticipated a lot of the criticism, such as that it left something to be desired as a work of the modern age. There was also a view that my psychological depiction of those young men was not totally accurate. There were indeed 'thin patches' where I had not been fully able to grasp things myself.

I had the map included at the front of the book to help convey the life of a young man who rarely went anywhere outside the limits of the area around Kumagaya, Gyōda, Miroku, Hanyū, and his birthplace of Ashikaga.

I've often seen people from the Kantō Plain region with a copy of 'Country Teacher'. I saw a young woman, who looked like a teacher, reading it as she was travelling along in a coach, and I saw it lying on the reception desk of an extremely unlikely-looking inn. I've also heard comments like "It seems the bit about going to the brothel district in Nakada isn't true. Novelists do write some terrible things, I must say!"

The part about the licensed quarters in Nakada is indeed conjecture. I believed that at some point in a young man's life there had to be an episode essentially like that, even if it might have been somewhat different in form. There was a break of a year or so in the diaries, and this too helped lead me to conjecture along those lines. That part also reflects to some degree the considerable intertwining of author and protagonist.

I used my imagination to depict the scenery of the lower Tone River — that is to say, the part between Ōgoe and Nakada — and when I later visited the area I discovered to my great regret that it was in fact very different. This convinced me that the best method is indeed on-the-spot depiction. By contrast, my depiction of the pines on the bank near Hotto was based upon actual observations I had made, so consequently it was highly praised by people who had visited the area.

The part where I listed all those flowers on the banks of the Tone might give the impression that I know a great deal about botany, but in fact I simply quoted from the diaries.

Anyway, I was pleased that I had depicted the aspirations of that young man. I was far more pleased than I had been with the portrayal of my mother in 'Life', perhaps because I wasn't too closely attached. I felt as though I had dealt with the human soul, and as though I'd resurrected that young man's soul from the grave.

Even nowadays, whenever I go to the temple in H, I always make a point of visiting his grave, with its headstone of natural rock, and offering flowers. For me it is no longer simply the grave of some stranger. His grave is now shaded by the cypress tree which his friends planted. On my last visit I did however notice that the fence around his grave had fallen into disrepair and that the division from the other graves nearby was no longer clear.

The Ibsen Society

"All we ever do at the Ryūdokai meetings is eat, " said Y.[611] "If we're going to have meetings, we should at least have meaningful ones." So it was that the Ibsen Society was formed, its first meeting being held at the Gakushikai [Hall] in Hitotsubashi.[612]

We were still young in those days. O was a fresh-faced young man who still had to make a name for himself, and he cut a dashing figure when he turned up in his splash-pattern haori and hakama.[613] I can still clearly picture H's plump face, the tall I-'s beaming face, A's face.....[614]

I- and M were messing around with a ball or something.[615]

We discussed 'Ghosts', 'The Wild Duck', 'Little Eyolf', and two or three other works. Y's refined, self-confident features stood out clearly in the gentle rays of the afternoon sun as it came slanting into that Western-style room. A was sprawled out on a settee, offering his opinions from time to time. "I wonder what it symbolises? It's strange, that white horse." He talked about the symbolism in 'Rosmersholm'.

The discussion grew heated when it came to 'Wild Duck'. We argued whether it was a good thing to come out openly with what one had to say, and whether it was good or bad to disrupt a quiet life of compromise. "I just don't know where Ibsen's sympathies lie in this work," said Y. "It does seem at this point as if he was aware of something very wrong."

We also argued heatedly about new ideology. Everyone gave their own personal views, and it was very informative as we had all studied various magazines and critical works and often came up with very useful material. O was particularly informed on drama, and brought lots of photographs of Western actors playing roles from Ibsen's works.

We talked for a couple of hours, decided the agenda for the next meeting, and then retired to the Japanese-style room at the rear of the building, where we had a Western-style meal of beef. Here too we talked heatedly about literature.

---

[611] Yanagita Kunio.

[612] The first meeting was held on February 1st 1907. The society was formed at Yanagita's instigation, although Iwano Hōmei also played a constructive part. The first concrete plans had been proposed on December 20th the previous year. According to Yanagita's diary, those present at the first meeting were, apart from himself, Katai, Tenkei, Maeda, Shūkō, Shunyō, Hōmei, Ariake, Osanai, Tōson, and Nakajima Kotō (1878-1946, novelist and critic). Katai's account (elsewhere) adds Hakuchō.

[613] That is, Osanai Kaoru.

[614] Hasegawa Tenkei, Iwano Hōmei, and Kanbara Ariake.

[615] Iwano and Maeda.

It was shortly before the opening performance of O's 'Free Theatre', so we talked a lot about that.[616] And what with us being young, we got carried away in our conversation, and talked till after ten o'clock.

"So, the next meeting is the first Thursday next month."

We left the premises. The sky was filled with stars, and we felt as though a bright world of boundless hopes lay before us. I remember A and I- walking back together.

The Development of Tōkyō

The recent development of Tōkyō has been quite remarkable. When you're actually in the middle of all the changes you tend not to notice them, but if you were to come up from the country you'd be sure to wonder where exactly you were. The remodelling of the city has been completed, and the roads widened, and electric trains now go everywhere, with the hum of the lines filling the air.

So what was Tōkyō like around 1881 — Tōkyō with its broughams and its 'Entarō carriages' dashing through the mud, and its many little food and drink stalls around the bridges?[617]

The trains have resulted in a gradual change in the location of the shopping centres. People living in the suburbs no longer have to shop locally, but can come on the trains right into the city-centre. Consequently dry-goods stores such as Mitsukoshi, Shirokaya, and Matsuya have expanded greatly.

Generally speaking, the intersections of the train-lines have become particularly busy, as a result of all the people getting on and off, and this too has brought about changes in the city. Places such as the corner of Owarichō in the Ginza, and Sudachō in Kanda, and Hirokōji in Ueno, and the various old castle approaches have all changed drastically from what they were in days of old.

If you look carefully you can see the biggest change of all has been in the types of people — an inevitable change brought about by the spread of transport.

---

[616] 'Jiyū Gekijō' was founded in November 1909 — two and a half years after the meeting of the Ibsenkai (Katai has obviously confused his description with a later meeting) — by Osanai Kaoru and the kabuki actor Ichikawa Sadanji (1880-1940). (The latter had just returned from a study-tour of European theatres.) The aim of the 'Jiyū Gekijō' was to introduce Western dramas, and for the first performance it was planned to stage Hauptmann's 'Vor Sonnenaufgang' (Before the Dawn). However, censorship problems caused a revision of plan, and at Tōson's suggestion Ōgai's translation of Ibsen's 'John Gabriel Borkman' was staged instead. The performance was held on November 27th 1909, at the Yūrakuza. The 'Jiyū Gekijō' continued till 1919.

[617] 'Entarō carriages' were a type of horse-drawn carriage named in popular speech after the comedian Tachibanaya Entarō the Fourth (?-1898), who frequently mimicked the mannerisms of the coachmen.

The main roads have lost all remnants of old Edo. There was once a time when the flurry of demolition and construction seemed strange and disorganised, but now things seem to have settled down — at least, after a fashion. The procession routes, Hibiya Park, Tōkyō Station — all these seem to have changed completely.[618]

Hibiya used to be a military drill-ground, and there was a large gingko tree standing there in the very middle of the fields. It was exposed to the sun in autumn, and to the dust-storms in summer, and in winter it was a sea of mud and not at all easy to cross. The road that ran along the moat from present-day Yūrakuchō to Sakuradamon used to get particularly bad when it rained, and the rickshawmen used to grumble about getting their feet covered in mud. That's how it was till at least the mid 1890's. There was also a tiny little Western-style hotel on the way to the Great Shrine of Hibiya, called the Grand Hotel, which was so small you wouldn't be able to find anything like it nowadays. I used to pass by there every day on my way to the Chūō Newspaper.[619]

When I first went to Tōkyō the Prefectural Office was in Dobashi.[620] Of course, in those days there was still an air of old Edo about in places, with tall fire-towers and old-style gates and tile-and-mortar walls. If I remember correctly the old prefectural middle-school was in that area too. Anyway, twice a year I'd go along to that office to collect the little pension my mother received following my father's death. The officials there had their desks in part of a Japanese-style building, with their bookcases beside them, and used to handle documents across a little glass window. Nowadays you can hardly find a set-up like that even out in the country.

Similarly, Marunouchi was a terribly dismal place, with a lonely, bleak, desolate air to it, and the Imperial Palace seemed shut away in the clouds. What a change nowadays! Now there are tramcars running busily all around the moat, and cars speeding about, and occasionally you even see aeroplanes flying overhead. There is nothing left at all of the old gloom and desolation. How it all looks fresh and alive, with the pines of the Imperial Palace, and the spring clouds drifting overhead,and the Shintenpu in the distance staring up at them![621]

[618] Hibiya Park was built in 1903 (see Note 448). Tōkyō Station (the building) was completed in 1914, construction having commenced in 1908. It was modelled on Amsterdam Central. The present building was restored in 1954.

[619] Katai had briefly joined the Chūō Shinbun staff in June 1895, resigning in September that year.

[620] Tōkyō, the capital from 1868, was a 'fu' (prefecture) from 1871, a mixture of 'fu' and 'shi' (city) from 1889, and 'to' (metropolitan region) from 1943. Dobashi is present-day Shinbashi 1 Chōme, but actually the office was in Uchisaiwaichō 1 Chōme.

[621] The Shintenpu is a building inside the Palace grounds which houses objects from the Sino-Japanese War of 1894-1895.

It's all changed completely too around where the trains run through Sotobori.[622] There used to be parsley and shepherd's-purse growing in spring on the banks of Tameike [Reservoir], and families often used to go there to pick them, but that was filled in and has become the busy red-light district it is nowadays.[623] The large Crown Prince's Palace has also been built, beyond Aoyama Palace.[624] The flowers alongside the [outer] moat here were indeed so splendid that they would now be thought of as one of the sights of Tōkyō. The green of the willows of Benkeibashi, too — especially in the haze of rain on a spring morning — was just indescribable.[625]

The three main roads of Yotsuya, Kagurazaka, and Hongō were once outer parts of the old castle and were therefore busy places. Yotsuya hasn't changed all that much from those days. Kagurazaka has also retained some of its old character. The stretch of road running along this part of the [outer] moat was long and uninspiring, and when the winds blew in early spring there would be dust-storms there, and the faded clothes in the second-hand clothes shops would flap about. You don't see anything like this nowadays. The Hongō road has mostly been widened. There used to be a shop there selling that well-known millet-cake, but it's not there any longer.

However, in the downtown districts — especially in the heart of Nihonbashi — it is not impossible even today to find a little something left of old Edo. If you go to the areas around Oyajibashi, Shianbashi, and Yokoyamachō I think you will find that the rows of storehouses and the big wholesalers give a suggestion of the three hundred years of prosperity of old Edo.[626]

The back-streets of Okachimachi and Takechō in Shitaya are surprisingly old-fashioned, seeming decades behind the times.[627] They give me the impression not so much of old Edo but of the early 1880's.

Generally speaking, the outlying parts of Tōkyō have been newly developed. They're new towns, where office-workers and students live. They have nothing of the old atmosphere about them. That old Edo at-

---

[622] The northern edge of present-day Akasaka 1-2 Chōme.

[623] Tameike was a man-made reservoir in this area, which was mostly filled in between 1886-1889, and finally filled in in 1910.

[624] The Crown Prince's Palace is the Tōgūgosho in present-day Motoakasaka 2 Chōme. Construction started in 1900, and was completed in 1909.

[625] Benkeibashi formerly spanned the Aizomegawa, in what is now Iwamotochō 2 Chōme in Chiyoda-ku, and was pulled down when the river was filled in in 1885. (Judging from this date, and from the fact that its location was on the opposite side of the Imperial Palace to the other items described in the paragraph, it is possible that Katai has mistakenly given this name instead of some other bridge.)

[626] See Note 47.

[627] Okachimachi and Takechō were parts of present-day Taitō 1-4 Chōme.

mosphere was overwhelmed by the enlightenment process, and can now only be found lingering on faintly in the heart of the city — or should I say rather the 'depths' of the city.

And thus times change, consuming in their wake all manner of people, and things, and dramas. New times bring new people, who tread the earth as if it had only ever been theirs alone. But what about fifty years from now? A hundred years from now?

A Man of Bygone Days

"When it comes to buying things, you can't beat the old establishments."

So says an old man I know, sixty-two or thereabouts this year, who has always gone shopping in the streets of Nihonbashi.

Ninben for dried bonito. Hanshige for fishcakes, Odaya for pickles, Inarizushi in Jikkendana for their special sushi wrapped in fried bean-curd, and there was also Kogetsu in the same area.[628] Mikawaya in the Kanda Myōjin temple-grounds for fermented soybeans, Eitarō for sweet red-beans, Hokakezushi in Nihonbashi for sushi, Nakagawa in Awajichō for beef......

However much the streets and buildings change, this old man can still picture the shops he used to go to in days of old. "People my age well remember how Inarizushi in Jikkendana used to be run by an old couple. When I was young it was just a tiny little shop, no bigger than a street stall. You could sit down and relax there. But it did very well for itself and in one generation grew into the big concern it is today." Not all his tales, however, were of such prosperity. He went on to tell me how one large Western-goods store, to which he had been apprenticed as a boy, had slumped badly and was now up for sale.

"All the food's fallen off in quality, especially tsukudani. And cakes too. Fūgetsu doesn't sell the same sort of stuff as it used to. When it comes to cakes the best place is Tazuki in Jikkendana, or Kogetsu in Hamachō — the old shops....."

He went on to tell me a lot about the old shops, including which ones had pretty girls working there, or an attractive proprietress. It was funny to think that these old-time beauties were now wrinkled old women. He also told me about the rice-cakes of Shinmei in Shiba.

---

[628] Inarizushi is given as the name of an establishment as well as the name of the type of sushi. It is not clear which took its name from which. Later on in this chapter Katai refers to a Kogetsu in Hamachō, which is not close enough to Jikkendana to be the same establishment, so presumably it was a chain of shops (as Fūgetsu).

"Daimaru's gone, too. It used to be a big concern, once upon a time. You could always hear the clerks and shopboys calling out when you passed by......"

He seemed to miss the old days very much.

Futabatei's Death

"Hasegawa's come," said H as he came up to me in the editing office.[629]

Hasegawa! Futabatei Shimei! I was only too happy to go to the reception-room and be introduced to him by H.

The man I saw before me was a tall man, of imposing appearance. I had wanted to meet him for a very long time, and now I was finally able to do so. I had not expected this famous literary personality — the author of 'Drifting Cloud', the translator of 'Rendezvous', the first man to introduce Russian literature, the first man to bring foreign literature to Japan — to be quite so unassuming.[630]

I was thrilled.

Hasegawa was about to go off to Russia. He was a man who felt unfulfilled, who did not feel happy with literature alone, who went deeply into life as well as into philosophy, and who, unable to find satisfaction in his own country, was about to set off for the distant climes of Russia.

If I remember correctly he had come on that occasion to discuss with H the plan to hold a reception for Danchenko at Yaozen, and it wasn't long afterwards that we held a party for *him* — a farewell party — at the Seiyōken [Restaurant] in Ueno.[631]

Hasegawa was just like a comet in the literary world. He had wonderful talent, surpassing all others on the literary scene at the time, but just never seemed prepared to reveal it. Nevertheless all the new writers were indirectly influenced by him.

---

[629] Hasegawa Tatsunosuke was the real name of Futabatei Shimei. H is also, confusingly, Hasegawa — Hasegawa Tenkei, who had joined Hakubunkan in 1897.

[630] For details of 'Drifting Cloud' and 'Rendezvous' see Notes 134 and 89 respectively. Though in a general sense Futabatei can rightly be thought of as the man most responsible for the introduction of Russian literature to Japan, the first actual translation was by Takasu Jisuke (1859-1909) in June 1883, when he did a partial translation of Pushkin's 'The Captain's Daughter', under the fanciful title (typical for translations of that time) 'A Strange Story from Russia: The Thoughts of a Butterfly in the Heart of a Flower' ('Rokoku Kibun: Kashinchō Shiroku').

[631] The reception for the Russian writer Vladimir Danchenko was held on April 28th 1908. Futabatei's farewell party, as he set off to Russia as an Asahi Newspaper correspondent, was held on June 6th (1908).

It's a pity Futabatei doesn't write more," we were always saying.

"But that's Russian literature for you," said someone else. "Just look at his friend Saganoya — you rarely find people like that in Japan, not worried at all about going around in dirty clothes."[632]

I'd always liked hearing from Takase Bun'en about Futabatei. Futabatei was one of the first to read Darwin and Haeckel. He believed that the general principles of science were not enough, and even went into such specifics as zoology. When most people were talking about Tolstoi and Turgenev, he was studying Artsibashev, Kuprin, and Andreyev. He was certainly one of the leaders of the Meiji literary world.

However, this comet-like figure rarely published anything. For a long time after 'Drifting Cloud' he wrote nothing. Then, some ten years later, he put out that excellent translation 'Unanswered Love'.[633] Then he withdrew again for another five or six years. Presently his translations of Gorki appeared, and then, more recently, the two works 'Images' and 'Mediocrity'.[634]

He had no real enemies. He was never in the 'rat-race' type of journalism that produced enemies. It is therefore only natural that his farewell party was one of the best in the Meiji literary world.

Apart from Ōgai, Rohan, and Sōseki, just about every writer from just about every faction attended, new writers and older writers alike.

Uchida Roan gave a speech. Then Hasegawa stood up and gave a reply of thanks. Both speeches were good. New and old alike extended the warmest feelings to Hasegawa.

So he went to Russia, fell ill with tuberculosis before he'd had chance to do anything, and died a lonely, miserable death in his cabin on board a ship bound for home in the Indian Ocean.[635]

If you compare his life to that of the characters in Russian novels, I believe that there was something of the Rudin about his life, but also something of Lermontov's Pechorin at the end. Rudin died in the revolu-

---

[632] Saganoya Omuro (1863-1947, also known as Yazaki Chinshirō), was a translator and novelist who like his friend Futabatei had studied Russian literature and was much influenced by it and by the Russian approach to life. From January 1906 (to September 1923) he taught Russian at the Military School of Russian and was largely withdrawn from the literary scene.

[633] See Note 294.

[634] The two works were respectively 'Sono Omokage' (October 10th-December 31st 1906, Asahi Shinbun) and 'Heibon' (October 30th-December 31st 1907, Asahi Shinbun). His translations of Gorki included 'Kain to Aruchomu' (Cain and Archom, February 1905, 'Taiyō'), 'Fusagi no Mushi' (Depression, January-March 1906, 'Shinshōsetsu'), and 'Haiirobito' (Grey People, April 1906, Asahi).

[635] He left Tōkyō on June 12th, sailed from Kōbe on June 15th, and while returning from Russia died on board ship in the Bay of Bengal on May 10th 1909. He was cremated at Singapore.

tion. Pechorin went to Persia and disappeared. And Futabatei died on the waves of the Indian Ocean, his hopes unfulfilled......

M went to Shinbashi Station for the arrival of Futabatei's remains.[636] "I just couldn't begin to tell you how moving it was. Just when new ideology has gained strength and when the old and the new are fighting so furiously with each other, he comes back in ashes....."

Kōyō, Doppo, Bizan, Hasegawa — they all died young, the sacrifices of the undeveloped world of Meiji literature. Their lonely graves have given new life to Japanese literature. Who can overlook them? Who can overlook their contribution to Japan's literature? Is it not true that Japanese literature has been built on their graves?

Social Intercourse amongst Writers

Social intercourse amongst writers is not the sparkling, lively thing it might seem to others. Of course, when one's young one feels the need for daily company, but in most cases the socialising gradually becomes less frequent, and writers end up mixing almost exclusively with just two or three close friends.

Naturally, this is because literature is essentially an independent business, and although there are times when alliances do figure prominently, each individual has always got to be ready to rely on his own strengths.

Also, in the main, writers are sensitive people, easily angered and easily pleased, and often prone to dwell on trivia. Accordingly they find it impossible to be patient, or to practice duplicity. They know only honesty and frankness, so they are not good at compromise in their relationships. They don't really care about socialising.

Moreover, whatever their differences, they tend to attach importance to some things and not to others. Matters such as wealth and fame are important to them. But observation and analysis have fostered in them a profound understanding of things, which affects their reactions to those things. For them, beggars are not necessarily humble. High offices are not necessarily impressive. In other words, their sense of values is very different from that of the world at large.

It might therefore seem that social intercourse amongst writers is in fact almost non-existent after all. However, this is not the case either, for it is a fact that on the inside there is a profound understanding that forms a bond even between enemies. The sympathies of people writing for the same cause of literature are stronger than those of academic colleagues,

---

[636] M is Maeda Akira.

or work colleagues. Thus, even though they may not fraternise very often, writers do understand each other. It is not the sort of relationship that needs holding together by superficial exchanges of gifts or by wives getting to know each other.

Social intercourse seems more conspicuous amongst foreign writers. Russia's Elisseeff has said that the social life of Japanese writers is a lot more subdued than that of writers in Russia, but in fact, even overseas, it only seems to be amongst the younger writers that socialising is conspicuous, and once they get to be middle-aged they don't seem to be as interested in it. The meetings of Flaubert's group, for example, could certainly not be called lively. On the contrary, they were lonely affairs.

In the thirty years of socialising that I have observed amongst Japanese writers I think it was the Genyūsha group, centred round Kōyō, that was the liveliest and appeared the most interesting. They used to drink together, talk together, and go on trips together. But it is a fact that their fraternising and their trips and so on were based on interest and were not aimed at manual encouragement or mutual edification. Their trips were trips of cheap witticisms and pleasure and entertainment. It is for this reason that their fraternising appeared so interesting, but it was only an appearance. Bizan later frequently complained to me how silly it was.

The socialising of writers like myself was centred on the Ryūdokai, and that's about the sum of it — though of course one always has two or three permanent close friends. But for all that, it was only the sort of relationship where, if you met after a year or two, you'd shake hands and say "It's been a long time."

Moreover, apart from with close friends, writers do not have to keep up relationships regardless of their own tastes and attitudes. There are indeed many cases where they have to argue in order to preserve their own principles. There must be complete mutual recognition of personal freedom.

There has always been gossip circulating in the literary world. I think in fact that it was worse in the old Genyūsha days than it is now. Indeed, there were people who specialised in it, such as Shōjiki Shōdayū. There was also Fuchian, who wrote 'How to Become a Man of Letters'.[637] The 'Mesamashigusa' joint-criticisms, too, displayed a talent that one simply cannot find nowadays. There were also a lot of newspapers and journals prepared to print such stuff.

There were some writers who deliberately used this gossip as a means of self-promotion — or at least, there were not a few who appeared to

---

[637] See Note 220.

do so. Thus, gossip possessed a power to bring, rather unexpectedly, a certain fame to writers, albeit basically trivial....

On the other hand there were writers for whom gossip was extremely damaging, and a major obstacle. There were some who lost that precious will to write as a result, and some who lost heart and never got to show their true ability. Bizan's suicide was to an extent brought on by this sort of thing.

"You have to be strong to survive in the literary world," said a certain writer, and his comment is indeed true. Once you let the gossip and the criticism get on top of you there's no end to it.

In the Genyūsha days it was a very common thing for critics to get entertained. This was known as the 'wining and dining policy'. The same sort of approach still seems to be around nowadays as well, though the term might have changed. Unless you establish yourself the literary world can be a difficult place to tread. Of course, to an extent this is true of the world in general, but I think it is a more prominent feature of the world of letters because of the latter's honesty [sic], sensitivity, and simplicity.

In thirty years I have seen the rise and the fall of many writers. Looking back, I find myself wondering why certain writers stopped writing. There are some who produced marvellous first works and who should have gone on to become top-class writers. On the other hand there are some totally unexpected figures who have gradually become excellent writers. There are some very talented writers who unfortunately fell ill and died young. There are some who, despite great enthusiasm in their early years, suddenly switched to some other field of activity. There are others who still continue to labour away, plagued by worldly worries but never abandoning their initial hopes. When I think about all these things I feel glad that I myself managed to come through all this 'Sturm und Drang'.[638]

For me personally, art is something I could never give up. I have no other ability, no other field I could enter, and so, self-indulgently, I have clung to art and somehow or other made it my life. I feel strange to think that this simple reason, this 'no going back' attitude has allowed me to survive for so long in the literary world. It was not a few times that I had thoughts such as "No matter how incapable, no matter how untalented, if you study hard enough, you can at least make it as a country newspaper reporter, and that's better than nothing...."

After establishing myself as a writer I always used to compare myself with other writers at more or less the same point as I was. I'd always

---

[638] Given thus in German.

think things such as "K's done very well — I must achieve the same for myself," or "I don't think I can write as well as F, but somehow or other I've got to try and see what I can do," or "I wish I had S's ability — even just half of it....."[639]

It was once said of my persistence as a writer that "It's straightforward, easy, not like the complexities in Doppo's case." That may be true, but I think that one can only say that my lack of ability to do anything else did not give cause to believe otherwise.

When I think about those thirty years of writers and novelists and novices, there are a lot of things I would like to write about. It certainly makes me feel strange to realise that I have reached the point in life where I am now.

Apart from the Ryūdokai I didn't socialise very much, but I did make a number of trips with colleagues.

On one occasion, in late spring, we held a Ryūdokai meeting on the banks of the Tone River.[640] Kanbara, Oguri, Nakazawa, and Kosugi Misei were all there, and I think Iwano was too.

Oguri got drunk, and became argumentative. This upset Kosugi, who clouted him one on the head. But Oguri was drunk so he didn't get all that angry. The racket that night at the inn was quite remarkable, till we went off to sleep.[641]

There were a lot of tales to tell too about the trip I made with Nakazawa, Tamura from the 'Chūō', and Kosugi to the Sugita villa in Minato in Hitachi, which Doppo was renting.[642] That Gurendō was there too, and we seemed to do nothing but drink.[643]

I once went with Shimazaki to Kōzu Takeshi's house in Shiga Village in Shinshū.[644] It was the start of winter and cold, and snow glistened on

[639] According to Maeda Akira, these are Kōyō, Fūyō, and Shimazaki. However, while Kōyō was close to Katai in terms of age, he was incomparably ahead in terms of status, and Kunikida seems a more likely contender for 'K'.

[640] Actually July 7th 1906. Katai had been appointed chairman for the meeting, and decided to hold it for a change outside Tōkyō. As well as those mentioned below, Maeda Akira, Ōta Gyokumei, and several others were also present.

[641] According to contemporary reports Kosugi was also drunk, and proceeded to jump naked into the Tone to swim across and back (no small achievement when one considers it was several hundred yards wide). They are also reported to have spent the entire night in revelry, accompanied by geishas, and not to have gone to bed at all.

[642] To try and recover his health Doppo stayed from September — November 1907 in the villa of a Sugita Kyōsuke (a friend of Kosugi's) in Minato, Ibaraki Prefecture.

[643] Sakamoto Gurendō (1866-1925), essayist noted for his heavy drinking and debauched life-style.

[644] Shiga Village is near Saku, Nagano Prefecture. The trip was November 2nd-5th, 1906. Kōzu Takeshi (1882-1946) was a young banker-cum-landowner who became a close friend of Tōson's from April 1903 (Kōzu's wife's family were neighbours of Tōson's in Komoro) and who helped fund the publishing of 'Broken Commandment' and 'Spring'.

the distant Japan Alps. Nevertheless, there were still red leaves in his garden, and it was a very quiet and pleasant trip. We later decided to go on another trip, of three or four days, with Kanbara and Takebayashi, and we went to Izu in March.[645] This trip is described in detail in 'Trip' in the 'Tōson Collection', and it too was another interesting and pleasant trip.[646]

I also went on a walking tour with Maeda Akira, Kubota, Kanbara, and Yoshie, from Iga to Tsukinose, Yagyū, Kasagi, Nara, Uji, and Kyōto.[647] I was the 'tour leader' on that occasion, and tried to do it as cheaply as possible and to get in as many places as possible. "Now I know how the old express messengers must have felt!" said Kanbara. Kubota and Yoshie seemed fairly exhausted as we went over the mountains from Tsukino to Yagyū.

I've been on various other trips, but my memory of them is not too clear nowadays.

A Photograph

There is a certain postcard-size snapshot in my box of photographs. I came across it the other day, and it brought back all sorts of memories.

That photograph had been called 'a stringful of writers'.[648] The date and place are written on the back — '10th February 1903, at home'.[649] That was when I was living in Haramachi in Ushigome, and by then I had already written works such as 'The End of Jūemon'.[650]

We are all lined up in a row — Kanbara, Kawakami, Kunikida, Oguri, Hasegawa [Tenkei] and me — under some plum trees, and a washing line that happened to be fixed between the trees seems for all the world to be stringing us together through the eyes.[651]

---

[645] Takebayashi Musōan (1880-1962), novelist and translator. The trip was actually in February, specifically 21st-26th, 1909.

[646] 'Tabi', in 'Taiyō' of April 1909 and included in 'Tōson Shū' of December 1909 (Hakubunkan).

[647] Kubota Utsubo (1877-1967), poet. The trip was March 18th-24th 1910.

[648] 'Bunshi no Mezashi'. A 'mezashi' (lit: eye-piercing) is a number of objects strung together, used usually of fish strung through the eye sockets.

[649] Doppo has recorded the date as March 8th 1903. However, this is one case where Katai appears to be the correct party, as the traditional plum blossom season (see below) is February 5th-25th.

[650] 'Jūemon no Saigo', May 1902, Shinseisha, was one of Katai's major early works. Katai used the fee from this work to move into the quite expensive rental house (fourteen yen per month) in Haramachi against the wishes of his family. (They also employed a maid at the house.) They stayed there from September 11th 1902-October 15th 1903.

[651] It is actually a pole, obtained by Miyato, but I have taken the liberty of referring to it as a 'line' to keep the metaphor of 'stringful'.

"This is a good photograph — a veritable stringful of writers," Doppo had observed in his usual witty way.

Of the figures in the photograph Kawakami looks the tallest, and Doppo and Fūyō the shortest. This bothered Doppo. "Short people always lose out," he said. "I look as though I'm about to fall off the string."

It was still cold, those February days. When I sat at my desk upstairs in the house in Haramachi and noticed the pale plum blossoms out beyond the balcony I was filled with a terrible sense of sadness and a need for company. I felt even worse in the evenings. The sight of the pale plum blossoms being swallowed up by the evening seemed so awfully sad, and made me feel all the lonelier.

"Why not hold a get-together?" I said to myself, and promptly sent off various postcards inviting people to come and view the blossoms together.

Of course, in those days I had no money, and nothing I could offer by way of refreshments. Nevertheless I felt I ought to provide something, moreover something a little out of the ordinary, so I went off to Kagurazaka to see what I could find. I came back having purchased a duck.

At the time we had a fat maid called Okin — she's the woman described in the short story 'Maid.'[652] There was also a student, K — well, I call him a 'student' but in fact he didn't have any literary ambitions, or any ambitions at all for that matter, and he was a young man who had had a lot of experience of domestic difficulties.[653] We also had two children by that stage.

"How much saké will you need?" asked the student.

"Hmm, well, let me see..... Kawakami and Oguri and Kunikida will all be drinking. And Tenkei likes his saké too. I think we should allow about one and a half pints per person."

---

[652] Katai gives the title of the work as 'Kahi', but I have been unable to trace it. The same maid appears in Katai's novel 'Wife' as Okiku, and to judge from events depicted in that novel she came to work for the Tayama family around 1899/1900 (ie., presumably after the death of Katai's mother in August 1899), having arrived from the country as a young woman, and was dismissed by Katai in March 1904 as he did not like her criticisms of Okada Michiyo, who arrived in February 1904.

[653] Katai refers in passing in several works to this student, but precise details are unclear. Though Katai did later have students of his own — Okada Michiyo being the best-known and earliest of them — this student was actually a student of his elder brother Miyato, who (according to 'Wife') looked after him for about a year before losing his job in March 1902. (Miyato was dismissed in a controversial incident over plagiarism, in which he appears to have been made a scapegoat.) Katai then assumed responsibility for the student, who was a law student in his early twenties and with considerable experience of the ways of the world. So experienced was he (according to 'Wife') that Katai looked upon him as an adviser. He too was 'displaced' from the Tayama household in March 1904 following Okada Michiyo's arrival. He appears in 'Wife' as Yamaguchi.

So, we bought that much saké in.

The guests arrived.

"It's a bit small, but I thought we could hold our gathering upstairs. You can see the blossoms from there. It's very moving, you know, watching the blossoms get swallowed up by the dusk."

"The blossoms really are a fine sight, I must say!" said Kawakami.

We had the trays of comestibles set out in that little six-mat room, and spent the rest of the afternoon there drinking. I remember Oguri singing his favourite song, 'Sweet Narcissus', and then reciting some poetry with the odd bit of English mixed in. Doppo too was in good health in those days. I also remember Kawakami making some remark like: "Well, as for that — !!" and the light playing on his gold-rimmed spectacles. His upper-class features were bright red as he spoke. By the time we clattered downstairs for that 'stringful' photograph we were fairly tipsy.

Kanbara did drink to some extent, but in comparison with the others was not really able to hold his drink. It was the time of his 'Lonely Lament', and he was in good spirits and laughed out loud a lot.[654]

When they'd all gone home the student said in amazement: "Good grief — you got through a lot of drink!" Apparently one and a half pints per person had not been enough, so he'd gone for another three pints, and then had to go yet again, for another six pints.

"You can certainly all drink — especially Hasegawa!" he said.

Now, fourteen or fifteen years later, Kawakami and Kunikida are no longer alive. I've lost track of how many years it is since I last met Oguri. I still meet Hasegawa from time to time at Hakubunkan, but we rarely get together and talk like we used to. Thus time rolls on. It's only the plum trees that keep on blossoming as before.

Hakuchō and Shūkō

I'd known for some time that Masamune was considered a real genius at Waseda.[655]

One day, in the editing section at H, I heard Takayama Chogyū say to someone, "Yes, that Masamune's a very capable fellow. He's a genius all right, and leaves the others behind." This reminded me that I had heard on a previous occasion that Takayama was often being asked probing questions by a student called Masamune.[656]

---

[654] See Note 450.

[655] Hakuchō was at Waseda 1896-1901.

[656] After graduating from the Imperial University in July 1896 Takayama became a lecturer there, and also lectured at Waseda and other institutions. He also joined the Hakubunkan staff in 1897.

"He must be a very talented person indeed," I said to myself.

Then, at my poetry teacher's house, I noticed in the register of his students the name of Masamune Somebody-or-other from Bizen. "Ah, so that's Masamune, is it!?" I thought to myself, but then I heard that it was in fact the younger brother, and not the one going to Waseda.[657]

It seems that in the early days Masamune often went to Y's house, because of the proximity of their home towns and the connection through the younger brother.[658] Therefore I later learned about Masamune from Y, too.

It was from then on that Masamune started reading foreign literature. The first time I met him was, I think, when I was still in Kikuichō.[659] He was a short, small-framed person with a rather cold manner. My wife often imitated him. "Masamune — " was all he'd say to announce himself, and he'd just stand there. He never bowed. If I wasn't at home he'd go away without saying a word, just like that. "He's a strange person," my wife would say.

And Masamune would say, in his typical manner, such things as "Wherever I go I see young wives — none of them are especially nice, but at least they're young and look nubile. It makes me very envious."[660]

Masamune did borrow foreign books from me, but he also lent me various books of his own, such as Sienkiewicz's 'Quo Vadis'. It was he who informed me that Turgenev's complete works had arrived in the Ueno Library, and he also lent me Miss Crawford's 'Studies in Foreign Literature'.[661] It seems that at that time Masamune read a lot of new books.

But whenever we met he never seemed to find it easy to talk, and generally listened in silence, merely contributing the occasional smart remark. His remarks were always negative.

I can more or less understand his period of struggle between leaving school and establishing himself in the literary world. He was a writer for

---

[657] Hakuchō's younger brother was the poet Masamune Atsuo (1881-1958). Both were born in the Wake area of eastern Bizen (Okayama Prefecture). The poetry teacher here is Matsuura Tatsuo, but Atsuo also studied under Inoue Michiyasu (1866-1941), the elder brother of Yanagita Kunio (see below).

[658] Yanagita was born in neighbouring Hyōgo Prefecture. It should also be remembered that Yanagita was himself studying under Matsuura.

[659] That is, before September 11th 1902.

[660] Masamune finally married in April 1911.

[661] I have been unable to trace this work ('Gaikoku Bungaku Kenkyū': it appears to have been written in a language other than Japanese, probably English), or any woman writer called Crawford who is likely to have written such a work. It is possibly a reference to a critical work "The Novel: What Is It?" (1893) by the American MALE writer Francis Marion Crawford (1854-1909), whom Katai may understandably have taken to be a woman.

the Y Newspaper, and a drama critic, and did quite a lot of translations too. I remember him saying to me in those days, with an earnest expression on his face, "Whatever I do it's no good, a waste of time. I can't seem to do anything worthwhile. What good is it my trying to be a writer?!"

Nevertheless, Masamune and I once had a very lively and interesting dispute over subjectivity and objectivity. Masamune wrote his views in the Sunday supplement of the Y Newspaper, and I wrote mine in the weekly journal 'Taiheiyō', which I was working on at the time.[662]

If I remember correctly we continued the argument through a number of issues. Masamune was working on the Sunday supplement of the Y Newspaper in those days, and Hōgetsu was also publishing his laconic criticisms in its pages.

I believe Masamune's first work was probably 'Old Friend' — if I've remembered the title correctly.[663] It was in that work anyway that I first felt I'd seen his true talent.

I got to know Tokuda Shūkō at about the same time as Masamune.[664] At times I could hardly even think of Masamune without thinking too of Tokuda, so similar were they in my mind. Tokuda hadn't got Masamune's talent, however, and there was something of the flatterer about him, something rather 'cloying'. They were classmates, and graduated together, as well as coming from neighbouring home towns, so I thought it was particularly interesting to observe their emergence together onto the literary scene.

Tokuda is now an excellent writer, but I think his struggle to establish himself in the literary world was a lot more severe than in Masamune's case.

"I just can't seem to write well at all," he would say, brushing the long hair from his pasty face.

However, unlike Masamune he lived next door to my elder brother's house, near the hill as described in 'Life', and for that reason he was on more familiar terms with me and my brother and my wife than Masamune was. My brother's wife also seemed to know him quite well.

---

[662] This exchange of views took place in the second half of 1901 following Katai's famous introduction to 'Flowers of the Field' (see Note 270) and Hakuchō's criticism of his statements regarding subjectivity. Writing in a series entitled 'Seika Yokō' (The Abundant Fragrance of Western Flowers) in 'Taiheiyō' Katai went on to expand his views on subjectivity, and his differentiation between the id and the ego is of great importance to naturalism in Japanese literature. Hakuchō's column was in fact in the Monday issues of the Yomiuri.

[663] 'Kyūyū' (Old Friend) was in the September 1906 issue of 'Shinshōsetsu'. Strictly speaking his first work was actually 'Sekibaku' (Loneliness) in the November 1904 issue of the same magazine.

[664] That is, Chikamatsu Shūkō. Shūkō was also from Wake in Okayama, and furthermore was a classmate of Hakuchō's at Waseda.

One day, when my wife went to my brother's house, there happened to be a fire nearby and the firebells were ringing. Apparently Tokuda got a ladder out, climbed up onto the roof, and sat there flirting with his wife as they watched the fire. My wife often talks about this incident.

It's the house described in his 'Doubt'.[665] I also spoke to his wife on a number of occasions, so I can visualise particularly clearly the background of that novel. I feel I have shared many of Tokuda's anxieties.[666]

By contrast with Masamune's rise to fame, it was a long time before Tokuda's novels were recognised. Or rather, he was for a long time unable to express himself fully. It was with 'Letters to my Estranged Wife' that he really did this, and it shows his talent, his poetic skills, and his lyricism.[667]

I believe at any rate that his relationship with his wife led him deeply into the realm of art, and while I sympathise with him in his suffering, I also believe it to be a cause for congratulation. I have been able to appreciate fully his anguish and desperation.

I don't know all that much about Masamune's life, but he too seems to have suffered loneliness. He put out such excellent works as 'Setting Sun' and 'Glimmer', but both of these reveal to me a dispirited, miserable author.[668] I feel that the author had his eyes half-closed to the world, and was staring sadly into space. The horror in 'Poison' may have been small in scale, but it was a tormented, wretched bitterness from the innermost reaches of human life.[669] And then, as if by way of a complete recovery of spirit, from time to time he'd write such works as 'Two Families' and 'First Trip'.[670]

It was very interesting to me to see the different directions taken by these two classmates, Masamune and Tokuda. It was like seeing a fan

---

[665] 'Giwaku', September 1913, 'Shinshōsetsu', in which Shūkō wrote of his suspicions of his (first) wife (see below).

[666] Shūkō married Ōnuki Masuko in 1903 (though he appears to have lived with her for some time before that), and she left him in 1909 (August). Their life had been a troubled one, including a failure in a haberdashery business. He remarried in 1922, to the masseuse Inose Ichi. Though Katai's expression here largely implies involvement in Tokuda's 'wife trouble', there is also a suggestion of a more personal sympathy. This should not however be interpreted as suggesting any infidelity on the part of Katai's wife Risa, but rather on the part of his mistress Iida Yone, whom Katai came to look upon as a second wife (though he and Risa never actually separated). Such doubts figured prominently in Katai's works from 1912 to 1923.

[667] 'Wakaretaru Tsuma ni Okuru Tegami', March-July 1910, 'Waseda Bungaku'.

[668] Respectively 'Rakujitsu' (September 1909, Yomiuri) and 'Bikō' (October 1910, 'Chūō Kōron').

[669] 'Doku', November 19th 1911-March 3rd 1912, Kokumin Shinbun.

[670] 'Nikazoku' (September 1908-May 1909, 'Waseda Bungaku') and 'Hatsutabi' (January 1914, 'Chūō Kōron').

spreading out, watching them draw further and further apart — one to the right, the other to the left.

Masamune will always be lonely man. He's the sort of person who can live with his loneliness, the sort of person who can come to your doorway and then promptly go away without a murmur if you're not in. Tokuda is also a lonely person, but unlike Masamune he feels the need to do something about his loneliness. He always has to try to do something to dispel it. This difference is clearly detectable in their writings, too.

It was with the emergence of writers such as these two that Meiji literature was able to free itself completely — in the real sense of the word — from all restrictions, such as traditions of character-usage, vacuous words, complications of form, and a romantic disposition. They had complete liberty. Kōyō, naturally, and even Futabatei were still caught up to an extent with old stereotypes and old modes of writing. Doppo managed relatively early on to break away to a degree, but still had something of the old-style morality [sic] about him. Shimazaki, Shūsei, Hōmei, and I myself have also been unable to shake off completely that flavour of a previous age. Our terminology and character-usage are still restrictive, as too our ways of thinking and arranging material. It was with the emergence of writers such as Masamune and Tokuda that the old traditions were finally left behind.

The Asphalt Road

For many a long year I used to get off the train at Sudachō and walk down a long road sealed on both sides with asphalt.

It was the same road on which, thirty years ago, that unusual large Western-style building had towered, the one with Asahiya and a place selling Xerez Wine.[671] It was a road along which rickety old carriages had ploughed through the mud, blowing their horns. Nowadays, although the ground is the same as in those days, the buildings along the road have changed so much you'd think it was a different road. The people going along the road also seem very different.

Though on occasion I caught a connecting train as far as the corner of Hongokuchō, usually I walked along that road. Nine o'clock in the morning, four o'clock in the afternoon.....

There I'd be, plodding along every day on my way to and from my boring job as a magazine writer, wearing tweed in winter and alpaca wool in summer. I wore red shoes, and carried a walking-stick, and looked rather pleased with life. But in fact I was generally in a state of

---

[671] See Note 2.

depression. I felt as if the world was against me, as if it was going to swamp me with its turbulent waves. I was caught between the old and the new, and suffered the sneers of the major established writers on the one hand and the prodding of the most recent writers on the other. I was also plagued incessantly by things connected with my family, and with day-to-day life, and with my associates.

There were gingko trees along the asphalt pavements. They'd only recently been planted, and only had a scanty covering of leaves, which were discoloured with grime and dust. On one side of the road there were shops such as seaweed wholesaler's, a hardware shop, a little restaurant, and a little dry-goods shop. There were a variety of people there too, all of them busy, such as aging shop-clerks, and bald old shopkeepers, and young proprietresses with their hair done up attractively in the downtown style, and apprentices who reminded me of my own younger days. There were also numerous customers. There was an auction hall too, and a shop specialising in 'comma design' baths. According to the large advertisement, which was highly conspicuous in the summer sunshine, they were very economical baths that only took forty minutes to heat up. There was also a bun shop, with 'Yone Buns' written up in large letters, and a large, long-established sugar shop that was always packed with customers.[672] Into the midst of such an atmosphere I used to bring my own confused mixture of boredom, and distress, and anxiety, and love.

The display-window of a large dry-goods shop, M, used to break the monotony of the long walk along that road.[673] Everyone would stop and look there. The beautiful designs of the obi and parasols and 'going-out' clothes, as well as the seasonal pictures in the background, were always eyecatching. I used to make a point of stopping to look.

Then it was across the bridge.....the bridge where the train line crossed. After that it was the corner of Hongokuchō, and then Jikkendana with all its doll shops. In spring there'd be really beautiful dolls on display there, and in May carp-streamers and Kintarō dolls.

When I reached here I always felt oppressed by the prospect of another boring day at the office. If the sky was blue I'd feel sorry for myself that I wasn't free to go on a trip somewhere, and if it came on to rain I'd worry about not having an umbrella to go back with, and feel thoroughly fed up and miserable. Misery, restrictions, irksome socialising......

---

[672] Yone manjū is a type of manjū (beanjam bun) that was first sold in Asakusa. There are several theories as to the name 'Yone' — that it is the name of the maker, simply a word for 'rice', or that it was favoured by prostitutes (also 'yone') working in the area.

[673] M is Matsuya.

There was a little post-office on the corner. From there I turned left down a narrow street. I walked on for another hundred yards or so. Then I'd come to the rear door of the company. I grace it with the term 'rear door', but in fact it looked more like the entrance to some dark little cellar. I'd go in, and through to the room where I worked.....

Sometimes I'd walk back along that asphalt road with Maeda Akira, who worked with me at the office. "If you're going to walk I'll go with you," he'd say.

We nearly always talked about literature — about who'd done what, or whose work wasn't very good, or whose arguments were unconvincing, or else about plans for next month's magazine, or else about foreign literature.[674]

In later days we also talked about a beautiful geisha in a house along the river.

Sometimes I'd feel reluctant to go straight back to my gloomy home in the suburbs for a gloomy night, and would go instead to a little restaurant near S, and drink saké in the late afternoon sunshine, feeling miserable.[675] On other occasions I'd keep on walking, as far as Shinobazu Pond.

Nowadays I hardly ever walk down that wearisome asphalt road. When I have chanced to pass that way I've noticed how big the gingkos have grown, and how in spring time the shade of the fresh verdure dapples the parasols of the young ladies.

The Death of Emperor Meiji

The tone of voice of the newsboy selling extras was not the animated tone one hears during war time; nor was it the flippant tone characteristic of some trivial event being deliberately overplayed, or the intrigued tone of a political reform. Rather, it was a sad, despondent voice that one heard as the newsboy ran down the street.

"His Majesty's condition critical"....."His Majesty's state of health as of yesterday"......and then, over the next four or five days, it was reported that crowds had gathered near Nijūbashi to pray constantly for His Majesty's recovery.[676]

The whole nation was stricken with grief. Everyone spoke in hushed tones, with a look of sorrow on their face.

---

[674] Katai and Maeda (who had joined the company in 1906) had particular responsibility for 'Bunshō Sekai', started in March 1906.

[675] S is Sudachō.

[676] Nijūbashi [Bridge] is in the southeast part of the Imperial Palace grounds. The Emperor was suffering from kidney complications.

It was impossible to stop nature's forces entering the Palace grounds and into the very heart of the Palace itself to where the Emperor lay. The best doctors in the nation were powerless.

Who could fail to be moved to tears by the thought of the illustrious life of His Majesty Emperor Meiji, 'Mutsuhito the Great', Lord of the Restoration, who despite being raised in adversity surmounted all manner of obstacles and perils to lead Japan to the state of wonderful international nationhood it enjoys today?[677]

There comes a time when one must bid farewell even to an emperor. It was not just me who felt this. The whole nation felt the same way. I had been too young to pay my respects at such ceremonies as the accession and the change of capital, but every time the Imperial Guard of Honour went in procession through the streets I was always to be found standing amongst the crowd at the roadside, paying my respects to His Majesty in an indirect way.[678] And on the occasion of His Majesty Emperor Meiji's move from Aoyama Palace to the Imperial Palace, and of His Majesty Taishō's investiture as Crown Prince, and his marriage, I went to Akasaka Mitsuke to watch — on the last of these occasions with my wife.[679] I had never dreamt that the Imperial Funeral would take place so soon, without our even being able to celebrate the fiftieth anniversary of the accession.

I will never forget that terribly hot day at the end of July when the Emperor's passing was announced.[680] Living away out in the suburbs I had to wait till the following morning to read the extras. It was a quiet morning. I got up early as was my habit and, breathing deeply in the cool shade of the young trees in the garden, I went as usual to the mail-box by the gate.

The extra edition was there.

"So, the Emperor has finally passed away," I thought to myself, overcome with a whole host of feelings.

---

[677] Mutsuhito (born November 3rd 1852) was the real name of Emperor Meiji. 'Mutsuhito the Great' is given in English by Katai. The rather obviously overstated praise of Emperor Meiji and of the Japanese cause in general, both in this paragraph and later in the chapter, is possibly an attempt by Katai to exculpate himself from any possible accusation of harbouring treasonous thoughts. This became a problem following the Treason Incident of 1910-11 (see later section 'A Certain Grave' and notes thereto).

[678] Both the accession and the change of capital took place in 1868, so for Katai to say he was 'too young' is something of an understatement: he was not even born at the time. His term ('osanakute') definitely implies that he was an infant at the time, which is most peculiar.

[679] The move from Aoyama Palace took place in 1888, Emperor Taishō (Yoshihito, 1879-1926) was invested in 1889, and he married Sadako (Teimei) in 1900.

[680] Mutsuhito died on July 30th 1912.

There was the Seinan Civil War, in which my father had died.[681] Then there was the war with China, followed by the war with Russia, in which I had participated as a member of a photography team. I saw an awesome display of the Emperor's august and virtuous power as it spread afar. I positively leapt for joy when I saw the Rising Sun flag flying from the enemy strongholds at Chin-chou and Nanshan, and realised how the blood in my veins too was Japanese blood. Ideologically I am a free-thinker, but my spirit is that of a Japanese nationalist. Naturally I was full of reverence towards the august might of His Majesty Emperor Meiji. And now......

I stood there in silence. Our dear, beloved, gracious Emperor Meiji, whom we had made our strength and support, had passed away!

I went to work as usual on that day. I saw many faces full of profound grief. The streets were quiet, and lacked their normal bustle and activity. Black flags of mourning hung miserably from the rooftops.

Thinking back over what had happened sinse the Restoration, I could visualise numerous events. There were the upheavals of the Restoration itself, the eastern expedition of the Imperial Forces, the vacating of Edo Castle, and then the Emperor's move to Tōkyō.[682] When I first came to Tōkyō the meritorious figures of the Restoration were still young, there were still vestiges of old Edo about the castle, and you could often see councillors riding in their carriages through Marunouchi. Prince Itō was still young, and Marquis Ōkuma had still not met with that bombing incident.[683] His Majesty too was still young, and used to have his councillors gather round him for discussions.

Those dignitaries have now grown old, and disappeared into obscurity. Prince Itō's death at Harbin must have been a big blow to His

---

[681] The Seinan (Southwest) War, February 15th-September 24th 1877, was an insurrection against the government by Saigō Takamori (1827-1877), who disagreed with government policy towards Korea. Katai's former-samurai father Shōjūrō volunteered for the special police force that took part in the action, and was killed near Kumamoto on April 14th.

[682] From February-November 1868 the Imperial Forces were sent to the northeast provinces to subdue the remaining supporters of the Shōgunate. The forces were commanded by Arisugawa no Miya Taruhito Shinnō (1835-1895).

Emperor Meiji was based in Kyōto from December 1868 to March 1869. He had been temporarily in Tōkyō Castle/Palace in October 1868, which was when the name was changed from Edo Castle (the former residence of the Tokugawa Shōgun). Though the Emperor was in theory based at the Palace from March 1869, much of his time till 1888 was spent at Aoyama Palace. The move to Tōkyō referred to here is almost certainly that of March 1869.

[683] Itō Hirobumi (1841-1909). Ōkuma Shigenobu (1838-1922), a leading political figure and in 1882 founder of the Tōkyō Senmon Gakkō (later Waseda University), lost his leg in 1889 when a fanatic threw a bomb at his carriage. He was at the time Foreign Minister, negotiating the revision of the treaties with the foreign powers.

Majesty.[684] I was greatly saddened by the thought that death should follow remorselessly such distinguished achievement.

That summer was a very wet one. Thick grey clouds covered the sky, as if even the very heavens were sad, and rain streamed miserably from the gutterings. It was unpleasantly chilly.[685] There were days when it was impossible to dry the washing. The road to the suburban railway station was deep in mud.

The white water-lilies in the garden often had it raining on them all day long.

The events at the Palace were reported each morning in the papers. Those people who had been in constant attendance on His Majesty, those who had seen such great achievements, must have been particularly moved. They now came to pay their respects to the departed Emperor.

Arrangements were made for the funeral. The late Emperor was to be returned to his home town of Kyōto, and the day of the sad farewell ceremony drew near. I will never forget that night, that sad ceremony.

However, it remains in my memory rather for the fact that it took place in the grounds at Aoyama, near my home. I did not actually set foot outside that night. I am therefore unable to describe the scenes in the streets.

A dismal rain was falling on that night too. Late at night I heard the funeral salute being fired, and realised that the departure was imminent. My wife and I sat gloomily facing each other across the kotatsu. It was a sad night.

I was taken aback by General Nogi's suicide, and was overcome by sadness and feelings of heroic tragedy.[686] I felt as though it was a revival of the spirits of those many heroes who had given their life in battle for their country.

I didn't think that General Nogi's attitude would be something that foreigners could understand. While on the one hand I regretted the sentimentality of the Japanese nation, on the other hand I felt that it was because of this very sentimentality that there was life and vitality in the nation. I felt very much that we were a sentimental, emotional people.

The passing of Emperor Meiji and the death of General Nogi made me think further about the tragedy involved in achievement. Achievement necessarily destroys people. It necessarily calls for sacrifice.

---

[684] Itō Hirobumi was assassinated at Harbin Station (Amur River Province) on October 26th 1909, by An Jūkon (1879-1910), a Korean nationalist.

[685] Sic. Since Katai has earlier said that the day of the Emperor's death was a very hot one, it is odd that he has not drawn attention to the exceptional nature of the weather on that occasion.

[686] General Count Nogi Maresuke (1849-1912) killed himself by ritual disembowelment on the day of the funeral of his liege lord Mutsuhito, September 13th, in the tradition of a loyal retainer. His wife Shizuko (born 1858) also killed herself.

The sadness of the victor, the loneliness of the hero — such were the thoughts that filled my mind.

Crisis at Forty

I went through the crisis of reaching forty.

I was beset by awful weariness, and boredom, and anxiety. I could take no interest in anything I wrote. The sluggishness of the literary world does indeed stem from the sluggishness of the writers themselves.

There had been calls for a fresh start, but had such a start actually been made? There had been declarations of opposition to the falsehood of society, but had that falsehood actually disappeared entirely? There had been cries for naturalism, but had there actually been a form of art produced that would change everything?

Had we allowed ourselves to be content, even smug, with cheap confessions and petty defiance and childish results?

It was when I crossed the forty mark that I first felt the blinkers removed from my eyes, that I first felt I had come to realise something about life.

"It's a waste of time writing novels like this," I'd think to myself.

I'd also think things like "It's a waste of time reading foreign literature. Where's the value in imitating the ideas of D'Annunzio and Oscar Wilde? Just what is 'new'?! Is it merely 'novel' or 'curious'? Just why are things old considered bad? The real issue is not whether things are new or old, but in the pursuit of truth. It's not a question of one's ideas, but of one's being. What good is it to read foreign literature and just produce imitations? We must relate to life in Japan. We must relate to Japanese people. Rather than reading, we should immerse ourselves more in Japanese life....."

But such thoughts left me feeling as though I had no base left to stand on, as though my once dependable citadel had suddenly crumbled. To add to it I suffered the weariness and boredom that everyone suffers around forty, and nothing I saw or heard seemed the least bit interesting. I realised I had lost that essential requirement of a writer — the ability to find things intriguing.

It was hopeless carrying on the way I was, writing short stories each month under pressure from publishers as deadlines approached. I searched desperately for a way out.

"I can't stand it!" I'd say. "I hate having to write to order. I hate publishers' demands even more than bills!"

There had also been a big change in Shimazaki's life at that time. He'd lost his wife. He had to look after his children by himself.[687] It seems that he too came to feel the weariness of life. He too seemed to want to break away from a life that left him shut away upstairs in his study, not wanting to go out as he had in his younger days but on the other hand being eaten away by loneliness.

One day Shimazaki said to me:

"It's a pity there's no means of getting educated when you reach middle age. There're all manner of means to educate YOUNG people."

"That's very true."

"I just feel that I'd like to go through a 'training course' again."

Shimazaki had already started thinking about going to France, about making a big break and bringing a change to his life. Before long his trip became definite.[688]

I too would have liked to go overseas, but I had things which I was worried about leaving.[689] And having had experience of going off to the war I knew the limited opportunity being overseas gave for coming into contact with material for a truly relevant Japanese novel. But, in a different sense, I heartily supported Shimazaki in making such bold plans to make a break and bring a change to his life.[690] Indeed, I was extremely envious. I too thought about making a break, and doing something like going overseas.

My daily routine and domestic life were just so terribly mundane. The days merely passed amidst monotony and troublesome restrictions. It was always the same — my wife's red face, my children all misbehaving, the soup for breakfast, the saké in the evening[691]..... MY children hadn't died. MY wife hadn't died. I hadn't even had such a stimulus as that to make me start out into a new life. I cursed the banality, the monotony.

---

[687] See Note 428 for details of the deaths of his wife Fuyu and his first three children. When Fuyu died in childbirth on August 6th 1910 she was giving birth to a fourth daughter, Ryūko, who survived, and she was the mother of three surviving sons — Kusuo, born October 20th 1905, Keiji, born September 8th 1907, and Ōsuke, born December 17th 1908. Thus Tōson was left to look after four very young children. From spring 1911 he was assisted by his niece Komako, with whom he had a relationship (discussed in his later work 'Shinsei' [New Life, in two parts, May 1st-July 10th 1918 and August 5th-October 24th 1919, Asahi Shinbun]) and who bore his child (a son) on September 3rd 1913. Kōzu Takeshi also assisted him.

[688] He left for France in April 1913, and returned to Japan July 1916.

[689] According to Maeda Akira, he was particularly worried about Iida Yone, who at this point in time was almost redeemed by another client.

[690] It is very doubtful that Katai knew at the time the full reasons for Tōson's trip overseas, notably the pregnancy of his niece. The relationship between Katai and Tōson was not quite as close as is commonly believed or as Katai tends to make out. Their conversation, for example, was for a long time generally conducted on the reserved '-masu' level.

[691] All Katai's five children had been born by this time, and all were still alive.

And so, in that sense, I envied Shimazaki his trip to France. To have lost his beloved children, and his wife, must certainly have been a bitter blow, but on the other hand he was able to achieve a certain freedom as a result, and I felt that that was at any rate better than the banality and monotony of my own life.

I was also saddened at having to part with Shimazaki for three or four years. I had just resigned from H-kan and become a free agent for the first time, and I'd said to Shimazaki that now I had time of my own I'd go over and see him more often.[692] We had travelled a long road together, which was quite unusual in literature, and were just at a time when we should continue to work together. That added to my despair.

I went with him from Shinbashi as far as Hakone, together with Kōzu from Shiga Village in Shinshū.[693] The spring rain was falling the night we parted. I wrote a poem on a handkerchief:

> "A quiet spring night
> In a hot-spring spa
> At the foot of the mountains:
> And here in the rain
> It seems we must part."

Then, at Kōzu Station, we watched him depart in a crowd of travellers.[694]

Shimazaki stayed in Kōbe for about a month, attending to various matters.[695] I myself went to the temple in H in Bushū, where I often went when I felt depressed, and sat drinking the local saké with O.[696] It was a lonely time.

"I must at least try doing SOMETHING!"

This thought never left my mind for a moment. I was worried about the children. I was worried about my wife. But more of a worry to me was my own situation. The more I thought about it, the more I felt the need to do something or other. My feelings at this time are described in some more detail in the work 'A Handful of Straw'.[697] The first title I had in mind for this work was 'Against the Stream', but I found that idea

---

[692] Katai resigned from Hakubunkan on December 23rd 1912.

[693] March 25th (1913).

[694] The station is a few miles *east* of Odawara and Hakone. It is possible that this particular station was chosen for the farewell as it is pronounced the same as the surname of Kōzu Takeshi.

[695] Tōson went from Kōzu to Kōbe, finally sailing from there on the French vessel 'Ernest Simon'.

[696] That is, the Kenpukuji in Hanyū, where Ōta Gyokumei was resident priest.

[697] 'Ichiaku no Wara' (sometimes read incorrectly as 'Hitonigiri no Wara'), January 1st 1914, 'Chūō Kōron'.

of going against the stream too depressing.[698] My mind was dwelling on Ibsen's 'Master Builder' and '[John Gabriel] Borkman'.

As the day for Shimazaki's departure from Japan drew near I went to a hot-spring spa at Yabuzuka in Jōshū.[699] Spring was by then well advanced. I could see red peach blossoms and white camellia blooming in amongst the bamboo behind the inn. One day it rained very heavily and drenched the double-cherry blossoms in the park out front. I could hear, somewhere in the distance, the faint sound of a gramophone, no doubt dispelling the ennui of some visitor to the spa. I thought about Shimazaki, and wrote him a letter. It was around this time too that I wrote the poem:

> ''Alone in spring
> In a village
> In the country,
> Thinking of my friend
> Crossing over the sea.''

My agitated state continued. I could not settle down at home. I went on one trip after another. I didn't even feel like meeting old friends. I just wanted to be alone with nature.

That May I went to an old temple in Nikkō, catering for myself and living alone.[700] I was full of thoughts about Huysmans' 'En Route'.[701]

Six Months in an Old Temple

I'd spend all day long in quiet meditation, sitting facing a water-bucket into which crystal clear water trickled from a bamboo pipe. I could hear the roar of rapids in the background, seething through a deeply scored ravine.

The temple I had gone to with Doppo had been completely destroyed by floods, and now, where the temple gate had stood, a tramcar ran happily along a large newly built road. Nevertheless, on the occasional walks I took over to the site, I had been able to discover vestiges of the old pond, the old stone steps, and the pretty little spring. Everything was in ruins, though. The old cedar grove that had stood behind the temple had

---

[698] 'Chōryū ni Taishite', probably inspired by Huysmans' 'Downstream'.

[699] Near Kiryū. Katai actually went there (in April 1913) with Ōta Gyokumei.

[700] The Inōin, not the Shōsonin (which had recently been destroyed by floods). Katai stayed there till October that year. See following chapter.

[701] From this point on Katai was profoundly influenced by the French writer J-K. Huysmans (1848-1907), the former Zolaist who turned in disillusionment to what he termed a 'spiritual naturalism', in which he searched for man's quintessence. 'En Route' of 1895 describes his stay in a Trappist monastery, meditating upon the above.

now been cut down, and the area was at present in a state of development that suggested nothing at all of the past.

I couldn't help comparing past and present. In the interval that had elapsed changes had occurred that I myself had never dreamt of. The changes were partly attributable to time, partly to man. In the old days I had had ambitions, a future. I found life intriguing. I dashed wildly ahead like a blinkered horse, thinking all that mattered was to go forward. Now the blinkers had been removed. I now had hesitations, reservations. The scenes from that period of life I had gone through now seemed to resemble those crumbling ruins lying buried in the grass.

I couldn't help thinking that we build a little more of our own graves with each passing day.

The river running through the valley also seemed very different from those days of old. There used to be a narrow stretch of stony ground in the very middle of the river, with willows and alders and oaks. There was also a long, rickety, wooden bridge, which often looked in danger of being swamped. The old lady from the temple used to go across it every day to work in the fields. There were mulberry saplings planted there too. Apparently the priest had intended building himself a little place there, to retire to some day. However, that little stretch of land had now been completely washed over, and was just a mass of tumbled rocks. It was enough to suggest the folly of human enterprise.

Some nights the moon shone brightly through the open shutters. Just as in the past, a hawk-cuckoo would fly past with its lonely cry. Occasionally I'd wake up in the middle of the night, feeling the sadness of solitude. Without thinking, I'd find myself reciting Chinese-style poems such as:

> "The people of old have passed without trace,
> In the vast unfurling of life:
> There are only the heavens, and the hills,
> And the moon that shines on my pillow."

The roof of that old temple leaked, the eaves were crooked, the joists were rotten, the floor squeaked and creaked, the mats were discoloured. Such were the surroundings of my solitude.

As if to emphasise rather picturesquely the surrounding decay, the little pond by the gate was coloured brightly by irises and rich green slender rushes. At night I could hear the frogs there, croaking out their songs of love's delights.

Sometimes a mist would set in, so thick I couldn't see more than a few yards ahead. At dusk the mountains were terribly lonely; people rarely passed by; and the tops of the cedars and the peaks of the mountains towered starkly into the deep blue sky. The door to the main building of the temple, where a triple Buddha was housed, was tightly shut, and gave me a feeling of profound mystery.

The Goncourts' 'Trap'

The first time I encountered the names of Flaubert and the Goncourts was when I read Daudet's 'Thirty Years in Paris'. I came across a considerable number of the works of Zola and Daudet fairly early on, but in the case of Flaubert and the Goncourts it was rather a question of respecting their reputations only, as it was not at all easy to obtain their works. Nevertheless, there were a few of Flaubert's works in the Ueno Library, so I was able to read — though not necessarily properly appreciate — 'Sentimental Education' and 'Salammbô'.

The Goncourts' works, however, were nowhere to be found. Moreover, there was no-one who had read them. And yet, according to Daudet, they were highly respected amongst the naturalist group, were very influential, and had an original approach to writing. I was desperately keen to obtain one of their works. Then I happened to notice their 'Germinie Lacerteux' listed in a cheap series of American publications, and ordered it straight away. It arrived about two months later.

Of course, it was an English-language translation.[702]

I read it at once. With my immature mind in those days I was unable to understand its true value, or to form a proper critical opinion of it, or indeed to appreciate fully its impressionism, but nevertheless I could see that there was something original about it. Having believed that naturalist literary art was characterised simply by Zola's cumbersome depictions and verbose descriptions I was amazed at the compact, crisp, concise descriptions in the Goncourts' writing.[703] How very different it was from Flaubert and Daudet, how superior an air it had about it!

---

[702] Possibly the now unobtainable 1906 translation by J. Chestershire, published by Page, Boston. Katai appears to have obtained the work early in 1908.

[703] This sentence contains two of the most remarkable statements Katai has ever made about naturalism. First, it is totally untrue that his view of naturalism was restricted to this narrow range, as his countless articles over the previous ten or so years blatantly demonstrate. I have deliberately translated the term 'bungei' by the awkwardly literal term 'literary art', rather than the normal term 'literature', in an attempt to lessen the sweeping nature of Katai's statement, but even if one does give him the benefit of the doubt and assume he is talking only about artistic expression, notably style, moreover even in France alone, it is still a bizarre statement. For many years, for example, he went to great pains to illustrate how Maupassant was a superb artist. (He also drew attention to the stylistic development of the German naturalists.)

The second statement, about the Goncourts' style, reveals the misunderstanding that did undoubtedly take place on occasion as the result of having to rely, in the main, on

That copy of 'Germinie' became one of the prized books in my study. People competed with one another to borrow it. And then, a short while later, I also obtained 'Sister Philomène'. I admired this work too.

I lent it to Doppo. I lent it to Shimazaki. Hakuchō also borrowed it.[704]

My knowledge of the Goncourts gradually increased. When I wrote 'Life' I wasn't influenced by them, but 'Country Teacher' is certainly full of them. I had obtained their 'Renée Mauperin' and kept it by my side as I wrote, referring to it from time to time.

I was always praising them: "The Goncourts are the most artistic of the naturalists. That's why their works never seem to age."

At the office I used to sit next to Maeda Akira, and I suggested to him that he put out a translation of 'Germinie' in the New Year edition of our magazine. Maeda readily agreed, and so the New Year copy duly carried a partial translation.

However, Ikuta Chōkō sweepingly criticised the translation as inaccurate and full of omissions. I thought this was a bit odd, and upon investigation I discovered that the English translation I had given to Maeda left a great deal to be desired. Maeda therefore suspended his translating.

It must certainly have been a frustrating annoyance to him. He searched for an unabridged edition of 'Germinie'. Chiba Kōtō happened to have one, which Maeda later borrowed.[705]

---

translations of questionable quality. Later in this chapter Katai does acknowledge that the translation was a poor one, and he also displays a new awareness when he describes the Goncourts' works as 'complex, esoteric, and sophisticated', but nevertheless this particular statement here must stand as a very inaccurate description of the Goncourts' style. Far from being 'compact, crisp, and concise' ('kanketsu na tekipaki shita byōsha to shōryaku'), the Goncourts' style must rank as one of the most difficult, intellectual, and exhaustively detailed styles to be found in any literature of any period of any country, which is no doubt one of the reasons that they have been relatively ignored by translators everywhere. For example, I give below a translation I have attempted (while bearing in mind the need for the utmost precision) of one paragraph of the original French publication, selected almost at random:

"A usual effect of organic nervous disorders is to derange the joys and the sufferings of the human being, to divest these feelings of their proportion and equilibrium, to push them to the extremity of excess. It seems that, under the influence of that malady of impressionability, these stimulated sensations, refined and spiritualised, surpass their natural limits and extents, reach out beyond themselves, and inject a type of infinity into the joy and suffering of the creature. Now the few joys that were still left to Germinie were mad joys, joys that left her intoxicated with the physical characteristics of drunkenness."

Elsewhere, as in the introduction to the novel, the Goncourts display such stylistic devices as the idiosyncratic use of capital letters. Clearly, as with his discovery of Maupassant earlier, Katai's initial impression was far from correct.

[704] It is not clear which of the two works is intended by 'it', but probably 'Germinie'.

[705] Chiba Kōtō (1878-1935, also known as Kameo), journalist. It is not clear whether this is an English translation or the original French. In view of the fact that Chiba's speciality was English, the former seems more likely.

Maeda was determined to complete a full translation of 'Germinie', and to that end he studied French. He was convinced that it was a waste of time working from an English translation, and would only settle for the original.

We advertised 'Trap' as one of the works in the series of foreign literature which H Company was planning to put out.

I don't think I've ever seen a translator labour as much as Maeda did with 'Germinie'. It took him over three years. His desk was covered with books — the original, two English translations, and a French dictionary — and he would painstakingly finish one line only to cross it out again. Just at that time he had resigned from H Company too, and his hardships in daily life seemed etched into those laborious lines.[706]

"Wouldn't it be better if you were to forget the idea?"

It wasn't just his friends who said this. I told him as much myself.[707] But, he laboured steadfastly on, determined to finish that translation of 'Germinie'.

It was November 1914. Maeda went off with his translation to a mountain temple in Nikkō.

I went with him.

I admired his determination. I also appreciated how lonely it was for him in that mountain temple.

It wasn't possible to stay in that old temple I'd been at the previous year, due to the appointment of a new resident priest, so I'd arranged for us to stay at the H Temple.[708] Maeda brought N along.[709]

H was a nice temple. There were still some red autumn leaves left there, while the snow lay white on the mountain peaks. Beyond a thick grove of cedars flowed the D River, sounding like a tumbling cascade.[710] Mixed in with its roar one could also hear the occasional passing tramcar.

Maeda and N set up their desks in separate rooms upstairs. N was working on a translation of Dostoevski's 'Crime and Punishment'.[711]

Looking out from the window in Maeda's room one could see, beyond the encircling cedars, the snow sparkling on Mount Nantai and Mount Nyohō.

---

[706] Maeda resigned in April 1913.

[707] This is a rather odd statement. The implication is that Katai was not a friend of Maeda's, but merely a (former) colleague or mentor. To judge from other writings, however, they were very close friends.

[708] The Hōmonin.

[709] Nakamura Hakuyō (1890-1974), translator, Russian specialist.

[710] The Daiyagawa.

[711] Published June 1915, Shinchōsha. Roan's 1892 translation had been from the English.

"This is nice! Really marvellous!" Maeda said to me from the window.

From the window in N's room one could see the range of little hills on the far side of the Inarigawa [River], as they rolled gently away into the distance, and, on the near side of the cedars, green fields of rape. The five-storeyed tower of the S Temple looked most picturesque as it stood there with an air of quiet composure.[712] Beneath the window were some cheerful red holly berries.

"Yes, this place is fine. I think I'll definitely be able to get something done here," said Maeda. He lengthened the string of the light so that it reached right to his desk, and sat there with a relaxed look on his face.

I returned to Tōkyō after a couple of days, but when December came round I thought Maeda would be a bit lonely, so I paid him another visit at the temple. I intended to stay for a fortnight or so this time, and prepared to do some writing there myself.

I occupied two rooms downstairs. I had a hibachi put in one of them, next to which I set my desk. I always got up early, whereas Maeda went to bed late and got up late. By the time he got up each morning and went for a wash I'd already written five or six pages.

Maeda's translating labours were pitiful. "I was up till two this morning," he'd say, "but I still only managed to do two pages. Translating the Goncourts is so difficult. They use so many adjectives, and not only that, they're all used so carefully. The more you consider them, the more complex their meaning becomes. It's a real problem when there aren't any suitable words in Japanese." He'd show me what he'd written, section at a time. It seemed that the more he followed the original the more difficult the translating became.

N had gone back to Tōkyō at the end of the previous month. He'd found that there in the mountains it was simply getting colder with each passing day, with frosts whitening the eaves and a piercing wind incessantly blowing. Maeda had written some poems to express his feelings while he was there with N, and now he showed them to me. "It's just unbelievable when the sun shines on the tower of the S Temple," he told me. "You can really appreciate silent labour when you're in the mountains like this. It's better than a Trappist monastery."[713]

By that stage Maeda had only completed about one hundred and forty or fifty pages of his translation. "I'd like to get beyond the two hundred page mark while I'm here, but I don't think I'll be able to," he said with a disappointed look on his face. And yet, by then he'd been working on the translation for some eighteen months.

---

[712] The Shihonryūji.

[713] Presumably a reference to Huysmans' stay in a Trappist monastery.

I'd get up while it was still dark. The old lady there at the temple would bring me some embers, and then presently breakfast. I'd finish the meal without waiting for Maeda to come down, and then get on with some writing.

Occasionally I'd find myself thinking about the time I'd gone to Nikkō with Doppo.

One day Maeda and I walked back from the bright lights of the town through the darkness of the cedars. As we watched the stars twinkling overhead we talked about the past, and sighed deeply over the indifference of nature.

We stayed till about the twentieth of the month.

It was still more than a year after that before the translation of 'Germinie' was published. Maeda had gone on a trip to the mountains of Shinshū, but things hadn't gone as smoothly as expected and so another year had passed.[714] Finally, however, it came out in the autumn of the third year.[715]

I read it at once. I was delighted. I was thrilled that this one and only Japanese translation of the Goncourts had actually appeared, despite the fact that even overseas the Goncourts were considered very hard to translate because their works were so complex, esoteric, and sophisticated. Moreover, the Japanese translation was far better done than the English ones, with superlative fidelity and patience.[716] One could tell the extent of Maeda's painstaking labours even in the details of phraseology and grammar, and one really felt as though one was reading the Goncourts' own so-called 'non-Académie' style.

When I next met Maeda I suggested to him:

"What about going on to try 'Renée Mauperin'?"

---

[714] Maeda spent three months in 1915 in Fujimi, Nagano Prefecture. Katai himself was to spend three months there (July-October) the following year (ie. 1916), in another period of meditation.

[715] It was published by Hakubunkan in August 1916, under the title 'Kansei' (Trap). See note below.

[716] I have not checked Maeda's translation and am unable to comment fully on this claim, but it is necessary to note that the dramatic title 'Trap' immediately switches the focus from the clinical personality study intended by the Goncourts to plot interest, and would probably lure unknowing readers into buying it on the assumption that it was some sort of rip-roaring yarn. This can only be condemned as misleading and inaccurate, and no better than the translations of the 1880's in this respect. Furthermore, in view of the extreme complexity of the Goncourts' French, one wonders to what extent Maeda was able to understand it after only three years' study of the language. It is hardly beginner's material. See also note below.

"Absolutely not!" he replied. "I've learned my lesson. Never again will I set my hand to a translation as difficult as that!"[717]

A Certain Grave

Nowadays a railway runs along beside the river and the area has been opened up, but until two or three years ago the road along the river was very lonely and countryfied. There was a bridge there, and a temple, and a graveyard a little way away from it, and the late afternoon sunshine used to slant peacefully onto the tiny needles of the pines there. You could also often hear the sutras being recited in the temple.

That riverside road went for a long, long way, with the occasional side road branching off at right angles. There was also a large gate along it, leading to the residence of a certain former feudal lord. In spring, bamboo shoots appeared in the thickets, and sunflowers bloomed on the riverbanks, and at night the fireflies flickered over the water.

I often used to go for a walk there.

One day I felt somehow drawn to the little temple-graveyard on the left bank. It was extremely small, only a hundred yards or so around the perimeter. I could see camellias there, and the red and white blooms of rose of Sharon. There were new wooden grave-tablets, and moss-covered headstones, and uncared-for graves, and graves with large marble headstones. Little pathways crisscrossed the cemetery.

I soon found the grave I was looking for. It was just a mound of earth, but nevertheless there was some star anise there so it looked as though someone had been to pay their respects. The anise leaves were half withered and black. There was also one grave-tablet there.

I was filled with emotion. I felt as though I were taking part in the final scene of a Russian novel. The more I thought about it the more I realised the significance of the fact that uncompromising women, new women had appeared in Japan. It was far more significant even than the pre-nihilist Bazarov.[718] I stood facing that grave in silence.

"I go to be beside my sister in the grave....." The woman who went to her death with these words on her lips was, although a new woman,

---

[717] Many years later he did in fact translate part of the Goncourts' 'Journal', and this was published in November 1948 together with a new printing of his translation of 'Germinie' — this time accurately titled 'Jeruminii Raserutō'. He also translated such works as Maupassant's 'Pierre et Jean', published in August 1922 with another disturbingly unfaithful tiue 'A Brother's Grief' ('Ani no Yūshū'). This episode too had a happy ending, however, as it was corrected to 'Pieru to Jan' in 1928.

[718] Sic. This is presumably a reference to Bazarov's being depicted before the emergence of the nihilist movement proper, but in fact he is often considered the perfect nihilist. (He is a major character in Turgenev's 'Fathers and Sons'.)

a woman full of sentimentality and emotion.[719] I looked around. There was indeed a grave nearby that looked to be that of her younger sister.

I imagined what it must have been like on that occasion, and felt I could see — as if fused into one — the fate of all the rebels of the world. I left the graveyard a short while later.

The next time I went there was with S.[720] He too had a sad expression on his face.

"It's certainly very significant, that's true...." he said. "There's definitely a meaning in her lying here, in a place like this."

As we left the cemetery we talked about the manifestation of individualism in republican government on the one hand and autocratic government on the other. These two major ideologies are the riddles [sic] of the modern world. Yet they are also major issues. We must base ourselves upon one of the two, yet this is easier said than done. One cannot put up with mere oppression. One cannot feel at ease in such a situation. One must consider things more thoroughly, more seriously.[721]

"Russia's very interesting, isn't it!" said S.

"But we also have to consider Germany," I replied, and with that we walked on in silence.[722]

It was spring. Brightly coloured flowers peeped out from between the cedars. Birds sang beautifully their songs of spring. Everywhere was full

---

[719] Though Katai does not name names, or even identify the location of the graveyard, most readers of the day would have recognised the woman in question to be Kanno Suga(ko) (1881-1911), who was executed as a result of the Treason Incident of 1910-11. Twenty-six socialists and anarchists were secretly tried by the government on alleged charges of conspiring to kill the Emperor. Twelve of them were executed, eleven on January 24th (1911) and Kanno Suga on the 25th. She was married to the alleged 'ringleader' of the anarchists, Kōtoku Shūsui (b. 1871), who was among those executed on the 24th. She was buried in the Shōshunji [Temple] cemetery in Yoyogi 4 Chōme, near Katai's home. (The railway line referred to in this chapter is the Keiō Line, of which the section running through northwest Yoyogi was opened in 1915.)

[720] This appears to be Shiraishi Jitsuzō (1886-1937), a novelist who was a pupil of Katai's from late 1909 and his travelling companion from around 1915.

[721] The notable vagueness of these political statements, and indeed of the chapter as a whole, is, I feel, a reflection of Katai's attitude following the Treason Incident. It has long been felt that the government's action in dealing so harshly with those suspected of anti-state thought also served to call the bluff of writers such as Katai who had been proclaiming individualism and criticising, albeit indirectly and largely philosophically, the restrictiveness of service to the state. Nagai Kafū later lamented the fact that, unlike Zola in his brave defence of Dreyfus, no major Japanese writer apart from Tokutomi Roka attempted to voice open opposition to the government over its action. Katai's reputation as a naturalist suffered considerably as a result of what was seen as the timidity of his failure to make a protest. A few years after the incident Katai wrote works such as 'Tokoyogoyomi' (Almanac, March 1st 1914, 'Waseda Bungaku') in which he tried to exculpate himself from any accusation of harbouring treasonous thoughts and made a case out that his apparent anti-state stand was purely on artistic and philosophical grounds.

[722] Katai's real sympathies lay with Germany in the First World War.

of the life-giving spring sunlight. From the pine woods beyond came the sound of a carpenter's busy adze.

After the railway was laid I hardly ever went walking along that road by the river. Once, when I did go, I noticed that the graveyard had been walled off, that the pines had been cut down, that the greenery had largely disappeared, and that the graveyard lay starkly exposed to view from the main road.

Aeroplane

The sky was filled with a humming sound, rather like that of a kite. The residents of the suburbs all dashed outdoors and looked up at the sky.

There were people on the street corners, in the treetops, on upstairs' balconies. "It's an aeroplane! An aeroplane!" yelled the children as they dashed off excitedly.

"Me too! ...... Me too!"

The youngest child was crying, having been left behind. Her sister, who had run outside, came dashing back, snatched her up, and then ran off again to where they could watch the aeroplane.

Fingers pointed up at it as it sped through the morning sunshine like some giant bird, its gallant droning filling the clear blue sky.

"Look! You can see people!" said the children.

"Where?! Where?!"

My wife also went out to look. "Are those black things people?! It looks very dangerous!" she said, face turned to the sky.

Sometimes as many as two or three planes passed together. We were close to the Yoyogi military training-ground, so we could observe the aeroplanes quite clearly as they circled to land nearby. Sometimes we also saw a large yellow airship, looking like some bizarre aerial fish. The children liked to watch the propeller turning, and to hear the noise it made, and to see the thin white smoke coming from the engine.

One day the voice of a newsboy selling extras broke the quiet of the suburban afternoon. "What?! Has that aeroplane crashed?! That aeroplane we saw just now? And all the people killed? What a disaster! You certainly have to be prepared to put your life at risk if you ride in one of those aeroplanes!"

The aeroplanes had plummeted to earth in a deserted green barley field in Musashi Plain. The two young flying officers had met a gruesome end......

Yet these sacrifices brought gradual improvement in aeronautics. And airmen gradually increased in number, attracted to the fame and the challenge. "When you see Tōkyō from the air it isn't just roofs and chimneys, you know!" said one airman. "There're a lot of trees, and greenery. It looks quite lonely, actually!"

Whenever some big event was taking place in Tōkyō you could guarantee that two or three aeroplanes would come flying over from Tokorozawa. Sometimes they would fly deliberately low over the buildings in the Ginza and Nihonbashi, often as low as one hundred and fifty or two hundred feet. On one occasion a large airship seemed to lose its steering over the Aoyama training-ground, and roamed about in the air over Shinanomachi Station like the lost soul of some strange and monstrous fish. Everyone in the train was watching from the windows. "It's big, isn't it!" they all said.

When I heard about what was going on in the pleasure-quarters of Tokorozawa I commented: "It doesn't surprise me. After all, they risk their lives, so they need that sort of indulgence. I'm sure it helps them run such risks."

When Smith came, and looped the loop despite the awfully windy conditions, the whole metropolis gasped in wonder.[723] I was watching from the gate at the back of the garden. I never believed he'd be able to do anything, because of the wind. But just then the stormy sky was filled with a frightful droning. The aeroplane appeared way up high, looking so very small and leaving a trail of wispy blue smoke. "He's good all right!" I thought to myself, and just at that moment he suddenly put the aeroplane through two or three large loops and then flew right up high again. I found myself applauding.

I also saw some loops — from a train window — when Miss Stinson came.[724] I admired her skill too.

It would have been totally unthinkable, in the Tōkyō of thirty years ago, that progress could have led to the sight of aeroplanes in the sky. Even telephones and electric trains seemed amazing, like some sort of magic....[725]

The newspapers also reported what the aeroplanes were doing on the battlefields of Europe. And then, Flying Officer S — reputed to be the best pilot and the leading figure in the world of aviation — crashed from a thousand feet while trying to do the impossible in a state of upset over

---

[723] The American aviator Art Smith (1894-?) arrived in Japan on March 18th 1916, and performed the stunts described here on April 10th.

[724] The American aviator Katherine Stinson (1897-?) arrived in Japan on December 12th 1916, and on the 18th did no fewer than six loops. According to some reports she was dressed in Japanese costume. It is rather strange that Katai has not remarked on her extreme youth.

[725] The first telephones in Tōkyō were installed in 1890 (telegraphs in 1869), while the first electric train was 1904 (see Note 446).

various rumours, and made people think about how serious aviators' attitudes were.[726]

Man has long cherished the ideal of flying like a bird. The idea is present in the work of people like Da Vinci, for example. I wonder how far progress will carry it? Even now, whenever my study window rattles to the sound of a passing aeroplane, I dash outside to look. Sometimes I've seen them fly very low over the parasol-tree in my garden.

---

[726] Sawada Hide (?-1917), a Japanese aviator of international repute, had recently returned to Japan and stated his intention to resign from military service. In fact he intended to enter a commercial company as a designer, but this was not understood at the time and rumours abounded regarding his resignation. The rumours were not kind, and included speculation about a love-affair, and Sawada was considerably upset by them. In a state of disgust with the world he acted with an unusual lack of prudence in a test-flight early on the morning of March 8th 1917, and plummeted to his death from over a thousand feet. At the time it was felt to be suicide, but this view is no longer generally supported.

GLOSSARY OF LESS FAMILIAR JAPANESE TERMS

Banchi	Sub-division of Chōme
Bungaku	Literature
-chan	Name suffix used of children and close friends
-chō	Sub-district of a ward (ku), also read 'machi'
Chōme	Sub-district of a 'chō' or 'machi'
Edo	Old name for Tōkyō
Edo (Period)	1603-1868
-gawa (kawa)	River
Gesaku	Satirical work of low artistic merit, 19th. cen.
Geta	Wooden sandals
Haiku	Traditional verse form of seventeen syllables
Hakama	Divided lower garment, usually of a formal nature, worn by both men and women
Haori	Short coat
-hashi (-bashi)	Bridge
Hibachi	Charcoal brazier
-ji	Temple
Jinja	Shrine
Jizō	Guardian deity of travellers and children
Kai (-kai)	Society, association
Katakana	Phonetic script
Kintarō	Legendary hero embodying boyhood prowess
Kotatsu	Table with brazier underneath
Koto	Harp-like musical instrument
-ku	Ward or district
-machi	Sub-district of a ward, as 'chō'
Marumage	Oval hairstyle of a married woman
Meiji (Period)	1868-1912
Mikan	Japanese orange
Nagauta	Long epic song
Nō (Noh)	Stylised classical drama
Obi	Waistsash
Rin	One tenth of a sen, ie. one thousandth of a yen
Sen	Ten rin, one hundredth of a yen
Sensei	Teacher, or used as term of general respect
Sha (-sha)	Society, association, company
Shamisen (Samisen)	Three-stringed musical instrument
Shimada	Type of swept-back hair style, usually of an unmarried woman
Shinbun	Newspaper
Shinpō	Report
Shizoku	Class of samurai retainers
Shōji	Sliding door or window, usually made of white paper
Shū (-shū)	Collection
Soba	Noodles
Sushi	Rice with vinegared filling
Taishō (Period)	1912-1926
Tanka	Traditional short verse
Tenpura	Type of fritter
Torii	Stylised entrance to Shintō shrine
Tsukudani	Various foods boiled in soy

Waka	Traditional verse form of thirty-one syllables
Yen	Main denomination of currency, equivalent to one hundred sen or one thousand rin
Yukata	Casual garment
-zaka	Slope
Zasshi	Magazine

SELECT BIBLIOGRAPHY

This bibliography is not intended to be complete. For original publication details of the literary works mentioned in the text the reader should consult the Works Index and the relevant note. Many of the works have since been published in numerous 'shū' ('collections'), 'zenshū' ('complete works'), and 'bunkobon' ('paperback pocket-series'), and in most cases the reader of such editions will also find useful commentaries and further bibliographical references. In this bibliography I have not listed any of the vast number of 'bunkobon', and have only listed a few of the more significant 'shū' and 'zenshū'. Similarly I have not attempted to list any of the vast number of research articles available, and have listed only works in book form. For a full list of translations the reader should consult 'Modern Japanese Literature in Translation: A Bibliography' by the International House of Japan Library, Tōkyō, 1979. Relevant post-1979 translations are given here in this bibliography. Works of European literature have been omitted. Unless stated otherwise, all Japanese publications are from Tōkyō.

BOWRING, Richard: 'Mori Ōgai and the Modernisation of Japanese Culture', Cambridge, Cambridge University Press, 1979.

DANLY, Robert Lyons: 'In the Shade of Spring Leaves' [Study and Translation of Higuchi Ichiyō], New Haven, Connecticut, Yale University Press, 1981.

'Encyclopedia Japonica', 23 vols., Shōgakukan, 1967-72.

FUKUDA Kiyoto and ISHIBASHI Tokue: 'Tayama Katai: Hito to Sakuhin', Shimizu Shoin, 1968.

'Futabatei Shimei Zenshū', 9 vols., Iwanami Shoten, 1964-5.

'Gendai Nihon Bungaku Daijiten', Meiji Shoin, 1965.

HISAMATSU Sen'ichi (ed.): 'Biographical Dictionary of Japanese Literature', Kodansha International, 1976.

—— (et al., ed.): 'Nihon Bungakushi: Kindai', Shinbundō, 1964.

HONMA, Kenshirō: 'A History of Modern Japanese Literature', Japan Science Press, 1980.

ICHIKO, Teiji (ed.): 'Nihon Bungaku Nenpyō', Ōfūsha, 1976.

—— (et al., ed.): 'Nihon Bungaku Zenshi: Kindai (vol. 5)', Gakutōsha, 1978.

IKARI, Akira: 'Kenyūsha no Bungaku', Hanawa Shobō, 1961.

—— : 'Kenyūsha to Shizenshugi Kenkyū', Ōfūsha, 1975.

INO, Kenji: 'Meiji no Sakka', Iwanami Shoten, 1966.

IWANAGA, Yutaka: 'Shizenshugi Bungaku ni okeru Kyokō no Kanōsei', Ōfūsha, 1974.

IWAO, Seiichi (et al., ed.): 'A Bibliographical Dictionary of Japanese History', trans. Burton Watson, Kodansha International, 1978.

KATAI KENKYŪKAI (ed.): 'Ai to Kunō no Hito, Tayama Katai', Kyōiku Shuppan Sentā, 1980.

KATAOKA, Yoshikazu (ed.): 'Nihon Bungaku: Kindai', Iwanami Shoten, 1958.

——: 'Shizenshugi Kenkyū', Chikuma Shobō, 1957.

KATŌ, Shūichi: 'A History of Japanese Literature: The Modern Years', trans. D. Sanderson, Tenterden, Kent, Paul Norbury Publications, 1983.

'Kawakami Bizan Shū', in 'Meiji Bungaku Zenshū' (Chikuma), Vol. 20.

KAWAUCHI, Kiyoshi (ed.): 'Shizenshugi Bungaku', Keisō Shobō, 1962.

KEENE, Donald: 'Dawn to the West: Japanese Literature in the Modern Era — Fiction', New York, Holt, Rinehart & Winston, 1984.

'Kenyūsha Shū', in 'Meiji Bungaku Zenshū' (Chikuma), Vol. 22.

'Kindai Bungaku Zasshi Jiten', Shinbundō, 1966.

'Kindai Nihon Bungaku Jiten', Tōkyōdō, 1954.

KOBAYASHI, Ichirō: 'Tayama Katai Kenkyū', 10 vols., Ōfūsha, 1976-84.

——: 'Shizenshugi Sakka Tayama Katai', Shintensha, 1982.

KŌDA, Rohan: '"Pagoda", "Skull", "Bearded Samurai"', trans. Chieko Mulhern, New York, Cornell University East Asia Paper No. 26, 1982.
'Kodansha Encyclopedia of Japan', 9 vols., Kodansha, 1983.
KORNICKI, Peter: 'The Reform of Fiction in Meiji Japan', London, Ithaca Press, 1982.
KUNIKIDA, Doppo: 'River Mist and Other Stories', trans. David Chibbett, Kodansha International, 1983.
'Kunikida Doppo' in 'Nihon Bungaku Arubamu' series (No.18), Chikuma Shobō, 1956.
'Kunikida Doppo Zenshū', 10 vols., Gakushū Kenkyūsha, 1964.
'Meiji Bungaku Zenshū', 99 vols., Chikuma Shobō, 1966-80.
MIZUTANI, Akio: 'Kindai Nihon Bungeishi no Kōsei', Kyōwa Shobō, 1964.
'[Mori] Ōgai Zenshū', 38 vols., Iwanami Shoten, 1971-5.
NAKAJIMA, Kenzō (ed.): 'Kindai Nihon Bungaku ni okeru Gaikoku Bungaku no Eikyō', Kawade Shobō, 1953.
NAKAMURA, Mitsuo: 'Modern Japanese Fiction', trans. D. Philippi and E. Fujimura, Kokusai Bunka Shinkōkai, 1968.
——:'Nihon no Kindai Shōsetsu', Iwanami Shoten, 1964.
'Nihon Bungaku Daijiten', 8 vols., Shinchōsha, 1952.
NIHON BUNGAKU KENKYŪ SHIRYŌ KANKŌKAI (ed.): 'Shizenshugi Bungaku', Yūseido, 1975.
'Nihon Bungakushi Jiten', Nihon Hyōronsha, 1954.
'Nihon Bungaku Shōjiten', Shinchōsha, 1968.
'Nihon Bungaku Zenshū', 72 vols., Shinchōsha, 1964-6.
'Nihon Bungaku Zenshū', 88 vols., Shūeisha, 1969-70.
'Nihon Bunkashi Taikei: Meiji Jidai', Shōgakukan, 1967.
'Nihon Chimei Daijiten: Kantō (Vol. 5)', Asakura Shoten, 1968.
'Nihon Chimei Daijiten: Tōkyō-to (Vol. 13)', Kadokawa Shoten, 1978.
'Nihon Jinmei Daijiten', 7 vols., Heibonsha, 1979.
'Nihon Jinmei Jiten', Shinbunkaku, 1914.
'Nihon Kindai Bungaku Daijiten', 6 vols., Kōdansha, 1978.
'Nihonshi Daijiten', Sōganshinsha, 1960.
'Oguri Fūyō Shū', in 'Meiji Bungaku Zenshū' (Chikuma), Vol. 65.
'Ozaki Kōyō Shū', in 'Meiji Bungaku Zenshū' (Chikuma), Vol. 18.
PAPINOT, E.: 'Historical and Geographical Dictionary of Japan', orig. 1910, Tuttle edition 1972.
ROBERTS,Laurance P.: 'A Dictionary of Japanese Artists', Weatherhill, 1976.
RUBIN, Jay: 'Injurious to Public Morals: Writers and the Meiji State', Seattle, Washington University Press, 1984.
RYAN, Marleigh Granger: 'The Development of Realism in the Fiction of Tsubouchi Shōyō', Seattle, Washington University Press, 1975.
——: 'Japan's First Modern Novel, "Ukigumo"', New York, Columbia University Press, 1967.
'Saitō Ryokū Shū', in 'Meiji Bungaku Zenshū', (Chikuma), Vol. 28.
SASABUCHI, Tomoichi: '"Bungakukai" to sono Jidai', 2 vols., Meiji Shoin, 1959-60.
'[Shimazaki] Tōson Zenshū', 17 vols., Chikuma Shobō, 1966-8.
SHŌWA JOSHIDAIGAKU KŌYŌKAI (ed.): 'Kindai Bungaku Kenkyū Sōsho' series (52 vols., 1956-81), esp. Vol. 32 (Tayama Katai), Shōwa Joshidaigaku Kindai Bungaku Kenkyūshitsu, 1969.
TAYAMA, Katai: 'Country Teacher', trans. Kenneth Henshall, Honolulu, Hawaii University Press, 1984.
——: 'The Quilt and Other Stories', trans. Kenneth G. Henshall, Tokyo University Press, 1981.
——: 'A Soldier Shot to Death', trans. Honma Kenshirō, Kyōto, Yamaguchi Press, 1982.
'Tayama Katai', in 'Nihon Bungaku Arubamu' series (No. 24), Chikuma Shobō, 1959.
'Tayama Katai Zenshū', 17 vols., Bunsendō, 1974.
'Tsubouchi Shōyō Shū', in 'Meiji Bungaku Zenshū' (Chikuma), Vol. 16.

WADA, Kingo: 'Shizenshugi Bungaku', Shibundō, 1966.
WALKER, Janet: 'The Japanese Novel of the Meiji Period and the Ideal of Individualism', Princeton, Princeton University Press, 1979.
YAMANOUCHI, Hisaaki: 'The Search for Authenticity in Modern Japanese Literature', Cambridge, Cambridge University Press, 1978.
YANAGIDA, Izumi: 'Tayama Katai no Bungaku', 2 vols., Shunjūsha, 1957-8.
'Yanagita Kunio [Zen]shū', 36 vols., Chikuma Shobō, 1969-71.
YOSHIDA, Seiichi: 'Kindai Bungei Hyōronshi', 2 vols., Shinbundō, 1980-1.
——: 'Shizenshugi no Kenkyū', 2 vols., Tōkyōdō, 1955-8.
—— (et al., ed.): 'Tōson: Katai', Sanseidō, 1960.
—— (et al., ed.): 'Shizenshugi to Hanshizenshugi', Kawade Shobō, 1956.

INDEX OF PERIODICALS

INDEX OF WORKS

INDEX OF PERSONS

This index lists only those places in the work where actual names are given. It does not include other references. Further, it does not include fictitious persons.